Daniel Webster and the
Oratory of Civil Religion

Daniel **Webster** and the
Oratory of Civil Religion

CRAIG R. SMITH

University of Missouri Press   Columbia and London

Library of Congress Cataloging-in-Publication Data

Smith, Craig R.
    Daniel Webster and the oratory of civil religion /
Craig R. Smith.
        p.   cm.
    Includes bibliographical references and index.
    ISBN 0-8262-1542-4 (alk. paper)
   1.   Webster, Daniel, 1782-1852—Political and social
views. 2.   Webster, Daniel, 1782-1852—Oratory.
3.   Civil religion—United States—History—19th century.
4.   Nationalism—United States—History—19th century.
5.   Political oratory—United States—History—19th century.
6.   Rhetoric—Political aspects—United States—Case studies.
7.   Speeches, addresses, etc., American—History and
criticism. 8.   United States—Politics and government—
1783-1865. 9.   Legislators—United States—Biography.
10.   United States. Congress. Senate—Biography.
I.   Title.
    E340.W4S597   2005
    973.5'092—dc22

                                    2004020732

DESIGNER: KRISTIE LEE
TYPESETTER: CRANE COMPOSITION, INC.
PRINTER AND BINDER: THE MAPLE-VAIL BOOK MANUFACTURING GROUP
TYPEFACES: GOUDY OLD STYLE

FRONTISPIECE: Southworth and Hawes, *Daniel Webster,*
c. 1851. Daguerreotype, 8-$\frac{3}{16}$ x 6$\frac{1}{8}$ in. Museum of Fine
Arts, Boston. Gift of Edward Southworth Hawes in
memory of his father, Josiah Johnson Hawes, 43.1402.
Photograph © 2004 Museum of Fine Arts, Boston.

This book is dedicated to all those professors who encouraged me to outgrow them

Contents

Introduction 1

Chapter 1 The Foundation of Webster's Civil Religion 7

Chapter 2 A Boston Lawyer 39

Chapter 3 The Lion Returns 64

Chapter 4 Civic Duty in the Romantic Age 84

Chapter 5 Liberty and Union 100

Chapter 6 Legal and Partisan Wrangling 120

Chapter 7 Abolition Confounds the Two-Party System 155

Chapter 8 Secretary Webster 175

Chapter 9 War with Mexico 191

Chapter 10 National Crisis, Capitol Gridlock 214

Chapter 11 Consummating Compromise 238

Chapter 12 Twilight Time 252

Chronology of Major Speeches 271

Bibliographic Essay 273

Bibliography 285

Index 293

Daniel Webster and the
Oratory of Civil Religion

Introduction

Daniel Webster was the consummate American orator. His career was punctuated with magnificent and effective speeches before the United States Supreme Court, the United States Congress, particularly the Senate, and assembled crowds celebrating national holidays. As a rhetorical theorist who studies public address and as a former presidential speechwriter, I have attempted to write an "oratorical biography" of Webster that not only places these rhetorical transactions in context, but also explains how they functioned to achieve persuasion. Webster's oeuvre is so large and so prominent that only a book-length study, which builds on the work of historians and public-address critics, can do it justice.

The method of this study is eclectic. Because the diversity of Webster's talent demands an inductive approach, I rely on the arsenal of rhetorical criticism to explain his effectiveness and literary merit. A contextual analysis of each speech places Webster's rhetoric in his times, thereby revealing the situational constraints he faced. The context of his speeches also reveals why some aspects of his rhetoric were controversial in his time and still are in our own. For example, Webster's success as a negotiator while serving as secretary of state in two different administrations gave him confidence that war could almost always be avoided. His role in crafting the Compromise of 1850 committed him to seeing that it was properly implemented; that meant enforcing the Fugitive Slave Law, which was unpopular in the North.

Of course, almost any study of public address begins with an analysis of the lines of argument used by the speaker. This study is no different in that regard. What is different is that Webster was an innovator when it came to argumentation. He understood that a single speech on a single issue is unlikely to achieve reform. Thus, on many topics, particularly his opposition to the war with Mexico and his support for the Compromise of 1850, Webster engaged in a campaign of persuasion, using many arguments in many speeches to achieve his goal. He often braided various genres as a way to develop a more fruitful arsenal of arguments and to achieve a sublime style. He initiated lines of argument early, and returned to them again and again to extend them.

Aristotle taught us that *ethos* is the most potent form of persuasion. Kenneth Burke expanded Aristotle's theory to include psychological identification between the speaker and the audience. These and other theories of credibility-building explain how Webster became so prominent in his age and how he used his reputation not only to advance the cause of Union, but also to embody it. His knowledge of history and literature enhanced his credibility. Reading Thucydides in college opened him to the great speakers and the great debates of ancient Athens, just as reading Gibbon opened him to the power of historical narrative. Webster shared his credibility with the Whig Party, playing a significant role in advancing its agenda and values.

Webster lived in a romantic era that was much more open to displays of emotion than our own. The Second Great Awakening occurred during his most influential period. Thus, his development of a civil religion resonated with the evangelism of the times. *Pathos* was a prominent feature in Webster's speeches, particularly his ceremonial addresses. He often sealed his persuasive message with an emotional peroration, bringing his audience to tears. My past work on Webster and the studies I have completed with Michael Hyde on a hermeneutics of *pathos* have proved helpful in completing this analysis.

Having studied Cicero, Webster was familiar with the Roman concepts of *decorum* and *ornatus*. The former was used to meet or create expectations in an audience; the latter provided the tropes and figures essential to fashioning the speech for the occasion. Webster's imagery often reinforces a powerful narrative that proves unusually persuasive. His effective use of these concepts helps to explain why he was considered one of the most literate men of his time. In the age of Wordsworth and Longfellow, Webster could hold his own arguing that Alexander Pope was the greatest poet of all time. Robert A. Ferguson claims that "[t]he writers of the American Renaissance cut their teeth on Daniel Webster." Ralph Waldo Emerson compared Webster to Shakespeare, another writer who understood the importance of Roman stylistic theory. In his study of Webster's style, Paul D. Erickson concludes that "Webster was beyond doubt an artist."[1]

---

1. Robert A. Ferguson, *Law and Letters in American Culture*, 238; Paul D. Erickson, *The Poetry of Events: Daniel Webster's Rhetoric of the Constitution and Union*, xii–xiii.

This study also examines Webster's speeches from the perspective of organization and delivery. His admiration for Cicero, for example, led him to imitate the great Roman senator in many ways. His sophisticated understanding of genre allowed him to combine Aristotle's three forms of public address—the deliberative (legislative), the forensic (legal), and the epideictic (ceremonial)—into braided masterpieces unsurpassed in American oratory. His skill at debate, so evident in his feisty replies to Robert Hayne, was supported by a fugal-like development of argument that was a throwback to the great speeches of Charles James Fox of the British Parliament, whose life overlapped Webster's. This rhetorical strategy gave his speeches a flow and unity that supported his campaigns of persuasion.

Webster believed that rhetoric worked; he believed a good orator could change minds and thereby change the course of events. It galled him when those untrained in oratory advanced to the presidency. It annoyed him when men rose in the Senate and embarrassed themselves with their weak arguments, ignorance of history and literature, feckless style, and lack of organization.

This study's rhetorical analysis supports several historical themes developed previously by myself and others while also providing new insights into Webster's successes and failures. Along with Henry Clay, Webster developed a coherent set of principles to guide the Whig Party. The Whigs endorsed a national bank, a tariff to fund national improvements, a diverse currency, public education, and limiting slavery to where it already existed, and they often opposed expansion and war.[2] But, like his friend and compatriot John C. Calhoun, Webster eventually became a victim of regionalism despite his adamant defense of the Constitution and Union. His loyalty to financial interests in New England influenced his tariff policy, alienating him from important voting blocs, particularly in the South. His presidential ambition was undercut by those who characterized him as a senator in the pocket of Nicholas Biddle and the National Bank. His opposition to the expansion of slavery reenforced Southern suspicions. When Webster tried to parlay his slaying of nullification (1830–1832) into a presidential nomination, he found that slayers make enemies. His opposition to the war with Mexico in 1846 and his dedication to George Washington's warning about foreign entanglements put him at odds with those preaching "manifest destiny." His arguments before the Supreme Court in favor of the individual, the propertied, and the federal government undermined his support among those who advocated states' rights. For these

2. See Daniel Walker, *The Political Culture of the American Whigs.*

reasons, Webster was unable to secure the nomination of his beloved Whig Party despite the fact that he was one of its chief architects and eventually its most qualified member.

Webster lived when the country was expanding rapidly, perhaps too rapidly for its own good. The expansion created centrifugal forces that would tear the country apart only eight years after Webster's death. His genius, in fact, was to help hold the country together during this difficult period. He accomplished that herculean task with a rhetoric that advanced an American agenda in the Whig platform that led to major improvements, particularly in transportation and commerce. He provided a lexicon of values that not only made Union a transcendent term but also reinforced the lessons of the founders, particularly Washington and Madison. Lincoln used Webster's call for the preservation of the Union as his touchstone. In fact, the end of the Gettysburg Address echoes a line in Webster's Second Reply to Hayne.

Early in Webster's life, especially during the War of 1812 and the battle over nullification, the survival of the Union was not a given. However, Webster's memorialization of the Union, often found in commemorative speeches on the occasion of beginning a monument, moved the Union into the public consciousness and concretized it. I will attempt to show that Webster transformed the civic republicanism of Washington, Adams, Jefferson, Hamilton, and Madison into a civil religion that transcended the political agenda of the times. A decade after Webster's death, soldiers gave their lives for his precious Union with his words in their hearts and on their lips. That kind of faith is rare in the civic arena. It can only be generated by a civil religion. In this case, it was the result of rhetorical acumen.

While for some there was a tension between liberty and Union—individual liberty versus taxation, states' rights versus national priorities—for Webster it was the Union that provided a guarantee of the pragmatic and metaphysical liberties the country embraced. From 1806 forward, Webster identified the Constitution with the Union; the former was the pragmatic architectural plan, the latter was the transcendent *telos* of nationhood. After his replies to Hayne in 1830, Webster was the high priest of American civil religion. However, he was to learn that compromise and religion do not mix. His failure to achieve the presidential nomination may have been a result of his compromising some of the principles of the civil religion he created.

In my attempt to explain Webster's effectiveness, I do not neglect his forensic triumphs. His speeches before the Supreme Court were so powerful that John Marshall borrowed from them when writing his opinions establishing the Court's review power and Federalist dogma. Like no other person in American history, Webster dominated the courts, the legislature, and the public-speaking circuit. Webster claimed that the law was his guardian angel. For him, laws constructed by humans transcended every form of human endeavor in terms of public policy and served only one master, natural law. By the end of his life, however, Webster believed that the Union created by the Constitution was the most transcendent law of all. He made it part of America's civil religion, and it has held that status ever since.[3] This offended those like Theodore Parker and Ralph Waldo Emerson, who believed that natural law was superior to the Constitution, or at least to the Fugitive Slave Law. Webster's comfort with the law came from its fixed and settled nature, and he attempted to pass this comfort on to the nation. In fact, he believed that election results were roughly akin to a jury verdict.[4]

His biography is the story of important speeches woven into a life of service to his country. He came to national prominence in 1812 and remained in the public consciousness well after his death in 1852. His success is a given; by accounting for that success, we can refine the theory by which we build speeches today, particularly speeches in those arenas where Webster did battle. Thus, this study is not only about the themes Webster developed and extended during his political career, but also about the rhetorical strategies he employed with such effect. In other words, this study looks at history through the lens of public address rather than the other way around.

Because Webster was so attuned to his audiences, it is possible that by examining the evidence, arguments, strategies, delivery, and style he used, we can obtain a clearer picture of American consciousness in the first half of the nineteenth century. The values expressed in his speeches were the same values held in the public consciousness. Webster, however, did more than adapt to the popular public mind; he changed it by reordering the priority of those values. By surveying his most effective addresses and analyzing the audiences to which they were delivered, we can reconstruct the public consciousness of the time. Such a reconstruction can be achieved only by the careful examination of speeches that are attuned to public attitudes. In short, rhetorical analysis refines our understanding of American society and thereby serves as an essential adjunct to any historical study of the time.

Ultimately, Webster's story is fascinating because it is about a man who was

3. See Sanford Levinson, "'The Constitution' in American Civil Religion."
4. Ferguson, *Law and Letters*, 208, 211.

self-made and who understood how important public speaking was to the process of self-creation. At almost every important juncture of his life, Webster delivered a speech that enhanced his reputation, saved the Republic, or changed the course of American constitutional law. He was addicted to language because he knew language shaped perception. It could bring reality into focus and it could convert division and disagreement into compromise. When confusion reigned and the truth was impossible to obtain, rhetoric could create what Protagoras called the better illusion. And what language could do for political issues, it could do for personal success. Webster was no romantic war hero; in fact, he believed soldiers were of little use in the political realm, where intelligent men understood the power of language and could wield it on the legislative and forensic battlefield. Webster polished and refined his talent for words; he sought to make his mark in a world where words were more important than swords and bullets. Luckily, he was raised in a country that believed in freedom of expression and where citizens had created a republican democracy in which deliberation and public speaking were highly valued. Webster's enormous success in that society should inspire those who seek a country committed to reasoned decision-making and who believe that an understanding of the state and the nature of public issues is important to the proper functioning of a republic.

Chapter 1

The Foundation of Webster's Civil Religion

The parallels between Webster's father and his father figure, George Washington, inspired some of his best ceremonial speeches. Like Washington, Ebenezer Webster fought in the French and Indian War. By age twenty-four he had led troops into Canada and risen to the rank of captain. For this accomplishment he was given land in New Hampshire which eventually became Salisbury, a cold and inhospitable town subject to invasions by bears, wolves, and Native Americans. It was there that his son Daniel would be born in 1782.

When the Revolution came, Ebenezer Webster was ready. He resumed his role as captain and assembled a group of some two hundred men who battled the British at Bennington, White Plains, and West Point at the time of Benedict Arnold's betrayal. In fact, Webster guarded Washington's tent on the night of the treason.[1] In 1788, he served as a representative to the New Hampshire constitutional ratifying convention. He was proud of the fact that New Hampshire put the Constitution over the top by becoming the ninth state to ratify the document. He also served as a judge for the Court of Common Pleas. The identification between Ebenezer Webster and George Washington was complete in young Daniel's mind at the time of Washington's death in 1799, even though the former president ended his life as a slaveholder. Daniel excused Washington's blind spot with several rationalizations: Washington was a hero of the Revolution; he did not purchase his slaves but married a woman who already owned them; and he freed them in his last will.[2]

---

1. Robert V. Remini, *Daniel Webster: The Man and His Time*, 32.
2. As we shall see, Thomas Jefferson lived well into Webster's adult life and the two met at one juncture, but Webster never condemned Jefferson's slaveholding, nor the fact that he would

Civil Religion

Daniel Webster was of the second generation of American leaders who came into prominence around the War of 1812 with Britain. These orator-leaders had a deep belief in the heroic nature of the birth of the United States, and they were not reluctant to valorize that past in their rhetoric. If not for the likes of Webster, John C. Calhoun, John Quincy Adams, Andrew Jackson, Henry Clay, and others of this second generation, America might not have developed its civil religion and civil war might have come earlier, while the South was strong enough to sustain itself against a Union that had a weak self-conception. Of these leaders, none was more important than Webster when it came to establishing a priority of values for developing nationhood. His talent was to use the founders, particularly Washington, to advance the Federalist agenda, often in the guise of making a ceremonial speech. Because of him, *the Union* became the God-term that Lincoln would use to justify the North's prosecution of the Civil War. The Union was Webster's heaven on earth; the Constitution was his Ten Commandments.

By civil religion I mean the mythos and rhetoric of nation-building that constitute a schema of values which in turn guides decision making. Whether one examines the nation-building techniques of the Egyptians, the Greeks, or the Romans, one finds the use of mythology to rationalize a vision of civic virtue and expansion. In each case there is a retrieval of the origins of nationhood or a tale of the rebirth of a nation. Hesiod and Homer provided the heroes, heroines, and gods that inspired Greek character and justified conquest. Speaking for democratic Athens, Pericles rationalized war against the Spartans; his rhetoric refined the Athenian sense of civic virtue. Virgil revised the story of Rome's founding to include Aeneas, a hero of Troy. The best of these values were merged into a call for civic republicanism based on the Roman republic as idealized in the speeches and writings of Cicero. Cicero's consistent defense of the Roman senate against the threats of Catiline and Marc Antony inspired not only Webster, but also the founders, particularly John Adams.[3]

---

not have won the electoral vote in 1800 if the three-fifths rule regarding slaves had not been in place.

3. The notion of civic republicanism and its role in scholarship is discussed in Daniel T. Rodgers, "Republicanism: The Career of a Concept." For its influence on John Adams, see Bernard Bailyn, *The Ideological Origins of the American Revolution*; J. G. A. Pocock, *The Machiavellian Moment: Florentine Political Thought and the Atlantic Republican Tradition*; Michael J. Sandel, *Democracy's Discontent: America in Search of a Public Philosophy.*

The United States was also a child of the Enlightenment. Thomas Jefferson had studied the French agitators and philosophers and the Scottish Enlightenment thinkers. However, most of the founders were more familiar with Locke's treatises on civil government. Locke's role as author of the British Bill of Rights after the Glorious Revolution of 1688 made him a natural source for civic republicanism.[4] The tension in civic republicanism is between the state's role as a dispenser of public goods, such as rights and national security, and the people's temptation to act in self-serving ways. Jefferson emphasized the benefits of a democratic republic while James Madison tended to focus on the need for checks and balances, and ultimately became the prime mover behind a bill of rights that protected minorities and curbed the voracious impulses of the majority.

Civic republicanism evolved into civil religion when the mythos of the founders was created from the lives of real people who delivered passionate speeches against the Stamp Act, wrote thoughtful treatises on independence, and led the new nation through a revolution. While myths emerged, they were much closer to actual events than were the narratives of the ancients. George Washington did not throw a silver dollar across the Potomac, but he did throw one across the Rappahannock. Paul Revere did ride through the countryside warning people that the British were coming. Betsy Ross constructed an American flag for one of the signers of the Declaration of Independence, and Nathan Hale died for it. American troops did spend a winter at Valley Forge with their feet bound in rags.

Which stories form a nation's civil religion is often determined by the orators who recall those stories for their audiences.[5] Few were better at glorifying America's immediate past than Daniel Webster. He clearly understood that the American revolution led to the rebirth of a nation first founded as diverse colonies in the wilderness. For Webster the Declaration of Independence served as the baptism of the new nation; the Constitution was its confirmation. These were sacramental moments in America's civil religion that could

---

4. See Louis Hartz, *The Liberal Tradition in America: An Interpretation of American Political Thought since the Revolution,* and Thomas L. Pangle, *The Spirit of Modern Republicanism: The Moral Vision of the American Founders and the Philosophy of Locke.* I do not mean to minimize the influence of the Scottish Enlightenment, particularly on Jefferson; see Joyce Appleby, *Capitalism and a New Social Order: The Republican Vision of the 1790s,* and Paul A. Rahe, *Inventions of Prudence: Constituting the American Regime.* Lance Banning, however, attributes most of the Jeffersonian philosophy to English opposition leaders; see *The Jeffersonian Persuasion: Evolution of a Party Ideology.*

5. See James Arnt Aune, "Public Address and Rhetorical Theory."

be shared again and again through the agency of Webster's oratory. His rhetorical ability allowed him to lead the public in mass celebrations that consecrated America's most sacred values. He became one of the high priests of American civil religion from at least 1820 to his death in 1852.

Civil religion not only recalls the past, it instructs on how to act in the present. As in Cicero's day, the speakers of Webster's day used celebratory rhetoric to shape current values. These values became guides to decision-making for the nation's leaders. The complication with such rhetoric is that audiences hold not only themselves but their speakers to the standards that are articulated. Thus, Webster took an enormous risk when he entered into compromise negotiations; they could undermine the more platonic themes of his civil religion. In fact, he was roundly condemned in New England because the 1850 Compromise included the Fugitive Slave Law, which was offensive to idealists who had supported Webster earlier.

The tension between civil religion and political compromise is a theme I shall pursue in this study. Its contemporary application should be obvious in an era marked by Manichaean presidential rhetoric that attacks "evil empires" and an "axis of evil." While good-and-evil dualities often prove attractive to the public, they can haunt those who rely on such tactics. Once politics is elevated to the level of religion, it tends to become uncompromising. That is a problem for those who believe, as did Webster, that politics is the art of compromising.

Finally, civil religion guides the nation toward a *telos*, an ultimate freedom, and, in so doing, takes on an ever stronger religious cast. Jonathan Winthrop's reference to a shining city upon a hill in 1630 not only recalled the prophet Micah and the Book of Revelation, it also provided a goal toward which the Massachusetts colony could strive. Centuries later when Ronald Reagan revived Winthrop's metaphor for political purposes, he recalled the Puritan adventure in the wilderness and provided a *telos* for the future by claiming dramatically that the United States was the last best hope of mankind. The conversion of the wilderness into a "civilized" place was a leitmotif of American civil religion that culminated in the call for manifest destiny in Webster's time. Appeals to hardship, sacrifice, battle, and martyrdom rallied the public to expansionism before and after the invention of the phrase *manifest destiny* in 1845. That idea was a natural extension of the belief that Americans were a chosen people with a mission not only to cultivate the land, but also to bring the "blessings" of civilization to a new continent.

While Webster recoiled from the dangers of expansion, particularly the unjust war with Mexico, he embraced the part of the myth that eulogized property. Like Jefferson, Webster believed that those who owned a piece of the nation were more likely to protect and defend it. A favorite quotation of landholding revolutionaries like Webster, who was a major defender of property rights before the Supreme Court, was Rousseau's comment "The first man who, having fenced in a piece of land, said, 'This is mine,' and found people naive enough to believe him, that man was the true founder of civil society."[6] Webster was also familiar with the *Second Treatise on Government*, in which Locke sets out his view on the subject of property:

> God, when he gave the World in common to all Mankind, commanded Man also to labour, and the penury of his Condition required it of him. God and his Reason commanded him to subdue the Earth, i.e., improve it for the benefit of Life, and therein lay out something upon it that was his own, his labour. He that in Obedience to this Command of God, subdued, tilled, and sowed any part of it, thereby annexed to it something that was his *Property*, which another had no Title to, nor could without injury take from him.[7]

Webster incorporated Locke's thesis into American civil religion.

When fully formed, Webster's patriotism called on the public to live up to the goals of the nation's founders and to venerate the sacrifices they made in bringing the nation to its ultimate fulfillment. Webster may never have been more effective in this regard than in his address celebrating the start of construction of the Bunker Hill Monument. Sitting near him were the survivors of that early revolutionary battle. He referenced them and those who died in the battle, coaxing his audience to lead better lives and achieve the dream for which those soldiers fought. Webster understood that civic cleansing, like religious cleansing, can be achieved by rebirth through rhetorical identification. Thus, he created a channel through which the audience became one with the soldiers who sat on the stage and with those who had given their lives. As audience members relived the sacrifice of the soldiers, they were purged, unified, and transformed into more perfect citizens.

Webster could achieve this transcendence because he was well educated in America's past. That past provided a foundation for his civil religion. Thus, to contextualize his oratory, we need to review the formation of the tenets of his philosophy—that is, his version of civic republicanism.

6. Jean-Jacques Rousseau, *Discourse on the Origin and Foundation of the Inequality between Men*, 192.
7. John Locke, *Two Treatises on Civil Government*, 309.

Webster's Evolving Federalism

Not surprisingly, the political philosophy of Webster and his contemporaries can be traced to past generations. For example, before the Revolution orators stirred the country from the pulpit and political stump with a mix of revivalist zeal and Enlightenment reason. This synthesis occurred most notably in the rhetoric of Rev. Jonathan Mayhew of Boston. His most famous sermon, "A Discourse concerning Unlimited Submission and Non-Resistance to the Higher Powers," was delivered in 1750. An examination of the sermon reveals why some have called it "the morning gun of the revolution." Its avowal of independence, natural rights, and individualism reflects Enlightenment thinking and is, in turn, reflected in the writings of Thomas Jefferson and George Mason twenty-six years later. This passage about the duties of the ruler and the ruled inspired Jefferson as he wrote the Declaration: "[I]t follows, by a parity of reason, that when [our ruler] turns tyrant, and makes his subjects his prey to devour and to destroy, . . . we are bound to throw off our allegiance to him, and to resist. . . . [T]o resist [our] prince, even to the dethroning [of] him, is not criminal; but a reasonable way of indicating [our] liberties and just rights." In 1763, Mayhew, ever the gadfly, authored the pamphlet *Observations on the Charter and Conduct of the Society for the Propagation of the Gospel in Foreign Parts*, which asked: "[I]s it not enough that they persecuted us out of the old world? Will they pursue us into the new to convert us here?"[8]

During the Revolution and in the debates over the ratification of the Constitution and the Bill of Rights, it was common for ministers to take political positions. They were particularly concerned about freedom of religion in the new nation.[9] This habit, which can be traced back to Jonathan Winthrop and forward to Jerry Falwell and Pat Robertson, also contributes to ways in which American political ideology merges with religious zeal.

No doubt Webster was also influenced by the oratory of Patrick Henry, which was spread through the colonies by underground presses. In Massachusetts Henry's published speeches led to the formation of the Sons of Liberty. Samuel Adams became the leading propagandist for a war of independence, particularly when a squad of British troops fired into a threatening crowd in Boston in 1770. Adams rhetorically recreated the "massacre" in

---

8. Charles W. Akers, *Called unto Liberty: A Life of Jonathan Mayhew, 1720–1766*, 85, 184.

9. See Craig R. Smith and David M. Hunsaker, "The Religious Clauses of the First Amendment," chap. 3 of *The Four Freedoms of the First Amendment: A Textbook*.

the *Boston Gazette* and used that newspaper's offices to print many powerful pamphlets.

American independence was based in part on the precedent of the Magna Charta of 1215 and the English Bill of Rights of 1689. Thus, when the colonies declared independence, most of them also called for a bill of rights. Pennsylvania in 1776, New York in 1777, South Carolina in 1778, and New Hampshire in 1783 all endorsed a bill of rights. In 1778 Massachusetts rejected a new constitution because it did not contain one. This history of the writing of new charters during the Revolution makes clear why so many colonists demanded a bill of rights when a federal constitution was written ten years later. These legal and political documents would allow Webster to declare that he understood the intent of the founders and thus could speak for them and act on their behalf.

These transitions from oratorical wishes to legal documents provided a nurturing environment for political parties. An atmosphere for debate had been established in which it was assumed that certain natural rights were inalienable and that reason would rule in the formation of law. In the interim, the Constitution of the United States was adopted in Philadelphia. The need for a new constitution to supersede the Articles of Confederation would prove important to the formation of the Federalist Party and to Webster. The leadership of the Federalist movement was composed of members of the merchant class, which wanted a strong federal government to protect shipping, to protect fledgling industries, and to extract taxes and tariffs that would pay for internal improvements. Webster inherited and defended this tradition for many reasons: his father was a Federalist; his law clients were mainly Federalists; the interests of New Hampshire and Massachusetts were mainly Federalist. Most of all, however, after defending Federalism in the courts and arguing for it in the House and Senate, Webster believed it was the only way the country could survive—economically, internationally, and ideologically.

Those opposed to Webster came out of the Anti-Federalist tradition. Reflecting their agrarian bias, the Anti-Federalists tried to lower taxes and tariffs, to protect minority and states' rights, and to reduce government interference. Later, embracing the civil religion of John C. Calhoun, some agrarian interests defended slavery and attempted to nullify tariffs using states' rights as their shield. The Federalists attempted to contain slavery and use tariffs to protect manufacturers, with the Union as their shield. The Federalists' rationale for a new constitution served Webster in his calls—in the Congress, before the

Supreme Court, and as Secretary of State—for curtailing states' rights. He believed that the Articles of Confederation failed because they gave too much
power to the states.

Webster also noted that among the former colonies sectionalism undercut
the Articles of Confederation. Before 1776, the colonies had divided into
three distinct groups, with different social, political, and economic interests.
The original New England states (Massachusetts, New Hampshire, Rhode Island, Connecticut) were called the "Eastern" states, as opposed to the four
"Middle" states of New York, New Jersey, Pennsylvania, and Delaware and the
five "Southern" states. By 1783, the Eastern states were using the threat of
forming a separate confederation to support their demand for a stronger central government.[10] New England again threatened secession in 1812 over "Mr.
Madison's war" with England, which the Eastern states did not support.
Webster played an important and controversial role in that debate; the roots
of his position can be traced back to the controversy of 1783.

Other animosities between the North and South were brought to the fore
in the summer of 1786 during debates in Congress over the navigation of the
Mississippi River.[11] On August 12, 1786, Virginian James Monroe wrote that a
group of New Englanders and New Yorkers had proposed dividing the confederation at the Hudson River. Noting that two Pennsylvania congressmen favored the idea, Monroe suggested, "It were as well to use force to prevent it as
to defend ourselves afterwards."[12]

When the Whig Party was under siege by Jacksonian populism, Webster relied on such Federalists as Alexander Hamilton to defend republicanism. According to Max Farrand, Hamilton "had no sympathy for the Articles of
Confederation." During the constitutional convention of 1787, he provided
the delegates with his own plan calling for a strong central government and

10. Nathaniel Gorham of Massachusetts, speaking in Congress, declared that if that body was
not given the ability to meet the demands of public creditors, the Articles of Confederation
would fail and "some of the states might be forming other confederacies adequate to the purposes of their safety." James Madison, notes on debates, February 21, 1783, in *The Papers of James
Madison*, 6:273. See also John P. Kaminski and Gaspare J. Saladino, eds., *The Documentary
History of the Ratification of the Constitution*, 13:55.

11. At one point, Rufus King, Benjamin Lincoln, and Theodore Sedgwick of Massachusetts
proposed a separate New England confederacy. Kaminski and Saladino, *Documentary History*,
13:55.

12. James Monroe to the governor of Virginia, August 12, 1786, in Edmund C. Burnett, ed.,
Letters of Members of the Continental Congress, 8:424-25.

limited popular participation through elected representatives. He said on June 18 that "the British government was the best in the world. . . . This government has for its object public strength and individual security." He went even further on June 26:

> All communities divide themselves into the few and the many. The first are the rich and wellborn, the other the mass of the people. . . . The people are turbulent and changing; they seldom judge or determine right. Give therefore to the first class a distinct, permanent share in the government. They will check the unsteadiness of the second, and as they cannot receive any advantage by change, they therefore will ever maintain good government.[13]

In the *Federalist Papers*, Hamilton, perhaps reflecting the thinking of Thomas Hobbes, argued that "the passions of men will not conform to the dictates of reason and justice, without constraint."[14] Like Madison, Webster shared Hamilton's view of human nature, and he incorporated it into his civil religion.

The Ratification Debates

When the Constitution was submitted to the states, many Americans registered their dissatisfaction with the omission of a bill of rights. Conventions had been an innovative idea at the time of the Revolution. However, since Americans had found them an effective way to draft state constitutions, it followed that ratification of the new Constitution should be accomplished by state conventions, assemblies of the representatives of the people.[15] Thus, cauldrons for political partisanship were forged even as the system rejected direct democracy.

During the convention Madison was not involved in the brief dialogue concerning the insertion of a bill of rights into the Constitution. His lack of concern grew out of his conception of Federalism. If the Constitution did not empower the federal government to promote or establish any religion or to restrict speech and the press, he believed, then all questions concerning freedom

13. Max Farrand, ed., *The Records of the Federal Convention of 1787*, 1:291, 288, 434.

14. Alexander Hamilton, *Federalist* (no. 15), 35.

15. Conventions would again be called in 1820 and 1821 when states sought to revise their constitutions. In 1831 the first party nominating convention was held, and all major parties have used them since.

of the press, speech, and religion would be left exclusively to the individual states to decide. If the Constitution contained a provision relating to those freedoms, reasoned Madison, it might be seen as an invitation to limit individual freedoms. Later, he would change his mind. At the time, he returned to Virginia from Philadelphia and became one of the Constitution's most ardent defenders, writing twenty-nine of the eighty-five articles that became *The Federalist Papers.* These editorials became the bible of the Federalist Party; each and every one was closely studied by Webster in his formative years.

Madison was but one participant in the Federalist campaign of persuasion. Federalists kept up a steady barrage of editorial opinion in the press. They succeeded in dubbing their opponents "Anti-Federalists," in place of the preferred "Federal Republicans." They out-organized and outflanked the Republicans as the crucial ratification debates began in state conventions. During those debates, however, the "Anti-Federalists" were able to sustain a call for a bill of rights, particularly in states that refused to ratify, such as North Carolina and Rhode Island, and in states that ratified reluctantly or conditionally, such as Massachusetts, Virginia, and New York.

One of the reasons for the high level of debate was that the founders were thoroughly familiar with the theoretical writings of Locke, Hobbes, Sir Philip Sidney, Milton, Montesquieu, Rousseau, Richard Price, and John Cartwright. Another influential rationalist was Algernon Sidney, whose *Discourses on Government* of 1698 were standard reading for the founders. James Burgh's popular *Political Disquisitions* (1774–1775), on nonconformist thought and natural rights, could be found in almost every sizeable town.

What the founders brought to Enlightenment thinking was know-how. Certainly Henry Clay and Daniel Webster understood that the founders converted the theories of European philosophers into the realities of the American political system. The founders were pragmatists who wanted the government to help them get things done. Like Aristotle, they sought an expedient system, not so much an ideal one. Clay's compromises and Webster's legal briefs are classic examples of how the second generation brought practicality to the theories of the first.

The Enlightenment thinkers derived many liberties from earlier documents that granted new rights to nobles. For example, the Magna Charta included due process, protection of unjust seizure of property and person, and trial by jury. The right to petition the government and to bear arms were included in the English Bill of Rights. It was, in fact, the English Bill of Rights that gave its name to our own even though many of the rights contained in the English Bill were first developed in the colonies.

As they evolved and decided to seek independence, the colonies also developed new rights that were never part of the English system of justice. In fact, some of the rights developed in the colonies predate Locke and other Enlightenment thinkers. As Webster often pointed out, Massachusetts' interest in a bill of rights can be traced to its early history starting with the Mayflower Compact of 1620 and the Pilgrim Code of Law of 1636. More important, however, was the Massachusetts Body of Liberties of 1641, the first civil document in the colonies to call for a guarantee of free speech, bail before trial, a jury trial, and the right to counsel. It was the first to protect individuals from double jeopardy, to provide for just compensation, and to reserve certain powers from government control. It was the first document in the history of the world to forbid unauthorized searches. In short, it contained many of the rights incorporated into the first ten amendments to the Constitution. The Body of Liberties was strengthened by the Laws and Liberties of Massachusetts, drafted in 1647. This may explain why Massachusetts was so adamant to add a bill of rights to the Constitution. Even before he became a lawyer in Boston, Webster was well aware of this tradition.

Partisan Strategies

While the Anti-Federalists numbered among their members some exceptional writers who published some important documents under various pseudonyms, they did not mount an effort equaling *The Federalist Papers*. In fact, the Anti-Federalists were about as diverse a group as one could imagine in the colonies. This may explain why George Mason was unable to form a committee of correspondents. Imagine what Mason, Patrick Henry, and Richard Henry Lee might have written in defense of their position had their effort been coordinated. Instead, Anti-Federalists too often had to fend for themselves, relying on infrequent letters from their leaders or gleaning what arguments they could from published rebuttals in the press. Furthermore, there was no consensus among Anti-Federalists on which form of government would work best. Elitists such as Luther Martin and Richard Henry Lee believed in a natural aristocracy that was tempered by democracy. Poorer Anti-Federalists tended to favor more direct democracy and to resent the elitists. In general, however, all Anti-Federalists opposed consolidation of the national government and unlimited powers for Congress; they favored states' rights and a bill of rights, particularly freedom of the press, speech, and religion.

On February 6, 1788, Massachusetts ratified the Constitution only after acrimonious debate and with the provision that a bill of rights be added. Although Maryland ratified the document on April 26 and South Carolina on May 23, Patrick Henry succeeded in delaying consideration in Virginia and Gov. George Clinton simultaneously delayed consideration in New York. If these two states held out, the Constitution would be mortally wounded, for they were the most populous and geographically imposing states. In June, New Hampshire became the ninth state to ratify, with Webster's father voting in the affirmative, and the Constitution was finally the law of the land, but Virginia and New York were needed to prevent the Union from being divided.

Before Virginians got word of the action taken in New Hampshire, however, Henry was defeated when on June 25, 1788, Virginia ratified the Constitution, believing it had provided the crucial ninth vote. New York followed suit on July 26. While some hope remained that the new states could still call for a new constitutional convention under the provisions of Article V, most leaders believed that the task of proposing amendments to the states would fall to the new Congress.

As a result of the state ratifying conventions, the Federalists got their Constitution, but the Anti-Federalists extracted a pledge for a bill of rights. Even though Madison opted for the legislative mode for drafting and ratifying amendments, his move to address them at all revealed that the clash with Henry had a significant impact on him.

Much to John Adams's horror, Jefferson mailed Thomas Paine's *Rights of Man* to influential opinion makers in support of the need for a bill of rights. Adams wrote to Jefferson claiming he had damaged the ratification process. This plaintive message contains one of the most interesting sentences in the history of American letters. Adams directly rejected Jefferson's olive branch concerning their "differences of opinion in private conversation." Wrote Adams, "You and I have never had a serious conversation together that I can recollect concerning the nature of government." This comes as something of a shock to those who have credited reports that Adams and Jefferson spent time at various junctures discussing the nature of government before the Declaration of Independence was written. When Webster rose to eulogize Adams and Jefferson in 1826, it made his task all the more difficult, as we shall see.

The founders believed that certain rights were inalienable, that they were natural or God-given, and that they were intended to protect the individual citizen from the federal government. The founders sought to preserve as much of states' rights as they could while building a viable Union. Only those items enumerated were to be the province of the Congress; it was not to assume any powers on its own. That predisposition would change with civil war and the passage of the Fourteenth Amendment, which was eventually used to enforce the first nine amendments against the states. At the time the Bill of Rights was being debated, however, Federalists gave Anti-Federalists assurances that the federal government would not overstep the checks and balances established by the Constitution. The Ninth and Tenth Amendments sealed that bargain.

Secretary of State Jefferson certified the Bill of Rights on March 1, 1792, when he announced that three-fourths of the state legislatures had ratified ten amendments to the Constitution. The road to ratification stretched back to the Magna Charta and wound through the works of Enlightenment thinkers into America's colonial experience, revealing each colony to be a distinct innovator of human liberties. The state constitutional ratification conventions heard cries for a national bill of rights.

The debates over the Bill of Rights had several important implications for Webster's interpretation of the Constitution. If one accepts the position of Madison and Jefferson that the Constitution should be interpreted in terms of its original intent, strict constructionists have a strong argument that their interpretation is the closest to what the founders had in mind.[16] In the ratification debates, the antagonists agreed that the federal government should be granted no powers that were not clearly enumerated. There was no endorsement of "implied powers," "penumbras" of meaning, or a "living constitution." To those who advance such notions, the vast majority of founders would probably have responded: If you don't like the Constitution the way it is, amend it. In one of his first speeches on the floor of the House, Webster began, "After the best reflection which I have been able to bestow on the subject of the bill before you, I am of the opinion that its principles are not warranted by any

16. Madison wrote that the Constitution must be interpreted according to "its true meaning as understood by the nation at the time of its ratification." James Madison to John G. Jackson, December 27, 1821, in Letters and Other Writings of James Madison, 3:244. Jefferson wrote that lawmakers ought to return "to the time when the constitution was adopted, recollect the spirit manifest in the debates, and instead of trying what meaning may be squeezed out of the text, or invented against it, conform to the probable one in which it was passed." Thomas Jefferson to William Johnson, June 12, 1823, Library of Congress, http://memory.loc.gov/master/mss/mtj/mtj1/053/1000/1004.jpg.

provision of the Constitution."[17] Webster's construction of the Constitution would often emerge in speeches in the Congress, though he was more than willing to give a little when it was in the interest of his clients before the Supreme Court.

Webster realized that the Constitution took Enlightenment themes and converted them into pragmatic realities. Building on the Magna Charta and the English Bill of Rights of 1689, Americans put European theory into practice with the Pilgrim Code, the Massachusetts Body of Liberties, the Pennsylvania Charter of Liberties, and the Virginia Declaration of Rights as the colonies evolved into a nation. After the Revolution, the debates over the ratification of the Constitution and the Bill of Rights established the two-party system. The Federalists held the presidency during Webster's formative years, using it to make judicial appointments that would last well into the nineteenth century. When John Adams succeeded George Washington in 1797, Federalists realized that they no longer had a charismatic leader. Adams soon found he could not rein in Hamilton, who strengthened the party by using the crisis of a quasi-war with France.

New immigrants to America moved into the party of Jefferson, the rebuilt home of the Anti-Federalists. When Jefferson was elected president in 1800, the two-party system was institutionalized and the Federalist Party began its decline, in part because the public began to turn against Hamilton's Alien and Sedition Acts. As a young Federalist, Webster would do all in his power to save the party and when that failed he would revive Federalist doctrine in a new National Republican (Whig) party. In this effort, he would rely on the Federalist credo, the interests of his state, and the guidance of George Washington.[18] In fact, Washington, despite being a plantation slaveholder, would emerge as the godhead of Webster's sect. Like other founders, Washington was a Freemason; Masonic symbols—reflections of builders of Egypt, Greece, and Rome— inspired the country's early architecture and still adorn U.S. currency. The founders downplayed their religion; like Pericles and Cicero, they devoted more time to their nation than to their church. Their vague deism allowed Webster to recast them into his civil religion. Before he could do that, however, he needed rhetorical and legal training. It is to that training that we now turn.

17. *The Papers of Daniel Webster: Speeches and Formal Writings*, ed. Charles M. Wiltse and Alan R. Berolzheimer, 1:20. The speech was delivered on December 9, 1814, in opposition to a conscription bill.

18. See Henry Weincek, *An Imperfect God: George Washington, His Slaves, and the Creation of America.*

The Education of a Citizen Orator

Daniel Webster's rhetorical prowess was not only the product of natural talent, it was also the product of a solid education and hard work. His mastery of
the techniques of Aristotle and Cicero served him well as he attempted to advance Federalist principles in the courts, in the Congress, and on the stump.
He did this by incorporating Federalist principles into the Whig Party and
into a civil religion that was most clearly and transcendentally expressed in his
ceremonial addresses. While Webster's pursuit of the presidency was a failure
of strategic thinking, he did enjoy much public adulation and certainly influenced the course of the nation. Much of this success was due to how his education refined his natural genius and talent.

With the Revolution over and the Treaty of Paris soon to be signed, the
United States was in its infancy in 1782. On January 18 of that year, Daniel
Webster was born in Salisbury, New Hampshire, to his father's second wife,
Abigail.[19] Daniel was two years younger than his parents' first son, Ezekiel,
who had been preceded by his sisters Mehitable and Abigail. (A third sister,
Sarah, was born in 1784.) The brothers became very close. Daniel's olive com-
plexion and black hair led his classmates to dub him "Black Dan"; that name's
meaning would be perverted by those who later condemned him as "Black
Dan," the man who sold out his values. Daniel's earliest lessons came from the
Bible as taught him by his parents.

A stern master, Ebenezer Webster required young Daniel to memorize
Watt's *Psalms*; when Daniel succeeded, his father knew he had a phenomenal
memory. These same passages would later float into Webster's consciousness
as he composed his speeches, and from there into the minds of his listeners.
When at the age of four Daniel began to show an interest in poetry, his father
provided outside tutors for him. Soon Daniel was reading Pope's *Essay on Man*
and Cervantes' *Don Quixote*.[20] Before he was ten, he was declaiming passages
from the Bible to citizens of the Merrimack Valley, who marveled at his clear
voice. Raised a Presbyterian, Webster would carry the marks of standard
Protestantism with him all his life. He used his understanding of individual
salvation to guide his adaptation of the Second Great Awakening, which developed around 1800 and lasted into the 1830s, moving from the South to the

19. Ebenezer Webster's first wife, Mehitable, bore three children who survived into adult-
hood: Suzannah, David, and Joseph. Mehitable died in 1774; five months later, Ebenezer married Abigail Eastman, a thirty-seven-year-old seamstress.

20. Remini, *Daniel Webster*, 15; Maurice G. Baxter, *One and Inseparable: Daniel Webster and the
Union*, 4.

North. That religious movement paralleled Webster's attempt to construct a civil religion out of America's respect for the civic republicanism of the founders.

By age thirteen, Webster was an intern in the local law office of Thomas Thompson, where he memorized and used legal phrases, many in Latin, that would serve him throughout his career and mark his published speeches. Thompson, a Harvard graduate, was the first of a series of mentors who took Webster under their wing. Older men of learning and skill were often so impressed with Webster that they not only accepted him as an apprentice, but also guided him in his later adventures. Thompson, for example, encouraged him to seek the best education available. These mentors, particularly the noted jurist Christopher Gore, became even more important to Webster after his father died.

Despite Thompson's help, Webster barely qualified for entrance into Phillips Exeter Academy in 1796. There, he was homesick and very insecure about public speaking. In fact, he had such stage fright that he often found himself unable to stand before the class. He would return to his room after these occasions and weep over his plight. In December of 1796, he dropped out of school.

This failure caused Webster to mount a major reexamination of his priorities. He believed he had failed his father and needed to provide income to the family. Thus, during the winter of 1797, he found himself trudging off to teach elementary school in Salisbury. Webster was a good teacher, but bored with his duties. He decided that he must attend college. In order to ready himself for the qualifying examinations, he took up study with Dr. Samuel Wood in nearby Boscawen. Wood stressed Cicero and Virgil; Webster was fascinated and had soon memorized Cicero's attacks on Catiline.

Next Webster took up Greek grammar with a Dartmouth senior named David Palmer in order to prepare for entry into that college. Though he never mastered Greek the way he did Latin, Webster learned enough to translate parts of the New Testament. He continued to work on his Latin and Greek, and is said to have memorized *Paradise Lost.* After a while, speaking began to come naturally to him. More important, the next year he excelled in enough subjects that his father agreed to send him to Dartmouth College if he could qualify. His efforts were rewarded in August of 1797; at age fifteen, Webster became a student at Dartmouth, only the third person from Salisbury to go to college.

When Webster attended Dartmouth, it was served by only four professors with three aides. In his freshman year he became more familiar with Cicero's

Select Orations and *De Oratore* and rhetorical theory and criticism.[21] In his next three years, he studied the Greek classics, Hugh Blair's *Lectures on Rhetoric and Belles Lettres*, moral philosophy, politics, and the law. Blair's book focused on creating the sublime, as Webster would do in his greatest orations. From the purity of Pericles to the florid style of Alcibiades, Webster learned that words can be the vehicles of great thought. Perhaps from Thucydides' account of the debates over the fate of Mytelene and Syracuse, he learned how argument can shape public opinion and decide the fate of nations. His talent was further refined by classes in oratorical composition and delivery and by membership in literary societies. He became the United Fraternity's top debater and formed the Federal Club to promote the party of Washington, Hamilton, and Adams. Again, he was nicknamed "Black Dan" because of his dark looks.

Receiving a charter from an earl of the same name, Dartmouth began as a school for Native Americans in 1769, and, when Webster entered, was a much lesser light than Harvard. However, classes at Dartmouth were perhaps some of the most rigorous in the new nation. They included instruction on all the elements of rhetoric with special emphasis on logic, the emotions, stylistic commonplaces, and organization. Webster quickly mastered these areas and in his junior year was given the privilege of delivering the 1800 Fourth of July address for the town of Hanover.

This assignment was heady stuff for an eighteen-year-old. Webster's first epideictic effort pleased the crowd, even though some of its phrasing was heavy-handed. He began:

> Countrymen, brethren, and fathers. . . .
>
> Twenty-four years have this day elapsed, since United Columbia first raised the standard of Liberty, and echoed the shouts of Independence!
>
> Those of you, who were then reaping the iron harvest of the martial field, whose bosoms then palpitated for the honor of America, will, at this time, experience a renewal of all that fervent patriotism, of all those indescribable emotions, which then agitated your breasts.

Clearly, Webster had a passion for the grand style. He also had a passion for Washington: "[W]here is our Washington? where the hero, who led us to victory—where the man, who gave us freedom?" He again recalled the martyrs of

21. David F. Ericson, *The Shaping of American Liberalism: The Debates over Ratification, Nullification, and Slavery*, 2; Herbert D. Foster, "Webster and Choate in College: Dartmouth under the Curriculum of 1796–1819," 511; Claude M. Fuess, *Daniel Webster*, 1:50.

the past: "For us they fought! for us they bled! for us they conquered." His awareness of world events was also evident, as was his chauvinism: "Columbia stoops not to tyrants; her sons will never cringe to France. . . . Let the sons of Europe be vassals; let her hosts of nations be a vast congregation of slaves; but let us, who are this day free, whose hearts are yet unappalled, and whose right arms are yet nerved for war, assemble before the hallowed temple of Columbian Freedom, and swear, to the God of our Fathers, to preserve it secure, or die at its portals!" Already the Federalist, Webster could not resist putting his take on the foreign crisis that Hamilton had used to force the Alien and Sedition Acts through Congress. In this election year, the young Webster would be shocked by the victory of the Democratic-Republicans.[22]

Though the speech was acclaimed by most who heard it, some groused that it was too florid.[23] Perhaps Webster was adapting to one of the distinguishing marks of his time, a reliance on emotionalism to persuade and entertain. People were far more emotionally active and responsive in public than we are today. Webster's adaptation to this emotionalism would be refined and would reemerge in many of his speeches, most notably in his First Bunker Hill Address. That Webster took the criticism to heart was evident in his next major address a year later, a eulogy for Ephraim Simonds, a fellow student. This speech was more austere, though it was one of Webster's most religious and sensitive.

Webster was required to take courses in public address every year he attended Dartmouth, culminating in legal and deliberative oratory in his senior year. Almost in revolt, he wrote poetry, which was well received by his classmates, if not by his instructors. His eyes were opened to the vices as well as the virtues of a college education. His social circle led him to gin, brandy, port, and gambling. The habits Webster formed at Dartmouth, particularly for drink and witty conversation, stayed with him all his life.

On October 6, 1800, Webster delivered an "Oration on Ambition" to the United Fraternity. In this speech he condemned the base ambition of Caesar but praised the virtuous ambition of George Washington.[24] The speech was

22. Daniel Webster, *The Writings and Speeches of Daniel Webster*, 15:475, 484.

23. Webster vowed never again to be so sophistic, and later professed embarrassment at his early effusions. *The Private Correspondence of Daniel Webster*, ed. Fletcher Webster, 1:52–53; *Writings and Speeches*, 13:582.

24. "Oration on Ambition," in Webster's original hand, can be found in the Dartmouth College Archives and online at http://www.dartmouth.edu/~dwebster/1801/ambition.html/.

widely praised and Webster was chosen to be one of the commencement speakers in 1801, but he turned down the opportunity because he believed he was not placed prominently enough in the program. Many agreed with his decision, believing that Webster was the best man in his class. So, on graduation day, Webster spoke instead before the United Fraternity on "The Influence and Instability of Opinion." The speech reveals his early talent for ceremonial oratory. In its praise of George Washington, it served as a precursor to later eulogies such as his speech at the centennial anniversary of Washington's birthday in 1832.

Becoming a Lawyer

Webster began the study of law on his own after his commencement from Dartmouth at age nineteen. Due to his father's financial difficulties, he was forced to teach school and delay his entry to the bar.[25] At Maine's Fryeburg Academy, Webster taught so well that he received a special bonus. The students were a wonderful audience for his remarkable expository talents. They allowed him to begin to hone his legal talent. He also continued to write rhetorical documents. For example, to celebrate New Year's Day in 1803 he branded President Jefferson a radical in "The News Boy's Message to the Patrons of the *Dartmouth Gazette*."[26] He studied Blackstone's *Commentaries* and often raised issues of common law in the classroom. These teaching techniques would prove helpful in addressing a jury, and Webster did not have to wait long for that opportunity. Once he was financially able, he returned to Salisbury and began an apprenticeship in the law under his old mentor Thomas Thompson. He stayed for two years.

In July 1804, Webster moved to Boston to tutor his brother in Greek and Latin and was luckily accepted as an apprentice by the great jurist Christopher Gore. Webster had arrived unannounced at Gore's office on Tremont Street after only a few days in town. Gore, a famous Federalist, commissioner, and lawyer, had just returned from Britain, having served under the Jay Treaty provisions. He hired Webster as a clerk. His incredible library was soon rifled by the young Webster, who worked diligently at improving his use of the English

25. As David F. Ericson points out, "41 percent of [Dartmouth] graduates became lawyers; 25 percent became ministers." *Shaping of American Liberalism*, 14.

26. Baxter, *One and Inseparable*, 11.

language. He read Gibbon, Boswell, Moore, and many others. He translated Latin and Norman common-law commentaries into English and worked to master case law. Gore taught Webster many useful things, not the least among them the ability to imitate the sound practices of other lawyers and to mix with high society in a civilized manner. The two men were not infrequently seen arm in arm, weaving down a cobblestone street together after an evening on the town.

Webster left Gore's office when he was admitted to the bar in March 1805. He took up the practice of law in Boscawen and was an instant success. He chose Boscawen because it was close to Salisbury, where his father lived in ill health, mourning the death of Webster's older sister Abigail. In the month prior to his admission to the bar, he found time to pen "An Appeal to the Old Whigs of New Hampshire," an attempt to rally the sagging Federalists. At Thompson's behest, Webster proceeded to campaign for the Federalist candidates in the area. His efforts went for naught as the Democratic-Republicans continued to make gains. Nonetheless, Webster defended even the Federalists' sins. His apologia for the Sedition Act of 1798 was published in the *Monthly Anthology* of Boston in 1806.

That publication signaled the fact that Boscawen was becoming too small for Webster; juries began to notice his arrogance.[27] So Webster was given his first full-fledged trial in Plymouth. Ebenezer came to watch the successful summation. Webster's triumph before his father built his confidence, but it turned to sadness when the old man died in April.

Webster was pulled out of mourning by an invitation to give a Fourth of July address at the new state capitol in Concord on Federalist contributions to the nation. In the speech, Webster defended American government as an unmatched political system, claimed that the island nation of Britain could never again threaten America, and attacked the French: "Ambition is the never-dying worm which feeds and fattens in the bosom of Gaul."[28] Webster's fame led to his being retained by several banks, a regular occurrence throughout his career for which he would be regularly criticized. In the fall of 1806, Thompson was elected to Congress, which fired Webster's ambition. Thompson's letters to him described a life on the Potomac for which Webster said he was ready to exchange the time he was spending on the

27. Remini, *Daniel Webster*, 78–79.
28. Webster, *Writings and Speeches*, 15:547.

Merrimack. Thompson let Webster know that he would have to achieve this goal one step at a time.[29]

First Webster gave his law practice to his brother, who had just finished law school. Then he relocated to Portsmouth, New Hampshire, where he partnered with Timothy Farrar, Jr., and became a contributor to the *Portsmouth Oracle*, the local Federalist outlet. In 1807, Webster was admitted to practice in the New Hampshire Superior Court, which traveled to various county seats. As he spread his wings, jurists found him more entertaining than arrogant. Webster's formula was to reinforce a clear statement of the facts and a reasonable argument with stylized emotional appeals.[30]

Portsmouth's bipartisan flavor reminded Webster of Boston, as did its harbor. He soon found another mentor in Jeremiah Mason, who often argued before the same courts as Webster. Mason, a strong Federalist, believed Webster to be a fine orator and actor, two essential talents for a great lawyer. Mason was superb at common law and clear argumentation. Webster was not above imitation. Combining his talents with those of Mason, he rounded his forensic ability into an even more powerful and effective instrument. He continued to deliver ceremonial speeches at Dartmouth on many a Fourth of July, and he expounded his Federalist philosophy at numerous dinners. He was soon known as "the Yankee Demosthenes."

In May 1808, Webster married Grace Fletcher after becoming a member of her Congregational church in Salisbury by writing his "confession." Still something of an idealist, Webster had taken a Calvinist turn even before moving to Portsmouth, which would serve him well in constructing the clear values of his civil religion. He and his wife rented a house from Jeremiah Mason in Portsmouth, where Webster's law practice was thriving.

The year 1808, of course, was a presidential election year, and Webster had high hopes for a Federalist resurgence, even though at this point in his life he greatly admired James Madison, the converted Democratic-Republican candidate, who had penned some of Webster's favorite *Federalist Papers*. Webster rightly believed that Madison was a reluctant Republican who was more concerned with checks and balances than with enhancing democracy. New Hampshire gave its electoral votes to Madison's opponent, Charles Pinckney, but this did not prevent Madison from ascending to the presidency.

29. *The Papers of Daniel Webster: Correspondence*, ed. Charles M. Wiltse et al., 1:7, 12, 74–82.
30. Peter Harvey, *Reminiscences and Anecdotes of Daniel Webster*, 46–50.

In 1809 the Federalists retook the governorship and both houses in New Hampshire. Webster campaigned for Federalist Jeremiah Smith, who won the governorship. By 1810 Webster was an official of the Federalist Party, regularly cajoling the faithful to work harder. In that same year, his daughter, Grace, was born, and Webster was chosen as one of three commissioners to revise the criminal code of the state. In March 1812, Webster became the first Federalist in thirteen years to be elected town moderator of Portsmouth; he won by twelve votes. He believed that agriculture was the foundation of all successful democracies, and quoted Aristotle to that effect.

The War of 1812

The year 1812 was a tumultuous one for Webster and the country. Madison asked for a declaration of war against Great Britain to protest the trade practices necessitated by its ongoing war with Napoleon's France. Madison could not have known that Napoleon's invasion of Russia would lead to his defeat, allowing Britain to focus its war power on its former colonies. On July 4, a few weeks after the declaration of war, Webster spoke at the request of the Washington Benevolent Society, a group of rabid Federalists. He was at his most dramatic: "We come to take counsel of the dead. From the tumults and passions that agitate the living world, we withdraw to the tomb, to listen to the dictates of the departed wisdom."[31] What could be more dramatic than the idea that the dead speak to us? It was right for the time and led into Webster's invocation of Washington and his theme of the development of the Union. This was significant since many in New England were calling for secession. Webster never did; he could later fall back on this speech for evidence of that fact.

However, the address did lead to Webster's appointment to a group that was assigned to write a "memorial" to the president condemning his conduct. When the Rockingham convention met on August 5 to organize Federalist opposition to Madison, Webster arrived with a draft of the memorial. It was accepted with only minor changes,[32] and proved so popular that the convention nominated Webster for the U.S. House. The nomination was made official on October 7 at the state Federalist convention. Webster's delivery of the memorial at the end of that convention and throughout the campaign became one of

31. Webster, *Writings and Speeches*, 15:583.
32. Baxter, *One and Inseparable*, 34.

the most popular political advertisements of the Federalists. Again, much to his credit and later credibility, Webster pulled back from secession: "We shrink from the separation of the states, as an event fraught with incalculable evils."[33]

The Federalists' Clinton-Pickering ticket swept New England, with the exception of Vermont. However, Madison had enough support elsewhere to win the electoral college, 128 to 89. Webster ranked second in the vote for the six at-large House seats available from New Hampshire.

As America went to war with England, Webster, at age thirty-one, arrived in the District of Columbia, a city he found appallingly dirty and swamplike. Two days after being sworn in, he met with the diminutive Madison at the "president's house," as it was called at the time.[34]

During the congressional session of the summer of 1813 Webster took quarters in a Georgetown boardinghouse, Crawford's Hotel, where his depression over the appearance of the city was relieved somewhat by his friends. Jeremiah Mason represented New Hampshire and Christopher Gore represented Massachusetts as senators; Gore lived at the same boardinghouse as Webster. These three stuck together and became part of the Federalist caucus that was outnumbered 114 to 68 in the House and 26 to 10 in the Senate. In light of the situation, Webster thought it best to offer his hand to the powers that be. During a special session of Congress, he met Speaker Henry Clay and Rep. John C. Calhoun, each of whom had supported an invasion of Canada in 1808 and Madison's war with Great Britain in 1812. (Calhoun was the same age as Webster, Clay five years their senior.) Webster was appointed to the foreign-relations committee, which was chaired by Calhoun. Clay ran the House, often giving angry speeches about the president's conduct of the war, thereby distancing himself from a policy he had supported. Webster also ran into Clay in the courtroom, where he occasionally took on a case. For example, Clay partnered with Webster on *Osborn v. Bank of the United States.*

These great minds formed an oratorical triumvirate that would dominate the first half of the century. Clay's speaking style was dramatic and lyrical, Calhoun's cold and rational. These men were easily as ambitious as Webster was. His relationship with Clay and Calhoun would outlive his relationship with most of the members of his family.

33. Webster, *Speeches and Formal Writings,* 1:3. The memorial was signed by 1,500 citizens and republished in the North.

34. It later became the "Executive Mansion," and then Theodore Roosevelt named it the "White House."

The war consumed the nation's attention. On June 10, Webster introduced five resolutions criticizing the war and suggesting that Madison had withheld information about France that would have made it less likely for the United States to declare war against England. Even Madison's supporters were impressed with Webster's skill at argument. He succeeded in getting the resolutions passed, and they were praised by the New York press.[35] Webster personally presented the resolutions to the president, whom he now found to be unimpressive. James Monroe, the secretary of state, wrote Madison's equivocal response to the resolutions and little more was heard about them.

As the Congress took up a tax bill to fund the war, Webster returned home to escape the July heat of the Potomac Basin and await the birth of his second child. Daniel Fletcher Webster arrived on July 23; henceforth, he was referred to as Fletcher. Webster took some time to tend to his law business because he was broke, a condition from which he rarely escaped.

He did not return to Washington until late December to attend the second session. News arrived from Portsmouth that Webster's house had burned to the ground, his wife and children barely escaping. Grace sent word that they were safe and that Webster should stay in Washington. The session continued into the new year, while the British blockade strangled American businesses. Webster's formal maiden speech in the House was well received; in fact, as he spoke congressmen left their desks and sat in the dock so they could see his every gesture.[36] William Plumer, a Republican representative from New Hampshire, wrote: "His manner is forcible and authoritative. Nothing is left at loose ends in his statements of fact or in his reasonings; and the hearer passes from one position to another with the fullest conviction that the result must be correct, where the steps leading to it are so clear and obvious."[37] Even Chief Justice John Marshall took notice of the speech, which was an attack on the war policy of the administration and demonstrated how committed Webster was to avoiding wars. The speech also made clear Webster's belief that the Constitution's main purpose was to stimulate commerce in America.

Even more impressive was Webster's "enlistment speech" of January 14, 1814. This address provides further evidence that Webster's anti-imperialism was early born. In it, he opposed any plan of invading Canada and condemned the administration for supporting an embargo on foreign goods:

35. *Annals of Congress*, 13th Cong., 1st sess., 149–51. See also Remini, *Daniel Webster*, 108; Merrill D. Peterson, *The Great Triumvirate: Webster, Clay, and Calhoun*, 41.

36. Charles W. March, *Daniel Webster and His Contemporaries*, 35–36.

37. Quoted in Richard N. Current, *Daniel Webster and the Rise of National Conservatism*, 27.

The army raised last year was competent to defend the frontier. To that purpose the Government did not see fit to apply it. It was not competent, as the event proved, to invade with success the provinces of the enemy. To that purpose, however, it was applied. The substantial benefit which might have obtained, and ought to have been obtained, was sacrificed to a scheme of conquest, in my opinion a wild one, commenced without means, prosecuted without plan or concern, and ending in disgrace.

The periodic style here is quite effective as it marches toward its goal. Later in the speech Webster sought to retain interest not only with inverted wording but with sarcasm: "All the evils which afflict the country are imputed to the Opposition. What possessor of political power ever yet failed to charge the mischiefs resulting from his own measures, upon those who had uniformly opposed those measures?" He accused the administration of accepting "rash counsels and feeble execution." When he moved to his attack on the embargo, he argued that "[t]he faith of this nation is pledged to its commerce, formally and solemnly. I call on you to redeem that pledge. . . . In the commerce of the country the Constitution had its growth; in the extinction of that commerce it will find its grave."[38] This wonderful antithesis brings to a close Webster's strong defense of New England's interests and his attack on the administration. In this speech, Webster developed a theme that he would return to in his opposition to wars of aggrandizement: a protest against those who question the minority's patriotism when it opposes the president. The speech called for a negotiated peace, a repeal of the embargo, and a stronger navy. This position went down to defeat 97 to 58. However, Webster edited, published, and sent the speech to commercial interests where he gained adherents.

Before the Supreme Court

Webster had his own commerce to worry about, which motivated him to take his first case to the Supreme Court. It was presided over by John Marshall and populated with such noted jurists as Joseph Story, who wrote the three-volume *Commentaries on the Constitution,* among other legal works. Webster's success with this court can perhaps partly be attributed to his feeling more at home among its Federalists than among the Democratic-Republicans who ran the House. He had already established a reputation for forensic achievement

38. *Annals of Congress,* 13th Cong., 2nd sess., 940–44, 950.

in the county courts of New Hampshire, the First Federal Circuit in Boston, and the Supreme Judicial Court of Massachusetts. The persuasive force of Webster's briefs would help Marshall build a consensus on constitutional questions. Marshall not only complimented Webster's arguments, he plagiarized them.[39] Webster's early Supreme Court cases centered on admiralty law. The knowledge of maritime jurisprudence he acquired would later give his deliberative speeches on trade, tariffs, and foreign policy added credibility. It may also explain his penchant in subsequent years for using nautical metaphors to open his speeches on the floor of the Senate. His expertise proved useful when he served as secretary of state under President Tyler and negotiated the Maine boundary compromise with England.

Of the 223 Supreme Court cases in which Webster appeared, he was the primary attorney for 168; of these, 24 involved precedent-setting constitutional questions, and of these, Webster won 13, most of them while Marshall was chief justice. Webster's fees varied widely. In *McCulloch v. Maryland* (see Chapter 2), he signed on for $5,000 but was given an additional $1,500 bonus when he won the case. His clients were diverse, including, at one point, the English banking firm Baring Brothers.

Along with Marshall and Story, justices Gabriel Duvall, Bushrod Washington, H. Brockholst Livingston, Thomas Todd, and William Johnson formed Webster's audience. Though Story and Livingston had been appointed by Jefferson, they were soon converted to Marshall's point of view, giving the chief justice a commanding majority on most issues. The Court's sessions in the basement of the Capitol building were often attended by lawyers and laypersons. In Webster's day there was no limit on how long an attorney could speak on behalf of his client. In the *McCulloch* case, for example, William Pinckney spoke for three days.

When Webster was admitted to the Supreme Court bar in January 1814, he wrote home to his brother about how much he admired Chief Justice Marshall.[40] He argued his first case on March 12, requesting a rehearing of a lower-court ruling against his client. Justice Washington delivered the opinion of the Court, which was in Webster's favor. (A year later the Court upheld Webster's client and reversed the lower court.) Webster was unsuccessful in his

39. Irving H. Bartlett, *Daniel Webster*, 75, 79, 80. Marshall was a fine persuader in his own right. He was forced onto the dissenting side in only eight cases and in only one constitutional case, *Ogden v. Saunders* (1827), where he sided with Webster.

40. Remini, *Daniel Webster*, 117.

second case, argued two days later. His third case, *Town of Pawlet v. Clark, et al.,* was eventually decided in favor of his clients. Justice Story's ruling in this case established the important constitutional principle that laws and precedents applying to the original thirteen states also applied to newly admitted states.

Meanwhile, with Napoleon's abdication, the threat from Great Britain was looming larger. Madison backed down on the embargo he had imposed on foreign trade. The move caused chaos in the New York and Boston markets. Webster attacked the administration on April 6:

> Sir, a Government which cannot administer the affairs of a nation without producing so frequent and such violent altercations in the ordinary occupations and pursuits of private life, has, in my opinion, little claim to regard of the community. . . .
>
> It is the true policy of government to suffer the different pursuits of society to take their own course, and not to give excessive bounties or encouragements to one over another. This, also, is the true spirit of the Constitution. . . . It owes protection to all. I rejoice that commerce is once more permitted to exist; that its remnant, as far as this unblessed war will allow, may yet again visit the seas, before it is quite forgotten that we have been a commercial people.[41]

The speech on the repeal of the embargo established Webster as a leader in the House. He was widely praised in Federalist circles and particularly among his colleagues.

The session soon came to a close and Webster returned to his home and a reelection campaign. The Republican press accused him of aiding the enemy, a charge that would reemerge when he opposed the war with Mexico three decades later. Webster was able to overcome this canard because the war was so unpopular in New England. In late August, the British invaded Washington, torching the Capitol and the presidential mansion. Madison, who had been visiting the front lines, fled to the Maryland countryside. His wife, Dolly, saved the most precious items in the mansion and escaped to the Virginia countryside. They were not reunited until late the next day because the First Lady was denied shelter by Virginians who opposed the war, proving that New England was not alone in its opposition to it.

The congressional election in New Hampshire was conducted just after this

41. Webster, *Writings and Speeches,* 14:35,46.

tragedy. Webster was reelected and turned his attention toward the English invasion. Portsmouth felt threatened since it housed a naval base. Webster's role as the chairman of the Committee on Public Safety stood him in good stead when he was accused of advocating separatism later that year. What led to those charges was the calling of a convention in Hartford in December to discuss secession. By then, Webster had returned to Washington because Madison had called for a special session of Congress. The burned presidential mansion saddened Webster; the Madisons took up residence in the Octagon House, which stands on New York Avenue to this day. The Congress met in temporary quarters where, despite his sympathy for the Madisons, Webster continued to beat the antiwar drum. His speech of October 24, 1814, strongly opposed administration policy. Madison, however, insisted he needed more money to prosecute the war against the barbarian British. His call stiffened New Hampshire's resistance to taxation. Of the taxes suggested, Webster supported only the tax on whiskey; he adamantly opposed raising land taxes. Webster allied himself with Calhoun in an effort to defeat the administration's banking bill. When they succeeded, the two men wrote the legislation for Webster's version of a national banking system, which passed on January 7, 1815, by a large majority. The president vetoed the legislation and it became an issue that would divide the parties for years to come.

The same session also considered Secretary of War Monroe's plan for a draft. Webster opposed it in no uncertain terms on December 9, 1814: "The Constitution is libeled, foully libeled. The people of this country have not established for themselves such a fabric of despotism. . . . Where is it written in the Constitution, in what article or section is it contained, that you may take children from their parents, and parents from their children, and compel them to fight the battles of any war in which the folly or the wickedness of government may engage it?"[42] Webster claimed that Congress did not have the power to make Monroe into a dictator. If such action were to be taken, Webster argued, the states would have the right to interpose in the way Jefferson had suggested during the Alien and Sedition Acts crisis. It was as close as Webster would ever come to Calhoun's doctrine of nullification. With the Hartford Convention about to convene, his words were given great weight. The irony of the situation did not escape the press: Why was the Federalist Webster invoking Jefferson, and the Democratic-Republican Monroe invoking Hamilton to

42. Webster, *Speeches and Formal Writings*, 1:20–21.

defend his draft?[43] Luckily, Webster never made it to the later-ridiculed Hartford Convention, and he was delighted when the conscription bill failed in the Senate. He claimed to have put the fear of God in some of the Democratic-Republican senators.

While Madison attempted to negotiate his way out of the war, Gen. Andrew Jackson, with the help of French forces led by the Marquis de Lafayette, defeated the British at New Orleans. Two thousand British were killed. Even before this victory, however, Madison's negotiating team had reached an agreement with the British in Ghent to reestablish the conditions that existed between the countries before the war. By March 1815 the British were focused on a new threat: Napoleon had escaped prison and was rallying his troops once more. Americans cheered their president and his party. Webster left the Capitol in gloom and vowed not run for reelection in 1816. In fact, he may have already decided to move to Boston; Portsmouth could not contain his ambition, nor satisfy his ego. He had led the Federalists in the House on some important issues: opposition to the war and conscription, opposition to tariffs, and support for a national bank. At thirty-two, it was time to decide where his future lay. Webster retired from politics, moved to Boston, and returned to the practice of law.

The end of the war with Great Britain marked the beginning of the Era of Good Feelings. Suddenly popular, President Madison said he favored a national bank, a protective tariff, and internal improvements. House Speaker Clay made that platform his own. His floor lieutenant, Calhoun, took up the unionist cry, even arguing for a more flexible view of the Constitution, a position that would come back to haunt him. In 1816, however, he and Clay were seen as nationalists and the Second Bank of the United States was approved.

Given his decision not to run for reelection, Webster could have sat back during the session and watched the action. Instead he provided correctives on the currency system, pushing through on the force of his oratory resolutions requiring a sound currency. He also succeeded in adjusting the tariff on cotton to suit the desires of industrialist Francis Cabot Lowell. The ensuing election proved that Webster had chosen just the right time to move to a new state. Congress had voted itself a raise, and in the fall elections of 1816 the public threw out a majority of each house of Congress. Webster realized that

43. Webster later defended his speech by arguing that interposition is not the same as secession, and that even Madison had joined Jefferson on the issue of interposition in 1798.

the Federalist Party was dying; the Democratic-Republicans even won New Hampshire, which would have an important impact on one of his most notable cases (see Chapter 2).

Webster moved his family to Boston, where he pursued a career in the law. He and his wife were in Washington in early 1817 for the final days of his term when they received word that their daughter was gravely ill. They returned to Boston, where she died of tuberculosis.

While grieving in Boston, Webster established himself as a member of two prominent churches. Soon he had recovered enough to join several social clubs. His wit and intelligence were in demand, and he recruited an impressive client list for an out-of-stater. It included Francis Cabot Lowell, George Cabot, John Jacob Astor, and James Otis. Webster practiced law in the courts of the area: Suffolk, Essex, Middlesex, Plymouth. He became prominent at the First Circuit Court of the United States. He generated a healthy income, yet still managed to overspend. He relied heavily on loans from benefactors.

Webster's clever use of narrative in the courtroom became legendary. He made sense of the facts in a way that helped his clients and beguiled the judge and jury. An early example occurred in the trial of Webster's clients Levi and Laban Kinniston. Elijah Goodridge, a respected citizen, had accused the two of shooting and robbing him. Goodridge had been treated for a wound in the left hand. Webster established the facts he needed in his cross-examination. Then, in his summation, he convinced the jury that Goodridge had actually shot himself in an attempt to fake a robbery and escape his creditors.[44]

In Boston, Webster was overwhelmed by a sense of freedom when he looked out to sea, the same sea that would provide him with a master metaphor for many of his speeches. Nearby was New Bedford, which provided the men who hunted whales. When Webster arrived he could have had no idea how prosperous whaling would become by the time of his death, but he lived long enough to see Herman Melville's *Moby-Dick*, based on the trials of the whaling captains, published in 1851. Whaling, however, was not the most important business in Massachusetts; creating cloth was.

The Mills

In 1780 an Englishman named Richard Cartwright developed a method for spinning cotton and wool into yarn. By 1789, the first American spinning

44. See Webster, *Writings and Speeches*, 10:173–93.

mills were sprouting up in Rhode Island. By the 1820s, waterwheels had turned these mills into power looms for the South's cotton and New England's wool. Francis Cabot Lowell, who invented the power loom and created the Boston Manufacturing Company, tried to create a better environment for his workers than that endured by workers in England.[45] "Lowell girls" were hired off the farm, where they made no money, and brought to the mill towns to work. They were not allowed to drink; they had to attend church service on Sunday, their only day off; and they had to work long hours, but that was no different from life on the farm. In fact, many of the women believed they had a much better life with the Lowell company.

In Lowell's factory town, bells called the women to their twelve-hour days. They were fed three decent meals a day and lived three to a room, often sharing beds as they had on the farm. Child labor was common, as on the farm. What these workers did not face on the farm was dust- and fiber-filled air, which choked their lungs, and the noise of looms, which often caused deafness. The press began to talk about the "lords of the lash" in the South, who produced the cotton that was spun by the "lords of the loom" in the North. In response, Lowell had his workers form an association known as the Daughters of Free Men. Throughout 1816, when tariff proposals were being hotly debated in Congress, Lowell rationalized support for selective tariffs and became instrumental in developing a new party out of the dregs of the Federalist movement.

Boston was a bustling city of 40,000 inhabitants. Webster and his family lived on Beacon Hill; his office was on State Street, near the State House. Francis Lowell provided financial support, betting that Webster had a future in Massachusetts politics. By 1819, Webster was earning over $20,000 a year, a sizeable sum at the time. Yet it was still not enough to support his extravagant lifestyle.

As Lowell watched approvingly, Webster practiced law with a small but talented fraternity. Arguing before the highest court in the land, he came into contact with the finest minds in America. His friend Joseph Story claimed to be a Jeffersonian but was a Federalist at heart.[46] William Wirt's use of humor and historical and poetic quotations impressed Webster. So did Wirt's defense of Jeffersonian principles. Wirt, who was attorney general from 1817 to 1829,

45. Even as late as 1860, "there were more cotton spindles in Lowell, Massachusetts, than in all eleven states that eventually made up the Confederacy." Louis Menand, *The Metaphysical Club: A Story of Ideas in America*, 10.

46. Maurice G. Baxter, *Daniel Webster and the Supreme Court*, 21.

joined Webster as often as he opposed him before the Supreme Court.[47] David Ogden appeared with or against Webster thirty-two times. And the eloquent Rufus Choate, a few years behind Webster at Dartmouth, joined him in *Rhode Island v. Massachusetts.*

These men helped sharpen Webster's abilities and refine his conceptualization of national conservatism. They forced him to find the best ways to defend his fundamental belief in due process, property rights, and federal protection of contracts. The defense was almost always rooted in constitutional issues because those issues were the most current before the Supreme Court. Furthermore, while a vague plan or an emotional argument might satisfy some in the Congress, only a tightly reasoned argument could pass muster before the Court. Any loose ends, contradictions, or holes would be noted by adversaries and the sitting justices. Thus, Webster's experience before the Court helped him to become the preeminent debater on the floor of the Senate. Webster was often to be seen running from the Supreme Court in the Capitol's basement up the steps to the House or Senate chamber. He would argue a legal motion on one level of the building and a legislative amendment on the next. Before that could happen, however, he needed to get himself elected to the Congress from his new home state.

47. Wirt opposed Webster in the *Dartmouth College* case and in *Ogden v. Saunders*; he joined Webster in *Gibbon v. Ogden* and *McCulloch v. Maryland.*

Chapter 2

A Boston Lawyer

Cast into a world of luminaries, Webster could not avoid political discussion. In fact, he soon became active in the search for a new structure to replace the Federalist Party. Being in at the beginning gave Webster the opportunity to set out the ideals of the new Union Party. It would be national and republican. It would stand for "measures, not men," unlike the demagogic Democratic-Republicans. National interests would be put before sectional interests. The great error of the Hartford Convention would be buried, or so Webster thought.

As Webster's career in Boston took off, so did the nation. In 1820 the United States comprised almost 10 million people; by 1830 that figure would be 13 million, by 1840 it would be 17 million, and by the time of Webster's death in 1852 it would surpass 23 million. The growth in the 1840s was due in part to the rise of the immigrant population, with a million and a half Europeans coming to America.

However, with the end of the slave trade, the ratio of African Americans to the total population began to decline. In 1820, about 25 percent of the population was African American; by 1840 the percentage had dropped to 20. While the South continued to rely on the plantation system for its wealth, the North expanded industrially, especially in terms of transport. With the completion of the Erie Canal in 1825, New York became the financial center of North America. Still not satisfied with the time it took to get farm products from Cleveland to New York and industrial products from New York to the Midwest, a group of New Yorkers opened a rail line in 1831, beginning a web of rapid transit that further revolutionized transport time in the United

States. By 1836, three rail lines ran from Boston to the South and West carrying goods from mills owned by Lowell and others.

These systems supported a burgeoning farm population that revolutionized the production of crops. In 1820, nearly 90 percent of the population lived on farms. With the development of the steel plow, farmers were able to plant and harvest more produce than ever. In 1831, Cyrus McCormick invented a mechanical reaper, cutting in half the labor needed to harvest wheat.

The worlds of property, invention, and transportation were badly in need of legal codification, particularly given the fact that the Constitution was written before these developments had an impact on the economy. The nation and its laws were at a formative stage, and Webster was positioned to take advantage. He was one of the men who would interpret the sacred document in order to develop pragmatic rules and regulations to guide economic growth. He would use the Constitution as a shield against the onslaught of state regulation and taxes that attempted to narrow personal property rights and infringe on long-standing contracts.

The *Dartmouth College* Case

By the time Webster had achieved a reputation in Boston, he was called back to New Hampshire for an important case. It involved his beloved alma mater. Dartmouth was caught in a struggle between its mostly Federalist Congregational trustees and its Presbyterian president, John Wheelock, son of founder Eleazar Wheelock. The elder Wheelock had been granted a charter by the Earl of Dartmouth to create a private college run by the board of trustees, but his son declared Dartmouth to be a public institution under the control of the state. Alumni and students lined up on either side depending on their religious and political affiliations; the five faculty members opposed their president, who had become something of an autocrat. The trustees set out to undercut President Wheelock's authority, particularly with regard to appointments to the board of trustees. He in turn penned a nasty attack on the trustees and called on the state legislature to intervene. In response, the trustees removed Wheelock and the legislature began an investigation of the situation in 1815. As the tempest grew, Democratic-Republicans tended to support Wheelock; Federalists supported the trustees. The *Dartmouth College* case became an election issue in New Hampshire in 1816. When the Democratic-Republicans won, they declared Dartmouth a public institution subject to legislative control. In his inaugural speech, the new governor, William Plumer, a reformed Federalist, declared that the college should be taken over by the state. Even a former Republican president got involved: Thomas Jefferson, believing the trust to be public, threw his support behind Plumer.[1] The legislature then imposed a new charter on Dartmouth. When the trustees refused to accept it, the legislature created Dartmouth University, and the trustees, with faculty and students in tow, continued to operate Dartmouth College in the homes of supporters in Hanover.

In 1817, the trustees sued the university and its treasurer, William H. Woodward, who had defected from the original college. Jeremiah Mason and Jeremiah Smith represented the reconstituted college; Webster made the closing argument and in the process reduced the audience in the courtroom to tears. Nonetheless, the judges claimed that the charter had enacted a public corporation, not a private one. Therefore, they ruled, it was not protected by the contract clause of the U.S. Constitution; it was in fact open to the reform imposed by the representatives of the citizens of the state. This ruling was sustained in superior court before the case reached the Supreme Court.

As we have seen, the Supreme Court was dominated by Chief Justice John Marshall, who had been appointed to the Court in January 1801 by John Adams. Though a cousin to Jefferson, Marshall, who had served in the Revolutionary War, was a Federalist through and through. He argued only one case before the Supreme Court, *Ware v. Hyton* in 1796; he had declined a seat on the Court in 1798 to become a member of the House of Representatives from Virginia, and was secretary of state briefly in 1800.

Marshall was known to be a master of the syllogism, and he believed in the power of logical demonstration. His colleagues referred to his "web of argumentation" as delicate yet ensnaring. He constructed justifications for his position and refuted the arguments of others. In closed chambers, Marshall gently riddled the positions of opposing justices and prodded them into consensus. He wrote 519 of the 1,215 opinions issued during his tenure as chief justice and was in the minority on only one case involving an important constitutional question.[2]

In 1801, Marshall instituted the practice of having the majority speak for

1. Thomas Jefferson to William Plumer, July 21, 1816, quoted in William Plumer, Jr., *Life of William Plumer*, 440–41.

2. Harold Chase, Samuel Krislov, Keith Boyum, Jerry Clark, eds., *Biographical Dictionary of the Federal Judiciary*, 176.

the Court through the chief justice or his designee. In 1803, he authored the landmark *Marbury v. Madison* decision, which established the Court's authority to review congressional and executive actions in terms of their constitutionality. Democratic-Republicans believed Marshall was undercutting state authority and stepped up attacks on his Court.

Marshall was surrounded by an able group of associate justices. Though they were appointed by different presidents, they had much in common. Most were related to the founders, most had fought in the Revolutionary War, and most had served in their state legislature or the Congress before being appointed to the Court. Marshall's strongest ally was Bushrod Washington, appointed to the Court by John Adams in 1798. Washington had served under his uncle George during the Revolution and had inherited Mount Vernon when his aunt Martha died. He had been a strong supporter of ratification of the Constitution during the Virginia debates of 1788.

H. Brockholst Livingston had been a classmate of James Madison's at Princeton, then known as the College of New Jersey, where he became a states' rights Republican. Prior to his appointment, he served on the Supreme Court of New York, where he was known for his Jeffersonian views. He was an active Anti-Federalist and particularly distrusted Alexander Hamilton. Perhaps no justice was more hostile to Webster's positions during the period from 1817 to 1824.

Thomas Todd was appointed by Jefferson in 1807; he had been chief justice of the Kentucky court system. He allied himself with western landed interests and specialized in real estate law. He followed Marshall's lead on constitutional questions, much to the dismay of Jefferson.

William Johnson was the brother of a South Carolina bank president. In 1804, Jefferson promoted him from the South Carolina Court of Common Pleas, to which he had been elected in 1798. Though he often disagreed with Jefferson's presidential policies, he remained close to Jefferson and wrote a flattering eulogy upon the founder's death in 1826.

Joseph Story, appointed by Madison in 1811, believed the Constitution should protect propertied interests. Such interests were, in his mind, the bulwark of representative democracy. Story had socialized with many of the justices prior to his appointment, and his addition to the Court strengthened its sense of camaraderie. At thirty-two, Story was the youngest person appointed to the Court to that time. He had served in the Congress for one year during the 1808-1809 session and then returned to the Massachusetts Assembly. He had strong ties to the banking community, and that association threw him together with Webster. He respected Webster's mind and ability to argue, but criticized his sentimentality before the Court. Webster was partially responsible for Story's strong commitment to the sanctity of contracts. Even though they were from different parties, they were willing to work together: Story wrote the Crimes Act of 1825, which Webster succeeded in getting passed into law. It was the first reform of the Criminal Code since 1790. Story and Webster became close friends, which helped Webster convert Story to the Federalist point of view.

Like Story, Gabriel Duvall was appointed to the Court in 1811. Duvall was from Maryland and had served with its militia in the battles of Brandywine and Morristown. He was elected to Congress in 1794 from the Maryland House of Delegates. He served two terms and then became chief justice of the Maryland General Court and Jefferson's comptroller of the Treasury. After Story and Duvall, no new appointments were made until 1823. Thus by the time of the *Dartmouth College* case, the seven members of the Court knew one another well and had a set way of working. They were a group that held key values in common. They respected the Constitution, they believed in natural rights, and they espoused certain liberties obtained through the Revolutionary War. They were close friends and had many friends in common. Webster was a part of their social world, and they were a part of his. This intimate audience of seven provided most lawyers with a difficult persuasive challenge. However, Webster's burden in the *Dartmouth College* case was reduced by the fact that Marshall had written two rulings that supported his interpretation: *Fletcher v. Peck* (1810) and *State of New Jersey v. Wilson* (1812).

As a graduate of Dartmouth College, Webster had a particular interest in seeing that the institution carried the day.[3] The State of New Hampshire, newly controlled by the Democratic-Republicans in 1816, had placed the college under the jurisdiction of a new board of trustees. However, the original board of trustees argued that Dartmouth held a royal charter that predated New Hampshire's becoming a state, and that since Dartmouth was a private eleemosynary institution, the state could not regulate it.

Webster's closing in the superior court became the basis for his concluding argument when the case reached the Supreme Court in 1818. He argued that contractual obligations were based on natural law and were therefore immune

3. Fuess, *Daniel Webster*, 1:220–21.

to man-made law. A right, such as the charter of Dartmouth, once invested, became a natural right and could not be divested through legislation. The New Hampshire legislators argued that Dartmouth had become a public corporation because it served the people of the state. Webster said that argument was radical and ludicrous; by such reasoning, almost any private entity could be converted to a public property or interest. While Webster relied on the briefs of Mason and Smith, he added eloquence and emotion, and drew heavily on English common law.

The forces arrayed against Webster in this case were impressive. They included William Wirt and the colorful William Pinckney, who realized they were in trouble before a divided Court and asked that they be allowed to bring in new arguments and evidence at a rehearing. Marshall denied the request but permitted a delay in the case. He may have needed to form a consensus on the important arguments, and he did not want to appear to be trampling on the rights of the New Hampshire legislature.

The delay from February to March for the presentation of arguments not only gave Webster extra time to prepare but a chance to celebrate a little longer the birth of his daughter Julia. As was the case with his contemporaries, Webster's public persona was a reflection of his private life. We talk now of "family values," but in Webster's time, a person's private life had to stand in a correct, that is to say consistent, relationship with his or her public life. Webster took enormous pride in his family and was close to his children. The tragedies that befell that family were well known and earned Webster the sympathy of a sentimental public, befitting the expectations of this romantic age.

When the time for his appeal arrived, Webster appeared in what was becoming a uniform for him: cream-colored vest, white tie, and navy-blue jacket with brass buttons, reflecting the colors of the Revolution. During his four-hour speech, he covered all of the law necessary to make his case, particularly English common law, which was on his side. He was defending both a prerevolutionary charter and property rights in general. He cited Article I, Section 10 of the Constitution on contracts and the precedent of *Fletcher v. Peck,* arguing that contracts and compacts are one and the same as far as the Constitution is concerned. This bedrock defense of the Constitution was pure Federalist dogma, one of the ways by which Federalists restrained the power of the states in favor of the Union.

Webster's argument to the Court was first and foremost a call for reversal of the state court. From the outset he attempted to create sympathy for the trustees of Dartmouth College by arguing that the legislature had acted "without their acceptance or assent."[4] Webster then established the credibility of the charter with a long historical narrative on its creation. Along the way, Webster won sympathy by pointing out that Eleazar Wheelock had established a charity school that "clothed, maintained, and educated a number of native Indians, and employed them afterwards as missionaries and schoolmasters." It was for actions like these that Wheelock was singled out by the proprietors of New Hampshire for a special charter. The charter empowered twelve trustees to oversee the operation "forever." And the charter was granted by the king not for a time certain, but "forever." The college then operated for fifty years without interruption until the legislature of New Hampshire intervened. Thus to the theme of sympathy Webster added the test of time and the guarantee of eternity, two lines of argument drawn from the father of conservatism, Edmund Burke, a somewhat hidden saint in Webster's civic bible.

Webster next accused the legislature of tearing the institution down. He took care to identify Dartmouth College with history and permanence and the legislature with transience. The legislature would impose "nine other trustees, and twenty-five overseers." On top of that, "[t]he college is turned into a university" with the power to create new colleges.

In the next few paragraphs, Webster added texture to his portrait of the legislature as a radical agent of change. He outlined the powers they had given away and those they imposed. He documented their recklessness in trampling so many rights, "franchises, property and privileges." He portrayed the New Hampshire legislature as more mad with power than even the British parliament, which rarely used its "unlimited powers," claiming that even the "illegal proceedings in the reign of Charles II were under color of law." He identified those who supported the legislature with the Restoration autocracy, a sure way to alienate them from patriotic Americans. Later in the address, he compared the legislature to the emperor Justinian: "Our constitutions do not admit the power assumed by the Roman prince." In this way, Webster inverted the state's argument that, with the Revolution, the powers of the British king devolved to the State of New Hampshire. While the legislature might act like an unruly monarch, he argued, they do not have the right to do so. He relied on the noted jurist Lord Mansfield to reinforce his point: "[T]he corporations of the universities are lay corporations; and that the crown cannot take away."

Returning to his strategy of creating sympathy for the college, Webster

4. All quotations from this argument are from Daniel Webster, *Speeches and Forensic Arguments,* 1:110–37.

compared it to a hospital both in legal terms and symbolic ones. While hospitals tend to the sick, colleges "breed up persons in the world." After quoting more legal authorities, Webster clinched the argument by pointing out that "[t]he New Hampshire bill of rights declares that no one shall be deprived of his 'property, privileges or immunities,' but by judgment of his peers, or the law of the land." He invoked Blackstone and the Magna Charta to demonstrate that the state may not take these things away in the name of the public. Instead, he asserted, the law of the land is transcendent, like the Constitution.

Next, Webster argued that contributions to Dartmouth College, including a land grant from the State of Vermont, were not intended for the State of New Hampshire. It was quite clear, he said, that the New Hampshire legislature had seized property over which it had no claim. He then detailed how certain articles of the New Hampshire bill of rights had been violated by the state legislature. The parallel structure of Webster's introduction of each of these indictments—"They infringe the twentieth article. . . . They infringe the twenty-third article"—no doubt helped them stick in the minds of the justices.

Employing a strategy that he would use with great effect throughout his career, Webster extended a theme from earlier in his speech. Having compared the state legislature to the autocratic regimes of Charles II and Justinian, Webster turned to James II and his attack on Magdalen College at Oxford. When the king tried to impose a president on the college, he was met with resistance. The legal electors refused to give up their rights and surrender their keys to the king's men, so the doors were broken down. This was considered the king's most arbitrary act, and he eventually repented it. Once again, "franchises were regarded . . . as private property." The relevance of this narrative to the *Dartmouth College* case was striking, as was Webster's reinforcement of the property-rights argument: "The principle is the same, and in point of fact, the result has been the same." Webster refuted his opponents' case by reiterating his main points in terms of case law.

As we have seen, several important rhetorical themes surface and are extended throughout this speech. There is sympathy for Dartmouth and its trustees, a portrait of the state legislature as disruptive and dictatorial, a sustained appeal to common law and property rights, and a sustained appeal to the New Hampshire bill of rights. Each of these themes is introduced and then amplified. And it is to the strategy of amplification that Webster returned in his famous peroration. With the gallery and justices listening intently, he delivered his conclusion:

This, sir, is my case. It is the case, not merely of that humble institution, it is the case of every college in our land. It is more. It is the case of every eleemosynary institution throughout our country—of all those great charities founded by the piety of our ancestors, to alleviate human misery, and scatter blessings along the pathway of life. It is more! It is, in some sense, the case of every man among us who has property of which he may be stripped, for the question is simply this: Shall our State Legislatures be allowed to take that which is not their own, to turn it from its original use, and apply it to such ends or purposes as they in their discretion shall see fit? Sir, you may destroy this institution; it is weak; it is in your hands! I know it is one of the lesser lights in the literary horizon of our country. You may put it out. But if you do so, you must carry through your work! You must extinguish, one after another, all those great lights of science which, for more than a century, have thrown their radiance over our land! It is, sir, as I have said, a small college. And yet there are those who love it. . . . Sir, I know not how others may feel, but, for myself, when I see my Alma Mater surrounded, like Caesar in the Senate house, by those who are reiterating stab upon stab, I would not, for this right hand, have her turn to me, and say, *Et tu quoque, mi fili!* And thou too, my son!

Webster made Dartmouth represent larger and larger categories of private privilege. It stood for all colleges, then all charities, then all private property. Nearly in tears, he paused before portraying Dartmouth as a small, simple school that could be snuffed out by the powerful court. The aposiopesis was contagious; many in the audience fell into weeping.[5] The emotion was reinforced by Webster's careful style. For example, woven through the argument is the "light" metaphor, a standard symbol of learning that served to unify the logic of his position into a stylistic whole.

Webster was successful, as he usually was when he appeared before the Supreme Court presided over by Marshall. In fact, Marshall often had his decisions ready before Webster presented his oral arguments to the Court because he was so influenced by Webster's legal briefs. Despite William Wirt's fine defense of the superior court's opinion, Marshall seized the opportunity to reinforce the Federalist commitment to protect the federal government and private institutions from encroachment by the states.

Because Webster believed in the power of opinion leaders to influence future

5. Remini, *Daniel Webster*, 156.

political and judicial opinions, he had his speech printed and distributed. Timothy Farrar, Jr., Webster's former law partner, published the *Report of the Case of the Trustees of Dartmouth College against William H. Woodward*. This persuasive tract rallied support for the college and resulted in Webster gaining the title "Defender of the Constitution." Because Webster departed from his prepared remarks when he delivered his emotional peroration, the pamphlet did not include this section. Thanks to Professor Chauncey Goodrich of Yale, who transcribed it, the peroration eventually overshadowed the *Report*. More important to this study, it initiated a technique that Webster used again and again. After delivery, he polished the texts of his speeches and then published them for general consumption in order to gain adherents to his cause. This tactic would be used to good effect after the Webster-Hayne debate of 1830 and the Seventh of March Address of 1850.

Almost a year after hearing the case, Marshall formed a consensus of justices who agreed with Webster that the original charter had been violated. All but one of the justices agreed that the contract clause of the Constitution prohibited the states from enacting laws that impaired "the Obligation of Contracts." Marshall, writing for the majority, held that the charter was a contract and therefore the covenants in the charter were inviolable even though the holders of the charter, the board of trustees, had no beneficial interest in the instrument. Story and Washington wrote concurring opinions more sympathetic to the states; Duvall dissented without comment. Given that the Democratic-Republicans had controlled the presidency since 1801, and Congress as well for most of that period, Marshall was the last Federalist in a position to convert ideology into public policy. Louis Menand has quite correctly concluded, "As Webster and Marshall intended, the decision expanded the privileges of private property against the claims of the public interest, and it helped to unleash capitalist enterprise in nineteenth-century America."[6] The most lasting tribute to Webster's effort in this case can be found on a bronze plaque at Webster Hall on the Dartmouth campus that reads, "Founded by Eleazer Wheelock, Refounded by Daniel Webster."

Webster's brilliant stylization of his arguments and his appeal to the sentiments of his listeners were credited with inducing the landmark decision, which made his reputation as a constitutional lawyer and a national figure.

6. Menand, *Metaphysical Club*, 243.

McCulloch v. Maryland

McCulloch v. Maryland, which was decided in the same year, was very different from the *Dartmouth College* case. Just three weeks after the Dartmouth victory, Webster defended the constitutionality of the Bank of the United States, for which he received a fee of $2,000. The original national bank had been dissolved in 1811. As we have seen, a second national bank was chartered by President James Madison to deal with the economic woes caused by the War of 1812. Many states were opposed to the bank, which began operation in 1817, because it preempted their ability to operate their own banks and collect tax revenues. Matters were brought to a head when the Second National Bank was held responsible for the Panic of 1819. Maryland enacted a tax on notes from banks not chartered by that state, thereby taxing the national bank. When the national bank refused to apply for a charter or to pay the tax, Maryland brought an action against James W. McCulloch, the cashier of the Baltimore branch of the national bank. Maryland won in the lower courts.

Alongside Wirt and Pinckney, Webster represented the national bank before the Supreme Court. They were opposed by Luther Martin, Walter Jones, and Joseph Hopkinson. How small this fraternity of lawyers was should be readily apparent from the fact that Wirt and Pinckney opposed Webster in the *Dartmouth College* case, and Hopkinson worked with him. Ironically, Webster had voted against the bank bill in April 1816, fearing it gave too much power to the president. The bank was established anyway and Webster found himself becoming its avid defender.

Webster's argument before the Court was short, to the point, and not nearly as stylized as some of his other rhetorical efforts. He opened for the defense and looked straight at Marshall throughout his presentation. His statement reveals the arsenal of argumentative tools he kept at his disposal when before the Court. He enhanced the credibility of his position, increased the gravity of the situation, inserted an important argumentative summary, used precedent, created winning definitions, argued from analogy to specific cases, extended arguments established earlier, and built a case from Aristotle's topic of "more or less."

From the beginning, Webster made sure the Court understood the gravity of the questions involved. He told the Court that it faced not only the question of state versus federal power, but the question of who controlled private property. To settle these questions, Webster was forced to go back to the First

Congress, where, he claimed, this issue had been decided. He invoked Alexander Hamilton, who favored a national bank as early as 1791. The Federalists knew where they should stand: a national bank was necessary to carry out the powers that had been delegated to the Congress.

Webster enhanced the credibility of his position by arguing that until this case, the issue had been decided in everyone's mind in favor of the federal government. Using negative evidence, he argued that neither the House nor the Senate had ever challenged federal preemption on the question of a national bank to collect revenue. Quoting Hamilton, Webster defended the proposition that Congress had the power to create a national bank. The First Congress did just that, the courts sustained it, and those who opposed the decision later agreed with it. These opening passages reveal Webster at his very best. He built the credibility of his case, reinforced it with precedent, and then argued that even those opposed to his position had been won over. His summary was powerful and clear: "When all branches of the government have thus been acting on the existence of this power for nearly thirty years, it would seem almost too late to call it in question, unless its repugnancy with the constitution . . . were plain and manifest."[7] The government's method of operating had been in place for so long that to change it would be disruptive and fly in the face of precedent.

Webster reinforced his position that Congress did in fact have the power to create a bank. His argument was multifaceted in order to capture every possible justice's opinion. It was based on an "even if" strategy: The Congress is sovereign "within the scope of these powers." But even if one does not accept that premise, the "general clause" gives Congress the power to create a bank. And even if one does not accept *that* premise, the power to declare war gives Congress the power to collect money for a war and that means it can create a bank to do the job. Overlaying this basic structure was the argument that Congress can use "all usual and suitable means for the execution of the powers granted." Finally, Webster extended the argument to the question of original intent in order to preempt an attack by the other side. He claimed that the founders did not define every means the government could use to carry out its commission because they were not clairvoyant and could not determine every eventuality. Instead they established a framework adaptable to new situations and new inventions. This framework allows Congress to use any means "not being specifically prohibited."

7. Quotations are from Webster, *Writings and Speeches*, 15:261–67.

With that line, Webster touched on one of the most important constitutional issues in American history: Is Congress limited to specifically delineated powers? Or is it limited only when specifically precluded from taking action by language in the Constitution? These questions are important because the answers determine which side must carry the larger burden of proof in the debate over implied powers. Webster shifted the burden to the states—Maryland, in this case. This position flowed directly from his "framework" analogy: If the Constitution is meant to be a flexible frame built to last through the ages, then Congress must have the widest latitude in adapting to new eventualities. Should the Constitution be limited by narrow interpretations, the government would fail in a short time. This argument set the tone for the rest of Webster's statement.

First, he demonstrated that a bank is "a proper and suitable instrument" for the government to use. It is Congress's right to determine the nature of the bank, not the Court's. All the Supreme Court can settle is whether creating a bank is constitutional. Next, he preempted an opposition point and advanced his argument by showing that creating a corporation is a normal activity for a government. All governments use corporations to conduct business; they are merely a means to an end. Furthermore, since state governments have the right to use corporations, the federal government should have even more of a right to create and use them. One should not deny a method of operation to the federal government that is granted to the states. At this point, Webster again felt the need for a summary to reinforce his position so that the justices would have time to digest his argument.

He then moved to the second major question: Did Maryland have the right to tax the federal bank? Webster argued that the people divided sovereignty between the states and the federal government. Since the bank was carrying out the will of the people, the states had no right to interfere with the bank. The federal government was supreme in this case because it is charged with carrying out its obligations under the Constitution, which is the "supreme law of the land." On this question, the Supreme Court could and must rule or else the system would fall into chaos.

To put it another way, the Court should rule for the defense because if it did not, the states would have the power to destroy the national bank. Webster reduced the opposition's position to absurdity by arguing that if the Court allowed some taxation, it must allow any taxation, and if it allowed any taxation, the states could tax the national bank out of existence: "An unlimited power to tax involves, necessarily, a power to destroy; because there is a limit beyond which no institution and no property can bear taxation." He applied this argument to other government properties that the states could attack, including bonds, lands, "permits, clearances, registers, and all other documents connected with imposts." Webster was not far from the position he would take years later in his reply to Robert Hayne: state power is dangerous because it will destroy the federal government if left unchecked. The case here was state taxation of federal property; the case in 1830 would be the nullification of federal laws.

Webster forced the Court to choose between causing the collapse of the federal system at the hands of the voracious states or strengthening the young government by allowing it to create and use a national bank to carry out its functions. Having exaggerated the danger, he quickly retreated to a reasonable position that enhanced his credibility and gave the Court a way out of the dilemma:

> A bank may not be, and is not, absolutely essential to the existence and preservation of the government. But it is essential to the existence and preservation of the government that Congress should be able to exercise its constitutional powers at its own discretion, without being subject to the control of state legislation. . . . To hold otherwise, would be to declare that Congress can only exercise its constitutional powers subject to the controlling discretion, and under the sufferance of the state governments.

The bank, then, was just an example of a larger problem that the Court must address to save the nation. Thus Webster concluded as he began, by bringing as much gravity to the case as the situation would allow.

Led by Hopkinson, the respondents argued that if the national bank was allowed to open branches willy-nilly, it would trample the states' right so clearly protected in the Tenth Amendment. Furthermore, if the states had the right to tax a corporation—a right clearly upheld in case law to that date—then they had the right to tax the national bank, which was incorporated. Martin followed with three days of arguments that, much to the annoyance of Marshall, proved to be no more than variations on the same theme.

Pinckney's conclusion of the bank's case also lasted three days, but it was highly stylized, and it upstaged Webster in the gallery and with some of the justices.[8] Nonetheless, it was Webster who influenced the thinking of Marshall,

---

8. Baxter, *Daniel Webster and the Supreme Court*, 173–75. Justice Story believed Pinckney's speech to be better than any he had ever heard before the Court.

who wanted to widen the scope of the government's powers, much in the way Alexander Hamilton had first envisioned them.

In a decision announced less than a week after the arguments, Marshall accepted Webster's argument that the "necessary and proper" clause of the Constitution established the legitimate role of the federal government in dealing with national problems. Consequently, the Maryland tax was unconstitutional. Marshall noted three distinct areas of federal power: the federal government draws its authority from the people, not the states; the "necessary and proper" clause gives Congress broad powers to implement the enumerated powers of the federal government; and any state legislation that interferes with the existence of legitimate federal powers is invalid. Marshall shamelessly borrowed Webster's allusion to Hamilton and the argument that an "unlimited power to tax involves, necessarily, a power to destroy." Webster was delighted to have won the case and took great pride in pointing out Marshall's plagiarism to friends. Given how quickly the decision followed on the oral arguments, Marshall must have written his decision before oral arguments began and simply lifted the phrase from Webster's brief. In any case the sweeping decision was quite controversial; Jefferson issued a letter critical of Marshall and the Court.

Webster participated in several other cases involving the bank. He often defended the bank on the floor of the Senate after receiving a hefty retainer from Nicholas Biddle, the president of the bank. Webster also held stock in the bank. Between 1819 and 1839, he defended the bank ten times and opposed it twice. When in Osborn v. Bank of the United States, for example, he was joined by Henry Clay, they defeated the State of Ohio's attempt to tax the bank. These bank cases expanded the rights of corporations to operate across state borders and to seek federal protection from state taxation.

The Missouri Compromise

In 1819 while Webster was appearing before the Supreme Court, he would stroll up to the House or Senate chamber and listen to the debates that culminated in the passage of the Missouri Compromise. The Northwest Ordinance of 1787 had prohibited the introduction of slavery above the Ohio River. Now northerners were calling for a prohibition of slavery in all new territories, particularly Missouri. Clay's compromise would allow slavery in Missouri as well as below a line extending from Missouri's southern border. After Webster returned to Boston, he gave a speech in December 1819 outlining the history of slavery and arguing that it was a "great evil." Because of this speech, and because he had proved effective in the *McCulloch* case, Webster was selected to head a committee of concerned Bostonians that would pen a memorial to Congress on the subject of slavery and southern attempts to expand it. This became "A Memorial to the Congress of the United States, on the Subject of Restraining the Increase of Slavery in the New States to Be Admitted to the Union." While the arguments are solid and almost irresistible, the language is subtle. Webster seemed to want to avoid offending southern members of Congress who would reread the memorial once it was converted to pamphlet form. However, there are lines in the memorial that preview what Webster would say at Plymouth Rock a year later in much sterner language. The issue rose to the constitutional level, according to the memorial, because it affected the nation, the "general welfare" of its citizens, and their liberty. Furthermore, since Congress had peremptory power to organize the territories, the issue was part of its domain, not that of individual states. As Webster and his associates made clear, "The creation of a new State is, in effect, a compact between Congress and the inhabitants of the proposed State."[9] This position would be strengthened in Webster's address at Plymouth Rock in 1820.

In that year, Maine petitioned for statehood and Clay's compromise was passed; Maine would be admitted as a free state and Missouri as a slave state. Slavery would be banned in future states north of the 36° 30' parallel—that is, in the remaining territory of the Louisiana Purchase. Webster was distracted from this legislation by the birth of his son Edward and by his thriving law practice. However, political interests remained in his mind. As a member of the electoral college from Massachusetts, he cast his vote for James Monroe and the Era of Good Feelings, since there was no Federalist candidate in 1820. During the campaign, Webster had given a major speech in Faneuil Hall on the issue of the tariff, his first of several important addresses in that great room. Webster opposed the use of the tariff for new industries, arguing that industries should be forced to survive on their own if they were to become strong. The tariff should not be used to create a dependent culture, but to raise revenue in case of an emergency. Lowell and Cabot would see to it that Webster altered this position once he returned to Congress.

9. Webster, *Speeches and Formal Writings*, 1:46, 50. The Congress held to this position through the 1850 Compromise; however, that legislation foisted the issue of whether a state wanted to enter the Union as slave or free on the voters of the state. The consequences would be tragic for the nation.

When Massachusetts decided to rewrite its charter, Webster was among those chosen to represent the Boston area. Though Democratic-Republicans held a majority in the state convention, the Federalists were more prominent, especially since they could count former President John Adams among their number. The convention gave Webster a chance to rub elbows with the Massachusetts elite and demonstrate his technical writing skills. He became a leader in the reform movement, heading various influential committees. At thirty-eight, he was emerging as a major player in Massachusetts politics. Oratory was still his most important asset, as he proved at the convention. It was a ceremonial address, however, that provided Webster with the occasion that would most add to his luster in 1820.

The "First Settlement" Address

The speech was given at a time when America was riven with emotionalism due to a second wave of religious revivals. The First Great Awakening of the early 1700s had marked a shift from intellectual appeals to the understanding in sermons by such "old lights" as Cotton Mather to appeals to the emotions by such "new lights" as Jonathan Edwards.[10] There was also a tension between those who retained a belief in predestination and those who, like George Whitefield, taught that believers could find redemption through Christ. The Second Great Awakening expanded on this theme by making the conversion process a deeply personal one. In both cases, there was a sharpening of individualism, which led to an increase in entrepreneurship and calls for direct democracy. Certainly, it was a time of economic development and expansion that would be spurred on by the Whigs' American Plan.

The second movement began stirring before the turn of the century and by 1820 it had permeated urban areas. The revivals became popular in the North by stressing free will, inner piety, and an outwardly moral life. By the 1830s, the movement would spawn the abolitionist movement in the North, which would play a role in Webster's career to the end of his life. The revivals were cooperative ventures, usually with one Protestant church serving as host for others in the community. This practice contributed to a growing sense of unity and nationalism, which played right into the Union plank of Webster's civil

---

10. See Craig R. Smith, "Charisma Generated by *Pathos* and Style," chap. 6 in *The Quest for Charisma: Christianity and Persuasion*.

religion. While some saw the country as several assembled states, Webster contributed to a growing sense of nationhood—one America, as he called it. Though Webster did not favor direct democracy, he did understand the need for a country to have one spirit. By making his speeches resonate with the new religious fervor, he could advance his agenda. Publications such as the *New-York Evangelist* and the popular periodical *Lectures on Revivals* covered the revivals in some detail, thus providing free publicity for the movement; coverage of the emotional responses to preachers was particularly vivid. Also important for Webster was the fact that religious figures began to treat the Declaration of Independence and the Constitution as holy documents inspired by God. Picking up the theme of a shining city on a hill articulated by Jonathan Winthrop for the Puritans, the new evangelists saw America as a chosen country that was destined to bring moral order to the world.[11] Webster added the notion that Americans became a people when they declared their independence and wrote their Constitution. He sought to overcome the more accurate picture of diverse colonies in order to conjure up his version of a homogeneous public. In his Plymouth address, Webster, the converted Congregationalist, had a chance to strengthen the narrative of nationhood.

The question of genre is particularly important in Webster's case since he was a master of all three: the deliberative, the forensic, and the ceremonial. One must be careful, however, not to confine Webster, as some have done, to a single genre for any one speech.[12] We have seen that Webster's forensic arguments before the Supreme Court influenced Justice Marshall's decisions on deliberative matters and reflected Webster's own political positions.[13] In his argument in the Dartmouth College case, there are elements of praise and blame normally associated with ceremonial speeches. Webster not only disguised one form of address in another, thus making his appeal more subliminal, he also used more than one form to develop complex schemes of rhetorical and liter-

---

11. George M. Thomas, *Revivalism and Cultural Change: Christianity, Nation Building, and the Market in the Nineteenth-Century United States*, 1, 67, 70, 78. Many other scholars have made this point, including H. Richard Niebuhr, *The Kingdom of God in America*; Robert N. Bellah, *The Broken Covenant: American Civil Religion in Time of Trial*; and Timothy Smith, *Revivalism and Social Reform in Mid-Nineteenth-Century America*.

12. William S. Howell and Hoyt H. Hudson begin their discussion of legislative speeches with this remark: "Turning now to Webster's deliberative oratory, as Aristotle would have classified speeches in Congress . . ." "Daniel Webster," 692. See also Glenn E. Mills, "Daniel Webster's Principles of Rhetoric."

13. See Fuess, *Daniel Webster*, 1:231–35.

ary invention. His ceremonial addresses demonstrate that effective discourse often has elements of all three forms of address and that interaction among forms within an address may explain its effectiveness. This sophisticated approach allowed Webster to advance the National Republican (Whig) agenda as a civil religion while playing to themes of the Second Great Awakening, particularly emotionalism, individuality, free will, and the sacredness of the founding documents.

"The First Settlement of New England" was delivered in 1820 to celebrate the bicentennial of the landing of the Pilgrims.[14] This speech, like many other of his ceremonial addresses, revealed Webster's growing sense of ecumenical Protestantism. Despite his conservative Congregationalism, Webster was friendly with the likes of William Ellery Channing, Boston's leading Unitarian minister. Webster attended Unitarian services at the church on Battle Square; but he was also on the building committee for the new St. Paul's Episcopal Church. Webster's belief in God, the Ten Commandments, and the righteousness of revenge was softened by his faith in New Testament redemption, a position more in line with the revivalists. Just as Webster was advancing a national unionist ideology, he was hoping, it would seem, for a national union of Protestants. However, he would find it difficult to achieve either goal because his speech in Plymouth wedded him to his condemnation of slavery, a position that would deprive him of southern support when he sought the presidency and that would cause major consternation among abolitionists when they believed he had abandoned it.[15]

Webster had been asked to speak at Plymouth while at the Massachusetts Constitutional Convention. The address gave him the opportunity to become a true son of Massachusetts and to shed his New Hampshire skin. After careful preparation, he left Boston for Plymouth on a very cold December 21. After dinner, Webster and his friends inspected the Rock and other points of interest; the next morning, Webster insisted on examining the place for the oration, the old First Church. Against the advice of his friends, he chose to speak below the pulpit. Ever the showman, Webster knew that speaking at the

14. This address was followed in 1843 by the lesser-known "The Landing at Plymouth," and in 1850 by "The Pilgrim Festival at New York." Webster also made reference to the Pilgrims in his Bunker Hill Addresses of 1825 and 1843. For an analysis of the use of the Pilgrim theme in these speeches, see Erickson, *Poetry of Events*, 63–86.

15. Webster never abandoned his position on slavery, but in 1850 embraced a compromise that required the returning of fugitive slaves.

communion rail demonstrated humility while moving him closer to the audience. His first words on the following day synthesized the history, emotion, and religion of the moment: "Let us rejoice that we behold this day. Let us be thankful that we have lived to see the bright and happy breaking of the auspicious morn, which commences the third century of the history of New England."[16] Webster was looking forward, the first hint that this ceremonial address might have deliberative overtones.

The rhetorical questions that followed led the audience to his purpose: "Who would desire the power of going back to the ages of fable? Who would wish for an origin obscured in darkness?" Slavery was part of that dark past. Rejection of the old times should not be read as a rejection of history or prudence, but as a rejection of dark crimes. Thus, Webster used the dialectic between past and future to extract the good and expunge the bad. Only in this way would a moral future be assured in the third American century.

Webster's respect for past generations and traditions is traceable directly to Edmund Burke, whom he greatly admired. History, tradition, and generational loyalty are the mystical cords that bind a people into a nation:

> Standing in this relation to our ancestors and our posterity, we are assembled on this memorable plot, to perform the duties which that relation and the present occasion impose upon us. We have come to this Rock, to record here our homage for our Pilgrim Fathers; our sympathy in their sufferings; our gratitude for their labors; our admiration of their virtues; our veneration for their piety; and our attachment to those principles of civil and religious liberty with which they encountered the dangers of the ocean, the storms of heaven, the violence of savages, disease, exile, and famine, to enjoy and establish.

This passage reveals the periodic cadence that typified Webster's grand style. The repeated "our" pulls the audience in and smoothly advances the theme. Unity and the Rock become one. They stand out against a sea of troubles as Webster calls up the emotions of the times in a tasteful yet romantic manner.

This perspective on what citizens owe their ancestors framed the obligation that Webster's audience owed to their descendants. "Advance, then, ye future generations!" called Webster. His religious values gave a decorous patina to his

16. All quotations from this address are from Webster, *Speeches and Forensic Arguments*, 1:25–56.

political philosophy, which had been enriched by his reading of Bacon, Macaulay, Dryden, and Moore. He used those values to fuse his romantic notion of America with the memorial moment. This allowed him to organize the speech in a progressive fashion, moving from the Pilgrims' intentions to demonstrations of their *ethos*, the progress of America as a nation, and finally to the legacy his audience embraced, which included free education, access to property, and an end to slavery.

However, the attack on slavery came only after Webster had reinforced transcendent values and a sense of linkage with the past. Only near the conclusion of the speech did he move to the course he believed the nation should take. Fusing deliberative argument with epideictic form, he believed that protection of property was a foundation of constitutional law, but did not include slaves in his definition of *property*. And what better place to emphasize property than on this shore with its noble rock, the material symbol of New World values? The Pilgrims had come to colonize a new land, not in an imperialistic way, but in a holy way. There was only one thing that defiled that holiness, and Webster sought to expunge it with this powerful and emotional passage:

> If there be, within the extent of our knowledge or influence, any participation in this [slave] traffic, let us pledge ourselves here, upon the Rock of Plymouth, to extirpate and destroy it. It is not fit that the land of the Pilgrims should bear the shame longer. I hear the sound of the hammer, I see the smoke of the furnace, where the manacles and fetters are still forged for human limbs. I see the visages of those, who by stealth, and at midnight, labor in this work of hell, foul and dark, as may become the artificers of such instruments of misery and torture. Let that spot be purified, or let it cease to be of New England.

Webster was at his best in using imagery to bring his thoughts close to the audience. Hearing, sight, smell, and touch are invoked in this short passage, which played to the visceral emotionalism of the times.

In recommending a course of action for the country at the same time he condemned slavery, Webster concealed a deliberative and a forensic argument in the epideictic form by reinforcing the seminal value of New England's Puritan founders, who sought to cleanse impurities in the body politic. His attack was also veiled by his references to Christianity and its values, further reinforcing the epideictic tone of the speech.

Webster's magnificent conclusion brought his audience back to the introduction by dancing to the theme of time:

> The hours of this day are rapidly flying, and this occasion will soon be passed. Neither we nor our children can be expected to behold its return. They are in the distant regions of futurity, they exist only in the all-creating power of God, who shall stand here, a hundred years hence, to trace, through us, their descent from the Pilgrims, and to survey, as we have now surveyed, the progress of their country, during the lapse of a century. We would anticipate their concurrence with us in our sentiments of deep regard for our common ancestors. We would anticipate and partake the pleasure with which they will then recount the steps of New England's advancement. On the morning of that day, although it will not disturb us in our repose, the voice of acclamation and gratitude, commencing on the Rock of Plymouth, shall be transmitted through millions of the sons of the Pilgrims, til it lose itself in the murmurs of the Pacific seas.

Having looked back over two centuries, Webster looks forward one hundred years and envisions a nation running from sea to sea, an evocation of the manifest destiny he would later reject. He envisions the Pilgrims' seed multiplying into a new nation that will dominate the continent. It is a wonderfully transcendent moment, after which Webster begs "future generations" to "advance" in hopes of an even better nation. Webster obviously was cognizant of the tensions that existed at the time between loyalty to the past and marching forward to innovation and expansion. His very first sentence sets a rather disingenuous tone: "Let us rejoice that we behold this day." There follows a litany of blessings, so that the audience is caught off-guard by the condemnation of the slave trade that comes late in the speech.

Another significant strategy of the address is to use time in several different ways. First, the audience is taken back and forward in time as Webster uses proxemics to bring his narrative sections closer to his listeners. The third paragraph of the speech begins, "It is a noble faculty of our nature which enables us to connect our thoughts, our sympathies, and our happiness, with what is distant, in place or time." While time plays a key role in the structure of the address, so does place. In fact, Webster devotes some paragraphs to the unique nature of the season and the place at which his audience has gathered. In this way, he unifies them and identifies with them: "We are here at the season of the year at which the event took place." Eventually, the place becomes the Rock, "hallowed in the esteem of the Pilgrims."

Some points are keyed to the past, while others are keyed to the future, which carries yet another subliminal message. The first clue to this strategy comes in the third paragraph: "We live in the past by a knowledge of history; and in the future by hope and anticipation." The history that Webster constructs includes religious toleration, which by 1631 had pretty much vanished in the colony at Massachusetts Bay. That may be why he concentrates his revisionist approach on the Pilgrims instead of the Puritans, trying to expunge intolerance.

Later in the speech, the past is what we learn from so that we can provide future generations with the "civil and religious liberty" that has sustained the nation. Webster foreshadows his conclusion when he dedicates his efforts to "future generations." Also in these early sections, there is a telling contrast between the Pilgrims, who came to New England of their own free will, and the slaves, who came by force. For both groups of immigrants, however, suffering was a hallmark. As the "scene passes before us," Webster weaves a narrative of self-sacrifice to which his audience owes a great debt. This suffering becomes another theme that weaves through the speech; first there is the suffering in the wilderness, then the suffering under the British, the suffering of the French and Indian War, and, finally, the American Revolution.

Webster expands his vision to the introduction of English-speaking peoples to the colonies and compares this to the Greek and Roman colonization of the ancient world. This allows him to ally colonization with commerce and advance one of his deliberative themes, the expansion of commercial opportunities in the United States. He returns to this theme and extends it in different ways throughout the speech.[17]

Yet Webster was always careful to keep a celebratory veneer on his recommendations; in this case, it was praise. He makes the case that the American system of government surpasses in its ideals and operation the governments of Greece, Rome, and England: "The New England colonies differ quite as widely from the Asiatic establishments of the modern European nations, as from the models of the Ancient States." What were once colonies have become a "home" to a new form of moral democracy: "Here was man, indeed, unprotected and unprovided for, on the shore of a rude and fearsome wilderness; but it was polite, intelligent, and educated man." This Anglo-Saxon heritage allowed the colonists to tame the wilderness and build a new home for themselves, creating a government of inalienable rights along the way. Webster

17. See, for example, the section on navigation laws. *Speeches and Forensic Arguments*, 41.

returns to this theme several times, weaving it into the fabric of the address. For example, in the latter part of the speech, he speaks about the value of free education for all New Englanders, in contradistinction to the English and French, who educated only the select few. After this effusive praise for New England, Webster turns to the "contamination" of slavery. It suddenly rises like a blight on the beautiful and evolutionary picture of the perfect society that he has painted. The contrast is overwhelming and hence particularly effective.

In the middle of the speech, Webster turns to the future with a clear transition: "The nature and constitution of society and government, in this country, are interesting topics, to which I would devote what remains of the time allowed to this occasion." The ensuing civics lesson is full of the common wisdom of the day and the pride of American ingenuity. Underlying these high-minded thoughts are Webster's commitments to property: "The property was all freehold. The entailment of estates, long trusts, and the other processes for fettering and tying up inheritances, were not applicable to the condition of society, and seldom made use of. . . . The consequence of all these causes has been, a great subdivision of the soil, and a great equality of condition." Once again, the contrast to a slave society cannot be missed. Webster extends his theme by arguing that the division of property has led to the division of the state into townships, from which a strong sense of democracy emerges. Again, Webster returns to the past to show New England's superiority over Rome.

"The First Settlement of New England" takes on a spiritual tone in many ways, not the least of which is to turn the founders into spiritual fathers. Webster tells his audience that they will learn history only by reliving the past, and that they can then apply the lessons they learn to the present in order to achieve their destiny. That destiny emerges from the fact that the law holds history and destiny together in the present.[18] Thus, the audience, America in 1820, is the focal point, the synthesis of past and future. Natural law reveals the slave trade to be a creation of the devil. The law of God and the law of the land must become one: "Whatever makes men good Christians, makes them good citizens." There is here no subtlety to Webster's civil religion; it is at once civic and religious.

This early Webster speech is remarkable for its sophistication, which is achieved in at least four ways: fusing genres, making time existential, playing to the emotionalism of the era, and introducing and developing themes in a

---

18. See Ferguson, *Law and Letters*, 219.

fugal form. It is also clear that the catechism of Webster's civil religion was now in place; liberty over slavery, union over division, the guidance of past generations, the march of future generations into a better destiny, individualism, the protection of property, and responsibility for one's actions are all brought to the forefront at various times in the speech. The speech is far more religious in orientation than the memorial of the previous year; the church setting allows for appeals to the "Eternal Father," "religious duty," and "moral feelings," and to religious values that were inappropriate for a memorial to Congress but quite relevant to Webster's condemnation of slavery near the end of the address. Webster signals this move early in the address when he speaks of "ourselves being but links in the great chain of being." He lays down a foundation of moral values upon which he can construct his forensic condemnation of slavery and his deliberative call for its abolition. It is one of his most priestly moments.

John Adams was effusive in his praise, calling Webster "the most consummate orator of modern times." Adams said the speech would live for "five hundred years hence." (This was high praise indeed, since Adams's son, John Quincy, had delivered the address commemorating the Rock in 1802.) In fact, the speech made Plymouth Rock into a national shrine.[19] Stephen Howard Browne concurs with my judgment that the speech advanced Whig virtues with which future party leaders could identify. The speech was effective because of the way it inscribed the national memory. It strengthened the mythology surrounding the Pilgrims while bringing a new sense of high-mindedness to the national purpose. Browne parses Webster's conservative thesis to be: "[W]e are bound in memory to the past and future by collective duty."[20]

After his two-hour oration, Webster was mobbed all the way back to his hotel. He rose above the praise and merriment at the dinner that followed, maintaining the public persona of a saint. It wasn't until after dinner, when he was alone with close friends, that he cut loose. The speech was published in the fall of 1821 in amplified form. The schoolboys of New England were required to memorize long passages from it. Webster took pride in the fact that his version of America's civil religion was on the lips of students across the North and the South. He had contributed to a sense of singular nationhood.

19. John Seelye, *Memory's Nation: The Place of Plymouth Rock,* 79.

20. Stephen Howard Browne, "Reading Public Memory in Daniel Webster's *Plymouth Rock Oration,*" 468, 470.

Chapter 3

The Lion Returns

In 1821 Webster was busy filing petitions for his clients before the Spanish Claims Commission, which had been established when Florida was sold to the United States. These cases meant more travel to Washington for Webster, and he was unhappy about leaving his wife, who was once again pregnant. His absence forced her to manage the children and household affairs late in her pregnancy. In fact, Charles was born in December while Webster was again traveling to the nation's capital to argue the case of *Cohens v. Virginia*.[1] The Congress permitted a lottery in the District of Columbia, and the Cohen brothers sold tickets for it across the Potomac in Virginia, where lotteries were illegal. Virginia saw this as an opportunity to curtail the impact of the *McCulloch* decision by reasserting states' rights. Justice Marshall had tried to prevent the case from reaching the Court. It necessitated writing one more decision that, like *Marbury v. Madison*, kept the Court's power of review intact.

Luckily Webster was selected to represent Virginia. He argued that because the lottery law did not apply to Virginia, the federal government had no jurisdiction in the case. Marshall led a unanimous Court in support of Webster's client, but the decision was written in such a way as to assert that the Court could have intervened in the case had the federal government made lotteries legal nationally instead of only in the District of Columbia. Thus, Virginia won the case against the Cohens, but, thanks to Webster's decision not to argue the question of whether the Supreme Court had jurisdiction, the ruling did not make a dent in *McCulloch*.[2]

1. See Henry Wheaton, *Digest of Decisions of the Supreme Court of the United States, 1789–1820*, 6:264.
2. Federal preemption of state authority remains an issue to this day. For example, the Su-

In February 1822 a remarkable event occurred during arguments before the Supreme Court. Webster was engaged in a case on the opposite side of his sometime rival William Pinckney. One of Pinckney's favorite techniques was to harass his opponents, often embarrassing them. He was a colorful but arrogant man who was the equal of Webster before the Court. In this case, Pinckney tried Marshall's patience by speaking for nine hours. Just as Webster was given the opportunity to reply, Pinckney suffered a heart attack. He was rushed from the Court and died a week later, leaving Webster as the most prominent Supreme Court lawyer in the land.

Midway through Monroe's second term politicians began vying for the presidential nomination. The election of 1824 would be hard-fought because by 1822 Henry Clay, John C. Calhoun, and William Crawford had joined the list of candidates. Though they were in disarray, Massachusetts Federalists put John Quincy Adams, the secretary of state, in nomination. Adams, however, believed it was not decorous to campaign for the presidency. If he had done a superior job, and he had, then the office should devolve upon him as it had upon other secretaries of state.

In the fall Webster increased his influence among the Federalists by getting himself elected to the lower house in Massachusetts. He led the Federalist ticket in vote-getting. Thus, when Rep. Benjamin Gorham of Boston resigned, the Federalists saw fit to nominate Webster to the seat. In response, Webster made it clear that the Federalists would have to cover his expenses for giving up part of his lucrative law practice. Webster's supporters decided to solicit funds for that purpose from business interests, mainly in Massachusetts and New York. The process worked well for the rest of his career, though it opened him to charges of being influenced by contributors.[3] It is a measure of Webster's magnetism that he was able to move to a new state and come to represent it in Congress a short six years later. In the same year, he was also named an overseer of Harvard University.

At the end of 1823, Congressman Webster, his wife, and their children arrived in Washington to celebrate the holidays and conclude the first session of

---

preme Court has regularly upheld the Federal Communications Commission's right to regulate the cable television industry. When the state of Oklahoma sought to ban the advertising of alcoholic beverages on cable stations, the FCC overruled the state and was sustained by the Court.

3. As a congressman and then as a senator, Richard Nixon used the same kind of support system from 1947 to 1951. He answered accusations of impropriety with his famous "Checkers" apologia in 1952.

the Eighteenth Congress. On New Year's Day they were guests at the presidential mansion. By this time, Webster believed that the Federalist Party was dead. He wrote to Joseph Story that it was crucial to form a fusion with Jeffersonians who supported the national-improvements agenda.[4]

Greek Independence

After a seven-year absence from Congress, Webster felt obligated to deliver another "maiden" speech. It would be a combination of epideictic praise, forensic prosecution, and deliberative proposals, a braiding of genre that was becoming his hallmark. The topic was Greek independence. As the founders of Western civilization, the Greeks had a great deal of sympathy in the United States and Europe, particularly among Romantics. Lord Byron would lose his life fighting for Greek independence, a struggle that began in 1821 when the Greeks sought to break the yoke of Ottoman rule. Webster, of course, had referred to Greek colonization in his Plymouth Rock address. Edward Everett, no mean orator himself, had written on Greek independence and now contributed to Webster's research. The writing of the new speech strengthened their budding friendship. Everett began as a man of the cloth, became an academic at Harvard, and took on government positions, but went down in history as the long-winded speaker who preceded Abraham Lincoln to the lectern at Gettysburg.

The Monroe administration, which had laid down the doctrine opposing European influence in North and South America, was careful not to contradict itself by offering direct aid to Greece. This delicate diplomatic balance provided Webster with the opening he needed. Of course, Webster did not have to worry about establishing his *ethos*. He was known as the best Supreme Court lawyer in the land, and his speeches, particularly "The First Settlement of New England," were nationally known. On top of that, Speaker Henry Clay had made Webster head of the Judiciary Committee, in part because of his forensic prowess and in part because Clay wanted Webster's support in the coming election.

In December 1823, a week after the announcement of the Monroe Doctrine, Webster called for the appointment of a representative of the United States to the new government of Greece to recognize that country's bid for in-

---

4. See Sydney Nathans, *Daniel Webster and Jacksonian Democracy*, 20.

dependence. On January 19, 1824, this rather thin resolution gave Webster a rationale to speak on the values he cherished. To a packed gallery, he began in an epideictic fashion by praising the contributions of Greece to Western civilization. Switching to a local context, he referred to the architecture of the new Capitol building as Greek in origin. He then attacked the Holy Alliance of 1815 for its deals and loyalty to monarchies instead of democracies. This narrative took on a forensic cast as he detailed the sins of the alliance: it forced other nations into submission by interfering in their internal affairs and it forced the signatories' own citizens into submission by depriving them of their rights.[5] Webster led the audience to the crucial point of the speech with a fusillade of rhetorical questions: How were we to proceed? "Are we to go to war? Are we to interfere in the Greek cause, or any other European cause?" The audience leaned forward to hear. No, came the answer; instead America should condemn the Holy Alliance and the Turks with moral force:

> It may now be asked, perhaps, whether the expression of our own sympathy, and that of country, may do them good? I hope it may. It may give them courage and spirit. It may assure them public regard, teach them that they are not wholly forgotten by the civilized world, and inspire them with constancy in the pursuit of their great end. At any rate, Sir, it appears to me that the measure which I have proposed is due to our own character, and called for by our own duty. When we shall have discharged that duty, we may leave the rest to the disposition of Providence.

Webster mixed religion and diplomacy. He continued to use this tactic in describing the barbarities being visited on the Christian Greeks—"ruined cities," "accursed slavery"—and in concluding that "by the common faith, and in the name, which unites all Christians, [America should] extend to them at least some token of compassionate regard."[6] The audience, once again witnessing an appeal for an American civil religion, erupted with applause. The members of the House itself were less impressed. They did not pass Webster's resolution. So intense was the feeling of noninvolvement in European affairs that even sending an emissary was out of the question.

On the domestic front, the nettlesome tariff would provide the major

5. This portion of the speech is said to have inspired Sen. Henry Cabot Lodge's successful attack on the League of Nations Treaty a century later.
6. Webster, *Speeches and Formal Writings*, 1:83–112.

controversy in the Eighteenth Congress. In part because he was beholden to the merchants of Boston for funds and political support, Webster considered modifying his opposition to tariffs. He allied himself with Clay, who forced a protectionist agenda onto the floor to provide funds for his American System, the platform of the emerging National Republicans, soon to be dubbed the Whigs. The South was in immediate opposition because tariffs led to higher prices for manufactured goods. At the end of March, Clay rose to defend his measure and overreached by naming as wholehearted supporters congressmen such as Webster, who was quick to correct the record. Webster said that all economic interests are part of a whole and that to separate some from others was a disservice to the national market organism. He pointed out that England was moving away from mercantilism and toward free trade, and that perhaps the United States should encourage such steps not with a tariff but with a more open policy. He did support the right of Congress to impose a tariff and complimented other provisions of Clay's bill. The bill passed the House by only five votes, with Webster voting against. That was all the signal the Senate needed; it promptly amended the bill to Webster's liking. It was then approved all around and the president signed it.

Gibbons v. Ogden

Late in 1823 Smith Thompson was nominated to replace Justice H. Brockholst Livingston on the Supreme Court, the only change in the Court since 1819. Thompson had been secretary of the navy for President Monroe and was politically ambitious. While sitting on the Court, for example, he would run against Martin Van Buren for governor of New York in 1828. This was viewed by many as unseemly, and Thompson lost what little credibility he had with his colleagues. Nevertheless, throughout this period he would attempt to advance the Democratic agenda, which often conflicted with Webster's Federalist ideology.

Just before Justice Thompson was sworn in, Webster argued his most important case of 1824. As in his previous cases, Webster attempted in *Gibbons v. Ogden* to expand the powers of the federal government by extracting implicit meaning from explicit language.[7] In this case, he argued that the Constitution granted the Congress exclusive power to regulate interstate commerce. He be-

7. See Wheaton, *Digest*, 9:1.

lieved the founders had taken this position because the state legislatures had mismanaged commercial affairs, particularly those between states. It was a dispute between Virginia and Maryland over fishing rights in the Potomac River that had led to the Annapolis Convention of 1786, which recommended a constitutional convention to amend the Articles of Confederation. The inability of the articles to solve interstate problems reinforced the need for a new national constitution. The commerce clause, according to Webster, was perhaps the most strongly mandated, given the way the Constitution evolved. Webster recreated the context in which the commerce clause was written and then interpreted the clause in light of this context. Since the clause was written into the Constitution to solve a serious problem regarding the relationship among the states and between the states and the federal government, Webster drew the logical implication that it was meant to grant to the federal government preemption with regard to interstate commerce.

The case involved historic figures, one of whom was Robert Fulton, the inventor of the steamboat. He and his business partner, Robert Livingston, had been granted exclusive rights to operate a steamboat line on New York waters. The New York courts reaffirmed that right in 1812. In the absence of a federal law to the contrary, no action was taken to restrict that license. Livingston and Fulton sold their rights to Aaron Ogden, a New Jersey lawyer. However, Thomas Gibbons, Ogden's former partner, operated a steamboat between New York and New Jersey, and refused to shut it down when Ogden claimed Gibbons was stealing his business. Gibbons argued that his license under the Federal Coasting Act justified his action and negated the monopoly granted to Fulton by New York. Ogden sued Gibbons for encroachment, and Gibbons appealed to Webster.[8] With the talented William Wirt at his side, and after two years of delay, Webster argued Gibbons's case for five hours before the Supreme Court on February 4, 1824. The date seems to have been set to preclude Smith Thompson from hearing it since, as we have seen, he had yet to be sworn in.

Webster claimed that congressional regulatory power in commerce was complete and exclusive, that the Coasting Act was commercial regulation, and that the State of New York was in conflict with this power. The genius of Webster's position is that he was handing the Court the right to decide which powers Congress has when they are not defined but clearly implied: "[T]he

8. Before his death, William Pinckney had represented Ogden.

extent of the grant [of powers] must be judged . . . by the nature of the power."[9] The founders, he argued, never intended to give the states the power to set up monopolies. Again he relied on quotations from Hamilton—particularly from *The Federalist*, no. 32—to support a Federalist interpretation of the Constitution. These passages no doubt pleased Justices Marshall and Washington.

Webster went on to recite the reasons for the failure of the Articles of Confederation and argued that this motivated the founders to insert the commerce clause into the Constitution: "Henceforth, the commerce of the States was to be a unit." If the Congress had not been granted this power, the Constitution would not have been worth ratifying: "The people intended in establishing a constitution to transfer, from the several States to a general government those high and important powers over commerce." Because of the nature of these powers, they must be "exclusive." That is, if the government is to have the power to regulate interstate commerce, it must have that right exclusively if it is to have any right at all, because commerce is such an interdependent operation. The states would be allowed to interfere with all transportation unless the Court remedied the situation. In a series of rhetorical questions, Webster raised horrible hypotheticals in the minds of the justices: states giving monopolies inside their borders; states closing ports to outside shipping. That is why what New York had done was "insidious."

Attacking states' rights from the people side of the equation, Webster added that the consumers of New York needed to be protected from their own government, which was causing them to be gouged by monopolies. Once again he was advancing the classic Federalist position: Strengthen the powers of the federal government and protect the rights of individuals against their states. The pincer movement against states' rights continued throughout Webster's career and was sealed by the Civil War after his death.

Webster concluded with another interesting argument. Since the Constitution gives Congress the power

> to promote the progress of science and the useful arts, by securing to authors and inventors, for a limited time, an exclusive right to their own writings and discoveries, . . . [t]he States might . . . exercise their own bounty toward authors and inventors at their own discretion. But to confer reward

9. All quotations from this argument are from Wheaton, *Digest*, 9:10–31.

by exclusive grants . . . was not supposed to be a power properly exercised by the States. Much less could they, under the notion of conferring reward in such cases, grant monopolies, the enjoyment of which should be essentially incompatible with the exercise of rights holden under the laws of the United States.

Clearly, in the area of commerce, copyright, and patent, the federal government was meant to be superior to the states.

The lawyers for Ogden and New York argued for concurrent powers based on the fact that while the Constitution granted Congress the right to regulate interstate commerce, it was not an exclusive right. Wirt rose in rebuttal on February 9 and reasserted Webster's position on exclusivity. However, he gave the Court an escape hatch. He argued that while the branches of interstate commerce that were high on the tree in all probability were meant to be under the exclusive control of Congress, the lower, less entangled branches might be shared with the states. In this case, the Court was dealing with the higher branches. Wirt asserted that what Webster had intended with his all-or-nothing argument was to control the important upper branches of interstate commerce, which this case concerned.[10] It was a brilliant revision of Webster's absolutist position, and may have saved the day.

On March 2, Marshall sided with Webster and Wirt, as did the majority on the Court. Congress had the power, Marshall wrote, to regulate "that commerce which concerns more states than one." Therefore, New York could not limit the scope of federal powers by creating a state monopoly over an interstate waterway, since that would effectively render the federally conferred license useless. While Marshall again borrowed from Webster's brief, the Court did not go as far as Webster desired. It did not decide the issue of exclusivity; instead, it found the State of New York in conflict with the Federal Coasting Act of 1793. Nonetheless, the case was a historic victory because of its affirmation of congressional power over interstate commerce.[11] It would provide a strong rationale for the new Whig agenda of internal improvements paid for by a national tariff. Eventually this ruling was used to justify legislation proposed during the New Deal.

Webster argued more than twenty cases before the Supreme Court from

10. See ibid., 9:165, 180–81.
11. Ibid., 9:187–221.

1819 to 1824. The most important ones strengthened the hand of the federal government and further confined the power of the states to regulate their own internal affairs and control their own citizens. Thus, Webster's forensic position complemented the political position he would espouse as a senator. Both in the courts and the Congress, Webster stood for the Union, for individual rights, and, most of the time, for property and contracts. Individual rights were made sacred in the Declaration of Independence and the Bill of Rights. The protection of property and contracts was made sacred in the main body of the Constitution.

Ogden v. Saunders

In the years that followed *Gibbons v. Ogden,* Webster argued many other cases before the Court, perhaps the most important of which was *Ogden v. Saunders* (1827).[12] The defendant, George Ogden, had refused to pay certain bills and claimed he was protected by a New York insolvency act dating from 1801. A team of seven lawyers, including David Ogden, William Wirt, and Henry Clay, defended him. Henry Wheaton, the longtime reporter of the Supreme Court, and Webster were on the other side. The main question in the case was: Could a state enact bankruptcy laws that affected future, private contracts? The secondary question was: Does the contract clause of the Constitution protect people against their states? Again the question of federal jurisdiction came to the fore.

The defense argued that the states should have the right to enact bankruptcy laws so they could control local contracts. Webster and Wheaton argued that bankruptcy law should be the exclusive domain of the federal government. To do this, they had to also argue that the precedent set in *Sturges v. Crowninshield* (1819) be overturned. Webster claimed that the intent of the founders was to protect citizens against their states and to protect their contracts. The contract clause is the tenth section of Article I of the Constitution. Advancing the Federalist position, Webster argued that the clause implied that bankruptcy laws are the exclusive right of the federal government. Moreover, no regulation, state or federal, could be triggered until a contract was broken. Thus, the New York law was invalid because of its prospective nature. In making the best case he could, Webster relied on a broad interpretation of the con-

12. Ibid., 12:213.

tract clause, in much the same way he had done with the commerce clause in *Gibbons v. Ogden*. Webster attempted to wed the Constitution to natural law, which he held to be higher than man-made law, particularly the laws of the states, which were often contradictory.

Supported by Story and Duvall, Marshall agreed with Webster and found himself on the dissenting side of a major constitutional question for the first and only time as chief justice. Though the majority was splintered, with each member filing his own rationale for his ruling, they put positive state law above natural law.[13] The decision caused many states to institute new and differing bankruptcy laws. The confusion that resulted helped cause the Panic of 1837. After that depression, Webster, claiming vindication, called for a national bankruptcy law to bring order out of the chaos. It was one of many instances where his legal experience influenced his legislative agenda and gave his deliberative speeches more credibility than other senators enjoyed.

The Election of 1824

If there was an Era of Good Feelings, it certainly collapsed with the election of 1824. Andrew Jackson led a populist-frontier revolt after being nominated by the Tennessee state legislature. South Carolina nominated Calhoun despite the fact that he had suffered a stroke; Virginia nominated William Crawford, the secretary of the Treasury and, despite his ill health, Monroe's handpicked successor. Kentucky nominated Henry Clay. John Quincy Adams, the son of the last Federalist president, was nominated by the legislatures of several New England states, but even he called himself a National Republican, avoiding the taint of Federalism.

Theodore Lyman, publisher of the *Boston Republican*, wrote to Webster in April 1824: "[T]he increase of democratic talent, respectability, and wealth in Boston the last two years, entirely owing to gradual secessions [from our party], is very great. . . . What can we do, therefore having lost our own fortress, but take the enemy's?"[14] Lyman eventually became a Jacksonian, turned his newspaper against residual Federalists, and in 1828 libeled even Webster in his new newspaper, the *Jacksonian Republican*.

---

13. See Baxter, *Daniel Webster and the Supreme Court*, 115.

14. Theodore Lyman to Daniel Webster, April 12, 1824, microfilm edition of Papers of Daniel Webster, Library of Congress, Ann Arbor, MI, 1971, frame 4096.

After appraising the political situation, Webster indicated his support for Calhoun; after all, at this juncture they shared a "free trade" point of view. Due to his ill health, Calhoun soon withdrew from the campaign, which embarrassed Webster with his New England friends, who supported Adams. Jackson had arrived in Washington as the new senator from Tennessee and had impressed Webster. Thin as a rail at 147 pounds, his six-foot frame was capped with a shock of white hair; Jackson looked presidential, and certainly was a hero for these romantic times.

In the meantime word of Crawford's health spread; then he was caught in a scandal, further reducing his chances of election. Clay hoped to fill the gap by wooing Webster. He knew that Webster did not trust Adams because Adams had accepted an appointment in the Republican administration of Monroe. He also knew that Adams despised Webster for, among other things, supporting Calhoun instead of New England's favorite son. Webster's sense that Adams felt himself to be above him reinforced the enmity between the two; Adams was not shy about letting people know he belonged to one of Boston's noble families. On his part, Adams distrusted Webster's ambition and rhetorical prowess. Yet Webster kept Clay at arm's length so as not to upset his Massachusetts constituents.

In November Webster easily won reelection to Congress, but no presidential candidate received a majority in the electoral college. Though Jackson had a plurality of the popular vote, he did not receive enough electoral votes to secure victory, nor did anyone else.[15] The election was therefore thrown into the House of Representatives. During his Christmas vacation, Webster traveled into the Virginia countryside to visit Jefferson and seek his advice on the presidential selection process. After stopping at Madison's home for a courtesy call, Webster and his close friend George Ticknor, who had been a student of his brother, went on to Monticello. (Webster would have been uneasy with the use of slaves at both of these plantations. The servants who straightened up his room and laid out his clothes were slaves, as were the cooks and maids who placed his food before him.)

From a hill in front of his mansion, the gentleman farmer Jefferson greeted Webster's party.[16] During their meeting, Webster learned that Jefferson believed Andrew Jackson to be dangerous. Jefferson said: "I feel much alarmed at

15. Jackson received 99 electoral votes, Adams 84, Crawford 41, and Clay 37.
16. Fuess, *Daniel Webster*, 1:303.

the prospect of seeing General Jackson president. He is one of the most unfit men I know of for such a place. He has very little respect for laws or constitutions and is, in fact, an able military chieftain. His passions are terrible." This view reinforced Webster's belief that Jackson threatened established institutions as "the people's candidate in the West and Southwest."[17] Jackson was no civic republican; he was a demagogue. As Webster rode back to the capital, he decided he had better work on behalf of Adams. Politics was put aside, however, when on reaching the capital he learned that his son Charles had died in his absence. Webster was crushed.

The election proved to be one of the most controversial in America's short history. With the election thrown into the House, each state's delegation voted as a unit. Jackson lost the House vote to John Quincy Adams, who had secured the support of Henry Clay. In fact, Clay and Webster worked closely during the caucusing to secure votes for Adams, after Adams reassured Webster that he would have a Federalist administration. Webster and Rep. John Randolph tallied the votes in the House and were pleased to announce that Adams had carried thirteen states to Jackson's seven. Clay and Webster were rewarded shortly after Adams took office; he made Clay secretary of state and Webster his leader in the House.[18]

The apparent deal between Adams and Clay was an instant scandal. The press and Democrats condemned the appointments as a "corrupt bargain"; Adams never recovered. Jackson was almost immediately nominated for president by the Tennessee legislature and began his campaign for the 1828 election. It was clear to Clay and Webster that Jackson was not part of the continuous chain that could be traced back to the founders. He had not served in any president's cabinet, as had all others who had become president after Washington. Jackson was a populist disruption, a clear threat to Webster's national conservatism. Jackson's attacks on the president, his call for a "judicious tariff," his frontier mobs, and his romantic press disgusted Webster.

On April 3, 1825, less than a month after Adams's inauguration, Webster spoke in Faneuil Hall. He had joined Adams and Clay in the National Republican Party, which he preferred to call by its Whig name. The Jacksonians soon took the Democratic half of the old Jeffersonian party and added Crawford

17. Jefferson quoted in Webster, *Writings and Speeches*, 17:371; Bartlett, *Daniel Webster*, 103.
18. Webster had wanted to be ambassador to the Court of St. James, but that plum fell to Rufus King. Other Federalists also received appointments.

and Calhoun's followers to their ranks. In his speech, Webster made a plea for political harmony as the Massachusetts state elections approached. The *Boston Courier* reported that Webster called for "union and conciliation," themes that would pervade his rhetoric henceforth. Like Edmund Burke, he also noted that "new parties . . . might arise. . . . Associations formed to support *principles* may be called *parties;* but if they have no bond of union but adherence to particular *men,* they become *factions*" (Webster's emphases). He was referring to the difference between National Republicans and Democrats, and he reinforced the point by explaining that Adams's inaugural address had been based on and often articulated conciliatory principles. He defended the appointment of Clay as secretary of state and set out to demonstrate that "republican institutions" were a model to the world.[19] By implication, he endorsed the American System and the prosperity it brought to each region of the nation.

The National Republican and the National Union parties would eventually coalesce into the American Whig Party, but in 1825, the merger was less than assured. Webster dared not move too far ahead of Massachusetts' voters, so he kept his speech short on details. He was specific only in his call for the formation of a "Union ticket" of like-minded Republicans and Federalists. A new party was needed to balance the excesses of Jacksonian democracy. A major step was taken when Levi Lincoln, a former Jeffersonian and recent convert to National Republicanism, accepted Federalist support from Webster's fusion banner and went on to win the governorship in the election of 1825.

As we have seen, Webster had inherited his Federalist beliefs from his father, whom he often resurrected in his epideictics to George Washington. Starting in 1814, these values were given pragmatic application in Webster's illustrious career before the Supreme Court, particularly while John Marshall was chief justice. The two men not only preserved Federalist doctrine but launched a two-pronged attack, as we have seen, on states' rights. On one hand, Webster defended federal powers, as in *McCulloch v. Maryland.* On the other hand, he defended private property and contracts, as in the Dartmouth College case, and individual rights, as in *Gibbons v. Ogden.*

But Webster's legal briefs were not the stuff of which party platforms were constructed. The Whig platform would rise from an amalgam of the old Federalist doctrines and Clay's appealing American System. The values of the new party would emerge from national oratory, notably the epideictic speeches

19. *Boston Courier,* April 5, 1825.

of Daniel Webster. This is not to say that there weren't southern Whigs who supported states' rights; even Clay, who hoped to lead, differed with Webster's stringent Unionism. Webster, however, could build a political constituency north of the Mason–Dixon line which he would inculcate with a civil religion that sometimes moved the whole nation.

The First Bunker Hill Address

One of the occasions on which Webster advanced his civil religion was the laying of the foundation of the Bunker Hill Monument. Webster had been elected chair of the association that would raise the funds and plan a tribute to the victory of Revolutionary forces at Bunker Hill. He worked hard on the speech, but his correspondence reveals that he was not happy with it prior to its delivery. This unease may explain why he felt obligated to edit the speech before its formal publication. More likely, however, the address was never in fixed form until it was delivered from Webster's notes.

On June 17, 1825, over twenty thousand people came to hear the First Bunker Hill Address, also known as "Laying the Cornerstone of the Bunker Hill Monument."[20] Fifty years earlier, the first major battle of the Revolutionary War had been fought on nearby Breed's Hill. (The battle was popularly known, however, as the Battle of Bunker Hill.) Webster's father had been close by, in charge of a company of volunteers. Webster's adoration of his father colored his narration of the Revolutionary War; the heroes of the war were his martyrs and saints.

Webster sat a dais at the bottom of the hill in Charleston, across the river from Boston. The Marquis de Lafayette was seated near him. The crowd spread out before him for more than a mile. The cornerstone was laid and a funeral march was played to commemorate the dead. Veterans of the Revolution were guided to their seats by young army officers in full regalia. The centerpiece of the ceremony was a group known as the Old Hundred, who had defended the hill and who would be addressed directly in the speech. The crowd sang an anthem, a prayer was uttered, and then Webster came forward. Just as he began, an awning over some of the attendees collapsed. Webster immediately called for order, and, by dint of his personality, the crowd was calmed and a stampede avoided. As Webster began anew, he realized that the hill worked as an

---

20. Remini, *Daniel Webster*, 248; Peterson, *The Great Triumvirate*, 108–10.

amphitheater, making for excellent acoustics. Many at the back of the crowd claimed they could hear him clearly.[21]

Webster's themes were not original. He argued for national defense, individual liberty, the Union, preservation of the Constitution, and Greek independence, and he speculated on South American revolutions. What was different in this speech was his valorizing of revolutionary heroes in religious terms. While he spoke, Webster often looked to the Marquis de Lafayette, the most noted foreign ally of the war, and the two hundred veterans of the battle who also sat on the stage. This allowed him to place the moment in the context of the American heritage and to reinforce the most important values in civil life: "We consecrate our work to the spirit of national independence, and we wish that the light of peace may rest upon it forever."[22] This use of *consecrate* was not the first nor the last time that religious terminology was injected into the address, in a nod to the Second Great Awakening that was sweeping New England.

Webster set the scene by demonstrating again his ability to integrate the local context into his speeches. He celebrated the occasion by applying a ceremonial veneer to his discourse. Then he excited the enormous crowd by creating an expectation of what was to come in the speech: "If, indeed, there be anything in local association fit to affect the mind of man, we need not strive to repress the emotions which agitate us here. We are among the sepulchres of our fathers. We are on ground distinguished by their valor, their constancy, and the shedding of their blood." Webster played to New England pride as he had in his address on the Pilgrims' landing.

Moving to a broader scale, he demonstrated that his narrative and descriptive skills were gathering a literary quality hardly equaled in American public address, as he described the scene

> when the great discoverer of America stood on the deck of his shattered bark, the shades of night falling on the sea, yet no man sleeping; tossed on the billows of an unknown ocean, yet the stronger billows of alternate hope and despair tossing his own troubled thoughts; extending forward his harassed frame, straining westward his anxious and eager eyes, till Heaven at last granted him a moment of rapture and ecstasy, in blessing his vision with the sight of the unknown world.

21. Remini, *Daniel Webster*, 248–50.
22. All quotations from this speech are from Webster, *Speeches and Forensic Arguments*, 1:57–70.

The movement between nature and the human mind is facile, as is the appeal to the unknown under the ocean, on the land ahead, and in the mind of Columbus. This sublime passage led into others that took the audience through the landing at Plymouth and the Revolutionary War to the very moment that was being consecrated that day. The religious imagery serves to tie America to a larger and older tradition: Christian transcendence. In this way the speech seems aimed at assuring the nation that it is part of the continuity of a universal *telos*: "We rear a memorial of our conviction of that unmeasured benefit which has been conferred on our own land, and of the happy influences which have been produced by the same events on the general interests of mankind." The dedication is punctuated by seven sentences that begin with the words "We wish." The paragraph about the monument then concludes, "Let it rise till it meet the sun in his coming; let the earlier light of the morning gild it, and parting day linger and play on its summit." The biblical tone reinforced the religious feeling of the moment.[23] It is important to remember that the audience was not reading the words; they were hearing them, and could easily associate the Second Coming with the line, "the sun [Son] in his coming."

Webster then proceeded to describe the events that were being celebrated. He began by denying exactly what he was about to do: "The occasion does not require of me any particular account of the battle of the seventeenth of June, nor any detailed narrative of the events which immediately preceded it." Having established a contrary expectation in the audience, Webster then brought the battle to life in a moving narrative. By returning to the event, he employed a strategy that Aristotle claimed was essential for effective epideictic oratory; he emotionally called out the names of the leaders of the battle, bringing the scene alive for the crowd:

> You see the lines of the little redoubt thrown up by the incredible diligence of Prescott; defended to the last extremity, by his lion-hearted valor. . . . You see where Warren fell, and where Parker, Gardner, McCleary, Moore, and other early patriots fell with him. Those who survived that day, and whose lives have been prolonged to the present hour, are now around you. . . .

23. The passage recalls Matthew 5:45, among other biblical verses, and was well remembered after Webster's lifetime. On April 3, 1865, just days before he became president, Vice President Andrew Johnson gave a speech at the War Department to celebrate the fall of Richmond, and said, "May not I be permitted on this occasion, to indulge substantially in the language of another, in referring to the Stars and Stripes of our country, which now waves in triumph, that it may continue to rise higher and higher, until it meets the sun in his coming, and may departing day linger and play upon its ample folds."

> Behold! they now stretch forth their feeble arms to embrace you. Behold! they raise their trembling voices to invoke the blessing of God on you and yours forever.

This metaphysical appeal worked because of Webster's sincerity, because the crowd was with him, because it was a romantic age filled with religious zeal and piety, and because sitting on the stage with him were the withered survivors of the battle whose "feeble arms" and "trembling voices" gave substance to Webster's rhetorical ghosts. The battle on the hill behind Webster was re-created in the minds of his listeners, who gladly received the benediction of the dead patriots.[24]

His main task complete, Webster turned to his deliberative agenda. Allying himself with the ongoing economic expansion, he praised America's fifty years of growth and newfound strength: "We have a commerce that leaves no sea unexplored; navies which take no law from superior force; revenues adequate to all the exigencies of government, almost without taxation; and peace with all nations, founded on equal rights and mutual respect." One of the reasons Webster was so convincing in this passage was that he reinforced his message with a periodic and parallel construction that progressed to a natural conclusion. (Speaking the words aloud helps one appreciate how style and thought flow together to make the message irresistible.)

In the next section of the speech, Webster contrasted American values and successes with European ones, again asserting a special American mission:

> The great wheel of political revolution began to move in America. Here its rotation was guarded, regular, and safe. Transferred to the other continent, from unfortunate but natural causes, it received an irregular and violent impulse; it whirled along with a fearful celerity; till at length, like the chariot wheels in the races of antiquity, it took fire from the rapidity of its own motion and blazed onward, spreading conflagration and terror around.

Thus France stands condemned in contrast to the prior, enlightened American experience. Webster claimed that the Revolution was only the beginning

24. In the Eulogy to Adams and Jefferson, discussed in the next chapter, Webster "became" Adams and uttered what has been called the greatest "ghost speech" in American public address. Perhaps his success at Bunker Hill gave him the courage to be even more daring with invented dialogue at Faneuil Hall a year later.

of a great victory that the New World would achieve over the Old World—not only in terms of military might, but also in terms of legislation, commerce, arts, letters, "and above all, in liberal ideas." While Europe fought wars to maintain alliances and power, America fought for freedom. Webster praised the Greek Revolution and the revolutions under way in Latin America as part of a new wave of freedom sweeping from the cradle of liberty to the New World.

Webster's two-page conclusion is a celebration of the ideals he believed would deliver America to her destiny. These included liberty, progress, duty, defense, peace, and Union. He concluded by paraphrasing the well-known legal oath each witness must take in a court of law: "Let our object be our country, our whole country, and nothing but our country. And, by the blessings of God, may that country itself become a vast and splendid monument, not of oppression and terror, but of Wisdom, of Peace, and of Liberty, upon which the world may gaze, with admiration, forever!" Webster therefore ended by identifying the Bunker Hill Monument with the monument of American values. It is a neat turn of phrase, but certainly not the only indication that Webster had mastered the ceremonial form. The speech is marked by its high style, full of tropes and figures. There are apostrophes: "Veterans!" There is a direct involvement of the audience. There are self-fulfilling prophecies: "I perceive that a tumult of contending feelings rushes upon you." There are well-formed balances: "Death might come, in honor, on the field; it might come, in disgrace, on the scaffold." And as we have seen, there is a magnificent use of metaphor to sustain interest and religious allusions to reassure. Throughout the two-hour address, Webster rarely glanced at the few scribbled lines he kept on a small lectern beside him. When he finished, the crowd exploded in applause, and many were in tears. They rushed the platform, seeking to touch him, to talk to him, to experience his presence. Through it all, he remained aloof, the godlike Daniel.

Like most of Webster's ceremonial speeches, this one was polished, then published and widely distributed. It was even translated into French and published in Paris at Lafayette's insistence. Schoolboys had yet another Webster speech to master. Proceeds from the sales were donated to the Bunker Hill Monument Association. Most important, the speech helped to establish the genre of ceremonial speaking in America. The *Dictionary of American Biography* states of Webster: "Achieving another great oratorical triumph at the laying of the cornerstone of the Bunker Hill monument on June 17, 1825, he made popular the occasional oratory that was to thrive for decades."[25] Events of a mystical nature would soon give Webster a chance to reinforce this achievement.

The Legislative Agenda

First, however, the business of the nation called; it was time to return to Washington for another session of Congress. Webster arrived with his family in December 1825. The Websters resided on Capitol Hill near the Library of Congress. When the library caught fire on December 22, Webster was there in the bucket line along with other local residents and a fire crew.

In his message to Congress, John Quincy Adams, clearly influenced by Clay, endorsed a program of national improvements. Southerners were skeptical and feared that it was a hidden attack on states' rights. How were these improvements to be paid for? Not, it was hoped, with a higher tariff. They of course had an ally in John C. Calhoun, the new vice president, who had reentered the presidential contest after recovering from his stroke.

Of lesser national consequence was Webster's attempt to reform the badly overworked judicial system. It was his second try to get reform legislation passed. The centerpiece of the legislation was the expansion of the Supreme Court to nine members. Webster jobbed the legislation around to his friends and then met with President Adams to discuss it. The bill was amended in committee to expand the Court to ten, a ridiculous notion that could easily result in tie votes. Nonetheless, despite southern cries for a smaller court, the bill passed the House after Webster spoke in its favor. The Senate, however, came up with its own bill and refused to compromise with the House. There was no way it was going to give the unpopular Adams the chance to appoint new justices to the Supreme Court; his father's midnight appointments of March 1801 were still part of the political consciousness. Thus, once again, Webster was frustrated in his effort to reform the court system.

He and Adams were also frustrated in their attempt to gain ratification of a treaty with the Cherokee of Georgia. The governor of the state intervened and claimed that Indian relations were an internal matter, despite the fact that the agreements signed with the tribes had been given treaty status even before the United States was formed. Again, the Senate supported the southern states,

25. Arthur C. Cole, "Daniel Webster," 19:588.

which would soon turn to Andrew Jackson, that old Creek and Seminole fighter, as their savior on this issue in the next election.

The end of the session turned acrimonious when Calhoun, as presiding officer of the Senate, allowed John Randolph to attack Secretary of State Clay in a vicious speech. Many thought Randolph was mentally ill, and Webster was angered by Calhoun's bad judgment. Clay was so affronted by the speech that he challenged Randolph to a duel. The two met across the Potomac in Virginia on April 8. Randolph missed his mark. Clay put a bullet in the lining of Randolph's cloak, declared victory, and went home.

The standoff between Adams and the Senate marked a new partisan and sectional division. Though the rather stiff president represented the old guard and the old ways, Webster would build a new party around his leader. America was in a religious and romantic mood, and Jackson would become its embodiment, much to the consternation of Clay, Webster, and eventually Calhoun. Jackson had survived a lightning strike, battles with Native Americans, and duels with his enemies. He had led American forces to a decisive victory over the British at New Orleans. He had led his party to a plurality victory in 1824; next he would seek an absolute majority in 1828.

Chapter 4

Civic Duty in the Romantic Age

Throughout 1826 Andrew Jackson met with allies and broadened his support across the country. His romantic persona seemed right for the season. Wasn't it time for a general to be president again? Hadn't the string of dry Enlightenment rationalists, who usually came to the presidency after being in the cabinet, denuded the presidency of its glamour? John Quincy Adams seemed stuffy, out of sorts, an elitist who disdained the populace, and was clearly in league with that "devil" Henry Clay.

Webster was distracted from presidential politics when Congress adjourned in May because he had several cases to argue before the Supreme Court. This came on top of being elected to the board of directors of the Bank of the United States at the behest of his patron, Nicholas Biddle, a brilliant man who had graduated from Princeton at age fifteen. This fact impressed another Princeton graduate, James Madison, who had appointed Biddle to the board of the first Bank of the United States from his position in the Pennsylvania legislature. From there, Biddle rose to president of the bank, in which position he revealed his love of Greece by instructing his architects to build his banks in the Greek Revival style, setting a precedent that lasted well into the twentieth century.

When Webster returned to Boston at the end of the spring, a Senate seat opened in Massachusetts. Webster avoided the appointment since it would last only for the current session of Congress. If he were to go to the Senate, he wanted a full six years. Webster thought he had a chance to enjoy the summer, but fate intervened.

The Eulogy to Adams and Jefferson

On July 4, 1826, exactly fifty years after the publication of the Declaration of Independence, both Thomas Jefferson and John Adams died, in a seemingly mystical concurrence. A eulogy was required and Daniel Webster was the orator that leapt to many people's mind.[1] He was deeply honored but not surprised when the Boston City Council asked him to deliver the speech in August. Edward Everett, who was gaining a reputation for oratorical skill himself, was planning to speak about the deaths in New Hampshire a few weeks earlier, but Webster talked him out of it, not so subtly implying that speaking on the subject before he did would be unwise.

There was hardly a prominent citizen of Boston who had not heard of Webster; the glow from the Bunker Hill address was still warm. Furthermore, Webster had had an association with John Adams, whose Federalist positions he admired. Adams had worked closely with Webster in 1820 at the Massachusetts Constitutional Convention and praised Webster's speech at Plymouth that year. As we have also seen, Webster had at least a passing acquaintance with Jefferson, having visited him a few years earlier.

Aristotle wrote:

> To praise a man is in one respect akin to urging a course of action. The suggestions which would be made in the latter case become encomiums when differently expressed. . . . Consequently whenever you want to praise anyone, think what you would urge people to do; and when you want to urge the doing of anything, think what you would praise a man for having done. Since suggestion may or may not forbid any action, the praise into which we convert it must have one or other of two opposite forms of expression accordingly.[2]

Recognizing that the interplay of the various genres can produce a unique speech for a rhetorical situation, Webster had often concealed one form of public address in another. His famous eulogy of Adams and Jefferson, however, is his most clearly ceremonial speech. His apparent faithfulness to the epideictic form in this case is a function of several factors. The address came

1. See Joseph Story to Daniel Webster, July 11, 1826, in *Papers of Daniel Webster: Correspondence*, 1:126–27.

2. Aristotle, *Rhetoric*, 1367b37–1368a10. For Aristotle's explanation of how forensic judgments are useful in epideictic discourse, see 1368b10–20.

six years after the Missouri Compromise and at least eighteen months before the tariff issue would ignite southern rage. The slavery issue was at low ebb. The occasion was midway between presidential election years, thus somewhat removing it from partisan politics. Furthermore, in 1826 Webster was not sure his future would be a political one; he remained in the House, unselected for the Senate. Deliberative policy and forensic condemnation were less likely to surface in this address than in his others.

The deaths of Adams, the last Federalist president, and Jefferson, the first Democratic-Republican president, marked the passing of a generation. It seemed that Providence had intervened to take the two leaders to their rest exactly fifty years after the Declaration of Independence was published. The country was so focused on these national heroes that an epideictic speech was required to meet the expectations of the audience and to celebrate the transcendent nature of the deaths. Deliberative and forensic elements might demean the occasion. The more priestly Webster could appear, the better. Once again he was presented with an opportunity to define a civil religion for the public by exhibiting the virtues of dead leaders and how they speak to us.

As usual Webster sought the advice of many friends in preparation for the address. He had his own notes on Jefferson's involvement in the Declaration of Independence,[3] and he pored over letters of Adams written in June and July of 1776. Timothy Pickering, secretary of state in the Adams administration, supplied the letter that may have inspired the famous "ghost speech" in the address. (Pickering served in the House with Webster and had been a client of his.)

On the day of the eulogy, August 2, 1826, businesses were closed in Boston. Thousands of people tried to crowd into Faneuil Hall in the financial district near the harbor. The doors were closed at noon, the dignitaries were seated, and the mob outside began a loud protest. To prevent a riot, Webster strode to the front of the stage and shouted, "Let the doors be opened!" Many in the mob squeezed into the hall; the rest quieted and strained to hear. For the first time, the balconies of the hall were draped in black, the decor of mourning. Near Webster on the stage sat Gov. Levi Lincoln, Maj. Josiah Quincy, and Harvard president John Thornton Kirkland; John Quincy Adams led the funeral service for his father. It was a daunting moment, complicated by the fact that Adams and Jefferson had very different personalities and represented very

---

3. *Papers of Daniel Webster: Correspondence*, 1:375.

different political philosophies. Webster's challenge was to weld the occasion and his subjects into one civil religion and one piece of discourse.[4]

Webster enhanced the mystical nature of the occasion by addressing the audience's expectations regarding the themes of death and resurrection in national memory. Aristotle can help us understand Webster's effectiveness; he indicates that discussions of virtues are used to support claims of honor or dishonor, and to make these claims believable. One way to make them believable is to ascribe to the subject those "qualities an audience esteems."[5]

Aristotle's recommendations for arrangement in epideictic speaking begin with a call for a preview of ideas. He suggests that themes be integrated into the text to ensure continuity. Consistent with this advice is a recommendation that narration be intermittent throughout the speech and that eulogy and argument be interwoven. Aristotle is concerned not only with finding an organizational structure appropriate to the occasion, but also that the structure demonstrate some sense of proportion. He realizes how easy it is for a speaker to exclude his audience while eulogizing the dead or a past event, or while vilifying an opponent, so he advises the speaker to bring his audience into the occasion. Of the three forms of public address, Aristotle claims that the epideictic "is the most literary, since it is meant to be read."[6] We find support for this claim among modern critics, in Webster's practice of not publishing his speeches until he had revised them, and in the success those published speeches enjoyed.

While Aristotle's commentary on epideictic speech is groundbreaking, it is not the only source that is helpful in assessing Webster's effectiveness.[7] Webster, particularly in this eulogy, uses Plato's notion of epideictic wherein lessons from history are reinforced and politics is merged with ethics. Webster also

4. Howell and Hudson, "Daniel Webster," 682. Much has been written about the difficult relationship between Adams and Jefferson. They rubbed each other the wrong way during debates on the Declaration of Independence, during debates over the ratification of the Constitution and the Bill of Rights, and during Washington's and Adams's administrations. Their "feud" was known to the public. For example, in 1789 they exchanged cool letters regarding the Publicola affair, in which a writer using the pseudonym "Publicola" had attacked Jefferson for endorsing Paine's *Rights of Man*. Jefferson accused Adams of being Publicola; Adams denied it and told Jefferson to stop slandering him. Jefferson indicated in his notes that Publicola may have been John Quincy Adams. If this was true, John Adams's denials were disingenuous.

5. Aristotle, *Rhetoric*, 1358b28, 1367a31.

6. Ibid., 1414a15–18.

7. See Lawrence Rosenfield, "The Practical Celebration of Epideictic"; George A. Kennedy, *Classical Rhetoric and Its Christian and Secular Tradition from Ancient Times to Modern Times*, 73–75.

read Cicero's advice that the epideictic speaker should reinforce "statements that are certain."[8] In fact, Webster's discussion of civic virtue in the eulogy reflects Cicero's and Quintilian's paradigm for the "good speaker."

Webster's eulogy meets the content-related criteria of the form by dealing with a present occasion and praising its subjects, but it meets the standards of structure in more subtle ways. The proportioning of the speech is almost poetic. If A represents the discourse devoted to Adams, J the discourse devoted to Jefferson, and AJ discussions of the two together, the following general pattern emerges:

Introduction	AJ
Body	A, J, AJ, A, J, AJ
Conclusion	AJ, digression, AJ, peroration

This metarhythmic progression directs Webster's line of thought, which is clothed in appropriate style throughout the address.

The introduction is concerned with describing the extraordinary coincidence that has brought the audience together. From the first sentence, Webster calls attention to the hall itself. He then connects the mourning in the hall to his conservative sense of history: "The tears which flow, and the honors that are paid, when the founders of the Republic die, give hope that the Republic itself may be immortal." Death reinforces life. This sublime contrast is matched by another when Webster notes that Adams and Jefferson "took their flight together to the world of spirits" in the midst of national rejoicing over the fiftieth anniversary of independence.[9] The common practice of merging religious and civic themes emerges early in the speech and is certainly justified in a eulogy to fallen patriots. The parallel lives of the two founders are explored generally as a preview of what is to come. Throughout this section, the audience is described and drawn into the speech.

Already, Webster has created a pattern that will guide him through the speech. The audience will be involved in the "account of the lives" by means of refer-

8. See Bernard K. Duffy, "The Platonic Functions of Epideictic Rhetoric," 79, 85; Cicero, *De Partitione Oratoria*, 365. For evidence of Cicero's advice in nineteenth-century epideictic speaking, see Richard Weaver, *The Ethics of Rhetoric*, 172.

9. All quotations are from the manuscript in Webster's own hand, New Hampshire Historical Society, Concord. This text is considered the most authentic since the published version was revised. The text is reproduced, with the revised passages set in brackets, in *The Papers of Daniel Webster: Speeches and Formal Writings*, 1:238-71.

ences to the occasion. The occasion will be explored with references to the parallel lives of the two patriots. Also unveiled in the introduction is a wonderful metaphor that surfaces several more times in the speech and culminates near the end. The stars in the sky—and, later, the planets and their orbits—provide a unifying image for the address: "These suns, as they rose slowly and steadily, amidst clouds and storms, in their ascendant, so they have not rushed from their meridian to sink suddenly in the west. . . . [T]hey have gone down with slow-descending, grateful, long-lingering light."

The introduction is also ordered by the forward movement of Webster's argument: "They live in their example; and they live, emphatically, and will live, in the influence which their lives and efforts, their principles and opinions, now exercise, and will continue to exercise, on the affairs of men, not only in their own country, but throughout the civilized world." Again, death reinforces life; it perpetuates "the stream of time."

The introduction is marked by the grand periodic style of Webster at his most literate. Metaphors and antitheses abound; semicolons and prepositional phrases march across the page. Just at the right moment, short, simple sentences offer relief from the onslaught of tropes and figures. "We are not deceived. There is no delusion here," concludes Webster after two train-length sentences.

The first section after the introduction is devoted to John Adams's life to the year 1776. The section that follows explores Jefferson's life to the same year. Webster knew Adams better than he knew Jefferson, and certainly preferred the politics of the former to those of the latter. This familiarity and the fact that the speech was delivered on Adams's home turf explains why Adams's biography is nearly three times as long as Jefferson's. The praise of both men centers on their particular accomplishments as evidence of honor. Jefferson's role as leader, statesman, philosopher, and Founding Father is compared to Adams's political commitments and service on the Massachusetts Supreme Court. Other accomplishments are used to demonstrate virtues attendant upon honor. For example, Adams did not cower when faced with having to defend Captain Thomas Preston, whose troops fired into a mob of Bostonians in 1770. Jefferson is said to have received the highest honors at William and Mary College, but his "love of letters" was "postponed" when duty called. Adams's educational career led to his having argued before his state's supreme court at the early age of twenty-four and writing a distinguished series of essays at thirty. Jefferson is portrayed as just in representing his constituents. In the case of Adams, Webster is direct: "Mr. Adams himself seems never to have lost the feeling [justice] produced, and to have entertained constantly the fullest conviction of its important effect." The biographies are written in a plain, declarative style that allows them to speak for themselves; they provide a much-needed contrast to the florid introduction.

Webster has little difficulty imputing courage and sacrifice to the two patriots in the early sections of the speech and then reestablishing these virtues toward the conclusion. Praise is contained in equal proportion in the AJ sections and reasserted to maintain continuity and consistency. Webster refers to certain virtues throughout, thereby reinforcing a feeling of unity in the address. He also creates a sense of unity with three striking metaphors. We have already reviewed the first, concerning the universe. The second appears in other Webster speeches as well: it involves a mariner bringing his ship safely home over a turbulent ocean. This metaphor had great appeal to Americans at the time because the bulk of the population lived in such ports as Boston, New York, Philadelphia, Baltimore, Charleston, and New Bedford, which by this time had established itself as the whaling capital of the world.

The third metaphor concerns the growth cycle. In its simplest form in speeches of the time, this metaphor referred to the past, the present, and the future. In this speech, it concerns the seed, the sapling, and the tree. The seed is the accomplishments of the two patriots; the sapling is the present and the audience's understanding of virtue; and the tree, which reaches to heaven, is the future, guiding the living and providing a lasting tribute to the dead patriots. This stream of time leads Webster and his audience to transcendence. It allows him to say that while Adams and Jefferson "are no more," "they live" nonetheless. The oxymoron is transcended by the metaphor of time and the reality of memory.

Webster also manipulates certain themes to achieve cohesiveness. His use of "liberty" is typical. The concept, which is introduced in paragraph 1, reappears in paragraphs 9 and 15, and is still evident in paragraphs 69, 71, and 72 at the end.

Webster shows great skill in making the virtues he attributes to his subjects believable. The next major section of the speech is a case in point. It combines the lives of Adams and Jefferson, and consists of a nearly forty-five-minute review of the writing and approval of the Declaration of Independence. Jefferson's involvement in writing the Declaration was easily researched; historians knew that Jefferson was the major drafter of the document. Webster acknowledges as much in a few phrases, making Jefferson's contribution to the Declaration quite clear. He even rebuts the charge by Timothy Pickering in an oration of 1823 that Jefferson's draft contained "nothing new."

Webster next discussed the relationship between the colonies and England in an effort to set the scene for what will follow. The issues of the day and the context of the debates over the Declaration were key elements of his daring strategy. Though no record of the debates was extant, he contended that Adams's debating skill was crucial to the passage of the Declaration: "John Adams had no equal."

But how was Webster to convey Adams's contribution? There had to be some way to provide a counterweight to Jefferson's writing of the Declaration. To accomplish this task, Webster first cited Jefferson's praise for Adams as a "colossus . . . not elegant, not always fluent" but capable of "thought and expression, which moved us from our seats." Second, Webster heaped praise on Adams and described his eloquence: "It was bold, manly, energetic." These passages undoubtedly created an expectation in the audience that Webster then fulfilled with his famous "ghost speech." Webster wrote this section in the plain, bold, manly style he attributed to Adams. Those in the audience who were familiar with the acerbic Adams were willing to accept this portrayal; those who did not know Adams's oratory were primed by Webster's foreshadowing. What is truly remarkable about these passages is that they bring Adams alive, in stark contrast to the early sections of the speech, which make clear that he is "dead," "no more," "lost," "fallen." Webster declares the death of the two founders and then resurrects them where they intersect in history. The strategy demonstrates his ability to create an expectation in the audience through word choice. He evokes a setting in the imagination of his audience and then steps into that setting to deliver a stirring portrayal of Adams.[10]

The opening of the "ghost speech" is stunning and powerful: "Sink or swim, live or die, survive or perish, I give my hand and my heart to this vote." The hail of rhetorical questions that follows holds the attention of listeners. The extended temporal and celestial metaphor at the end is all the more glorious because it rises from the declarative desert that precedes it: "Through the thick gloom of the present, I see the brightness of the future, as the sun in

10. In his *Life and Character of Patrick Henry* (1817), William Wirt had reconstructed Henry's "Liberty or Death" speech with such eloquence that it had become an assignment for every schoolchild in America. Webster's "ghost speech" for Adams may have been meant to provide a New England model.

heaven. We shall make thus a glorious, an immortal day. When we are in our graves, our children will honor it. . . . On its annual return they will shed tears, copious, gushing tears, not of subjection and slavery, not of agony and distress, but of exultation, of gratitude, and of joy." And then comes the last line, which presages Webster's magnificent conclusion to the debate with Hayne in 1830: "It is my living sentiment, and by the blessing of God it shall be my dying sentiment, Independence *now, and Independence for ever.*"[11]

Webster claimed to have written the "ghost speech" over breakfast at his home on Summer Street and that his stationery was wet with tears when he finished. Other records indicate that he was unsure about this section of the speech. The day before he was to deliver the eulogy, he rehearsed the section in front of George Ticknor and asked him if it should be deleted. Ticknor told him to retain it,[12] and he ended up expanding it by almost one-third in the published version of the eulogy. Aside from its fitness for the occasion, the impersonation of Adams works because it is explosive and dramatic, in marked contrast to the dry exposition of Jefferson's involvement in writing the Declaration, and because it refutes the arguments Webster presents on behalf of Adams's opposition.[13] Furthermore, the use of ethopoeia reinforces the AJ structure, keeping the lines of organization clear while filling the individual units with exciting discourse.

After paying homage to the other patriots present at the debate, particularly those from the "commonwealth," Webster resumes his narrative of the life of Adams, briefly outlining various accomplishments and honors. This section was almost doubled in length in the pamphlet version; both versions end with the claim that the last words "which trembled on [Adams's] lips" were "Independence forever!"

A recounting of Jefferson's life from 1776 to 1826 follows, concluding with the creation of the "infant seminary," the University of Virginia. Again, a plain style allows the narrative to speak for itself. Webster then returns to his grand style to paint a moving picture of the man of letters beholding "his last sands . . .

11. For a close look at the use of tropes in the "ghost speech," see James M. Farrell, "The Speech Within: Trope and Performance in Daniel Webster's Eulogy to Adams and Jefferson."

12. Fuess, *Daniel Webster,* 1:302.

13. These arguments heighten the drama and add to Webster's credibility. It can be argued, though, that Webster's zeal in setting up the debate is excessive. The case he makes against independence is very strong. This may have been what prompted him to expand Adams's reply in the published version.

falling." He quotes as Jefferson's dying words a Latin phrase from Tacitus's tribute to Agricola. Legend has it, however, that Jefferson, under a mistaken impression, actually said, "I have but one regret, that Adams has outlived me."

Webster then unites his subjects again, discussing their successive presidencies and comparative merits in plain style. His "faint and feeble tribute," as he calls it at the beginning of the conclusion, is inadequate, but Adams's and Jefferson's "fame . . . is safe." He marks the passing of a generation by pointing out that only one signer of the Declaration remains, like "an aged oak, standing alone on the plain." This metaphor signals a return to the grand style; parallel structure, extended metaphors and similes, apostrophes, repetitions, periodic rhythms, and alliteration fill the final paragraphs in anticipation of the closing lines: "Washington is in the clear, upper sky. These other stars have now joined the American constellation; they circle round their centre, and the heavens beam with new light. Beneath this illumination let us walk the course of life, and at its close devoutly commend our beloved country, the common parent of us all, to the Divine Benignity." Thus, Webster places Adams and Jefferson in the firmament, but keeps his beloved Washington at the center of his pantheon, which hovered over the audience.

The speech was an enormous success. Richard Rush, the secretary of the Treasury, wrote to Webster: "The speech . . . made my hair rise. . . . Nothing of Livy's ever moved me so much."[14] The Boston press and persons of political and literary accomplishment from Mayor Josiah Quincy to Joseph Hopkinson joined in the praise. Webster had achieved his desired persona in the Boston media as the "Godlike Daniel," encouraged by his reference to Adams as "godlike." His fusion politics and civil religion would soon propel him into the Senate. As Stephen Howard Browne writes, Webster's speech "does this work . . . by inscribing the tenets of Whig tradition into itself and by putting on display the competencies defining that tradition."[15] Webster had moved beyond being a great congressman and lawyer; he had become a man of letters, a force in American literary circles. Few political leaders have equaled that achievement. The most noted, Abraham Lincoln, never produced the variety or volume of work that Webster did, although he was able to match the quality of Webster's best poetic lines.

Within the epideictic form of the speech, Webster satisfies the needs of the

14. Quoted in *Speeches and Formal Writings*, 2:129.
15. Stephen Howard Browne, "Webster's Eulogy and the Tropes of Public Memory," 42.

particular rhetorical situation with proportion and grace. He treats his subjects separately and then unites them: "Both had been presidents, both had lived to great age, both were early patriots, and both were distinguished and ever honored." Paragraph 28 provides an example of the same strategy but with the use of historic events instead of thematic material: "Mr. Jefferson . . . had received the highest and Mr. Adams the next highest number of votes. The difference is said to have been but a single vote." Near the end of the address Webster expands the strategy to include the occasion, when he speaks again of the common day of death. Thus, the A, J, AJ structure is evident both in substance and in form.

Clearly this address is Webster's most ceremonial. However, elements from other genres do subtly surface. He encapsulates deliberative advice inside the AJ structure: "They live in their example; and they live, emphatically, and will live, in the influence which their lives and efforts, their principles and opinions, now exercise, and will continue to exercise, on the affairs of men not only in their country, but throughout the civilized world." This passage appears early in the speech (paragraph 6) and foreshadows Webster's use of "principles and opinions" for deliberative ends while playing to the audience's need to enshrine the founders in the national memory. Subsequent paragraphs reinforce this preview, which seems both to justify and to mask Webster's deliberative remarks. When Webster finally translates the patriots' "principles" into a course of action, the deliberative advice seems natural to the discourse: "Be it remembered . . . that liberty must, at all hazards, be supported."

Later, he reasserts his commitment to continuity: "And now, fellow citizens, let us not retire from this occasion without a deep and solemn conviction of the duties which have devolved upon us. This lovely land, this glorious liberty, these benign institutions, the dear purchase of our fathers, are ours; ours to enjoy, ours to preserve, ours to transmit." In the last paragraph, Webster admits that he might have spent too much time on these themes, but continues to discuss them anyway.[16] He argues that America is a model for the world, that it embodies a new approach to government, that its citizens must preserve its institutions, and that all must be guided by God. Webster's references to the occasion and the forefathers maintain an epideictic veneer over a delibera-

---

16. Just as in the first Bunker Hill address, Webster denies doing exactly what he is doing. The most famous example of apophasis is Marc Antony's eulogy in Shakespeare, where Antony says, "I come to bury Caesar, not to praise him," and then goes on to praise Caesar.

tive message concerned with ways to achieve and preserve happiness, with the good in society, with forms of government, and with the duties of citizens. Each of these themes is treated by Aristotle under the deliberative heading in book 1, chapters 5–8, of the *Rhetoric*.

Even less apparent are the forensic elements. While accusation and defense rarely appear, Webster does employ them to set the scene for the all-important "ghost speech." Throughout the speech, he uses his defense of the founders as reinforcement of praise and as a backdrop for deliberative themes. A passage near the end of the speech exemplifies Aristotle's belief that any praise of a person is closely akin to forensic pleading: "No men, fellow citizens, ever served their country with more entire exemption from every imputation of selfish and mercenary motives, than those to whose memory we are paying these proofs of respect. A suspicion of any disposition to enrich themselves, or to profit by their public employment, never rested on either." The setting and the audience make this passage epideictic; however, were the same passage uttered before a jury, it would be transformed into a forensic pleading.

The issue of England's treatment of the colonies is more clearly forensic. Paragraphs 29 through 32 condemn the unjust actions of Parliament and King George III, while vindicating the actions of the patriots. Webster uses this section to establish his probity regarding the debate over the Declaration, its intent, and composition. Thus, the masking of forensic elements works to make the epideictic persuasion more effective.

This analysis reveals several important strategies that Webster used in ceremonial addresses from his first Fourth of July address, in 1800, to the year of his death in 1852. The overlap between genres occurs in two theoretically distinct ways: through a masking process in which purposes proper to one genre are developed in a speech ostensibly belonging to another genre, and through a borrowing process in which the purposes of one genre are served by using devices from another. The latter case is exemplified in the eulogy to Adams and Jefferson, in which Webster uses deliberative and forensic elements to reinforce the epideictic *telos*.

At the same time, there seems always to be one controlling or dominant form. Audiences that gather to hear a speech are called upon to serve in a loose sense as jurors, observers, or deliberators, but they may also serve a secondary function, with or without the encouragement of the speaker. For example, those gathered to hear Webster's eulogy could function as jurors sitting in judgment of England, as policymakers on the course of the Union, or merely as observers of the display. Thus, the role of the audience is one of the major components by which we can identify the controlling genre. Setting is also useful: whether a speech is given in court, in Congress, or in celebration of a holiday helps determine the dominant form shaping the discourse. While one setting may dominate, another may be called to mind. Webster's transformation of Faneuil Hall into the Continental Congress for the "ghost speech" is a case in point.

Aristotle also uses time as a determinant of the controlling form. If one intends to issue a judgment about the past, the forensic form is most useful. Speaking to the future necessitates deliberative utterance, and endorsing values for the present is epideictic. Again, while one time period may be emphasized and thereby help to identify the controlling form, secondary time periods often appear. Webster's vindication of Jefferson's past in the eulogy is part of an overall strategy to reinforce present values so that future policies will be improved.

Form explains why Webster was so successful. He adapted epideictic rhetoric to fit the audience, subject, time, and setting. He understood that Aristotle's three genres cast three different lights on the persuasive situation. Each light reveals a different "available means of persuasion" and Webster employed them all, which explains why his public address was complex, effective, and enduring.

Through Webster, the Federalist virtues of Union, liberty, opportunity, and propertied rights not only survived but also flourished with the birth of the new Whig Party. The success and fame of the Eulogy to Adams and Jefferson, along with Webster's subsequent election to the Senate, made him a leader in the new party and further endeared him to the leaders in Boston. His ceremonial speeches brought the Whig platform to the public and reinforced values that devolved from the Revolution and the ratification of the Constitution and its Bill of Rights. These same values would serve Lincoln as he preserved and protected the Union less than a decade after Webster's death.

Politics as Usual

During his term as president John Quincy Adams was forced to endure the independent vice presidency of John C. Calhoun, who opposed the National Republican agenda. The Whigs needed to maintain some sort of party if their ideology was to survive, and Webster was forced to gravitate into Henry Clay's orbit. The Whigs endorsed tariffs to protect manufacturing and fund internal improvements; the funds would be administered by a secure National Bank of the United States. They defended the property rights of individuals, believing with Aristotle, Rousseau, and Jefferson that individual ownership of land is the key to good citizenship and development of the hinterlands.

As Webster considered Francis Cabot Lowell's claim that British imports were endangering his mills, Jacksonians challenged Webster's claim to a House seat. Webster, however, overwhelmed his opponent by a margin of 15 to 1 in the election of 1826. Promoting a fusion ticket in Massachusetts had paid off in this single-district election. When Webster returned to Washington, he was surprised at the activity of the Jacksonians; they were in full campaign mode with almost two years to go before the presidential election. Webster learned that Calhoun and Martin Van Buren had entered into an arrangement whereby they would support Jackson for president. Calhoun would retain the vice presidency, and Van Buren would join the cabinet if he delivered the state of New York to the ticket.

As Congress gathered in February 1827, Webster pushed a woolen protection bill through the House, much to Calhoun's displeasure. The vice president let it be known that he favored free trade and states' rights. When the bill came to the Senate, a tie vote arranged by Van Buren allowed Calhoun to cast the deciding vote and defeat it. The issues of free trade and states' rights would merge over the next few years to form the dividing line between North and South, driving senators back to their states for instructions. The confrontation would eventually lead to civil war, in part because the agricultural South needed lower tariffs and slaves to produce its raw goods.

In the same session, as we have seen, bankruptcy legislation failed, forcing the Supreme Court to side with the states on the bankruptcy issue that year by a close vote, with Marshall and Story dissenting on Webster's side; states could pass bankruptcy laws as long as those laws applied to commerce inside their boundaries. Despite Webster's best efforts, there was no national bankruptcy law until 1841, but even that one was repealed two years later.

With another do-nothing session behind him, Webster took off to campaign in Maryland, Pennsylvania, and New York for the fusion National Republican Party. Clay did the same in the South and the West. In fact, Clay and Webster would never be closer than during the run-up to the 1828 election. However, they were disappointed to find that their party did not have the same organization or grassroots support enjoyed by the Jacksonian Democrats. Webster suggested that a media campaign was in order to counter the threat.

A second strategy was to get President Adams to use his patronage powers to the party's advantage; but the high-minded Adams refused to go along. The "spoils system" would not come into its own until the Jackson presidency, and American politics would never be the same.

A third strategy was to raise funds in the business community to support the Whig campaign. At this Webster was the master, especially in New York and Massachusetts. The monies were quickly laundered through intermediaries and delivered to friendly newspapers or those that were wavering, such as the *Richmond Whig* and the *Cincinnati Gazette*.[17]

Meanwhile, Webster concerned himself with getting selected to the Senate from Massachusetts, a nettlesome process given the diverse interests at work in the state legislature. Clearly, he was the most qualified and articulate candidate, but in America that has never guaranteed selection. In fact, the Massachusetts legislature was deadlocked between the incumbent and the Jacksonian candidate. In April Webster spoke at Faneuil Hall in opposition to the Jacksonians. He called for support for President Adams while rationalizing the fusion of the old Federalists and Jeffersonian Republicans.[18] Their old animosities were at an end; they faced the united threat of Jacksonian populism being used by the South to advance its agenda.

The speech led to Webster being added to the list of candidates for the Senate seat. Uncharacteristically, he developed doubts: Why should he move from leadership in the House to isolation in the Senate? Would the legislature support a candidate born and raised in another state? What made up his mind was the strategic effectiveness of the Jacksonians in seizing issues that worked to their favor. For example, they had passed a bill in the Massachusetts legislature that provided for the confiscation of the Charles River Bridge from its toll-charging owners and made it a free passageway. Gov. Levi Lincoln vetoed the popular legislation, giving the Jacksonians a new issue with which to attack him. The veto also eliminated Governor Lincoln as a possible nominee for the Senate seat. Since Jacksonians had the edge in direct elections, the Whigs needed to hold the Senate seat. Webster was the only nominee with enough credibility to do it. He was selected by over two-thirds of each house on June 7, 1827. His illustrious Senate career was about to begin.

As Webster began to plan a national campaign of support for his emerging party, his wife fell gravely ill. Then his chief aide died, leaving him in a tangle

17. Remini, *Daniel Webster*, 277.
18. See Webster, *Writings and Speeches*, 13:24–30.

of bills and legal briefs. By the end of the summer, he was back on the campaign trail, had a new aide, and was encouraged by reports that Grace was recovering. In fact, she felt so well that she agreed to accompany her husband to Washington for his swearing in. By the time they reached New York, however, both were ill—Webster with rheumatism and Grace with a cancerous tumor. Grace could travel no farther. She believed that if she could just rest for a few weeks she might return to Boston, and she bade Webster go on to Washington. He arrived there on December 16, was sworn in the next day, and became one of the forty-eight senators serving in the new Capitol Building.

The Senate chamber was an impressive Greek-style amphitheater with a draped gallery surmounted by a soaring eagle. Webster believed that the concentric semicircles of small mahogany desks facing the vice president's massive seat were crowded and not made for effective speaking. More to his liking was the small room he acquired, where he took other senators for wine when business on the floor was slow or adjourned. It was here that he worked his private persuasion, bringing his dark presence or affable wit into play according to his needs.

The new Senate had formidable players such as the bullying Thomas Hart Benton of Missouri, the gentlemanly Robert Hayne of South Carolina, and the mannered John Tyler of Virginia. Webster struck up a friendship with Tyler that would prove important when Tyler acceded to the presidency in 1841. Hayne, on the other hand, was to become Webster's most important opponent.

During the holiday break in the session, Webster returned to New York to be with Grace, who had taken a turn for the worse and had not returned to Boston as planned. Her tumor had grown and she was in and out of terrible pain over the next two weeks. She finally died on January 21, 1828. Webster delivered the news to his son Fletcher, who arrived too late: "Poor Grace," Webster said, "has gone to heaven."

Chapter 5

Liberty and Union

U rged on by his children, Webster attempted to reduce his depression by returning to Washington. By mid-February he was on the floor of the Senate. A bogus judicial-reform bill caught his attention and he requested the opportunity to speak. His two-hour speech killed the bill by revealing its insidious intent: a vote for the bill would give the appearance of a vote for reform, while the actual bill did little to remedy corrupt practices.

Webster's glory was short-lived. When he toyed with the idea of accepting an appointment as ambassador to the Court of St. James, the Democrats howled that the offer was part of the "corrupt bargain" that had made Adams president. So Webster returned to Senate matters, chief of which was the tariff. The tariff proposal of 1828 was even higher than the one of 1827, and therefore more intolerable to the South. It affected the importation of flax, hemp, iron, lead, molasses, and raw wool. Webster represented Boston shipping and wool manufacturers in Senate negotiations, confident that rewards in the tariff bill would provide enough votes for passage. The bill was tied to Clay's American System of internal improvements, his hemp farm, and a set of incentives for westerners to support the tariff. Webster ensured his constituents that money was appropriated for dredging and maintaining harbors important to Boston shippers. New Englanders saw the advantages of the internal improvements supported by revenues from the tariff, and they encouraged Webster to continue cooperating in the design of the legislation. The American System, which would speed the opening of the West and help farmers move their produce to eastern markets, became a firm plank in the

National Republican platform and gave Webster a way to prevent an alliance between southern and western senators.[1]

On the other side, the Democrats were trying to construct the tariff in such a way that it would penalize New England for supporting Adams and reward the South for supporting Jackson. This was one of the largest bribery schemes in the history of American politics to that date. For example, the rate on woolens, an interest of New England, was reduced by three cents, while the rates on molasses and spirits were raised to protect southern interests.

Obviously a compromise would have to be crafted. On May 9 on the Senate floor, Webster spoke on behalf of New England interests. Why were we protecting raw goods such as hemp and wool, and not providing corresponding protection for manufacturers of rope and woolens? The next day, on Van Buren's motion, the bill was corrected to Webster's liking. The amendment passed on a very close vote, disappointing Vice President Calhoun, who had expected a tie. Webster then voted for the full Senate-House version, which passed by five votes, and President Adams signed it. Webster's manufacturing constituency, particularly the textile manufacturer Abbott Lawrence, was delighted. The South condemned the bill as the "Tariff of Abominations." Congress adjourned on May 26 to begin the campaign season.

The Campaign of 1828

Sen. Robert Y. Hayne of South Carolina argued that Webster's and Van Buren's changing of the bill was a blatant attack on the emerging alliance between the South and the West. Calhoun agreed and responded with the South Carolina Exposition. This essay claimed to advance Jefferson and Madison's famous Resolutions of 1798 by calling for the protection of a minority represented by a state government and by giving that state the power to nullify heinous federal acts. The instrument of nullification was to be a state convention, not unlike the conventions that had ratified the Constitution. Calhoun, now the preeminent philosopher of states' rights, would complete his interpretation of civic republicanism with his *Disquisition on Government*, written in the mid-1840s; it would refine his call for concurrent majorities in the Congress and reaffirm that the Constitution was a "compact" among the states, not a "contract" granted by the people. In 1828, however, Van Buren and others began

---

1. Bartlett, *Daniel Webster*, 114–16; Current, *Daniel Webster*, 52.

to wonder whether Calhoun could serve in a Jackson administration, given his states' rights position.

In the meantime, Jackson was well into his bandwagon campaign. Voters no longer needed to own land to have a vote, so the franchise was spread to many more citizens, many of them poor and uneducated. The new Democrats attacked the "corrupt bargain" of 1825, the tariff of 1828, and the person of the president. Webster was not only accused of arranging the "corrupt bargain" between Clay and Adams, but also of having supported secession in 1812. He responded with a libel suit and a letter from Adams exonerating him on all counts.[2]

This was just one of the unfortunate incidents in the dirty campaign of 1828. The Democrats spread a rumor that when Adams was ambassador to Russia he engaged in a prostitution ring. The Whigs countered with attacks on Jackson and his wife, Rachel. When Jackson met Rachel Donelson, he was a twenty-one-year-old lawyer in North Carolina and she was the wife of Lewis Robards, an army officer. Sensing that Jackson was falling for Rachel, Robards chased him off. Eventually, Rachel returned to her family in Tennessee and Robards returned to his native Virginia, where he obtained permission to file for a divorce. In 1791, mistakenly thinking the divorce was final, Jackson took Rachel as his wife. Two years later, Robards sued for divorce on grounds of adultery. Jackson and Rachel remarried in 1794, and later adopted an abandoned Native American child. Over the years, while Jackson's military career advanced, Rachel wavered between depression and deeply religious spells.

By 1828, Jackson hoped the scandal surrounding his marriage was water over the dam. However, the Whigs went on the attack, often yelling out at Jackson rallies that he had married a whore. Rachel took to a sickbed. Nonetheless, Jackson won the election with 56 percent of the vote—no candidate would surpass that percentage for the rest of the century—carrying the South and the West for 178 electoral votes. Adams garnered 83 electoral votes, all from his New England base. Webster was obliged to return to Washington for the last session of the old Congress and the impending inauguration of the general.

Tragedy struck Jackson a few weeks before the inaugural when Rachel collapsed and died. Jackson blamed her death on Whig campaign tactics. On

2. The publisher who printed the accusation, Theodore Lyman, won the libel case only because the jury was hung, voting 10 to 2 for conviction. Focusing on the stated positions of players in the War of 1812 was common. Calhoun had been a Unionist at that time and questioned the patriotism of those who opposed the war.

March 4, wealthy friends of the widowed president threw an inauguration like nothing the capital had ever seen. The city was overwhelmed by frontiersmen and common folk, who, it was claimed in the Whig press, made the presidential mansion's floors slippery with wine and cheese. Webster was disgusted by the mobocracy.

The selection of the cabinet presented no surprises; Van Buren would be its senior member as secretary of state. Calhoun had been reelected vice president, the only man to serve in that position under two presidents of different parties. It was an alliance that would not last.

In April 1829 Webster suffered the loss of his brother, Zeke. It brought back his melancholy, and his friends became concerned about his drinking. His friend Sarah Goodridge, a noted painter, cheered him and brought out his emotional side. She had painted his portrait just a few years before, and they exchanged letters regularly, even before the death of his wife.[3] The most unusual moment between the two occurred after Grace's death when Goodridge sent Webster a self-portrait of her breasts. Like most of her paintings, it was a miniature, but quite racy for the time.

Webster began to court other women, casting an eye on the lovely Catherine Van Rensselaer, for example. In New York City, he met Caroline LeRoy, the daughter of a rich businessman. She was fifteen years younger than Webster and had a fiery temperament. Though she was plain of feature, Webster found her attractive. He was not averse to another marriage; remarrying after the death of a spouse was common at the time, and Webster himself was the child of such a marriage. In December 1829 he and Caroline were wed. Webster's sons, Fletcher and Edward, chose not to attend the service, but his daughter, Julia, was there to tend to her father and to be sure the first $10,000 of the promised $25,000 dowry was properly deposited. Eventually the boys warmed to their stepmother, and Caroline developed a particularly close relationship with Fletcher.

Back to the Senate

In the same month, President Jackson sent his first message to Congress urging some changes, the most important of which was that presidential appointees be permitted to serve only four years. Jackson believed that new

---

3. Remini, *Daniel Webster,* 306.

presidents should have the right to make new appointments; he wanted to strengthen the patronage system for his second term. He also called for a single six-year term for the president and for the abolition of the electoral college, having suffered at its hands in 1825. He urged Congress to cover the national debt, reform the "Tariff of Abominations," curtail the national bank, and move Native Americans west of the Mississippi River. It was a bold agenda that smacked of populism. It came on top of Jackson's festering relationship with Calhoun, which was strained because of the latter's call for nullification of the tariff. While Jackson wanted the tariff trimmed, he would not brook the states rebelling against legitimate federal functions. His relationship with Calhoun deteriorated further when Mrs. Calhoun led the other cabinet wives in snubbing the wife of Secretary of War John Eaton because of questions about her past. Remembering how the rumormongers had "killed" his beloved Rachel, Jackson defended Mrs. Eaton against the snobby cabinet wives. Van Buren seized this moment to become even closer to the new president; he would be rewarded with the vice presidency in Jackson's second term, when candidates finally ran on tickets. For now, however, the split in the Democrats gave the National Republicans hope.

The possibility of another split was emerging, and it was Webster who would drive in the decisive wedge. In late 1829, Senator Hayne encouraged the West-South axis by attacking the North as a conspirator against the South. Webster, because he had supported internal improvements, could join the fray as a friend of the West and give the lie to Hayne's charges. Furthermore, the call for Union above separatism, reinforced by the American System and the tariff, was irresistible to the patriotic frontiersmen and farmers of the West, most of whom considered slavery a necessary evil at best.[4] Jackson's civil religion could compete with Webster's; Calhoun's version could not. In fact, the attack on Webster by Hayne, the acolyte of Calhoun, would give Webster the moment he needed to press his catechism over Jackson's.

What began in December as a debate over one senator's resolution on the disposition of public lands in the West spilled over in January 1830 into questions about the tariff, states' rights, and slavery. Sen. Samuel Foot of Connecticut had proposed legislation to halt surveys and sales of western lands at cheap rates. Senator Benton took this move as an assault on the growth of the West. He referred to Foot and his compatriots as "yankees" who were trying to maintain control of Congress by preventing population expansion in the

4. Current, *Daniel Webster*, 59–60.

West. Those on the Senate floor were astonished. Was this the same Benton who had supported Clay for president in 1824? Was this the same Benton who started a fistfight with Andrew Jackson and then had to move to Missouri to avoid reprisals? Was he now supporting the president and courting the South? Calhoun saw that the feisty Benton was agitated, so agitated that he yelled loudly during his speech—even rattling the windows, by some accounts.[5]

Calhoun advised Hayne to use this moment to attempt to create a West-South alliance. As Hayne reached the middle of his speech on January 19, 1830, Webster arrived on the floor of the Senate from the Supreme Court downstairs.[6] Taking his lead from Benton and his thoughts from Calhoun, Hayne alleged that there was a conspiracy among manufacturing states to retain poor laborers in the North by discouraging their emigration to the West. In this way, the North was continuing its efforts to "consolidate" the Union, which Hayne condemned: "The very life of our system is independence of the States." Hayne believed that the government should use western land to attract farmers, not to produce revenue for federal projects. The fact is that the cheaper the land was, the easier it would be for poor southern farmers who did not own slaves to move west to homestead it. In other words, contrary to Hayne's claim, the current policy actually allowed slaveholders to consolidate their hold on the southern states. Ignoring this fact, Hayne launched an attack on the taxing and tariff policies of the government. Via the tariff and improvement systems, he complained, wealth from his section of the country was being redistributed to other areas, and that was unfair to the South.

Webster was appalled and asked to reply formally the next day, since by the time Hayne finished it was time to adjourn. Webster woke up early the next morning, as was his custom, and jotted three pages of notes. In his short reply, Webster carefully avoided antagonizing the West while drawing Hayne out on the issue of states' rights. He also alluded to Calhoun's role as Hayne's mentor. Calhoun glowered from the presiding officer's chair throughout Webster's remarks.

In his speech, Webster claimed that New England had always supported western development. Nathan Dane of Massachusetts, a delegate to the Continental Congress, had composed the Northwest Ordinance of 1787, which not only allowed development of the West, but also precluded slavery in the new territory.

5. Remini, *Daniel Webster,* 317.
6. The case was *Carver v. Jackson,* involving a dispute between John Jacob Astor, who had retained Webster, and the state of New York.

This passage was clever because it brought the slavery issue to the fore; Webster knew it was the Achilles' heel of Hayne's position.

Webster demonstrated the unity between the North and the West with a discussion of the tariff of 1816. He justified his support of the tariff of 1828 by arguing that tariffs had become established national policy thanks to support by the South in general and Calhoun in particular. The question was not whether or not there would be a tariff, but rather on what goods and at what level. Furthermore, the tariff provided funds for internal improvements, which were important to the nation as a whole but particularly to development of the West, and for enhanced manufacturing capacity, which, while important to the North, also benefited the national treasury and American commerce in general.[7]

Webster then proceeded to attack disunionists in South Carolina. He moved his rhetorical guns away from Benton and Hayne's concern for land in the West and toward Calhoun's Exposition, which attempted to justify nullification. Hayne's talk of a conspiracy provided the rationale for this shift in tone. Webster claimed that this so-called conspiracy was nothing more than a national—and natural—tendency toward consolidation. "Consolidation!" he yelled in stentorian tones that jolted the galleries. "That perpetual cry both of terror and delusion,—Consolidation!" Since George Washington, America had consistently moved toward "true, constitutional consolidation," by which Webster meant "whatever tends to strengthen the bond that unites us and encourages the hope that our Union may be perpetual." With that sentence, Webster made it clear that his notion of Union had evolved into a permanent fixture that was the *telos* of the government. Ironically, this was a position that would be embraced by President Jackson, as we shall see. Its later impact on Abraham Lincoln is hard to underestimate. They, like Webster, would argue that the Constitution made the Union permanent; a retreat back toward the Articles of Confederation or Calhoun's government by concurrence was not an option. Webster concluded, "I am a unionist, and in this sense, a national republican."[8] Again, Webster defined the Whig *ethos*, one that would serve the

7. Quotations from the First and Second Replies to Hayne are from Webster, *Writings and Speeches*, 5:248–69 and 6:3–75, respectively. Wiltse's edition of the *Speeches and Formal Writings* contains two versions of the Second Reply to Hayne (285–394), but omits the First Reply.

8. Calhoun regularly claimed to be a Republican in the Roman sense. He praised the Roman tribunate in his *Disquisition* as a forerunner to his theory of concurrent majority; however, the tribunate of Rome was much more like the House of Representatives than an assembly of singular states.

conscience of National Republicans well, especially those that became just plain Republicans in 1854.

In his most provocative argument, Webster asserted that slavery and nullification did not support America's dream of unity and nationhood, a dream he traced back to the founders. He also burdened Hayne with the attack on the East that had initially come from Benton. Needling Hayne, he pointed out that the tariff of 1816 had been a southern tax, not an eastern one. In 1825 it was South Carolina's representative who had argued for a tariff higher than the one Webster proposed. Webster then moved back to the issue of slavery to ensure that westerners would not ally themselves with Hayne. Thus, in his first reply to Hayne, he managed to shift the debate from land policy to how the Constitution was to be interpreted and to taint the South with the suggestion that it desired to spread slavery into the West.

In replying to Webster, Hayne attempted to burnish his reputation as a polished and literate orator. In his opening paragraph, he asked: "Has the gentleman's distempered fancy been disturbed by gloomy forebodings of 'new alliances to be formed,' at which he hinted? Has the ghost of the murdered coalition come back, like the ghost of Banquo, to 'sear the eye-balls' of the gentleman, and will it not 'down at his bidding'? Are dark visions of broken hopes, and honors lost forever, still floating before his heated imagination?"[9] This sarcastic challenge to Webster would not go unrefuted. Worse yet, Hayne made the mistake of dwelling on the issue of slavery. While his speech brought nods of approval from Calhoun, it helped Webster frame the debate around issues that were splitting the West from the South, mainly states' rights, nullification, and slavery. Hayne was a small man who could become shrill on occasion. At one point he grabbed his heart and said that Webster's speech "rankled" in his bosom. He proclaimed that Webster "had discharged his fire in the face of the Senate," and that he now sought "the opportunity to return the shot." From his desk, Webster shouted out, "I am ready to receive it. Let the discussion proceed." Benton interceded, however, insisting on giving his own speech, which allowed Webster to run down to the Supreme Court to finish his business there.

When Hayne finally won the floor back on January 25, he declared he would reveal Webster's true motives. He rightly pointed out that he had not attacked the East or Massachusetts. He complained that Webster had "pour[ed] out all the vials of his mighty wrath upon my devoted head" instead of on Benton,

9. *Register of Debates*, 21st Cong., 1st sess., 43.

who *had* attacked the East. He continued, "When I find a gentleman of mature age and experience,[10] of acknowledged talents and profound sagacity, pursuing a course like this . . . and making war upon the unoffending South, I must believe . . . he has some object in view that he has not ventured to disclose." That object, Hayne asserted, was to use slavery to incite prejudice against the South. Hayne argued that the South made less profit from slave labor than northern manufacturers made from their workers. Unable to resist, he then claimed that slavery benefited the nation as a whole. Webster looked up and then jotted a note. In his zeal to defend the South, Hayne had overshot his mark.

Hayne next went after Webster on the tariff question, arguing that Webster's activities since 1828 put him squarely behind those trying to penalize the South. He clinched the argument by tying Webster to the Hartford Convention, which had considered secession. Hayne was painting Webster as a hypocrite of the first order. Why, he asked, had Webster's love of the Union not been present in Hartford?

Hayne was calmer when he defended Calhoun's Carolina doctrine. He repeated Calhoun's arguments about the Tenth Amendment and what Madison and Jefferson had meant in the Kentucky and Virginia Resolutions of 1798. Webster sat at his desk taking copious notes, for he knew that this was the weakest plank of Hayne's platform. Hayne's defense of interposition undermined all he had worked for because the majority in the Senate, in the House, and in the nation would not give a single state the ability to unhinge the Union. While Hayne believed that nullification could keep the government honest and prevent the usurpation of powers, most in the room saw nullification as the road to anarchy. Hayne was clearly wrong to assert that the states and the federal government were on a par and that the Union was a creation of the states. That possibility was removed when the Constitution was written to begin, "We the people."

While Hayne spoke, said some who were present, Calhoun was not above passing notes to him to help him defend slavery.[11] When Hayne extended his accusations of conspiracy to all who opposed slavery, Webster knew he could force the West to choose between embracing a slaveholding ally or one who supported Union and the American System. After Hayne finished, Webster told associates that he would "grind" him into a "pinch of snuff."[12]

---

10. At forty-seven, Webster was ten years older than Hayne.
11. Nathan Sargent, *Public Men and Events*, 1:175.
12. Bartlett, *Daniel Webster*, 117; Fuess, *Daniel Webster*, 1:372.

The Second Reply to Hayne

Webster's Second Reply to Hayne was the most memorable speech delivered on the floor of the Senate to that time, and perhaps of all time. Anybody who was somebody in Washington attended the speech on the afternoons of January 26 and 27. Webster dressed immaculately in his dark blue coat with brass buttons, buff-colored vest, and white cravat. His highly stylized oratory pleased the bonneted ladies in the gallery. His lines of argument impressed his colleagues on the floor. His strong voice filled the room. Webster was animated and confident as he strode around the floor, not infrequently shaking a finger at Calhoun to punctuate his case.

One of the most remarkable features of the Second Reply to Hayne is its structure. On the surface, it appears to contain the usual elements recommended by Hugh Blair, Richard Whately, and the Roman rhetorical theorists: exordium, statement of case, explication, argument, and peroration. This apparent structure was appropriate to the decorum of the occasion.[13] However, the actual structure of the speech is highly refutative in nature. Webster, like most good parliamentary debaters, knew that it is more effective to argue on your own ground than on your opponent's. There are, in fact, several allusions to this strategy in the speeches of both Hayne and Webster. Why, then, did Webster rely so heavily on Hayne's organization of his argument in this second reply?

First, Hayne's second speech was a response to Webster's first, and, as such, refuted Webster's arguments. Thus, Hayne was already on Webster's ground. Webster followed Hayne's outline in his Second Reply not only because it gave the appearance of fairness, but also because Hayne's points were the very ones Webster wanted to raise. Second, the element of bravado increased Webster's credibility with the audience. He as much as said, "I will not only win this debate, but I will win on my opponent's terms." Third, and most obvious, Hayne's speech was still clear in the minds of those present. Webster might have risked confusing them if he reorganized the sum and substance of the arguments at issue.

Webster therefore accepted the organization of Hayne, refuting him point by point, but all the time also advancing lines of argument useful to his persuasive strategy. This structure forced Webster to use his patented fugal form of argumentation. When he introduced an argument, he did not develop it

---

13. See Ferguson, *Law and Letters*, 224. Webster was enamored of Bishop Richard Whately's *Elements of Rhetoric*. Webster, *Writings and Speeches*, 17:463-65.

fully; when he reintroduced it later, he extended it a little further; later still, he extended it even further. This method gave the speech a feeling of progress based on persuasion by repetition and extension. Webster's best arguments built to a crescendo at the conclusion.

Using one of his favorite metaphors, Webster began by comparing the legislative debacle to a storm-tossed sea. He sought to bring calm to the situation, he announced. No sooner had he said this, however, than he began to ridicule Hayne, a tactic that is evident throughout two-thirds of the speech. In the best parliamentary tradition, Webster's first complaint was ironic. He said that Hayne had talked about "everything but public lands," which was the ostensible topic of the debate. Of course, to achieve his persuasive purpose, Webster had to wrench the debate from the issue of public lands to the questions of slavery and states' rights. This bit of subterfuge served Webster well.

Webster pointed out that though Hayne claimed he "had a shot" to discharge, Webster was still standing. Hayne interrupted to clarify his remark, but Webster waved him off, arguing that it was not what he said but what he intended that was important:

> I will not accuse the honorable member of violating the rules of civilized war—I will not say that he poisoned his arrows. But whether his shafts were, or were not, dipped in that which would have caused rankling, if they had reached [their target], there was not, as it happened, quite strength enough in the bow to bring them to their mark. If he wishes now to gather up those shafts, he must look for them elsewhere; they will not be found fixed and quivering in the object at which they were aimed.

This passage set the tone for a running personal attack on Hayne. Webster opened with one of his favorite devices, an apophasis, or denial of what he was actually doing; then he developed an extended metaphor, dripping with sarcasm, that painted a picture of a weakly armed opponent using unethical tactics. The picture fit the diminutive Hayne and brought peals of laughter from the galleries.

From this moment on, the speech contained a vast array of stylistic devices and persuasive strategies; those seeking entertainment were not disappointed. Webster was intent on refuting every point Hayne had made. He even disputed Hayne's charge that Webster needed "to sleep" on Hayne's speech before replying. Webster said that he had been ready to reply but that Benton adjourned the Senate before a response could be made. He then answered Hayne's "taunt" about his seeking to debate Hayne instead of Benton: "Sir, the gentleman seems to forget where and what we are. This is a Senate; a Senate of equals."

With his opponent's reputation in tatters, Webster turned to Hayne's more serious charge that there was a conspiracy afoot. He ridiculed the charge by pointing out that Hayne's use of Banquo's ghost was misleading: "It was not, I think, the friends, but the *enemies* of the murdered Banquo, at whose bidding his spirit would not down." Webster carried on in this vein for several paragraphs, using Hayne's erroneous reading of "the classics" to reduce his credibility to pulp. The argument about a conspiracy would be introduced again and extended, but at this juncture the purpose of Webster's remarks was to damage Hayne's credibility as much as possible. By the end of this onslaught, the audience was left with the impression that Hayne was ill-mannered, weak, poorly educated, and unable to keep his mind on the legislation before the Senate.

Having demolished Hayne, Webster began to examine more substantive matters, still retaining the refutative organizational pattern for his remarks. Hayne had belittled Nathan Dane after Webster cited the New Englander in his first reply. Webster seized the opportunity to reinforce the ties between the West and New England while further ridiculing Hayne, who had claimed that Dane was not the author the Northwest Ordinance; Dane, said Webster, "is of Massachusetts, and too near the north star to be reached by the honorable gentleman's telescope." After citing the provisions of the ordinance, Webster claimed he had not said "a single word which any ingenuity could torture into an attack on the slavery of the South." While the federal government could not interfere with slavery in the South, Webster nonetheless regarded it as "one of the greatest evils." Webster turned Hayne's attack on the American System back on him and used it to isolate South Carolina: "'What interests,' asks he, 'has South Carolina in a canal in Ohio?' . . . On his system, it is true, she has no interest. On that system, Ohio and Carolina are different governments and different countries. . . . On that system, Carolina has no more interest in a canal in Ohio than in Mexico." Webster then defended New England's national approach; adding credibility to his cause was the fact that a few days earlier he had supported federal underwriting of the stock of the South Carolina Canal and Railroad Company. While South Carolina might not support improvement projects in the West, Webster, as the embodiment of New England, certainly did, and he supported them in South Carolina too.

As we shall see in his 1850 Compromise speeches, Webster liked to use the states as microcosms of geographic sections and build his arguments from that inductive position. In a way, the battle between Hayne and Webster was a synecdoche for the battle over how South Carolina and Massachusetts would be perceived, and hence how the South and North would be perceived. Webster claimed that South Carolina was taking advantage of the provisions of the Constitution on slavery: "[L]et it stand; let the advantage of it be fully enjoyed," he growled. He painted quite a different picture of Massachusetts, again denying exactly what he was about to do:

> Mr. President, I shall enter no encomium upon Massachusetts: she needs none. There she is. Behold her, and judge for yourselves. There is her history; the world knows it by heart. The past, at least, is secure. There is Boston, and Concord, and Lexington, and Bunker Hill; and there they will remain for ever. The bones of her sons, falling in the great struggle for Independence, now lie mingled with the soil of every State from New England to Georgia; and there they will lie forever.

South Carolina could not compete with that kind of valor in the Revolution.

Webster next explained the alleged inconsistency in his record on the tariff. Once the tariff became national policy, he worked to support his constituents' interests, but never, even when opposed to the tariff, did he threaten nullification. Hayne, claimed Webster, used "metaphysical scissors" to patch together a misleading version of his position. This argument was eventually extended into an elevated theme that pervades the speech. By the conclusion, New England's willingness to play by the rules was sharply contrasted with South Carolina's unsportsmanlike conduct.

Webster then undercut Hayne by quoting Calhoun's nationalistic sentiments of 1816 and later. This part of the speech is undoubtedly the weakest. Everyone knew that senators changed their minds, and the argument over the past positions of Webster and Calhoun was old territory. This passage seemed perfunctory to the senators, but probably had some appeal to the wider audience in the North.

Calhoun, sitting as the president of the Senate, interrupted to ask: "Does the chair understand the gentleman from Massachusetts to say that the person now occupying the chair of the Senate has changed his opinions on the subject of internal improvements?" Webster disingenuously responded that Calhoun had not changed but that South Carolina had, unless Hayne had "misled" him. In fact, claimed Webster, Hayne had misled people about Webster's position on the national debt and his reference to national consolidation. Webster explained that he meant consolidation of the Union, not of the North, as Hayne had alleged. A close reading of the First Reply bears out this interpretation of his earlier remarks.

Webster returned to his goal: to tie New England and the West to the cause of Union and to tie Hayne to Calhoun, South Carolina, and the cause of disunion. An internal summary brought things into focus: "The real question between me and him is: Has the doctrine been advanced at the South or the East, that the population of the West should be retarded. . . . Is this doctrine, as has been alleged, of Eastern origin?" Webster then explained his basic position on western lands: Lands should not be given away but used to help finance and promote internal improvements and education in all of the states. He contended that lands have historically been distributed to serve the common good. This question aside, Webster demonstrated that New England had "supported measures favorable to the West." In 1820, for example, New England favored reduction in the cost of public lands by a vote of 33 to 1 among its House delegation.

Webster then returned to the issue of the tariff and states' rights. He was sure that if he could make the issue one of patriotic loyalty to the Republic, he could carry the votes of western senators, who were highly dependent on a national system of roads, canals, harbors, and other internal improvements. They were frontiersmen and farmers who hailed mainly from the North; they knew that the federal government had protected and promoted their interests and that the individual states had not.

Webster defended New England against Hayne's conspiracy charges by extending the argument a little more. In this case, the extension constituted an attack on Hayne's evidence. Hayne had quoted from pamphlets, sermons, and speeches which he claimed proved that the North was out to diminish the influence of the South. Webster was disgusted with Hayne's selective use of evidence. He said he would not answer point by point nor would he stoop to using similar evidence from the South, of which he asserted there was an abundance: "I employ no scavengers; no one is in attendance on me, tendering such means of retaliation; and, if there were, with an ass's load of them with a bulk as huge as that which the gentleman himself has produced, I would not touch one of them."

Thus, Webster avoided Hayne's trap. It would not be consistent with the tone of his speech to insult the South and annoy the North by reading from inflammatory southern tracts. Instead he defended New England's loyalty to General Washington, to the Constitution, and to the Union, foreshadowing his stirring peroration. He then praised South Carolina for her past patriotism, introducing a strategy he would visit again before the end of the speech. He would seek an accord with southerners and westerners who supported Union and all the benefits it could bring. He would not be lured into partisan or sectional strife.

This was the appropriate moment, Webster said, "to state and to defend what I conceive to be the true principles of the Constitution." The question to be resolved was when and under what circumstances a state legislature could interfere with the authority of the federal government. Webster answered that it could do so only when "this government transcends its constitutional limits."

Did Hayne's case fit the criteria? To answer this question, Webster restated Hayne's position in four paragraphs, each beginning with the phrase, "I understand him to . . ." Hayne interrupted to point out that he had used the Virginia Resolution of 1798 as his authority. Webster explained that there was a crucial difference between the laws the Virginia Resolution was trying to resist, the Alien and Sedition Acts, and the current problem, a tariff. In the former case, the government had become too oppressive and the public had a right to resist; the latter case, however, was part of established government policy. Hayne interrupted again to say that "the right of constitutional resistance" is more important than "the mere right of revolution." He went on to say that "plain, palpable violation of the Constitution by the general government" justified interposition. Hayne attempted to place the right of the states to interpose above the right of citizens to revolt. Webster, whose whole argument was that the Constitution is for the people, not the states, would not allow Hayne to succeed with this ploy: "I say the right of a state to annul a law of Congress cannot be maintained but on the ground of the inalienable right of man to resist oppression. . . . But I do not admit that under the Constitution . . . there is any mode in which a State government, as a member of the Union, can interfere and stop the progress of the general government, by force of her own laws, under any circumstances whatever." In other words, states do not have the same rights as common citizens. Webster ridiculed Hayne's system, in which there would be "four and twenty masters, of different wills and different purposes." The decision as to whether the twenty-four states or the federal courts were dominant had been made when the Constitution was ratified as "the supreme law of the land." Furthermore, the federal government had been given judicial power over "all cases arising under the Constitution." Webster in case after case before the Supreme Court had helped to solidify this power, at the expense of the states. This power was the "keystone of the arch" for Webster. In a slashing attack on states' rights, he got to the nub of the issue: "It is, Sir, the people's Constitution, the people's government, made for the people, made by the people, and answerable to the people."[14] This remarkable sentence crystallized Webster's vision that "the people" had created the Constitution to support an eternal Union.

Hayne's plan for the Union was unworkable because the Constitution confined certain activities—such as making war, coining money, and agreeing to treaties—to the federal government exclusively. Webster scoffed at Hayne's selective notion of nullification. South Carolina would nullify the tariff of 1828 because she did not like it, but not the tariff of 1816 because it protected her cotton from imports from Calcutta. With a flurry of rhetorical questions, Webster reduced Hayne's doctrine to anarchy: "If there be no power to settle [questions between the states], independent of the States, is not the whole Union a rope of sand? Are we not thrown back again, precisely, upon the old Confederacy?"

He then compared the "New England school" of protest to the South Carolina school. Massachusetts responded to the Virginia Resolution of 1798 by defending the Union, and had not wavered from that course: "Misgoverned, wronged, oppressed as she felt herself to be, she still held fast her integrity to the Union." Massachusetts protested vehemently, then submitted to the will of Congress. That is the way it should be, Webster said. Such reasoned submission makes the Union work. He concluded the argument by pointing out that Madison did not believe the tariff to be an excessive exercise of federal power. Once again Webster turned Hayne's own authority against him. (After the debate, Webster and Hayne submitted their speeches to Madison. The former president sent a 4,000-word rebuttal to Hayne. He sent Webster a cautious letter that discussed the need for checks and balances. While he opposed secession, Madison thought Webster assumed too much power for the federal government.)[15]

As Webster moved toward his conclusion, he marshaled his various arguments into a major summary and extended the most important ones. If the South

14. The published version of the speech influenced the young Abraham Lincoln, who later paraphrased this line at Gettysburg.
15. Bartlett, *Daniel Webster*, 120.

Carolina doctrine had been exercised in the past, "The government would very likely have gone to pieces, and crumbled into dust." The Constitution formalized the Union, and the Union had its roots in the Revolution. The states ceded their sovereignty to the Union and to its people when they ratified the Constitution. Said Webster: "For myself, sir, I do not admit the jurisdiction of South Carolina, or any other state, to prescribe my constitutional duty; or to settle, between me and the people, the validity of laws of Congress for which I have voted. I decline her umpirage." He admitted that the federal government was limited, but insisted that it was supreme when operating within the limits imposed by the Constitution and that establishing a tariff was clearly within those limits.

At this point, Webster revisited the question of workability and reduced Hayne's position to absurdity by asking what the customs collector was to do when torn between federal and state authority. He compared nullification of congressional law to Fries's Rebellion and implied it was nothing short of treason: "If John Fries had produced an act of Pennsylvania annulling the law of Congress, would it have helped his case!" Realizing he had scored a point, Webster extended it with gallows humor, speculating on what might happen if the Senate refused to go along with Hayne: "[S]hall we swing for it? We are ready to die for our country, but it is rather an awkward business, this dying without touching the ground! After all, that is a sort of hemp tax worse than any part of the tariff." The remedy to any serious problem, said Webster, is not nullification, but rather amending the Constitution.

As a transition to his peroration, Webster sought unity by reminding the states that they had fought together in the Revolution and that if they had not, the enterprise would have surely been lost. Had not South Carolina and Massachusetts together defeated the tyrant George III? Webster dramatically underscored this historic loyalty to Union in his memorable peroration:

> Would to God that harmony might return! Shoulder to shoulder they went through the Revolution, hand in hand they stood round the administration of Washington, and felt his own great arm lean on them for support. . . . When my eyes shall be turned to behold for the last time the sun in heaven, may I not see him shining on the broken and dishonored fragments of a once glorious Union; on States dissevered, discordant, belligerent; on a land rent with civil feuds, or drenched . . . in fraternal blood! Let their last feeble and lingering glance rather behold the gorgeous ensign of the

Republic, now known and honored throughout the earth, still full high advanced, its arms and trophies streaming in their original luster, not a stripe erased or polluted, not a single star obscured, bearing for its motto no such miserable interrogatory as "What is all this worth?" nor those other words of delusion and folly, "Liberty first and union afterward"; but everywhere, spread all over in characters of living light, blazing on all its ample folds, as they float over the sea and over the land, and in every wind under the whole heavens, that other sentiment, dear to every true American heart—Liberty *and* Union, now and forever, one and inseparable!

And there it was for all to see, Webster's vision of hell and heaven, disunion and Union. He had come a long way from his position in the *Dartmouth College* case, in which he argued that the law of the land was supreme. Now he asserted that the Constitution had created the Union, and that to form a more perfect Union is the American *telos*. When he concluded, all present knew that he had elevated a legislative quarrel from the slag heap of regional advantage to a transcendent question of national spirit. He had done it in the past and he would do it again, particularly in 1850, but never as forcefully or as effectively as he did on that afternoon in January 1830.

Webster had spoken extemporaneously from twelve pages of notes that were the culmination of his thoughts on the subject of Union.[16] His arguments had been rehearsed in ceremonial speeches and in many cases before the Supreme Court. In 1830, however, they came together in one triumphant rhetorical moment. The speech thrilled those in the audience who longed for a defense of the Union. It established Webster as the chief advocate of Union and, once again, defender of the Constitution. He defeated the forces of states' rights by frustrating their attempt to link arms with the representatives of the West. Calhoun's doctrine of nullification was dead; he would soon resign the vice presidency to return to the Senate as the chief defender of nullification, forcing Hayne into the governorship of his state. Until his death in March 1850 Calhoun would battle against Webster.

Luckily for Webster, Joseph Gales, sometime editor and part owner of the *National Intelligencer*, took down the speech in shorthand and had his wife transcribe it.[17] Webster polished the text before having it published in three parts in the *Intelligencer* in late February. Edward Everett then reviewed the text

16. Ibid., 117.
17. Joseph Gales described this process in the *National Intelligencer*, March 20, 1841.

before it was published as a pamphlet. Demand was overwhelming; 60,000 copies were distributed by the spring. Unauthorized versions reached well beyond 100,000. It was undoubtedly the most widely distributed speech to that time. Webster was flooded with honors, requests to speak, and praise from established patriots. Madison said this "very powerful" speech had crushed secessionist sentiment. Even Hayne, in later years, said Webster had proven himself the greatest orator of all time with his pair of replies.

Most important in any assessment of the effectiveness of this speech is that it helped lead the American public toward freedom and Union, two pillars of Webster's civil religion. It helped reify public respect for constitutional order. It elevated the people above the states in phrases that Abraham Lincoln would echo at Gettysburg, just as the men who had fought there heard them in their hearts. This speech achieved the highest goal of rhetorical literature: it touched the actual consciousness of the immediate audience on a specific topic, and it moved the potential consciousness of a wider audience toward lasting, transcendent values.

Fighting for the American System

Webster's orations had revealed a philosophical cleavage among the Democrats. On April 13, Jefferson's birthday, they tried to make a show of unity by throwing a huge banquet. The effort came a cropper when President Jackson rose to make a toast: "Our Union. It must be preserved." Vice President Calhoun responded: "The Union: Next to our liberty, the most dear." The breach between Calhoun and Jackson was complete. Calhoun must have had resignation in mind so that he could become a more effective voice in the Senate for South Carolina and so that he could position himself to succeed Jackson.

The National Republicans watched, waited, and hoped for further division among the new Democrats. But it was not to come. Jackson had a working coalition in the Congress that threatened important National Republican initiatives. The coalition blocked any progress toward resolution of the western lands policy. The president asked that his Indian Removal Bill be acted upon. Despite Webster's objections, the cruel bill was passed and signed into law in May 1830. Only Chief Justice Marshall stood between the Cherokees and their march on the Trail of Tears. However, Marshall would prove to be only a momentary obstacle to the president's plan for Native Americans. By the end of his presidency, Jackson would launch a second Seminole war, one more devastating than the one he had personally conducted during his military career.

Emboldened by his success, Jackson decided to punish Clay and the National Republicans on May 27 by vetoing a bill to improve the Maysville Road with federal money. Van Buren wrote the veto message as a way to become even closer to his president. The message attacked the National Republican attempt to unify the country with transportation projects. Jackson's veto revived speculation that he was for states' rights after all.

On August 3, Clay responded by calling on Congress to override the veto. It was clear to many that the road, running from Kentucky to Ohio, would benefit Clay's state more than any other. Clay went to the "West" to defend his American System. In Cincinnati and several other cities, he tried to prove that Jackson had been inconsistent: "The veto message is perfectly irreconcilable with the previous acts, votes, and opinions of General Jackson."[18]

As we shall see, the Knapp-White murder case kept Webster away from this dispute. Like many in Congress, he was aware that this was a pet project of Clay's and that the president had, in fact, been fairly generous in his support of other projects. So he concentrated on preparing for a criminal case that would enhance his reputation as one of the most versatile and talented lawyers in America.

18. Henry Clay, "Speech on the Maysville Road Veto," 268.

Chapter 6

Legal and Partisan Wrangling

W ebster, the master of argumentation before the Supreme Court, was also persuasive in criminal and civil cases. In 1830, his summer vacation with his family was interrupted when he was called in to one of the most famous criminal cases in Massachusetts history. It would be the only time that he served as a prosecutor.

Capt. Joseph White, a well-to-do entrepreneur, was found murdered in his bed on April 7, 1830, in Salem, Massachusetts. White's housekeeper, Mrs. Beckford, was also his niece. Her daughter, Mary, had recently married Joseph Knapp, Jr., who was the captain of one of White's ships. The old man objected to the marriage, fired Knapp, and told Mary to leave his house, where she was living while her husband was at sea. On the night of the murder, Knapp claimed that he and his new bride were on her mother's farm in Wenham. Thus, while Knapp had a motive for murder, he also had the perfect alibi if his wife and mother-in-law were to be believed. Knapp's father was a well-respected shopkeeper in Salem and one of Knapp's brothers, Phippen, was a trusted lawyer, but his other brother, Frank, had had run-ins with the law. Frank became the crucial link in the conspiracy. He had shared a jail cell in Charleston with Richard Crowninshield, the son of upper-class parents and the nephew of Benjamin Crowninshield, secretary of the navy in the Madison and Monroe administrations. Richard and his brother, George, were often in trouble with the law.

The town of Salem formed a vigilante committee to aid in the investigation. When committee members interviewed inmates at the Charleston jail, they found some willing to testify that they had overheard the Crowninshield brothers plotting to kill Captain White and steal his "chest." The brothers were arrested based on this hearsay evidence and indicted by a grand jury.

On May 14 the committee discovered a blackmail letter addressed to the senior Knapp and threatening his son. The author was apprehended when he went to claim the response at a post office in Maine. He turned out to be John Palmer, who had also served time with Richard Crowninshield. This disclosure led to the arrest of Joseph Knapp, Jr., and his brother Frank since it connected them to Crowninshield. Furthermore, Palmer had mailed two more letters before his arrest claiming that Stephen White, Captain White's nephew, had killed the old man.

The worst panic since the infamous witch hunts swept Salem. The Reverend Henry Colman, who had married Joseph Knapp and Mary Beckford, was also Captain White's minister, and he urged Knapp to confess to a conspiracy. Under questioning, Knapp admitted to hiring Richard Crowninshield to destroy White's will, so that his fortune would be divided more evenly. Knapp mistakenly believed that White was leaving all his money to his nephew. The plot quickly spun out of control after the impatient Knapp destroyed the will and urged his brother Frank and Crowninshield to kill Captain White. He told the reverend that on the night of the murder he left a window of Captain White's house open before he returned to Wenham. Richard Crowninshield decided to act alone, sending Frank home. Unfortunately for Crowninshield, he was seen on the streets of the neighborhood on the night of the murder. (George Crowninshield was in a bar with two women who later testified on his behalf.)

Hearing about his brother's confession, Frank agreed to make a partial confession in exchange for immunity. Reverend Colman, who was a member of the vigilante committee, signed as a witness to the confession, which Joseph Knapp then signed. Colman took the document to the attorney general on May 29, 1830. The Knapp brothers retained Franklin Dexter and William Gardiner to represent them at the trial. Two weeks later Dexter visited Richard Crowninshield in the Salem jail. Crowninshield believed that his brother and the Knapp brothers could not be tried as accessories until he was convicted as the murderer. Dexter told him that his interpretation of the law was correct. That night Richard Crowninshield committed suicide, apparently to protect his fellow conspirators. Joseph Knapp retracted his confession and refused to testify when the grand jury met on July 20 in Salem. Thus, while severely weakening the case against him, Knapp also forfeited his immunity and would stand trial with the others. Separate trials were ordered because of the complexity of the indictments.

Because of the fervor in the community and at the request of Stephen White, the nephew of the deceased, the prosecution invited Webster to represent their interests in the trials. As special prosecutor, he would be paid one thousand dollars. Since this was lower than his usual fee, it is probable that he took the job as a favor to his friend and Supreme Court Justice Joseph Story, who was Stephen White's brother-in-law.

Frank Knapp was tried first and his trial began on August 3, which gave Webster a very short time to study the case. Wisely, Webster let others take the lead. With only Reverend Colman's memory and the less than certain testimony of witnesses to go on, the jury could not reach a verdict. Tension increased substantially in Salem and spread to nearby communities. At that point Webster took over the prosecution of a second trial for Frank Knapp, which was ordered one day after the close of the first.

The jury was drawn from the town's 14,000 inhabitants, twenty-seven of whom had formed the vigilante committee intent on capturing the murderer and finding evidence for the court. Most observers believed that Webster's summation to the jury turned a circumstantial case supported by unreliable witnesses into a narrative that produced a unanimous verdict. He built a coherent scenario of the crime. This stratagem was essential because one of the problems in the case was proving that both Knapp brothers were involved in "a cool, calculating, money-making murder."[1] Webster's ability to re-create scenes in the jurors' imaginations and to establish the credibility of Reverend Colman was the key to his success. Re-creating the scene also helped incite the jury against the conspirators, since the victim was eighty-two years old and helpless. To accomplish his goal, Webster relied on Aristotle's advice in the *Poetics* and the *Rhetoric* that making the scene real for the audience requires skill at word choice and narrative.

Webster began by talking about how unusual it was for him to be part of a prosecutorial team in a criminal trial. He had to lower expectations about his performance in light of his spectacular success against Hayne and particularly because there was no smoking gun in this case. Dexter, the defense lawyer, had already claimed that Webster was part of a prosecutorial attempt to rush the jury to judgment. Webster replied, "I hope I have too much regard for justice, and too much respect for my own character, to attempt" such a thing. The ac-

1. All quotations are drawn from the version of the proceedings in *The Papers of Daniel Webster: Speeches and Formal Writings*, 1:399–446.

cusation allowed Webster to praise the jury's intelligence and to reveal that he had taken the case out of a sense of civic duty. Establishing his own credibility, Webster claimed not to have any prejudice toward Frank Knapp: "I would not do him the smallest injury or injustice."[2] With the rhetorical essentials completed at the end of the second paragraph of the summation, Webster for the first time labeled the crime a "midnight assassination," an "enormous crime" that cried out for justice.

In the third paragraph, Webster employed one of his favorite tactics; he magnified the case into something special. The case had no precedent that he knew of because it involved "the weighing of money against life; the counting out of so many pieces of silver against so many ounces of blood." Hence, he broadened the significance of the crime until it was not only the worst ever committed in New England, but also analogous to the killing of Christ. The conspirators did not act out of revenge or anger, but out of greed. Having established his theme, Webster at various times during the summation extended, reinforced, and repeated it.

In the fourth paragraph, Webster began to paint his portrait of Captain White as "an aged man, without an enemy in the world." Webster was allaying any prejudice among jury members against the old man. It is a portrait to which he would return, but not before he pointed out to the jury that the crime was a blot on New England's record that they must remove: "Whoever shall hereafter draw the portrait of a murder . . . let him not give it the grim visage of Moloch, the brow knitted by revenge, the face black with settled hate, and the bloodshot eye emitting livid fires of malice. Let him draw, rather, a decorous, smooth-faced, bloodless demon." The passage is typical of Webster; the repetitious, periodic phrasing lends force to the image. More important, it reinforces the depiction of the conspirators as greedy, cool young men out to steal a fortune. Webster's object was to engrave the attitude of the conspirators on the minds of the jury.

By paragraph five, Webster was confident enough in his powers of narrative to present an account of how the murder was committed:

> The deed was executed with a degree of self-possession and steadiness equal
> to the wickedness with which it was planned. The circumstances now clearly

2. Here and in other passages, Webster seems to be concerned that the jury might have some sympathy for the young conspirators and some antipathy toward the old captain.

in evidence spread out the whole scene before us. Deep sleep had fallen on the destined victim and on all beneath his roof. A healthful old man to whom sleep was sweet, the first sound slumbers of the night held him in their soft but strong embrace. The assassin enters through the window already prepared, into an unoccupied apartment. With noiseless foot he paces the lonely hall, half lighted by the moon; he winds up the ascent of the stairs, and reaches the door of the chamber. Of this he moves the lock by soft and continued pressure, till it turns on its hinges without a noise; and he enters and beholds his victim before him.

Webster knew that the case would be won or lost on the question of motive, so he worked throughout the speech to reinforce this aspect of his argument. He brought to bear on the question not only scenic re-creation but also psychological analysis and the force of repetition. That meant creating a persona for each of the conspirators that was congruent with what the jury knew about him and could see in his face in the courtroom. It also meant creating a coherent story that functioned as a theory that would explain all of the relevant facts.

Thus in the opening five paragraphs Webster established the themes on which he would elaborate for the remainder of his summation. He continued by alleging that the conspirators believed that their deed died with Captain White. It seemed a perfect crime. Webster, however, argued that no guilty person is safe in God's world, where "murder will out." Playing on Knapp's now inadmissible confession and Crowninshield's suicide, he claimed that guilt drives a criminal to confess: "When suspicions from without begin to embarrass him, and the net of circumstance to entangle him, the fatal *secret* struggles with still greater violence to burst forth. It must be confessed, *it will be* confessed; there is no refuge from confession but suicide, and suicide is confession" (Webster's emphases). The jury, already aware of the retracted confession and the suicide, had these events brought back into their immediate consciousness.

Webster next digressed into an apologia for the vigilante committee, which had been criticized by the defense. The defense had complained about the rewards being offered, the unreliable testimony accepted, and the circus atmosphere encouraged by the committee. Webster justified each action of the committee on the grounds that the group did nothing extraordinary given the heinous nature of the case: "The committee are pointed at as though they had been officiously intermeddling with the administration of justice. . . . [W]hat must we do in such a case? Are people to be dumb and still, through fear of overdoing? Is it come to this: that an effort cannot be made, a hand cannot be lifted, to discover the guilty, without its being said there is a combination to overwhelm innocence?" These remarks led into a refutation of the case presented by the defense, beginning with the defense's procedural arguments and concluding with more substantive matters, the most important of which may have been the charge that the prosecution had cast Frank Knapp in the role of principal in the case only because of Richard Crowninshield's suicide. Webster denied this charge by asserting that the grand jury had made no disposition of the Knapps' case before the suicide: "They intended to arraign all as principals."

Webster seemed to suspect that some members of the jury admired the cleverness of the murderers. He asked the jury not to be blinded by awe at the calculations of the killers: "Gentlemen, this is an extraordinary murder, but it is still a murder. We are not to lose ourselves in wonder at its origin, or in gazing on its cool and skillful execution." On the other hand, the jury was not to engage in the business of revenge. It was simply to act in a way that would provide the strongest deterrent to future crime. In this way, Webster made the jury seem heroic and noble: "Every unpunished murder takes away something from the security of every man's life."

Webster argued that though his case was technically circumstantial, it was substantial enough for a conviction. Paraphrasing Shakespeare, he ridiculed the defense counsel's characterization of the evidence as "circumstantial stuff": "[I]t is not such stuff as dreams are made of. Why does he not rend this stuff? Why does he not scatter it to the winds? He dismisses it a little too summarily."[3] Webster proceeded to go through a litany of facts that pointed toward the guilt of Frank Knapp. It was critical that he make the jury see the conspirators gathering in the street near the house of Captain White. There they hatched a plot, a coldhearted deal for money. Webster turned to a *topoi* from the Roman *stasis* system: "If the Knapps and the Crowninshields were not the conspirators in this murder, then there is a whole set of conspirators not yet discovered."[4] Like Cicero attacking Catiline, he asked, If these weren't

3. Webster returns to this theme when he says sarcastically, "Fix your eyes steadily on this part of the 'circumstantial stuff.'" Webster, *Speeches and Formal Writings,* 1:414.

4. Webster also used the *topoi* of definition. For example: "There are two sorts of murder. The distinction between them is of essential importance to bear in mind: 1) Murder in an affray, or upon sudden and unexpected provocation; 2) murder secretly, with a deliberate, predetermined intention to commit the crime." *Speeches and Formal Writings,* 1:419.

the conspirators, then where were they? As for the defendants at the bar, Webster brought down a mountain of evidence on the side of their guilt. Each piece of evidence was meticulously examined and fitted into the conspiracy: "These facts are proved by Hart and Leighton, and by Osborn's books. On Saturday evening, about this time, Richard Crowninshield is proved to have been at Wenham with another person, whose appearance corresponds with Frank." (Hart and Leighton overheard the conspiracy talk in the Charleston jail. Osborn, a stable owner, testified about money transfers and rentals by the Knapp brothers.)

The strategy of making the conspiracy real pervaded the summation. In a hail of rhetorical questions, for example, Webster drew the jury into the scene on Brown Street: "Can any person doubt that they were there for purposes connected with this murder? If not for this purpose, what were they there for? When there is a cause so near at hand, why wander into conjecture for explanation? Common sense requires you take the nearest adequate cause for a known effect. Who were these suspicious persons in Brown Street?" Six pages later, to sum up the facts supporting a meeting of the conspirators, he said: "It was their place of *centrality*. The club was found near the spot, in a place provided for it, in a place that had been previously hunted out, in a concerted place of concealment. *Here was their point of rendezvous*; here might the lights be seen; here might an aid[e] be secreted; here was he within call; here might he be aroused by the sound of the whistle." The thesis that this was the location was reinforced by the repetition of *here*, and the opportunity for the crime was reinforced by the repetition of *might*. Again, the drumbeat of Webster's phrasing, combined with his sonorous delivery and the striking figure he cut, apparently proved irresistible.

This long paragraph was followed by another in which the word *considering* was used as a refrain to sum up each piece of damning evidence: "Considering that the murder was effected by a conspiracy; considering that [Frank Knapp] was one of the four conspirators; considering that two of the conspirators have accounted for themselves on the night of the murder, and were not in Brown Street; considering that the prisoner does not account for himself, nor show where he was . . . This proves *appointment, arrangement, previous agreement*." So it went until no other logical conclusion could be reached but that Frank Knapp had conspired to kill Captain White.

At this point Webster returned to the confession that he had only touched on earlier. He wanted it to appear that he didn't need Joseph Knapp's confession; it was simply an additional argument in the stack of evidence against Frank Knapp. He began by establishing the credibility of Reverend Colman and his relationship with the Knapps and by revisiting the scene of the confession in the jail cell. He told the jury that Colman was "on trial as to his veracity" and then attacked the credibility of the eldest Knapp brother, Phippen, who had disputed Colman's account. Once again, Webster brought alive the scene of the confession: "To judge of this, you must go back to that scene."

After his review of the confession, Webster moved to his conclusion, claiming to have presented the facts "plainly and fairly." He issued a litany of the case, beginning each sentence with "That you cannot doubt . . ." He told the jurors to do their duty and leave the consequences to others: "You are the judges of the whole case. You owe a duty to the public." Finally, he ended his summation with a transcendent appeal:

> A sense of duty pursues us ever. It is omnipresent, like the Deity. If we take to ourselves the wings of the morning, and dwell in the uttermost parts of the sea, duty performed or duty violated is still with us, for our happiness or our misery. If we say the darkness shall cover us, in the darkness, as in the light, our obligations are yet with us. We cannot escape their power, nor fly from their presence. They are with us in this life, will be with us at its close; and in that scene of inconceivable solemnity, which lies yet further onward, we shall still find ourselves surrounded by the consciousness of duty, to pain us wherever it has been violated, and to console us so far as God may have given us grace to perform it.

This poetic close is remarkable for its highly religious tone. Webster created a world in which people were held accountable for their actions before God in the hereafter.

Most important in this case was Webster's ability to take disparate facts and circumstantial evidence and weave them into a credible narrative. His penchant for homework served him well, and his five-hour summation to a packed courtroom won him acclaim. Frank Knapp was convicted of conspiracy to commit a murder. At the trial of Joseph Knapp, Webster also won, having taken on that case pro bono. The Knapp brothers were executed in November while a crowd of ten thousand looked on. Webster's legend grew.

Webster had gained national attention with his reply to Hayne in January 1830. With the Knapp-White case in August, he became the consummate lawyer. He had proven himself in the highest court in the land on constitutional issues and in a simple courtroom in Salem on criminal matters. In each situation, he had demonstrated an ability to link the specific issues of the case at hand with transcendent constitutional and moral issues. He had persuaded the justices of the Supreme Court and the jurors of Salem that his vision of those issues was the correct one.

Webster's forensic powers not only served his career well, they also helped strengthen the young Union and set a model for criminal prosecution. Late in life, he confessed, "You will find, in my speeches to juries, no hard words, no Latin phrases, no *fieri facas*; and that is the secret of my style if I have any."[5]

Jacksonian Democracy

At the end of 1830, President Jackson fired everyone in his cabinet and began to rely on Amos Kendall, an auditor at the Treasury Department who had switched allegiance from Clay to Jackson in 1828. It was Jackson's way of removing Calhoun's supporters. This coup was engineered by Martin Van Buren, who was nominated to be ambassador to the Court of St. James as a reward. Henry Clay seized on the disunion among Democrats to advance his candidacy for president. At the same time, Webster's stock had never been higher and he contemplated a run himself. In fact, he was approached by the Anti-Masons to head the ticket of their newly formed party. In part because Clay was a Mason, as was Jackson, Webster argued that the National Republican nominee should not be a Mason, in order that the party might form a fusion ticket with the Anti-Masons and pick up much-needed Catholic support.

On March 10, 1831, a banquet was held in Webster's honor in New York City, serving further notice that he was seeking the nomination. The effort came to naught, however, when the Anti-Masons made it clear that they were not interested in a fusion effort. They held the first political convention in U.S. history in September 1831 in Baltimore, nominating William Wirt for president. Webster believed the Anti-Masons' effort would work to Jackson's advantage because it split his opposition. In the meantime, Clay got himself elected to the Senate by the Kentucky legislature and in the summer of 1831 Calhoun issued his "Fort Hill Address," which endorsed a state's right of nullification.

Clay arrived for the December session of Congress and, together with Web-

5. Webster, *Writings and Speeches*, 13:582.

ster, encouraged Nicholas Biddle to apply for a new charter for the National Bank, even though the current one was good until 1836. Clay, correctly believing that Jackson would veto a new charter, planned to use the issue in the election of 1832. From his Greek Revival temple on Chestnut Street in Philadelphia, Biddle sent his request to the Congress on January 6, 1832. The election campaign was about to begin.

Jackson was a wealthy man who had built a mansion, the Hermitage, outside Nashville; however, his public persona was that of a frontier hero. By 1832 the Republic had taken a democratic turn that favored Jackson. Public opinion dominated the political scene; that is why Jackson addressed his veto of the Second National Bank to the public, not to the Congress.[6] His playing to the masses was offensive to Webster, whose private life reflected his republican tendencies. His public persona reflected the priestly distance he strove to maintain. His private persona revealed a more hedonistic Webster. Though again strapped for cash, in 1832 he bought Marshfield, a modest home on a large tract of land south of Boston. Rich foods and wine filled out his frame, and he became "prosperous" in both senses of the nineteenth-century use of the word: he was flourishing by reputation and also gaining weight. His new wife hung works of art throughout the house; he bought surrounding land to extend his holdings and forbade the killing of animals on his property.

Webster and Clay were of the opinion that presidential personas were formed in public institutions, the House, the Senate, and the cabinet. Jackson had changed all that. In his own way, he was a throwback to Washington, a general elected by the people. However, Washington had been involved in the formation of the nation, and his selection was made more by the elite than by the general public. There were other differences as well. Public political speaking in the age of Jackson was much more emotional and romantic. The venues for campaigning were changing too. Reflecting the religious revival, politicians appeared at more outdoor rallies, conventions, and public meetings. Webster was a successful public speaker because he was able to establish just the right distance between himself and his audience; he was the prophet Daniel. The new breed of speakers were much closer to their audiences. They were more likely to fire up an audience in anger or sorrow than to appeal to the intellect or inspire them.

6. John William Ward, *Andrew Jackson: Symbol for an Age*, 49; Kenneth Cmiel, *Democratic Eloquence: The Fight over Popular Speech in Nineteenth-Century America*, 64.

If Jackson presented the threat of a national demagogue, then Calhoun, who fit the elitist model, presented the threat of disunion, which was anathema to Webster. Thus, on the occasion of Washington's centennial birthday in February 1832 Webster gave a speech in the capital's Barnard Hotel to celebrate Federalist virtues. He was selected to be "President of the Day" and to preside over a dinner; other members of Congress served as his "vice presidents" at the affair.

In his "Character of Washington" address, Webster used an ostensibly epideictic occasion to attack Calhoun's doctrine of nullification. Two years earlier, in his debate with Hayne, Webster had soundly thrashed the doctrine, but it would not die as long as Calhoun was around to flog it back to life. While the speech was formally labeled "An Address on the Centennial Anniversary of Washington's Birthday," Webster preferred the title "The Character of Washington," which stressed the epideictic nature of the occasion while harkening back to Washington's "Farewell Address." (The replies to Hayne were full of praise for Washington, who provided ample support for Webster's call for Union.)

Webster began by focusing on the name of Washington: "That name was of power to rally the nation, in the hour of thick-thronging public disasters and calamities; that name shone, amid the storm of war, a beacon light, to cheer and guide the country's friends; it flamed, too, like a meteor, to repel her foes. That name, in the days of peace, was a loadstone, attracting to itself a whole people's confidence, a whole people's love, and the whole world's respect."[7] Using the grand style, Webster promoted his subject in periodic cadences and announced his commitment to a nation of one people, a theme he would extend the next year in refuting the nullification doctrine.

Webster moved from the character of the first president to the character of the nation by glorifying the immediate occasion: "We perform this grateful duty, gentlemen, at the expiration of a hundred years from his birth, near the place, so cherished and beloved by him, where his dust now reposes, and in the capital which bears his own immortal name."[8] As he had done in previous speeches, Webster cited the progress of the New World and praised its unique

7. Webster, *Speeches and Forensic Arguments*, 2:36–48.
8. Webster's right-branching sentence structure mirrored Washington's complex style in the Farewell Address. Washington claimed full credit for the ideas in the speech even though Hamilton and, to a lesser extent, Madison had a hand in the writing. See Victor Hugo Paltsits, *Washington's Farewell Address*; and Matthew Spaulding and Patrick J. Garrity, *A Sacred Union of Citizens: George Washington's Farewell Address and the American Character*.

values. In contrast, the Old World seemed stagnant. Again taking a theme from Washington's address, he explored the geographic blessings the United States enjoyed, not only because of its distance from Europe but also because of its own land mass. This argument reinforced the view that the founders had a special mission in settling the New World.

Many of the New World values Webster mentioned were supported in the biographical section of the speech. He used Washington's life to demonstrate those values and how they manifest themselves in national leadership. This strategy culminated in the following sentence: "We cannot wish better for our country, nor for the world, than that the same spirit which influenced Washington may influence all who succeed him." The line served as a turning point in the speech, foreshadowing Webster's underlying message: To honor Washington properly we must live by his principles, and those principles inevitably lead to Union, which embodies the national character.

Webster built to this message subtly and carefully. He began by associating Washington with simple values no one could reject: "[H]e told the country . . . that honesty is the best policy. . . . He had no favorites; he rejected all partisanship; and, acting honestly for the universal good, he deserved, what he has so richly enjoyed, the universal love of his countrymen." Note that when Webster spoke of simple values, he used simple phrases. Throughout the speech, style and structure echoed the meaning, and critical listeners delighted in its iconicity.

Once he had established his audience's admiration for and identification with Washington, his "great character," and his foreign policy, Webster reinforced his own agenda:

> The domestic policy of Washington found its pole-star in the avowed objects of the Constitution itself. He sought so to administer that Constitution, as to form a more perfect Union. . . . [T]here was in the breath of Washington one sentiment so deeply felt, so constantly uppermost, that no proper occasion escaped without its utterance. From the letter which he signed in behalf of the Convention when the Constitution was sent out to the people, to the moment when he put his hand to that last paper in which he addressed his countrymen, the Union—the Union was the great object of his thoughts.

The remainder of the speech supported Union, further identifying it with Washington, and stressed the values important to maintaining it. As in his reply to Hayne, Webster argued that all good things flow from the Union and that ending the Union would end its benefits as well.[9] In an emotional conclusion, he referred back to the opening of the address and prayed that in another hundred years the nation would still be moving toward its glorious destiny: "[A]nd then, as now, may the sun in his course visit no land more free, more happy, more lovely, than this our own country! Gentlemen, I propose— 'the Memory of George Washington.'" Webster was followed by other speakers at the dinner, none of whom matched his oratorical achievement.

Trapping the President

Back in the Senate, Webster found he had miscalculated the impact of the bank issue on the American public. It was one thing for him to urge Americans to embrace the values of George Washington; it was quite another to invoke those values in a debate over the rechartering of the National Bank, particularly when that bank had him on a lucrative retainer. No politician was closer to the National Bank than Webster; he served on its board and often "forgot" to repay its loans to him. Biddle had huge resources at his command and could "lend" money to politicians that favored the bank's position. He refused to alter the bank's charter to facilitate the president; in fact, at Clay's behest, he rejected an offer of negotiation from the secretary of the Treasury. Jackson's attorney general, Roger Taney, told him to fight. So began the bank war. Taney, who hated Biddle, was a regular informant for Senator Benton, who dubbed the National Bank an "Eastern Monster." The tariff was another major issue in Congress at the beginning of 1832. The National Republicans presented their plan; the administration presented its plan; and the southern states sought relief from the "Tariff of Abominations" of 1828.

In January, what should have been a routine approval of the nomination of Van Buren to be ambassador to England turned into the first skirmish of a political war. Clay announced his opposition, and Calhoun joined him behind the scenes. Webster spoke against the nomination on January 24, arguing that Van Buren was so close to the British that he supported English policy over the Monroe Doctrine. He used as evidence Van Buren's handling of trade in the West Indies. The next day, the senators present arranged a tie vote so that Calhoun could kill the nomination himself, extracting revenge against Van

---

9. This would be the thesis of his 1833 speech against Calhoun's doctrine of nullification, which is discussed below.

Buren. Incensed, Jackson made it clear that Van Buren would be his running mate in the next election.

In February, Clay introduced his new tariff bill in a speech that ran through three days of Senate business. The bill reasserted the American System and was clearly Clay's platform for election. While the overall tariff would be reduced, certain items would have higher tariffs placed on them. The South was opposed; New England manufacturers were unhappy. Negotiations over the bill dominated the cloakrooms of Congress over the next few months. Eventually Clay, Calhoun, and Webster were able to craft a compromise that protected the textile mills of the North and satisfied agricultural interests in the South. The president signed it in July.

This moment of consensus was short-lived. Because the bank battle was so contentious, political motives lurked behind every maneuver. Clay, Calhoun, and Webster, now recognized as "the great triumvirate," had humiliated Van Buren and achieved their tariff of 1832. Now it was time to go after the president. Senator Benton, Jackson's defender and something of a windbag, had given a long speech in January attacking the National Bank. Webster had taken extensive notes on Benton's speech and was ready to defend the bank bill, but it was stuck in committee. At Webster's behest, Biddle came to Washington from Philadelphia; after much wining and dining of committee members, the two men managed to spring the bill from parliamentary limbo. On May 25, Webster sought recognition to speak on the recharter of the National Bank. Calhoun was delighted to oblige.

Webster established his credibility immediately by confessing that he had opposed the chartering of the Second National Bank in 1816. Acknowledging Calhoun, he said that his senior colleague in the Senate had been right to support the bank in 1816. Webster now claimed to have seen the light and said he hoped Calhoun's example would pull other southerners into a majority for recharter. He linked the bank to a stable currency, and a stable currency to a stable economy.[10] He claimed to have no doubts about the constitutionality of the bank.

The next day when amendments were introduced to allow states to tax branches established in their territory, Webster rose to speak again. The amendments were clearly unconstitutional in light of *McCulloch v. Maryland*, and no one in the Senate could speak with more sagacity on this issue. Webster devastated the amendments. Indignant, he demanded that his colleagues refuse to

10. *Register of Debates*, 22nd Cong., 1st sess., 954-64.

give the states "a power to embarrass, a power to oppose, a power to expel, a power to destroy the bank. . . . [I]t is the *Constitution*, not the *law*, which lays the prohibition on the States."[11] The amendments went down to defeat on June 1, and it became clear that Clay and Webster had enough votes to carry the day. On June 11, the recharter bill was passed by a margin of eight votes in the Senate. The next month, the House passed the bill by twenty-two votes and sent it to the president, who vetoed it on July 10.

In a message suggesting the influence and wording of Amos Kendall and Roger Taney, Jackson claimed that the bank was a "hydra," a monopoly, and that the legislation was "monstrous." He also called for reversal of the *McCulloch* decision, which he claimed violated the "necessary and proper" clause of the Constitution.[12] He attacked the corrupt practices of the bank in general and Biddle in particular. He attacked the rich and the powerful, defending farmers and the poor. This was populism pure and simple.

Webster could not tolerate the veto or the attack on *McCulloch*. On July 11 he spoke for three hours refuting the message. He began by saying that the Senate now knew where the president stood, and that his stance threatened the bank and, therefore, the currency. If the bank was to be forced to give up its charter three years hence, as the president proposed, it would have to immediately start collecting its outstanding $60 million in loans. This would cause a financial panic in the nation as prices of real goods soared.

In the middle of his speech, Webster let fly with a beautifully written defense of National Republican principles in the negative. That is, he pointed out how the president had offended each one:

> This message calls us to the contemplation of a future which resembles the past. Its principles are at war with all that public opinion has sustained, and all which the experience of government has sanctioned. It denies first principles; it contradicts truths, heretofore received as indisputable. It denies to the judiciary the interpretation of law, and claims to divide with Congress the power of originating statutes. It extends the grasp of executive pretension over every power of the government. But this is not all. It presents the chief magistrate of the Union in the attitude of arguing away the powers of that

11. Ibid., 981–88.

12. This part of Jackson's message set off alarm bells among National Republicans. What kind of men, they wondered, would this dictatorial president appoint to the Supreme Court? Would his appointees undo all Federalist precedents?

government over which he has been chosen to preside; and adopting for this purpose modes of reasoning which, even under the influence of all proper feeling towards high official station, it is difficult to regard as respectable.

Webster then turned to Jackson's demagoguery: "It appeals to every prejudice which may betray men into a mistaken view of their own interests, and to every passion which may lead them to disobey the impulses of their understanding. It affects alarm for the public freedom, when nothing endangers that freedom so much as its own unparalleled pretenses. . . . It manifestly seeks to inflame the poor against the rich."[13] Jackson, in other words, was a Hobbesian nightmare.

Having secured his audience's attention, Webster defended the practices and perquisites of the bank as no different from those of other banks in the states. Then he turned to his strongest argument, the constitutionality of the National Bank. He cited previous congresses, prior presidents, and Supreme Court precedents and said all were arrayed against the current president. Since those congresses and presidents were sworn to uphold the Constitution, and since the Supreme Court determined what was constitutional, Jackson had violated the spirit of rule in America. Webster compared him to the Tudors and Stuarts, implying that he had become a despot.

Webster brought his themes together in his conclusion. The pretensions of the tyrant president had caused alarm and threatened the Constitution, he said. The populism of the president would divide the nation along class lines. Though Webster was ahead of his time in speaking of the Supreme Court's *exclusive* power to determine constitutionality, that too would come with the Civil War.

Clay continued the attack that the president had fomented with his veto message. On July 13, as expected, Benton rose in defense of his leader, in the knowledge that he had enough votes to prevent an override of the veto. The Congress then adjourned, knowing that Jackson had implied in his message that the 1832 election would determine whether the public was with him on the bank issue. Thus, to the consternation of National Republicans like Webster, the decision on rechartering the bank was left to a public referendum.[14]

13. Webster, *Speeches and Formal Writings*, 1:501–30.
14. At this time, Biddle paid off Webster's loans by consolidating them into one secret loan, thereby removing one sign of connection between the bank and Webster. But Biddle also paid for the publication and distribution of Webster's July 11 address.

The Election of 1832

The election presented an opportunity for South Carolina to call a nullification convention. The state commissioned Calhoun to explain its position to the other states. Calhoun soon issued another philosophical tract, "Address to the People of the United States," in which he condemned the consolidation of power in Washington. When the election was preceded by tariff riots in South Carolina, Calhoun again called for nullification, which neither Clay nor Webster could approve.

Jackson beat Clay by 215,000 popular votes and won the electoral college 219 to 49.[15] Worse yet for the Whigs, Van Buren would be the vice president. These events emboldened Calhoun to encourage nullification of the tariff, and a duly elected South Carolina convention did just that on November 24. Calhoun resigned the vice presidency and was selected to replace Hayne in the Senate, where he waited for the opportunity to avenge Hayne's humiliation at the hands of Webster. As we have seen, Hayne moved into the governorship of South Carolina, ready to confront Jackson's orders. On December 10, Jackson signed a proclamation to the people of South Carolina. He claimed that those opposed to tariff collections were guilty of treason and he threatened armed intervention to enforce the tariff. The document had been prepared by Secretary of State Edward Livingston, a Democrat with strong nationalist tendencies. By signing the document, Jackson abandoned all pretense of being a states' rights Democrat. In a private letter to Gen. John Coffee on December 14, Jackson wrote, "I will die for the union."[16]

On December 17 Webster spoke in Faneuil Hall to address this issue. Harrison Otis, Boston's former mayor, preceded him to the lectern and argued for popular democracy, not exactly the republicanism that Webster favored.[17] Dressed in his usual navy-blue and buff outfit, Webster spoke with great enthusiasm, and as always used the immediate scene to buttress his arguments: "When I look around me on the numbers who fill these galleries and crowd this hall, I thank Almighty God that I may still address them as citizens of the United States." He "approved" of the president's necessary action to put down

15. The Anti-Mason Party took over 100,000 popular votes, most of which probably would have gone to the National Republicans.

16. Quoted in Hofstadter, *Great Issues in American History*, 1:282.

17. Otis had been a staunch Federalist who helped develop the woolens industry. Once mayor of Boston, he became more of a populist.

"civil war." He once more championed his transcendent solution: "I say, when the standard of Union is raised and waves over my head—the standard which Washington planted on the ramparts of the Constitution—God forbid that I should inquire whom they have commissioned to unfurl it and bear it up: I only ask in what manner, as a humble individual, I can best discharge my duty in defending it."[18] The president must uphold the laws of the land; no state may secede from the Union; secession is rebellion. It was a simple, eloquent speech that proved effective with the crowd.

The crisis, however, did not abate nationally. Governor Hayne and the South Carolina legislature passed resolutions of defiance in the face of Jackson's threat. Hayne called for ten thousand men to come forward to defend the state.

Webster was reelected by the Massachusetts legislature in January 1833. When he returned to Congress for the winter session, he found Clay proposing yet another compromise, one designed to quiet South Carolina and assuage New England. Clay suggested a ten-year phaseout of the tariff, which would give northern manufacturers time to adjust and promise South Carolina an eventual end to the tariff. Webster thought the plan too audacious and opposed it, probably at Francis Cabot Lowell's request. The great triumvirate was again split. Clay and Webster would come together now and then, but Calhoun was lost for the most part to sectionalism. This division, with Clay, Calhoun, and Webster in their prime, made the Senate the seat of entertainment in the capital.

Calhoun's Revenge

Calhoun was lusting for a fight and the president obliged by sending a "force bill" to Congress. Basically, Jackson was asking the Congress to support his right to use martial force to make South Carolina collectors comply with the tariff. On February 8, Webster defended the president's request as reasonable and moderate: the president would take action only if provoked, and he sought only a minor change in previous laws governing the situation.

On February 15 and 16, Calhoun responded with his first speech on the Senate floor in sixteen years. To replace Clay's compromise, he advocated a

18. Webster, *Writings and Speeches*, 13:40–43. Though this speech was one of Webster's shortest, it proved to be quite influential, particularly with Abraham Lincoln.

"constitutional compact" to resolve the crisis: to win approval, legislation would have to achieve a majority of representatives of the North and South in *both* houses. This compact would paralyze the government, and Calhoun knew it. Philosophical consistency is not always sound political practice. Calhoun believed that sovereignty inhered in the states; they made the Constitution and they could enforce it. The Union, he asserted, could not be maintained by force. He defended the "peculiar" institution of slavery and the liberty of the minority against an oppressive majority. He attacked the corruption of the federal government that had led to factionalism and anarchy in the Congress. The republican virtue of the South was its unique culture, a theme Calhoun would embrace until his death as he separated himself and his region from the Union of Webster.

In response, Webster wisely chose not to answer the speech argument by argument as he had with Hayne. He realized that if one accepted Calhoun's initial premise—that sovereignty inhered in the states—all else followed. So he was forced to attack that premise, present a counterphilosophy, and then reveal the pragmatic implications of Calhoun's proposal. This address, though largely ignored by historians, is just as important as the Second Reply to Hayne because it extends and amplifies Webster's civil religion. It is his most radical defense of Union because it so marginalizes the states and romanticizes the people.

Webster began by claiming that he had already won this argument in the court of public opinion when he debated Calhoun's surrogate, Hayne. Since then, he said, the public "[has] become awakened to this great question; it has grasped it; it has reasoned upon it, as becomes an intelligent and patriotic community, and has settled it."[19] Then, relying heavily on his beloved *Federalist Papers*, Webster set out the thesis that the Constitution was not a *compact* between the states; it was a *contract* with the people, and, therefore, it was the supreme law of the land. Webster had been more and more extreme in defending this position since his success against Hayne. Many senators still believed that the Constitution was a compact between the states, but that the states had granted some of their authority to the national government.[20] Webster's lucid explanation of the Preamble to the Constitution, in which he undercut the compact theory, was aimed at just such thinking:

19. Quotations are from Webster, *Speeches and Formal Writings*, 1:571–620.

20. Ericson, *Shaping of American Liberalism*, 91. See "Daniel Webster's Patriotic Community," chap. 6 of Ericson's book, for his analysis of Webster's speech on the Force Bill.

They executed that agreement: they adopted the Constitution, and henceforth it must stand as a Constitution until it shall be altogether destroyed. . . .
The truth is, Mr. President, and no ingenuity of argument, no subtlety of distinction, can evade it, that, as to certain purposes, the people of the United States are one people. They are one in making war, and one in making peace; they are one in regulating commerce, and one in laying duties and imposts.

During the course of the speech, Webster made his philosophical position much less flexible. The law-abiding state, he said, was analogous to the law-abiding citizen. Violating the law was revolutionary and anarchistic. He defended majoritarian democracy and mocked Calhoun's proposal as "wholly unknown to our Constitution." He argued that republican government was far superior. By the end of the introduction, three themes had emerged that would be developed, supported, extended, and woven together: 1) the Union is superior to the states and is of the people; 2) republican federalism is superior to direct democracy; and 3) the Union has transcendent worth.

Relying on the *Federalist Papers*, Webster charged that nullification was a radical act tantamount to revolution, a theme that pervades the speech. While the Articles of Confederation visited certain hardships on the founders, Calhoun's doctrines would result in even more drastic harms, including disunion: "To begin with nullification, with the avowed intent, nevertheless, not to proceed to secession, dismemberment, and general revolution, is as if one were to take the plunge of Niagara, and cry out that he would stop half way down." One state alone cannot nullify or change the Constitution; it can legitimately be altered only by three-quarters of the states acting in concert. The compact that Webster did recognize was the one handed down from the Enlightenment: "The consent of the people has been called, by European writers, the social compact." Thus, Webster charged, the Constitution merely reflected what had been achieved by the Revolution: America was a union of "one people," not "separate States." He contended that some in the Senate had confused things with their misuse of the word *sovereignty*. It is the sovereignty of the people as a whole that the Constitution established, not the sovereignty of the states, he said.

Webster thus clashed directly with Calhoun's call for "divided sovereignty" vested in concurrent majorities. Webster's alternative was a republican approach that was historically grounded and pragmatically proven, as opposed to Calhoun's theoretical—some said metaphysical—system. Webster supported his vision with two pillars: "First, that there is so far a common interest among those over whom the government extends." He meant such things as defense and protection from oppression. "Second, that the representatives of the people, and especially the people themselves, are secure against general corruption."

If there was a failure in this speech, it was Webster's inability to articulate common interests in a detailed and compelling way. Instead, he called up a common sentiment among the one people: patriotism, or loyalty to the Union. The people were sovereign under the Union, not, as Calhoun would have it, under the states. Perhaps Webster was trying to transcend divisions as he had in 1830 and would again in 1850. More likely, he was preparing his audience for his move to questions of loyalty, the glue of the Republic. While citizens have a duty to pay taxes, to avoid treason, and the like, the "government owes high and solemn duties to every citizen of the country. It is bound to protect him in his most important rights and interests. It makes war for his protection, and no other government in the country can make war." This transaction was something the common citizen could understand, unlike the details of legislative agendas. Like Edmund Burke, Webster required loyalty from the public; however, he believed, the specific business of the country should be carried on by the representatives of that public. These representatives should be enlightened on the issues and held accountable for their performance at election time. When they address their constituents, they are duty-bound to give them a true picture of what is at stake in legislation. This requirement is one of the genuflections that Webster made to Jefferson's belief that a functioning democracy requires an educated public. But while the founders, particularly the authors of the *Federalist Papers*, claimed that citizens owed civic virtue in return for the benefits of Union—for example, liberty and security—Webster claimed they owed patriotism. He moved the public from enlightened participation to romantic commitment, from civil republicanism to civil religion.

In fact, in a passage in the speech about the state of South Carolina, Webster chastised Calhoun for misleading his constituents by presenting only one side of the equation to them. If they saw that nullification meant disunion, Webster said, he had every confidence they would reject Calhoun's formulation. He claimed that Calhoun's resolutions were built on sand, a series of unfounded, ungrounded "assumptions." Calhoun, he said, used a "theoretical and artificial mode of reasoning" that perverted the founders' triumph in converting Enlightenment theory into pragmatic reality (as discussed in Chapter 1). Webster compared Calhoun's resolutions to the failed and rejected Articles of Confederation, saying they "strike a deadly blow at the vital principle of the whole Union. . . . The gentleman seems not conscious of his opinion's direction or the rapidity of his own course."

Webster omitted any reference to the residual rights of the states; in this speech, unlike some of his others, there is no praise for the states. Thus, he laid out his most extreme version of Union, one many senators would modify by adding that the states do have powers—all of those not specifically delegated to the federal government by the Constitution. This is what they meant by "divided sovereignty."

Webster preferred the people to the states and believed that the benefits of Union flowed directly to them, just as their authority was granted directly to the federal government. The states, he believed, should not be arbiters between the people and their Union. Webster's praise of the loyalty and feelings of patriotism essential among the *demos* led to his transcendent view of the Union, in which he gave the Constitution a sense of active being: "The Constitution, Sir, regards itself as perpetual and immortal . . . for all time." In exchange for the patriotism it required, the Constitution dispensed liberty. That liberty would be reduced under Calhoun's scheme because a "small minority" could bring the government to a halt. By liberty, Webster meant the personal freedom to pursue happiness; he did not mean liberty for the states under the Union. This twofold concept of liberty is what made America the "last great experiment of representative government."

Webster pounded home his contention that the government was adopted by the people and that it was not a confederation of states. He reviewed the evolving relationship between the people and the government, and concluded that no state had the authority to sunder their ties and responsibilities: "What is a constitution? Certainly not a league, compact, or confederacy, but a fundamental law." The states, he said, were no longer in a position to dissolve it. Once set in motion—that is, once it was ratified—the Constitution was permanent. The Supreme Court, not the states, decided what was constitutional, and nullification was unconstitutional. The mission as Webster saw it was to preserve the Union, not to change it. Happiness and liberty flowed from the Union and that was why it must be preserved, especially when compared to what would flow from nullification.

Webster became emotional in his peroration:

> Disorder and confusion, indeed, may arise; scenes of commotion and contest
> are threatened, and perhaps may come. With my whole heart, I pray for the

continuance of the domestic peace and quiet of the country. I desire, most ardently, the restoration of affection, and harmony to all its parts. . . . But I cannot yield even to kind feelings the cause of the Constitution, the true glory of the country, and the great trust we hold in our hands for succeeding ages. . . . I shall exert every faculty I possess in aiding to prevent the Constitution from being nullified, destroyed, or impaired.

The Senate erupted with applause and cheers. Like many others, Madison sent Webster a letter praising the speech.

This address is important not only because it cut through the philosophical fog of Calhoun's resolutions, but also because it extended Webster's civil religion in at least two important ways: First, it emphasized that the people created the Constitution from sentiments and principles that go back to the Greeks. Hence the Constitution owes its loyalty to the people, not the states. To honor the past and succeed in the future, the people must remain loyal to the Constitution. Second, the form of this loyalty is patriotism. Webster thereby created a sentimental Union that was right for the times and badly needed by his party. This romantic Union was far more attractive than Calhoun's metaphysical system; in fact, Webster's Union could rival the best the populist Democrats could offer.

Webster tapped into the rich sentiment for the Union that gave heart to the men of the Revolution. Calhoun was attempting to end this love affair by interposing the states and making them an equal partner in the relationship. Webster rejected the triangle. He moved beyond the civic republicanism of the *Federalist Papers* to posit a transcendental love affair between the people and their Constitution. In part because of his rhetoric, the Senate passed the Force Bill, isolating South Carolina.

Calhoun, who had taken notes throughout Webster's speech, wrote a careful response. Speaking ten days after Webster, he put forward a syllogistic and effective rationale for his position. He rejected federal dominance and argued that the implication of Webster's position was the end of state sovereignty. The states were the home of liberty for Calhoun—they had defended individuals against an ever encroaching federal government—and he believed Webster was out to destroy that home.

Calhoun garnered enough support in the House to stop the Force Bill as it had been proposed. To appease him, the Senate softened the bill. In the meantime, Clay tried to work with Calhoun on tariff reform since few believed the compromise between Unionists and nullifiers would endure.[21] Given his previous speech, Webster had no choice but to attack the Calhoun-Clay compromise. His attacks impressed even Van Buren.[22] Nonetheless, Clay prevailed because some form of compromise was needed to calm the situation. The South needed some counterweight to set off the Force Bill. Ironically, the president signed the compromise tariff on the same day he signed the revised Force Bill. Along with other congressional leaders, Webster was invited to the White House for the occasion and enjoyed the recognition associated with his defense of Union.

The Bank Crisis

Because of the Force Bill, Webster had moved closer to Jackson and away from Clay. Given his antipathy toward Jackson, this indicated that Webster was more committed to principle than to personality. Nonetheless, word circulated in the Capitol that Webster would be appointed to the cabinet at the first opportunity. Reveling in the publicity, he undertook a western tour to consolidate support for the National Republican platform. Everywhere he went, he linked prosperity to Whig virtues. He dubbed the Great Lakes a "new bond" of the Union. He called for the protection of American labor against foreign interests. He defended property rights, education for all, sound currency through a national bank, internal improvements, and business competition. Like Jefferson, he believed that liberty must be intelligently managed and that property breeds patriotism.[23]

Strengthening speculation about a budding friendship, Webster interrupted his tour to greet Jackson in Boston on June 20; Jackson was on his own tour trying to reassure the nation about the Force Bill. Webster resumed his travels in July, spreading the Whig gospel to Pittsburgh and Cincinnati. The tour led to his name being bandied about as a presidential candidate. At the same time, he continued to be courted for a cabinet position by some around Jackson. The first opportunity for an appointment came when Louis McLane, the secretary of the Treasury, was transferred to the State Department for

21. Current, *Daniel Webster*, 67. See also Peterson, *The Great Triumvirate*, 214–15, 222–24, 228–30, 232–38.

22. Remini, *Daniel Webster*, 385.

23. See, for example, his speech in Buffalo on June 15, 1833. Webster, *Writings and Speeches*, 2:131–33.

refusing to remove deposits from the National Bank at the president's request. Van Buren, who had the president's ear, eliminated Webster for the position (if he ever had a chance at it) by pointing to his connections to Biddle. The appointment went to William Duane, whose father had published the Jeffersonian *Aurora* in Philadelphia. The Duane family, immigrants from Ireland, were critical of Biddle, thus winning Jackson's approval.

The National Bank again became a bone of contention between Jackson and the Congress when the president ordered his new secretary of the Treasury to take all government money out of the bank. Ironically, Duane balked, telling the president to notify Congress first. Amos Kendall was quick to intervene and began to examine which state banks could best house the government's reserve.

On September 30, 1833, Jackson announced that the monies would be removed and so would Secretary Duane, who promptly withdrew into private life and wrote a defense of his actions. Roger Taney was nominated to be secretary of the Treasury. On his small plantation near Frederick, Maryland, Taney owned a handful of slaves, whose quarters have been preserved to this day. He began his political career as a Federalist, serving one term in the Maryland House of Delegates in 1799. He broke with the Federalists when they opposed the War of 1812, but by 1816 he had retaken control of the Maryland Federalist Party and was elected to the state senate. He again broke with the Federalists in 1824 to support Jackson, an act that Jackson saw fit to reward, first making Taney his attorney general and then nominating him as secretary of the Treasury.

Biddle was astounded and began to cut back on the availability of loans from his bank. A panic swept the financial community. At Webster's behest, Biddle asked for help from Congress when it reconvened in December. He accused Taney of violating the bank's charter. Webster knew he would have to break with the president not only because of Biddle, but also because he believed that the constitutional provision that put Congress in control of revenue also put it in charge of government monies and where they were to be stored. Calhoun and Clay followed along, and the triumvirate was briefly reunited. They retained the key positions in the Congress: Clay sat on the Committee on Public Lands; Webster won the chairmanship, 21 to 18, of the Committee on Finance; and Calhoun used his prestige behind the scenes, refusing to sit on any committees. Biddle renewed Webster's retainer while consolidating support among merchants in Europe and America.[24] Petitions rained

24. Remini, *Daniel Webster,* 402, 406.

down on the Congress from those merchants in favor of the National Bank and reasonable tariffs.

Clay provided vehicles for the debate by crafting two motions of censure against the president and his nominee, Taney, for exceeding their authority. The debate over the motion began on December 26 and lasted three months. The president's chief defender, Benton, was no match for Clay, Calhoun, and Webster. Benton's opening salvo took the better part of three days; it was full of sound and fury, but probably did not change a single vote. Webster replied by reading resolutions from Boston and arguing that the president's action had penalized labor far more than capital. Public works were at a standstill; public money was in the hands of an unapproved secretary of the Treasury. Webster called for rechartering the bank immediately.

Biddle was attacked by Sen. Silas Wright of New York, who had run against Webster for finance committee chair. Webster defended Biddle by accusing the Democrats of fomenting class hatred. Echoing sentiments he had expressed on his western tour, he said: "[I]t shall not be till the last moment of my existence . . . that I will believe the people of the United States capable of being effectually deluded, cajoled, and driven about in herds, by such abominable frauds as this. . . . Sir, the great interest of this great country, the producing cause of all its prosperity, is labor! Labor! Labor!"[25]

By February 5, 1834, Webster had his committee's report ready for the Senate. It ended any chance of an alliance with Jackson by condemning Taney and the president. Taney's attacks on the Bank of the United States were found to be unsubstantiated and without merit. The report blamed the national recession on the actions of Taney and Jackson. As committee chair, it was Webster's task to make the case for indictment. As a free soul, Calhoun could attack the president directly, unhindered by the report.

Webster believed he could bring the crisis to a close by proposing to reform the currency system and to extend the bank's charter. His committee helped him craft legislation to force the president to restore the funds on July 1, to continue the bank for six more years, and to limit paper specie to twenty-dollar bills and higher. This compromise failed to win important adherents, however. Clay, for example, wanted blood and he got it at the end of March when both of his motions censuring Jackson were passed in the Senate. Compromise was impossible now.

Webster welcomed the recess in April and traveled north toward his beloved

25. Webster, *Writings and Speeches*, 6:269.

Marshfield. He stopped along the way to talk to local National Republicans, only to discover that they had picked up his habit of calling themselves Whigs. (As we have seen, Webster had written "An Appeal to the Old Whigs of New Hampshire" in 1805 and he greatly admired Edmund Burke and William Pitt.) Soon Clay embraced the name too; the party needed something respectable to counteract the new Democrats and their symbol, the jackass.

By the time Webster returned to the Senate in late April, Jackson had responded to the censure resolutions. If the president was to be censured, he said, the House, according to the Constitution, should have initiated the resolutions as it does in cases of impeachment. The Senate had no authority to censure on its own. Furthermore, as the representative of all the people, he resented the Senate's action, given that senators represented only their states and were not directly elected. Clay called Jackson a Napoleon and introduced measures of condemnation.

Webster's attack on the president proved more effective. He waited until May 7, by which time he had completely mastered the material and could destroy each of the president's claims. He began by praising Jackson's contributions to the nation and by separating the cause for action in this instance from Jackson's illustrious career as a general and a defender of the Constitution by means of the Force Bill. Then, in a lawyerly way, Webster made the case against the president, saying he must bear responsibility for the actions of Taney and others in regard to the National Bank. Jackson's reply to censure had come in the form of a presidential "protest." Webster played with this by asserting that it was clearly not written by the president, a fact that was obvious to every senator but not to those in the gallery, nor to those who would read Webster's speech in the press. Whoever wrote this protest, Webster intoned, "did not know what he was talking about." The Senate, he said, had the right to express its opinion of presidential conduct without consulting the House; this was not an impeachment trial, but rather a censure by one body defending the Constitution. The president was trying, Webster asserted, to take "freedom of speech" from the Senate. Webster, however, was not about to let "the writer of the Protest" take that freedom away. The senators were the representatives of the states and they had a duty to protect liberty, just as the president did. Jackson had become like Louis XIV, believing "I am the state." Webster concluded:

> In my judgment, the law has been disregarded, and the Constitution transgressed; the fortress of liberty has been assaulted, and circumstances have

placed the Senate in the breach; and although we may perish in it, I know we shall not fly from it. But I am fearless of consequences. We shall hold on, Sir, and hold out, till the people themselves come to its defense. We shall raise the alarm, and maintain the post, till they whose right it is shall decide whether the Senate be a faction, wantonly resisting lawful power, or whether it be opposing, with firmness and patriotism, violations of liberty and inroads upon the Constitution.[26]

Though the speech would not be among Webster's most popular nationally—after all, he was attacking a national hero—it impressed his colleagues, who gave him a standing ovation, as well as the elite. Ralph Waldo Emerson, for example, wrote in his *Journals* that Webster had shown himself to be a "true genius . . . Long may he live."[27] The Senate approved Clay's motion not to receive the protest of the president. It then rejected the nomination of Taney for secretary of the Treasury.

The president fared better in the House, where an investigation of the National Bank was ordered. Biddle did not respond to a request that he come to testify, nor would he open his books to be searched for any loans to members of Congress, which greatly relieved Webster. The House, however, found that the bank had caused the recession, and the bank's days were numbered.

In the summer, a Senate investigation was headed by Webster. It exonerated the bank, to no one's surprise, leading to new rumors that Webster was on the take. At least the nasty battle was over. Though the president had been censured, the bank charter would not be renewed, and Biddle was forced by the bank's board to loosen its purse strings. The Congress recessed for the summer.

26. Webster, *Speeches and Formal Writings*, 2:71.
27. Quoted in Remini, *Daniel Webster*, 420.

Daniel Webster. Lithograph by Francis D'Avignon after daguerreotype by Mathew Brady, 1850. National Portrait Gallery, Smithsonian Institution, Washington, D.C.

John Caldwell Calhoun. Lithograph by Francis D'Avignon after daguerreotype by Mathew Brady, 1850. National Portrait Gallery, Smithsonian Institution, Washington, D.C.

Henry Clay. Engraving by W. G. Jackman after daguerreotype by Mathew Brady, c. 1891. Used by permission, State Historical Society of Missouri, Columbia.

Zachary Taylor. Lithograph by Francis D'Avignon after daguerreotype by Mathew Brady, 1849. National Portrait Gallery, Smithsonian Institution, Washington, D.C.

Charles Sumner. Lithograph by J. A. Manger. National Portrait Gallery, Smithsonian Institution, Washington, D.C.

Millard Fillmore. Lithograph by Francis D'Avignon, 1850. National Portrait Gallery, Smithsonian Institution, Washington, D.C.

William Seward. Lithograph by Francis D'Avignon after daguerreotype by Mathew Brady, 1850. National Portrait Gallery, Smithsonian Institution, Washington, D.C.

Chapter 7
Abolition Confounds the Two-Party System

Calling themselves the Whigs, the National Republicans prepared for the congressional elections of 1834. That summer, Webster took several steps to signal his supporters that he wanted his turn at running for president. Rufus Choate, Edward Everett, Joseph Story, and Caleb Cushing, a member of the Massachusetts state senate, provided a kitchen cabinet that accepted Webster's other close associates: his minister, John Palfrey; George Ticknor; and Josiah Quincy, the president of Harvard College. Choate and Cushing then purchased the *Boston Atlas* and put a friendly editor, John O. Sargent, in charge; after the congressional elections, the *Atlas* would let Webster's intentions be known.

The first trick was to bring the Anti-Masons on board and to that end Webster encouraged them to support the Whig candidate for governor of Massachusetts, the incumbent John Davis. The Webster contingent expanded its operations to newspapers in Ohio and Pennsylvania, attempting to capitalize on their man's speaking tour. Webster also counted on support from Unionists in the South. By 1835 his banker friends were shipping money to newspapers in financial trouble in exchange for endorsements of Webster for president.

Webster watched the congressional election of 1834 with great interest. While the Whigs did well in Maryland and retained New England, their fortunes elsewhere were much less satisfying. Jackson held his party together and Vice President Van Buren proved more effective on the stump than people had supposed. Worse for Webster was the fact that many new presidential candidates began to crop up once the election was over. Many states nominated a "favorite son," one of their own, as a way of gaining influence at the newly established national conventions. The conventions' success in part resulted from the advertising benefits, the festive atmosphere, and the ability to gather the party faithful in one place. These conventions were in fact a throwback to the ratification conventions of the previous century.

Regional candidates soon emerged. In 1835 southern Whigs found a senator to their liking in Hugh Lawson White; westerners began to rally around William Henry Harrison, the hero of the Battle of Tippecanoe. The northern Democrats were solidifying around Van Buren. The Massachusetts legislature nominated Webster in January 1835, but a hoped-for endorsement from Clay never came. Webster feared his candidacy would be contained in New England in the same way that Calhoun's was bottled up in the nullification states of the South.

Webster returned to Washington for a session of Congress, where he criticized Jackson's rather aggressive demands on the French to pay for damages incurred during the Napoleonic Wars. Webster was quickly distracted, however, by charges of bribery and payoffs during his tenure in the Senate. On January 12, he called the charges, which had been generated by the Democratic press, "false and malicious." This only stirred the pot. The Democrats again raised the issue of his involvement in the Hartford Convention of 1812, forcing his friends to write rejoinders. The campaign for the nomination had begun in earnest, but these were not the issues that would prove decisive.

Abolition

The old issue of how to deal with slavery attained new prominence. In 1828 Benjamin Lundy, a Quaker who had created colonies for African Americans in Haiti and Canada, advocated using Texas as a home for freed slaves. In the process, he strongly condemned slavery, exciting mobs in the North and South. He had created the first antislavery association in 1815 and it became a model for the thousand or so similar societies that eventually followed. In 1835 Lundy met with John Quincy Adams, who had read many of his works. In fact, Adams credited Lundy on the floor of the Congress with supplying him with facts. In 1836 Lundy condemned the Texas Revolt, realizing that it might mean an expansion of slavery rather than providing a home for freed slaves. His fiery pamphlet *The Origin and True Causes of the Texas Revolution Commenced in the Year 1835* pulled his arguments together. These played right into the Second Great Awakening with its call for repentance. The moral cer-

tainty of the abolitionists annoyed Webster even though he had a strong dis-
taste for slavery. He believed the legislative process needed to be more pragmatic than the abolitionists' philosophy would allow. He realized that the
abolitionists were not calling for a civil religion, but rather for a religious ethic
to guide the government.

Even more influential than Lundy was William Lloyd Garrison, who began
publishing the *Liberator* in Boston in 1831, the same year that Nat Turner led a
slave revolt. The Jackson administration would eventually empower the post-
master general to refuse to mail the *Liberator* into states that wanted it banned.
By 1834 Garrison had the support of activists across the nation. Men and
women in Ohio, for example, signed a petition "against permitting the District
of Columbia to remain a mart of *human flesh* to the disgrace of our national
character, and to the cruel oppression of thousands of native Americans, who
are loaded with chains, immured in jails, and sold under the hammer like
brutes within the sight of the Capitol." Women of South Reading, Massachusetts, warned Webster and his congressional colleagues that the "extension" of slavery would "invoke the judgments of Heaven." Another petition
that made the rounds in Massachusetts listed the wrongs done to slave women
and children whose fathers had no legal recourse to protect them.[1] However,
even in Boston, Garrison had enemies; one day in 1835 they dragged him from
his office and attempted to hang him. He barely escaped when Theodore Lyman
rescued him.

One of the most dramatic episodes in the abolition debate took place two
years later in Webster's favorite hall. After the murder of Elijah Lovejoy, an
abolitionist newspaper publisher in Alton, Illinois, a meeting was held in Faneuil Hall on December 8, 1837, to consider resolutions of condemnation. The
attorney general of Massachusetts, James T. Austin, stunned the crowd of five
thousand by arguing that slaves were nothing more than animals and that the
citizens in the mob who killed Lovejoy were akin to Revolutionary heroes. He
said Lovejoy had died a fool's death since he had been warned several times

1. Petition of the Citizens of Ohio on Slavery in the District of Columbia, February 18, 1834,
HR23A-G4.3, District of Columbia Committee, National Archives box 3 of Library of Con-
gress box 48; Petition of the Female Inhabitants of South Reading, Massachusetts, against the
Admission of the Territory of Arkansas to the Union as a Slaveholding State, June 6, 1836,
HR24A-G22.4, National Archives box 12 of Library of Congress box 71; Petition of the Ladies
of Massachusetts for Abolition of Slavery in the District of Columbia, December 18, 1835,
HR24A-H1.3, National Archives box 3 of Library of Congress box 47.

about publishing inflammatory material. Wendell Phillips, a lawyer who had witnessed the attempt to lynch Garrison and who had recently spoken out on abolition for the first time, rose to answer Austin. His extemporaneous speech was so effective that he became known as the "golden trumpet" of abolition. Phillips remained on the scene well into the century; he vilified Webster for supporting the 1850 Compromise and attacked him again in an 1852 speech to the Massachusetts Anti-Slavery Society.

Race riots were common in the South and reached the District of Columbia in August 1835. Every politician was plagued by questions about abolition and many were asked to protect or restrict Garrison's right to freedom of the press. Webster consistently defended what the Constitution and the Northwest Ordinance of 1787 had set out: that the government could not promulgate emancipation in the South, but it could limit slavery to that region. This compromise position offended idealists and religious organizations in the South and in the North. Webster's supporters had their work cut out for them, especially since Clay's Compromise of 1820 had extended slavery into Missouri. In a major way, Webster was learning that advocates of a civil religion did not have much room for compromise on moral issues.

A Failed Candidacy

In 1835 in the Senate, Webster kept a wary eye on the activities of the abolitionists and did what he could to maintain his stature. He supported Calhoun's bill to reform the "spoils system," another slap at Jackson. With Webster leading them, the Whigs rejected Jackson's nomination of Taney to the Supreme Court to replace Justice Duvall and passed a bill to limit the size of the Court to six; the House wisely rejected it. The Whigs in the Massachusetts legislature followed Webster's advice and nominated Governor Davis for the Senate instead of John Quincy Adams, a slight for which the ex-president would never forgive Webster. Webster believed that Adams was moving too far to the left on the abolition issue and that he might still be harboring presidential ambitions.

At the end of the congressional session in March 1835, Webster finished up his legal affairs and campaigned through Pennsylvania on his way home. He attended a public dinner in the capital and a meeting of the party faithful in Lancaster, and paid the obligatory courtesy call on Biddle in Philadelphia. As the year progressed, however, Webster felt the presidential nomination slipping away. From his base in Tennessee, Senator White was consolidating his hold on moderates in the South. William Henry Harrison was not open to Webster's suggestion that he sign on for the second spot on the ticket. In December, Pennsylvania Whigs and mainstream Anti-Masons endorsed Harrison for president; Maryland followed suit, and all was lost.

Webster's depression was not helped in the new year when Adams launched a diatribe against him on the floor of the House. Despite a warning from the chair about unfair references to a member of the Senate, Adams continued for three hours, much to the delight and applause of Democrats on the floor. Webster had voted on constitutional grounds against an appropriation for fortifications for the District of Columbia. Adams shouted, "I say, there was only one step more, and that a natural and easy one—to join the enemy in battering down these walls."[2] With these words, Adams essentially accused Webster of treason.

Matters continued to deteriorate when President Jackson nominated Taney to be chief justice of the Supreme Court following the death of the great John Marshall. Could it be that the man who had so recently been rejected by the Senate on two occasions would now be approved for a more responsible position than either of the prior two? The president also nominated Philip Barbour of Virginia, a federal judge, to succeed Justice Duvall, whom Taney had failed to replace. Jackson had already appointed three justices to the Court, and the confirmation of Taney and Barbour would give him control of the majority. Webster won the first skirmish when the judiciary committee voted to table the nominations. However, the Democrats had gained a majority in the Senate, and on the fateful day known as the Ides of March, the nominations of Taney and Barbour were approved. Webster must have realized that his influence before the Supreme Court would be severely limited.

Soon news swept the nation that Texas had broken from Mexico. The Mexican government had invited Americans into Texas to help develop the region, but the program had been too successful. It was only a matter of time before the non-Mexicans sought independence from what they considered an alien government. On April 21, 1836, the Texas army, avenging the loss of the Alamo, defeated Gen. Antonio Lopez de Santa Ana and established a new republic.

On May 9, Webster called for U.S. neutrality on the Texas question. However,

2. *Register of Debates*, 24th Cong., 1st sess, 2270.

people were already talking about annexation, and that is just what the Texas Republic wanted. Webster predicted a war with Mexico and a collapse of the balance between the states if Texas was admitted to the Union. For once Jackson held his counsel and delayed any action, perhaps to reinforce Van Buren's chances of being elected in November.

Jackson did move forward with his Indian-removal plan. The Whigs, however, heard the pleas of the Native Americans and attempted to intervene. Webster spoke on their behalf and chided the Democrats for their shameful action. It was no use; Jackson's fraudulent treaty with the Cherokees was ratified by one vote. Justice Marshall had stopped the president before; now no one stood in his way. The Cherokees were removed from Georgia and many died terrible deaths along the Trail of Tears to Arkansas. At the same time, the president pursued his second Seminole war, this time as commander in chief. The war would last into the Van Buren administration because the Seminole were effective guerrilla fighters. In fact, after completing his course of study at West Point, William Tecumseh Sherman, named for a Native American hero, would see his first action in Florida.

The election went as expected. Van Buren won easily since the Whigs were divided among three viable candidates. The "Little Magician," as Van Buren was called, received 170 electoral votes, including those of Webster's native New Hampshire. Harrison received 73, White 26, and Webster only 14, all from Massachusetts. At age fifty-four, Webster had suffered a humiliation he would never forget.

In December he returned to Washington for the next session of Congress. Benton led the Democratic majority in the Senate in seeking to expunge the censure of Jackson. Calhoun spoke against the motion, then Clay, then Webster; the great triumvirate was momentarily reunited. Of the three, Webster's speech was the least emotional and the most factual. He ended by begging his colleagues to respect the rights of the minority and not expunge what it had done in a previous Congress. The triumvirate lost 24 to 19. The clerk of the Senate immediately drew a black box around the censure resolutions, and the Whigs walked out of the chamber.

While Webster toiled in Washington, the abolitionists continued to stir up the northern population against slavery. In 1837 they created a controversy by not only appealing to women to join the cause, but by also enlisting them as major speakers in the movement. Angelina and Sarah Grimke were the most effective of these new women. Hailing from South Carolina, these Quaker sisters had moved north in 1832 and been awakened to the cause by a pamphlet of the American Anti-Slavery Society entitled *An Appeal to the Christian Women of the South* (1836). They attended the society's select "Seventy" convention, spoke in New York City (to little effect), and became students of the abolitionist Theodore Weld for training in oratory.

The sisters were fast learners. They created a sensation in Massachusetts with their oratory, to which men and women flocked. In 1838 Angelina made three appearances before the Massachusetts legislative committee on antislavery petitions, winning the plaudits of legislators. William Lloyd Garrison was so impressed that he made suffrage part of his group's platform. That may have been a mistake since conservative clergy and members of the Massachusetts congressional delegation opposed the vote for women and the "obtrusive" effort of the Grimkes. John Greenleaf Whittier rightly feared a split in the abolitionist movement and quietly intervened, asking the sisters to be less controversial. The issue was resolved when Weld asked for Angelina's hand in marriage, and she and her sister renounced Garrison's platform plank. Soon after her marriage, Angelina fell ill and was forced off the lecture circuit. Sarah, the older of the two, wrote *An Epistle to the Clergy of the Southern States* (1838), which further inflamed opinion against her in her home state. In the same year, Sarah persuaded her mother to free her remaining slaves in South Carolina.[3]

Condemnations of slavery reached a zenith when Weld published *American Slavery as It Is* (1839), which reached a large audience. In this document, perhaps the most incendiary preceding *Uncle Tom's Cabin* (1852), Weld claimed to have a thousand witnesses to brutality in the South. He cited their most poignant tales and argued for human rights over southern privilege.

Charles River Bridge

Like the rest of the Massachusetts delegation, Webster opposed suffrage for women and believed the Grimke sisters were inflammatory. He hoped their fire would burn out before the next presidential election. Though the Grimkes would make some adjustments in their civil religion, Webster began to see the danger hard-liners could foster.

In the meantime, he turned his attention to his law practice. The Charles

---

3. Stephen Howard Browne, *Angelina Grimke: Rhetoric, Identity, and the Radical Imagination.* Lyman Beecher, the grandson of Jonathan Edwards and the father of Harriet Beecher Stowe, was one preacher who opposed slavery but did not favor suffrage. His daughter Catherine, who ran a school for girls, also opposed suffrage and recommended fighting slavery only with moral suasion in the home. Harriet took the same position.

River Bridge Company had been granted a sixty-year charter by the state of Massachusetts in 1785 on condition that it compensate Harvard College for a ferry Harvard had run across the Charles from Cambridge. The company was allowed to extract a toll, and it proved very successful. The state, seeing the potential revenue, decided to build a second bridge across the river. In 1828 it created the Warren Bridge Company, which was authorized to construct a bridge next to the existing bridge and, consistent with its charter, to charge a toll for six years before becoming a free bridge. The Charles River Bridge Company sued the state, claiming breach of contract. Jacksonian Democrats in Boston used the case to rally support against the pro-business Whigs, who defended the company.

Webster represented the Charles River Bridge Company and though he lost at the state level, as expected, the case was granted *certiorari* by the Supreme Court in 1831. Unfortunately, the Court could not decide the case; the only majority that emerged was one that favored rearguing the case entirely. By the time the case came back to the Court in 1837, Taney was chief justice; given that Webster had handled the case since 1828 and given that he had consistently opposed Taney for appointments, some argued that Taney should recuse himself in this case. In fact, it was on Webster's motion that Taney had been denied an appointment as an associate justice. Taney would not recuse himself, however, and Webster was forced to make the best of a bad situation.

During oral arguments, Webster reasserted the property rights of the Charles River Bridge Company, declaring that its charter gave it a monopoly. He appealed for the maintenance of the contract clause of the Constitution against the state's claim of eminent domain. Aside from facing a hostile majority, Webster had to contend with the fact that whatever its past, the Warren Bridge had become toll-free and state property. That allowed its defenders to argue that the case was one of public needs versus private rights, not private needs versus private contracts as Webster maintained.

A reading of Webster's rebuttal suggests that he was out of sorts. The speech contains needless personal attacks on the opposition, it lacks coherence, and it is often superficial. Nonetheless, Webster scored points that the minority opinion could refine, and those refinements eventually became law in later cases: Payment for performance is a kind of contract. Franchises are to be protected. Property may not be taken by the state without due compensation. In this case, Massachusetts had engaged in an "unjust taking," a clear violation of the Fifth Amendment. However, at this time most jurists believed that the Fifth Amendment applied only to the federal government, as did the other parts of the Bill of Rights. It would take the Fourteenth Amendment to incorporate the Bill of Rights against the states.

The Court voted just as Webster had predicted: the four Democrats voted against him and the three Federalists voted for him. (Because of Taney and the Democrats, Webster's winning percentage before the Court would drop to 48 percent by the end of his life for the 168 cases he argued.) Taney used the doctrine of states' rights to rationalize his siding with Massachusetts; it was a clear repudiation of Marshall's position that the federal government could protect private contracts, as in the *Dartmouth College* case. Taney also argued that competition is better for the economy and the consumer than are monopolistic franchises. He claimed he was not disturbing the precedents set out in the *Dartmouth College* case.

In his dissent, Justice Story affirmed Webster's position by coming down on the side of contracts and property rights. In concluding his dissent, he wrote, "I maintain, that, upon the principles of common reason and legal interpretation, the present grant carries with it a necessary implication that the legislature shall do no act to destroy or essentially impair the franchise." In private letters, Story lamented the loss of Marshall and complained that the ruling was one of the Court's worst.[4] While the decision was big news in Boston, the incoming president was the focus of national attention.

A New President

To the delight of Jackson, Martin Van Buren was inaugurated on March 4, 1837. Eleven days later (again on the Ides, he noted) Webster traveled to New York City, where he was greeted by a huge throng. One of the characteristics of great politicians is their resilience. Webster exhibited this characteristic, especially after speaking before an audience; the adulation revived him. In this regard, 1837 would be one of his better years. It needed to be, for he was strapped for cash again. His western land investments were not doing well and his outgoing revenue was exceeding his income by larger than normal amounts. So he traveled to New York to reassert his national role. The Whigs honored him with a parade up Broadway that was widely cheered.

At Niblo's Saloon, he gave a two-hour speech to a crowd of over four thousand. Overwhelmed by the adulation he was receiving, he identified with his audience: "You are for the Constitution of the country; so am I." He invoked the

---

4. Story's dissent and letters quoted in Hofstadter, *Great Issues in American History*, 1:306, 308.

Union, then moved to what the crowd wanted to hear. The Jackson administration had destroyed the economy by ruining the currency. Raw goods had
lost their value; western lands had plummeted in worth; unemployment was
rising. When the crowd interrupted him with shouts of encouragement, he
promised he would stay in the Senate to fight for their rights. Understanding
what free soil was all about even before the Free Soilers, he called for the low-
priced sale of more public lands in the West so that they might be developed
and saved from state governments encroaching on them.[5] He called for tariffs,
not to protect manufacturers but to protect the jobs of common workingmen.
He warned that annexation of Texas would lead to the expansion of slavery,
something that must never happen. Texas, he rightly claimed, would be a slave
state and that would throw Congress out of balance. He said that though slavery was a "great moral, social, and political evil," America had no choice but to
leave it where it already existed because the Constitution must be honored at
all costs.[6] The Constitution was his bible; even if it contradicted some higher
laws, it must be obeyed lest chaos reign.

For two days following the saloon speech, the leading Whigs of New York
wined and dined Webster. Meanwhile the stock market fell dramatically, just
as Webster had predicted. (The prediction might have been self-fulfilling, given
his stature in the Senate.) The prices of raw goods fell further, and people
flocked to their banks for hard currency. By May, bank failures were common.
Van Buren's honeymoon with voters was one of the shortest on record. Like
many presidents who followed him, he learned that pocketbook issues determined presidential popularity.

In the background, the drumbeat of the abolitionists continued. William
Ellery Channing wrote a public letter to Henry Clay condemning the plan to
annex Texas. Many abolitionists lobbied to prevent Texas from becoming part
of the Union. The New England states, led by John Quincy Adams, sent resolutions to Congress condemning the plan. The ensuing counter-resolutions of
Tennessee and Alabama revealed the deep divisions in the country. To the delight of Webster and Adams, Van Buren was eventually forced to repudiate the
idea of annexing Texas. Before that occurred, however, Webster went west to
discover the sentiment among the people there.

---

5. Some Free Soilers supported free land in the West, while others supported lands free of
slavery.

6. Webster, *Speeches and Formal Writings*, 2:130.

A Swing around the West

Webster was so encouraged by the reaction to his positions in New York City that he decided once again to take his message west. It would give him the chance to inspect his property and to test the electoral waters now that Van Buren's presidency was in serious trouble. Caleb Cushing, now a senator from Massachusetts, financed the tour, which began in Pittsburgh in May 1837. The tour took Webster to St. Louis, Chicago, Detroit, and many stops in between, including Lexington, Kentucky, where Henry Clay played gracious host. In Louisville, Webster spoke to a huge crowd for two hours, advancing the themes he had developed at Niblo's Saloon and trying to adapt them to a southern audience. The crowd was slow to warm to him, but by the end of the speech people were cheering. Webster moved on to Ohio, where he met with Harrison, and to Indiana, where Harrison had served as territorial governor in the early years of the century. Since Harrison was born in Virginia, he could claim to be the favorite son of several states, which is partly why he was the odds-on favorite to win the Whig nomination in 1840.

In his "Reception at Madison" address in Madison, Indiana, on June 1, 1837, Webster argued for western expansion, the American System, the Constitution, and nationalism. The hour-long speech was delivered from an elaborately decorated platform. Above the platform was a large banner that read "Liberty and Union, now and forever, one and inseparable" in tribute to the stirring conclusion of the Webster-Hayne debate. A reading of the Madison address reveals that it was easier for Webster to praise General Washington or a historic battle than to advance his own name. His attempts at adapting to his audience seem awkward and contrived. For example, he said he had "lived on terms of great intimacy and friendship with several western gentlemen, members of congress, among whom is your estimable townsman near me [Senator Hendricks]. I have never before had an opportunity of seeing and forming an acquaintance for myself with fellow-citizens of this section of the Union."[7] Beside the fact that the lines contradict one another, the wording is unusually wooden for Webster.

He devoted the first part of the speech to praising Indiana's accomplishments and making sure his audience understood that he had supported the American System of internal improvements that facilitated settlement in Indiana

7. Daniel Webster, "Reception at Madison Address," in *Selected Speeches from American History*, ed. Robert T. Oliver and Eugene White, 38-46.

and transportation of its crops to market. As in his other speeches, he made clear that the American System was made possible by a national Constitution.

Webster was known by 1837 as a spokesman for the propertied, industrial, and banking interests of prosperous Boston, yet his Madison audience was composed mainly of small landholders and farmers. Throughout the speech, his attempts to identify with these simple folk missed the mark. "[Y]ou far surpass in fertility of soil and in the widespread and highly-cultivated fields, the smiling villages and busy towns," he said. "[Y]ou will reap a rich reward for your investment and industry. . . . [Americans] plough the land and plough the sea."

Another problem Webster faced in this situation was the fact that William Henry Harrison, former and potential presidential nominee, had been military governor of Indiana. Webster avoided antagonizing Harrison's supporters by concentrating his fire on the legacy of the Jackson and Van Buren administrations. In the second part of his speech, he discussed national economic problems and how leadership was needed in the White House to overcome the financial depression. His answer was to facilitate commerce wherever possible and to continue to build roads, bridges, and canals all across the country. These improvements would not only spur the economy, they would also serve to unite the country, which meant a stronger Union.

When Webster returned to Ohio to speak in Cincinnati, the crowd was delighted to see that Harrison had come to introduce him. This rapprochement would serve Webster well once Harrison became the nominee. For now, however, Webster continued to have difficulties with campaign rhetoric. His deprecation of his former oratorical style never rang true. He was simply too bright and too eloquent to imitate the bandwagon-and-torchlight oratory of Jackson and Harrison.[8] He was also too aware of his place in history; the glow of the Webster-Hayne debate was all around him. To reduce his eloquence to the level of "western farmers" was too much to ask.

Webster's party traveled overland to the Mississippi and took a steamboat to St. Louis, where they followed a familiar routine: a parade up the main street with flag-waving crowds, a dinner speech that was well received, a retreat with friends for port and brandy. From St. Louis the party headed north to inspect Webster's land holdings, his son Fletcher having joined the tour to show the way. On June 19, they stopped in Springfield, Illinois, where Webster met with

8. Erickson, *Poetry of Events*, 29.

a young lawyer named Lincoln, an avid Whig. Webster gave an address to a large crowd attending a barbecue in his honor.[9] He inspected his property in the north of Illinois and then went on to Michigan and across the lakes to Buffalo. His last major speech of the swing was given in Rochester on July 20. The party returned to Marshfield, where by all accounts Webster was now resuscitated and considering another run at the Whig nomination despite General Harrison's popularity.

The grand tour of 1837 was a success in terms of publicity but less helpful in promoting Webster for his party's nomination. In fact, since the nomination was three years off, Clay took offense at Webster's show of ambition. So did southern Whigs who disagreed with Webster on Texas, the tariff, and slavery. They would bide their time as the country endured the depression. Van Buren called Congress into session in September to deal with the financial panic.[10] Webster arrived late since he was busy solving his own financial crisis and at the same time constructing a new dam at Marshfield.

The Senate tried to stabilize the currency but got caught in a fight between hard-money advocates in the West, such as Benton, and paper-specie advocates in the East, who were mainly Whigs. The Democrats refused again to extend the charter for the National Bank. Instead, Calhoun, of all people, presented a bill that would create an independent subtreasury, which the administration desired. On September 28, Webster rose to speak against the scheme. Though a member of the minority party, his credibility flowed from his expertise on the finance committee and his prediction of the panic at Niblo's Saloon. His speech was deductive in structure. He opposed the Calhoun and Van Buren initiatives, claiming they would do nothing to end the depression. The people had tried the Jackson currency, he lamented, and it had failed them. Citing President Madison's message to Congress of 1815, he argued that it was time to return to the founders' plan for a sound national currency, which Congress had established and Calhoun himself had formulated in 1816.[11]

Calhoun responded that he had been wrong in 1816 because Congress had

9. In November 1838, Lincoln wrote an editorial in the *Sangamo (IL) Journal* urging Whigs to support either Webster or Clay over Harrison. Lincoln compared Webster and Clay to Cicero, Pitt, and Washington.

10. One of the victims of the panic was the incipient union movement. The National Trades' Union, which was founded in 1834 and spread across six states, had already been damaged by courts ruling that it constituted a conspiracy and was an illegal combination.

11. For the full text of this speech, see *Speeches and Formal Writings*, 2:155–82.

gone beyond its constitutional limits. In a witty response, Webster said, "Government does interfere and place restrictions in a thousand ways upon every kind of individual property." This is done in the name of the common good, he said; that was why the senators were assembled. The results of private banking, which Calhoun had endorsed, were evident in the crisis the country faced. Furthermore, the administration's attempt to create one kind of currency for the government and another for the people was elitism of the worst order. Why should the people's government have a stronger currency than the people themselves? Webster lost this debate by six votes, and the subtreasury passed. However, the House came to the Whigs' rescue by tabling the bill; the congressmen wanted to wait for the results of the fall elections.

The Whigs came roaring back in those state and local elections, particularly in Van Buren's home state of New York. Webster celebrated with the Massachusetts Whigs at Faneuil Hall on November 10; notables present from around the country included John Bell of Tennessee, who would become a leading cotton Whig. There were so many speeches that Webster was not called upon until 2:00 a.m.; he spoke until nearly 4:00. By all accounts, he had the crowd's rapt attention.[12] The Whigs would never again demonstrate so much unity.

The first cracks in the resurgent party came not because of financial issues but because of slavery—specifically, the slave trade in the District. At the end of 1837, Calhoun brought a series of resolutions to the floor of the Senate reasserting his "compact" theory of congressional governing in connection with the slavery issue. Since the states formed the government, he said, they had a right to determine whether or not slaves were traded in the District of Columbia. Webster wisely avoided personal attacks but again attacked Calhoun's interpretation of the Constitution. Congress, in his opinion, had every right to govern the District as it saw fit. Slavery in the southern states, however, was the states' business exclusively.[13] The Senate turned down Calhoun's resolution, which would have deprived Congress of the right to determine whether territories could have slavery, but passed his resolution allowing slavery in the District. While the resolutions were nonbinding, they previewed the dominant issues of the next generation of congresses.

In March the subtreasury bill returned to the Senate, and Webster spoke for the better part of two days attacking the legislation. In the process he indicated

12. Remini, *Daniel Webster*, 474.
13. For the text of this speech, see *Speeches and Formal Writings*, 2:198–203.

his support for a diverse currency, dropping his opposition to the distribution of banknotes, now claiming they were in short supply. (He had earlier argued that bloated credit caused the Panic of 1837.) He again pointed out Calhoun's inconsistency on the National Bank issue and ridiculed his call for states' righters to "march off." "March off from whom? March off from what?" Webster asked. "[W]e have made these struggles here, in the national councils, with the old flag, the true American flag, the Eagle, and the Stars and Stripes, waving over the chamber in which we sit. He now tells us, however, that he marches off under the States rights banner! Let him go. I remain."[14]

In response, Calhoun turned the tables by pointing out Webster's inconsistencies, citing his support of Jackson's Force Bill. Calhoun claimed that Webster's real goal, whether in the courts or the Congress, was to wipe out states' rights altogether. Calhoun had remarked in his speech that he would carry the war to Webster even if he ran to Africa. Webster, however, was running nowhere; he replied that "Scipio Africanus South Carolineinsis" was welcome to bring the war to his shore.[15] With good humor, he referred to Calhoun's linkage to the states' rights movement as a "secret marriage" until very recently: "Where am I? In the Senate of the United States? Am I Daniel Webster? Is that John C. Calhoun of South Carolina, the same gentleman that figured so largely in the House of Representatives in 1816, at the time the Bill creating the National Bank passed that body? What have I heard today? The Senator attempting to maintain his consistency?" He characterized Calhoun as the "engine car" on the nullification train. Webster was at his most humorous, however, when he returned to the issue of who had been more inconsistent on the bank issue: "I followed him: if I was seduced into error, or into unjustifiable opposition, there sits my seducer."[16] That brought the house down.

Webster succeeded in getting the Treasury to view various kinds of specie equally when it came to collecting debts. Soon he had enough followers to repeal Jackson's Specie Circular. While the Independent Treasury Bill passed the Senate, the House killed the subtreasury bill. The Whigs had triumphed on financial issues because of Webster's leadership. Clay was clearly jealous. He was more political, emotional, and vindictive than Webster, and everyone knew that Webster had a better sense of humor and a better philosophical

14. Webster, *Writings and Speeches*, 8:236.
15. Scipio had defeated Hannibal to end the Second Punic War.
16. Webster, *Writings and Speeches*, 8:238–60.

rationalization of the legislation he supported. Webster debated Calhoun on a higher rhetorical plane than could Clay. Clay could claim his compromises, but he had nothing like the reply to Hayne in his collected works. When the Maine caucus, which had been expected to endorse Clay for president, decided at the behest of Webster's friends to keep their powder dry, Clay was furious. The division between Clay and Webster would further open the door to William Henry Harrison's nomination.

The busy congressional session ended in a muggy Washington July; Webster immediately retreated to his coastal enclave at Marshfield. Though by the end of the year he was reelected to the Senate by the Massachusetts legislature, it was becoming clear to him that he would not be the nominee of his party. The Whigs wanted a sure vote getter, someone who could rise above politics and form a fusion ticket. When Webster left for Europe in May 1839, his favorite paper, the *Atlas*, called for the nomination of Harrison. From London, Webster announced by letter that he would not be a candidate for president in 1840. This cemented the relationship between Harrison and Webster to the exclusion of Clay.

Webster was an Anglophile. He loved England and its best orators; by 1840 he favored English authors over Americans like Emerson, Thoreau, and Longfellow.[17] His reputation preceded him to England, where he was feted. He gave toasts and lectures, but only one formal speech (to the Royal Agricultural Society in July). He observed the British parliament in action, dropped in on the courts, went to the opera with the Duke of Wellington, and was the guest of Queen Victoria at a ball that did not end until four in the morning. He soon returned to the palace for a royal dinner. In September his daughter, Julia, was married in Hanover Square; her brother Edward was groomsman and Webster gave the bride away. In October he was off to France, where Lewis Cass, who had been Jackson's secretary of war, was serving as ambassador. He met with King Louis Philippe, who had a special admiration for America since it had provided a home for him in his exile.

The Whig Triumph

Webster left Europe on November 21, 1839, and reached New York City just after Christmas. There he learned that the Whigs would nominate Har-

17. Baxter, *One and Inseparable*, 116, 277–78.

rison and create a unity ticket with appeal in the South by putting former Democratic senator John Tyler of Virginia in the second spot, though some in the convention had supported Webster. It would be a Jacksonian campaign for the ticket of "Tippecanoe and Tyler Too." Harrison was the "log cabin" candidate who loved his "cider." Before the campaign could begin, however, work needed to be completed in the Congress. In January 1840 Congress again debated a subtreasury bill; it became law in July. On the Fourth, Van Buren took great pride in signing the bill in the midst of his campaign for reelection.

The new type of campaign undoubtedly annoyed Webster, but he did his best to adapt. He rode in a carriage with Clay in a parade in Baltimore during the Whig convention in May. Webster told the crowd: "Every breeze says change. Every interest in the country demands it." In June he attended a Whig rally in Alexandria, where he called for unity and praised Harrison as one of Virginia's children. In July he campaigned for the ticket in Vermont. John J. Crittenden, Webster's friend and colleague in the Senate, called the Whig campaign of 1840 a "Popular Insurrection."[18] One of the most important innovations made in the campaign was the incorporation of women along the Whig battlements.

In August, Webster pumped his campaigning up a notch and seemed more at ease with folksy humor. At a rally in Saratoga, New York, when the stage collapsed under the weight of the dignitaries and pitched the assembled Whigs to the ground eight feet below, Webster leapt up and declared that the Whig platform was much more solid than the one that had just collapsed. He climbed onto a wagon and carried on for two and a half hours more, enthralling the crowd.[19] Some passages brought tears to his eyes as well as the audience's:

> Gentlemen, it did not happen to me to be born in a log cabin; but my elder brothers and sister were born in a log cabin, raised amid the snowdrifts of New Hampshire, at a period so early that, when the smoke first rose from its rude chimney, and curled over the frozen hills, there was no similar evidence of a white man's habitation between it and the settlements on the rivers of Canada. Its remains still exist. I make to it an annual visit. I carry my children to it, to teach them the hardships endured by the generations which have gone before them. I love to dwell on the tender recollections, the kindred trees,

18. John J. Crittenden to Daniel Webster, October 27, 1840, in *Papers of Daniel Webster: Correspondence*, 5:60.

19. Current, *Daniel Webster*, 110–12.

the early affections, and the touching narratives and incidents, which mingle with all I know of this primitive family abode. I weep.[20]

Webster made over twenty-five speeches for the Whig ticket. He spoke to fifty thousand people at Bunker Hill on September 10, a crowd on Wall Street on September 28, and over ten thousand in Richmond on October 10. There Webster pressed home the Whig case in periodic prose: "Tell it to all your friends that standing here, in the capitol of Virginia beneath an October sun, in the midst of this assemblage, before the entire country, and upon all the responsibility which belongs to me, I say there is no power, direct or indirect, in Congress or the general government, to interfere in the slightest degree with institutions of the South."[21] This sentiment, expressed again and again in the campaign, further infuriated abolitionists.

The Richmond speech, like the others, strongly endorsed the economic principles of the Whig platform. The integrated American System required a national bank, western development, and a sensible tariff. The speech, as reported in the *New York Herald*, indicated that Webster had learned to leave the language of the U.S. Senate and Supreme Court behind. He was finally taking up the rhetoric of simplicity and sentiment when speaking to the common voter. He had learned his lesson from the Madison, Indiana, address: "I come to make no flourishes or figures, but to make a plain speech to the intelligence of the country."[22] Whig operatives distributed almost seventy thousand copies of this speech in pamphlet form.

True to the new Whig party, Webster set aside time during this campaign stop to speak to the "Ladies of Richmond." Like most Whigs, he did not advocate suffrage since women were to be protected from the rough-and-tumble of the political world. However, he did attribute the development of civic responsibility to women. Over a thousand women attended this "special address." Webster praised them by claiming that women are quicker and better than men at moral decisions. Women understood that there should be no line drawn between private and political morality, he said. It was the obligation of women to raise their children as virtuous Whigs. By staying above the political fray, women had the advantage of a clear view of right and wrong, which they

20. Webster, *Speeches and Forensic Arguments*, 3:472–497.
21. Ibid., 3:529–546.
22. Ibid.

could pass on to their children. Just as his mother had guided him to Whig virtues, he said, so too did these ladies need to guide their sons and husbands, especially in the critical election of 1840.[23] This speech indicates that while men must engage in political compromise, often to save the soul of the nation, women must prepare men for such battles by strengthening their sense of morality. Webster did not seem to realize, or perhaps he chose to ignore, the fact that a strong sense of morality is likely to reduce a person's desire to compromise.

By election day, Webster could rightly claim that he had helped elect the next president. Harrison won 53 percent of the popular vote to Van Buren's 47 percent; more importantly, he carried 234 electoral votes to Van Buren's 60. The Whigs captured the Congress by comfortable margins. It was their best showing ever.

Webster's campaigning had further endeared him to the president-elect. When he returned to Washington in December, Harrison asked him to join his cabinet as secretary of state. Webster's already fulsome résumé would now expand to include international affairs, particularly treaty negotiations. Webster accepted the invitation and, as the senior member of the cabinet, felt free to advise Harrison on other selections. He had at last become more influential than Clay, who smoldered as his own requests for appointees were denied.

Webster officially resigned from the Senate in February 1841, secure in the knowledge that the Whig-dominated Massachusetts legislature would replace him with a suitable candidate. When Harrison arrived in Washington for his inaugural, Webster greeted him and the two men became even closer, meeting almost every day and spending long hours together. Harrison consulted Webster on his inaugural address; unfortunately, he ignored Webster's advice that the speech be cut significantly. After riding his white horse to the Capitol on a cold and wet March 4, Harrison delivered the longest inaugural address ever; in his seventy-five-minute speech he revealed his intention to serve only one term, his penchant for ancient history, and his admiration of the Roman generals who had become consuls of the Republic. Harrison sought to embody the civic republicanism of the prior generation. His frontier, log-cabin background gave him a common touch. His military background gave his persona a military cast, much as Washington's had, perhaps further stirring Webster's admiration. To the audience, Harrison was Washington and Jackson rolled into one.

23. Ibid., 3:547–550.

Harrison participated in the inaugural parade, onto which the heavens dropped a cold rain. By the next day he had a severe cold, which developed into pneumonia. Harrison died one month later, serving the shortest term of any president. John Tyler, the Democrat turned Whig, was sworn in and Webster's dream of an ideal Whig administration began to fall apart. The unlucky Whigs would be after one another in a matter of months.

Chapter 8

Secretary Webster

Webster was confirmed as secretary of state the day after Harrison's inaugural. He immediately began to entertain foreign ministers and important members of Congress, the administration, and the Supreme Court. Parties at his new home were lavish and lasted into the morning hours. Living on the State Department's budget would not be the only challenge that Webster faced during his tenure. From Van Buren's presidency he inherited the crisis surrounding the seizure of the *Caroline* by British partisans in Canada. Several Americans on the ship had been killed, and one of the partisans was stupid enough to brag about it while on American soil. His name was Alexander McLeod and he was immediately jailed by the state of New York. The British demanded his release. Van Buren had left the matter to the New York courts. Webster tried to resolve the situation by ordering a writ of habeas corpus to extract McLeod from New York's jurisdiction. Unfortunately, William Seward, New York's new Whig governor, had other plans and let Webster know it in several sharply worded missives. It would not be the last time Webster crossed swords with Seward. McLeod would be brought to trial in October 1841.

In the meantime, President Harrison acceded to Webster's wish that Edward Everett be named ambassador to the Court of St. James. Almost as soon as this appointment had been approved, the president died. When John Tyler, a slave-owning, states' rights Democrat, became president, Webster assured Everett that the administration would speak with one voice on the matter of relations with England.

The Nettlesome Bank Bill

Unfortunately the new administration was less united when it came to Congress. In fact, Tyler had more difficulty with the Whigs than with the Democrats. His worst feud was with Henry Clay, who wanted a new national bank immediately. Tyler, who had favored a national bank in the past, was more restrained in 1841. That infuriated Clay, who was attempting to coalesce the Whig majorities in Congress behind his leadership. Eventually he got his subtreasury plan through Congress, and the president signed it in August. However, that was not the end of the matter. Clay and Tyler were divided over the enabling legislation to establish the bank's branches. Tyler wanted the states to have the right to refuse branches, which was in direct violation of the Whig platform and Webster's position in the *McCulloch* case.

Fearing Whig disunity, Webster had anonymously editorialized for compromise in the *National Intelligencer* in June. His editorials had little effect on Clay, who brought forth a bill to allow the subtreasury to establish branches without state consent. Tyler fumed that he would veto any such legislation, passing the word through Webster to Sen. Rufus Choate of Massachusetts. On the floor of the Senate, and without citing his source, Choate predicted a veto. Clay went after him, demanding to know where he got his information. The division among the Whigs was now an open matter. Webster found it hard to forgive Clay for his antics, particularly when the Fiscal Bank Bill, with its provisions trampling states' rights, reached the president's desk.

Tyler's veto was sustained in the Senate. Clay condemned the president and called on loyal Whigs to resign from the cabinet. Webster tried to negotiate a compromise on the bank bill, traveling to the Senate himself to work out the details. Webster's ability to produce an alternative, the Fiscal Corporation Bill, demonstrated that he was the real power in the executive branch; he was further vindicated when the House approved the bill on August 23. When the legislation arrived in the Senate, however, Clay gave a nasty speech in which he referred to Tyler as a "corporal." A horrified Webster lost all patience with Clay.

Though the Senate passed the bill, Clay's speech infuriated Tyler, who promptly vetoed the bill, claiming it still contained provisions to which he objected. The veto fomented a mass resignation from the cabinet on September 11, much to Clay's delight. Only Webster stayed, believing it was crucial to save the once promising Whig administration; he and his president were estranged from Clay in particular and from the Whig party in general. Democrats gleefully helped dissident Whigs approve a new cabinet on September 13, while Clay was in absentia—he was busy helping the majority Whigs draft a public resolution excommunicating Tyler from the party.

Webster explained his decision to stay with the president in a September 14 editorial in the *National Intelligencer*. For him, it was matter of national over partisan interest, or so he claimed. In fact, with his Senate seat given away, Webster had nowhere else to turn except to a law career. Furthermore, the position of secretary of state enhanced his résumé, making him ever more qualified for the presidency. He was not about to give it up simply to please Clay.

Just as Congress adjourned, the *Caroline* incident returned to the front page when British soldiers abducted James Grogan of Vermont, apparently hoping to force a postponement of McLeod's trial. The trial proceeded and McLeod was found not guilty on the grounds that he was falsely bragging about partaking in the *Caroline*'s seizure; he had an alibi for that time. Webster immediately renewed negotiations with the British to bring the issue to a close. He set out his position in a forensic argument on behalf of self-defense that he first broached in a letter to Henry Fox, the British ambassador to the United States. What could the possible motive have been, he asked, for the British to attack the *Caroline* at night, murder some of her crew, and set the ship on fire? This was a wanton act and thus the United States had a right to defend itself.[1] Combing common and admiralty law, Webster succeeded in convincing the British that its partisans had erred.

The Maine Boundary Dispute

Webster's success in the *Caroline* affair led him to attempt, with Tyler's blessing, to solve the Maine boundary dispute with Britain.[2] In 1755 John Mitchell drew up a map of the area that was inadvertently not attached to the treaty ending the Revolutionary War. The treaty provisions referring to the border with Canada along the St. Croix and St. Lawrence Rivers fell into dispute when the British planned to build a road from Halifax to Quebec that would run through land claimed by Maine. King William of the Netherlands tried to

1. *The Papers of Daniel Webster: Diplomatic Papers*, ed. Kenneth E. Shewmaker, Anita McGurn, and Kenneth R. Stevens, 1:58–68. This rationale of self-defense became part of international law and was cited in 1945 during the Nuremberg trials.

2. Webster was already familiar with this issue, having written a fourteen-point memo on it in 1839. Remini, *Daniel Webster*, 486.

resolve the dispute but neither side could persuade him of the legitimacy of its claims. In 1831, he therefore suggested that they split the difference. Britain was ready to accept the suggestion and cut a deal on the boundary, but the U.S. Senate refused to go along. The state of Maine claimed that it should control all of the territory to the St. Lawrence tributaries that drained into the Atlantic. Land and fishing rights were the paramount concerns.

Ten years later Webster prepared for negotiations by launching a public relations campaign in Maine favoring compromise. He enlisted the aid of Francis Smith, a former senator from Maine who may have come up with the idea in the first place.[3] Smith, now a publisher, agreed to plant newspaper articles and editorials for a fee of $3,500. He bet that the public would request an end to the dispute in exchange for certain fishing rights. Tyler approved payment to Smith from the secret newspaper fund. (As we shall see, this action would come back to haunt Webster when he returned to the Senate.) Officially, but behind the scenes, Smith was an agent of the State Department.

The strategy worked. The news articles and editorials were reprinted throughout New England and Webster, in his own editorials and through other agents, reinforced the call for a compromise that would allow the British to pay for their section of the disputed land. Maine would get its fishing rights; England would get a military highway.

In November, just as it seemed a treaty might be agreed upon, the U.S. slave ship *Creole* was seized by mutineering slaves, who took it to Nassau, a British territory. The British imprisoned the mutineers but freed the other slaves onboard. By December the *Creole* was free to leave for New Orleans. Newspapers across the South and some southern congressmen called for war with England. Calhoun claimed that the national honor had been compromised.

At the beginning of 1842, Webster passed an American protest through Everett to the British. Why wasn't the *Creole* returned immediately to its captain? Under international law and the U.S. Constitution, the slaves constituted property and should have been returned to their rightful owners. Webster demanded that the mutineers be returned to America for trial. The Senate printed this protest with Clay's endorsement. While the "Creole Paper"[4] added to Webster's credibility nationally, it hurt him with abolitionists who, only the year before, had won the infamous *Amistad* case before the Supreme

3. Remini, *Daniel Webster,* 539.
4. Webster, *Diplomatic Papers,* 1:524–27.

Court with the help of John Quincy Adams. In that case, the Court freed mutineering slaves because of the conditions they had endured. Webster's friend Justice Joseph Story now advised him that his interpretation of the law was not correct.

The British, however, were ready to resolve all conflicts and sent Foreign Secretary Lord Ashburton to negotiate a treaty in April 1842. Through Smith, Webster kept pressure on Maine to agree to a compromise. His most successful ploy was to send his agents there with a newly discovered map drawn in 1746; it was revealed to certain state leaders that the map supported the British position. Webster hoped they would realize that compromise was better than the truth in this case. Ironically, Ashburton soon learned of a map in England that supported American claims.[5] Given all the competing claims and parties, negotiations stalled in the humid Washington summer. When Ashburton seemed ready to call it quits and head home, Webster induced Tyler to invite the Englishman to the White House for a talk and dinner. Ashburton's belief that Webster and Tyler would be easier to work with than a new administration got the negotiations back on track.

By mid-July, Webster was able to report a compromise: of the 12,000 or so square miles in dispute on the Maine boundary, the United States would get about 7,000, the British 5,000. Maine would be allowed free navigation on the St. John River. The United States would pay Maine compensation for giving up its claims. In the Great Lakes region the British made more concessions, including St. George's Island, which contained large sections of good farmland. While Ashburton agreed that no future seizures would be made of American ships victimized by mutiny, Britain refused to return the slaves freed in Nassau.[6] Article VIII of the treaty spelled out a cooperative agreement between the two countries to suppress the slave trade from West Africa. (This noble effort came to naught when succeeding U.S. administrations refused to support it in deference to the South.) No resolution was achieved in the *Caroline* case, much to Webster's distress. Ashburton apologized for the burning of the ship, but claimed that it had been involved in harassment of British territory. In a separate exchange of notes, Ashburton and Webster agreed that the impressing of U.S. seamen into British service on the high seas would cease.

5. Remini, *Daniel Webster*, 549.
6. The *Creole* case came to an end in 1853; the owners of the slaves were paid more than $100,000 by an international commission that agreed with Webster's famous protest.

The successful treaty negotiations were celebrated at a dinner hosted by Webster. In a toast, President Tyler blessed "the peacemakers." The treaty was formally signed on August 9, 1842.[7] Newspapers across the country proclaimed Webster not only the "Defender of the Union," but also "Defender of the Peace." Even John Quincy Adams, still serving in Congress as chair of the House Committee on Foreign Relations, grudgingly praised Webster. The acclaim, combined with Webster's own public relations effort on behalf of the treaty, assured its ratification in the Senate by 39 to 9, the largest majority in U.S. history to that point.[8] Webster's herculean effort demonstrated his dedication to negotiated peace over military posturing. That commitment helps explain his opposition to the war with Mexico in the next administration.

Energized by his diplomatic success, Webster set about to correct other wrongs. One such problem was an Oregon border dispute that Ashburton and Webster had failed to resolve. The advantage of pursuing this issue was that it might distract the divided Whigs from the issue of slavery and focus them on a problem whose solution could produce national unity. No sooner had Webster embarked on this mission, however, than President Tyler, against Webster's advice, vetoed a tariff bill the Whigs had passed in response to the expiration of the Compromise Tariff of 1833, which had gradually reduced the tariff to almost nothing over a ten-year span. By the end of 1842, northern interests had secured a new tariff that mirrored the high rates of 1832, which offended southern Whigs and Democrats.

The Abolitionists

The more Tyler ignored Webster's advice, the more Webster's friends implored him to resign. Webster knew that Tyler had his eye on Texas and some of the territory controlled by Mexico. Webster was caught between his presidential ambition—he needed an office from which to be nominated for the election of 1844—and his strong disagreement with his president over national expansion.

The other horn to this dilemma became apparent when the abolitionists sniffed out the Texas problem and began to actively campaign against any plan

7. The agreement was dubbed the Treaty of Washington in accordance with the tradition of naming treaties after the cities in which they were signed. However, when another treaty was signed in Washington in 1871, the former became known as the Webster-Ashburton Treaty.

8. Remini, *Daniel Webster*, 567.

to make Texas part of the Union. Wendell Phillips continued to rally the abolitionists, though his mental condition was questioned even by moderates. Threats by his family to incarcerate him in an insane asylum had failed to temper him. Phillips advocated universal toleration of all people and ideas, including the rights of women. For him, all people were created equal.

A small group of Whigs—John Palfrey, Webster's former minister; Charles Francis Adams, the son of John Quincy Adams; and the lawyer Charles Sumner—disdained the connection between the New England mills and southern cotton. They divided themselves from these economic interests, calling themselves "Conscience Whigs" and dubbing their opponents "Cotton Whigs." While Webster's condemnation of slavery was well known, so was his connection to the Lowell mills. Should the Union collapse, Lowell would have to pay a higher price for southern cotton.

During the same time, Frederick Douglass was gaining prominence for his oratorical abilities. In November 1841, he spoke before the Plymouth County Anti-Slavery Society in Hingham, Massachusetts, ridiculing those in the South who justified slavery with quotations from the Bible. He attacked northern churches that had failed to condemn slavery, eventually taking his case to Webster's beloved Faneuil Hall in 1842 with his "Slaveholder's Sermon." Douglass kept up his criticism until his departure for Great Britain in 1845, which was motivated in part by a break with the more radical William Lloyd Garrison, who by this time was advocating extraconstitutional means to achieve his ends.[9]

Certain social groups also became more active at this juncture. For example, Boston was home to the prestigious Saturday Club, named for the day on which its eminent members dined together. The club included Dr. Oliver Wendell Holmes, Ralph Waldo Emerson, Henry Wadsworth Longfellow, James Russell Lowell, Richard Dana, Jr., and other prominent Brahmins. Emerson, a lapsed Unitarian minister, had delivered his lecture "The American Scholar" to a Harvard Phi Beta Kappa audience in 1837, calling slavery a terrible disgrace and a blot on the optimistic vision of transcendentalism. His 1838 "Divinity School Address" at Harvard, in which he denounced organized religion, sealed his reputation as something of a gadfly.[10] The members of the

9. See Gary S. Selby, "Mocking the Sacred: Frederick Douglass's 'Slaveholder's Sermon' and the Antebellum Debate over Religion and Slavery"; Gregory Lampe, *Frederick Douglass: Freedom's Voice, 1841–1845.*

10. Emerson was not invited back to Harvard for thirty years. Menand, *Metaphysical Club*, 18, 20.

Saturday Club discussed slavery among themselves as they sat down to sumptuous dinners served by the working poor of Boston, but they also took their opinions to others. William Ellery Channing, the city's leading Unitarian, did even more, chastising slave owners in his essay "Slavery"; however, he also called on abolitionists to moderate their positions. He believed persuasion was more likely to solve the problem than force. Like Frederick Douglass, Channing and his circle wanted slavery abolished through constitutional means.

The Boston Brahmins were well known to one another. For example, Benjamin Peirce, the great mathematician and astronomer, was married to the daughter of the senator who Daniel Webster replaced in 1827. Webster was a visitor to the Peirce home, as were Longfellow, Holmes, and Charles Eliot Norton. But Peirce provides a view of the ideological balance in Boston; he refused to admit abolitionists into his parlor. He believed Phillips, Sumner, and their ilk to be dangerous extremists if not outright insane.

Webster was therefore well aware of the anti-abolitionist sentiment in Boston. We have seen that in 1835 a group of citizens had pulled Garrison through the streets with a rope. Many of the faculty at Harvard opposed abolition and particularly its political form. As Louis Menand points out, "Only one member of the Harvard faculty enlisted to fight in the Civil War. He was a German 'emigre.' "[11]

The Massachusetts Whigs brought the matter to a head. They not only announced their opposition to the Tyler administration, they also voted to nominate Clay for president, a tremendous insult to Webster. On September 30, 1842, the lion left his den in the Executive Office Building, traveled north, and entered his favorite arena, Faneuil Hall. There he spoke at a reception in his honor to celebrate the treaty with England. In his address, he vented many of his concerns.

Perhaps because he was surrounded by friends on the stage, or because he believed the country owed him something for his success, he spoke his mind openly and plainly. Before establishing his credibility and allaying any latent hostility, he chastised his critics. Operating from a false sense of security, he misjudged the occasion. From the moment he walked onto the stage, the crowd of three thousand seemed to be grumbling about his loyalty to President Tyler. Webster stared down at the audience until the noise abated. The mayor of Boston provided an introduction that attempted to reestablish Web-

11. Ibid., 12–13.

ster's reputation and set the stage for a great epideictic moment, perhaps an apologia.

From the outset, though, Webster goaded the crowd. He began by praising Tyler for supporting his secretary of state during the treaty negotiations. He admitted that friends had asked him to resign to save his own skin, but he said he was free to do as he pleased and would not be coerced from office. He claimed that the country was better off with him as secretary of state than as a private citizen and that the recent Whig convention had acted rashly in voting to nominate Clay. He claimed that he was the real Whig, loyal to the party always, loyal to its presidents, and not ready to see it split apart. He would continue to place principles above personalities. He even suggested that the people of Massachusetts vote on who was the better Whig, he or those accusing the president. The political cast of this speech and its vindictive nature were clear. His acid soured the audience.

But Webster had not finished. He accused the Whigs of Massachusetts of forcing a divorce between his "parents," the president and the party. He was the child left in the breach, he claimed disingenuously. He digressed into a defense of Tyler's banking plan, which had led to the resignation of the cabinet in the first place. It was the last thing the audience wanted to hear. The Whig press did not like it either. Webster's rancorous tone was attacked by Thurlow Weed's newspapers in New York, by the *Boston Atlas,* and even by the *National Intelligencer* in Washington. Some of his most loyal friends—Harrison Otis, John Davis, and Massachusetts congressman Robert Winthrop, who had studied the law under Webster—deserted him for what they saw as arrogant pettiness. There were those, such as George Ticknor and Jeremiah Mason, who thought the speech was heroic; they helped Webster compound his error by having the speech bound and mailed. While Tyler was pleased, most Whigs were not. In Congress, Webster was excoriated; he was called a traitor to his party and to his principles.

The Oregon Border Dispute

Webster tried to ignore the criticism by returning to the Oregon question. There, Great Britain and the United States shared the territory between the 42nd parallel and the 54th at forty minutes. Hence the cry "Fifty-four forty or fight," meaning that the United States wanted all of the territory. While the British were willing to split the territory at the 49th parallel, they wanted to deviate from this line where it met the Columbia River and follow that to the sea. With California not yet a part of the Union, this meant that Great Britain was unwilling to give the United States a deep-water port on the West Coast. Webster would not stand for that; being farsighted, he wanted what would become Seattle.

Webster's negotiating position was not strengthened by rumors that he would resign as secretary of state to become ambassador to Britain, replacing his friend Edward Everett. Tyler could then appoint a new secretary to carry out his Texas ambitions. Trying to make the best of a bad situation, Webster put forward a compromise plan for England: If Mexico could be persuaded to sell San Francisco to the United States, the United States would cede everything north of the Columbia River to England except the Olympic Peninsula.

The plan came a cropper for several reasons. First, Britain did not want to offend Mexico. Second, as trouble on the Texas border mounted, it became clear that war with Mexico was more likely than compromise. White Texans favored expanding the Texas Territory and had been making raids on Mexican farms and stealing horses. Mexican authorities had retaliated by arresting Texans. The worst incident occurred when two hundred American settlers sent to Santa Fe by the president of the Texas Republic were captured and marched off to Mexico City. Their plight touched a nerve in the United States, especially when it was learned that some had died or been shot along the trail. Webster was able to put this fire out by arranging for the release of the remaining settlers, again demonstrating his preference for negotiation over retaliation. This, however, did nothing to reduce widespread disdain for the country south of the border.

Webster's next move was too clever by half. He talked Tyler into opening relations with China and naming Everett head of the mission. However, Everett suspected that the president wanted to move Webster to England to replace him as ambassador, and he turned down the request. Caleb Cushing received the appointment instead and Webster named his son Fletcher secretary for the mission. Webster took the mission's report seriously and recommended a policy that resulted in the Treaty of Wanghia of 1844, which opened China to American trade, and the Tyler Doctrine, which freed the Sandwich Islands from European domination, much to the delight of New England whalers and missionaries.[12] But Oregon remained undecided, and Texas was beginning to boil.

12. Webster's policy eventually resulted in the annexation of Hawaii and the McKinley administration's Open Door Policy.

Worse yet, Tyler began to angle for the Democratic nomination for president since only Van Buren seemed to stand in his way. Van Buren wanted revenge for his loss to Harrison. Tyler was unpopular with Whigs because of the national bank, and he was unpopular with Democrats for helping Harrison win in the first place. Nonetheless, in order to consolidate Democratic support, Tyler began to send signals to Webster that his usefulness was at an end; for example, he regularly ignored Webster's advice on congressional bills.

By early 1843, it became clear to Webster that he would have to resign. The abolitionists provided the crisis that permitted his exit. On May 4, John Quincy Adams argued in his "Address to the People of the Free States of the Union" that annexation of Texas would mean the end of the Union. Led by William Lloyd Garrison, abolitionists claimed that Tyler's plan to annex Texas was a plot to expand the institution of slavery. Webster submitted his resignation on May 8, 1843; the president accepted it with a letter of praise. Abel P. Upshur was named acting secretary of state; when Upshur died in an accident in February 1844, Tyler made Calhoun secretary of state.

Back to Bunker Hill

Webster's political clout was nearly gone. His dreams to serve Harrison and succeed him had evaporated in service to Tyler, the Whig apostate. At sixty-one, he had hit another low in his life and sought renewal with his family at Marshfield. It was not long, however, before his friends were arranging dinners at which he could express his desire to reunite with the Whigs. Then came what seemed a golden opportunity for Webster to erase the memory of the bitter anti–Whig Party speech he had given at Faneuil Hall and return to the transcendent themes that marked his most memorable oratory. The Bunker Hill monument had been completed, and since his speech had been such a success at the laying of its cornerstone in 1825, perhaps he could rival it with a speech at its completion in 1843.

Webster's friends let it be known he was available to deliver a major address to commemorate the event. And so, on June 17, eighteen years to the day after his First Bunker Hill Address, Webster returned to the site of his early triumph to speak again. Several factors gave him a case of nerves before the address. President Tyler had decided to attend the event with some of his slave-holding cabinet members, and in protest, John Quincy Adams absented himself. The crowd would be huge and Webster was preceded by his considerable reputation. Expectations were very high. Could he top himself once more?

Webster was so jittery that he downed a tumbler of brandy just before the address. Evidently, it worked to calm his nerves and soothe his vocal cords.

He began by establishing certain themes that he would extend throughout the address. He proclaimed, for example, that the completed "column stands for the Union." He trotted out the Whig values emanating from support for the Union. He asserted that the American experiment had produced a culture and political system superior to that of Europe and its former colonies, but he avoided in any way encouraging the president's hunger for Mexican territory. When he concluded, he downed another tumbler of brandy and enjoyed the adulation of the crowd. The speech, however, was not up to his usual standards.[13] The audience was already familiar with his arguments and themes. There seemed to be no compelling issue to drive the speech. And the occasion seemed mired in politics; Tyler's presence and Adams's absence reminded the audience that Webster had supported the former and often quarreled with the latter. In fact, Adams referred to Webster as "a heartless traitor to the cause of humanity" in regard to this speech.[14]

He fared better in September when he was cheered for a speech he gave in Rochester, New York, to rally the Whigs on agricultural policy. By this time, Tyler had finally declared for the Democratic Party. In November, Webster spoke to the Whigs at Andover, Massachusetts, and he concluded the year on December 22 by delivering a speech on the landing at Plymouth to the New England Society of New York. In short, Webster was trying to use his oratory to curry favor with the Whigs and rehabilitate himself in the North. It would prove too little and too late for the presidential nomination. The Whigs united behind Clay at their convention in May 1844, convinced that the Democrats were too weak to win. They believed that Van Buren would be the Democratic nominee and that he did not stand a chance of winning the South, let alone Whigs in the North. Van Buren's strength was among abolitionists, still a distinct minority. Webster's consolation prize in the midst of all this was that he was nominated for the Senate again to replace his own replacement and friend, Rufus Choate.

In the meantime, he had revived his legal practice. His most important case of this period was *Vidal v. Girard's Executors*, which involved the banker Stephen Girard, who had left a bequest to found a school for orphaned white boys.

13. See Bartlett, *Daniel Webster*, 196; Peterson, *The Great Triumvirate*, 355–56. The speech is included in *Writings and Speeches*, 1:259–83.

14. Charles Francis Adams, ed., *Memoirs of John Quincy Adams*, 11:384.

Girard insisted in his will that no religion be taught at the school. Webster represented the heirs who wanted the bequest overturned because they believed it defamed the Christian religion and was therefore invalid. In light of the First Amendment, Webster was in a difficult position. He argued the case for three days before the Supreme Court, building up to his strongest argument: The will was invalid because it overstepped its intention by excluding clergy from the school whether they taught religion or not. Webster's tactics probably would have offended Jefferson and Madison, who believed in strict separation of church and state. And yet it is important to remember that in Webster's time schools were not considered to be part of the state; they enjoyed the same right to preach religion as private schools do today.

Webster's appeal was so dramatic that a member of the House who was watching ran up to the Senate chamber and fetched his colleagues to hear it. When he returned with them, Webster was echoing Jesus: "Suffer little *children* unto me," he cried (Webster's emphasis). At one point the audience broke into applause, a most unusual event in the Supreme Court. Webster's central argument on the first day also impressed the audience: "[I]n any institution for the instruction of youth, where the authority of God is disowned, and the duties of Christianity derided and despised, and its ministers shut out from all participation in its proceedings, there can no more be charity, true charity, found to exist, than evil can spring out of the Bible, error out of truth, or hatred and animosity come forth from the bosom of perfect love."[15] Webster's periodic style, conjoined with his credibility on the issue of the rights of eleemosynary institutions stemming from his defense of Dartmouth College, won over the audience but not the Court. Even his friend Justice Story upheld the bequest, making the vote unanimous. The clergy of America, however, had a new and unlikely champion. Webster's remarks were quickly printed and disseminated. This outpouring of support from the religious community cemented Webster's return to a position of some influence in the Whig Party, though nowhere near that of Clay's.

The Election of 1844

Tyler continued to push for annexation of Texas, a position that was anathema to many northerners, especially after Calhoun's endorsement of the proposition. When Tyler appointed Calhoun as his secretary of state, he lost what

15. Webster, *Writings and Speeches*, 9:143.

little northern Whig support he had; he also damaged himself with northern Democrats, though to a lesser extent since they were more open to the annexation of Texas. Webster had already warned that annexation would throw the Senate—and hence the Union—out of kilter.

On April 12, 1844, Calhoun submitted the annexation treaty to the Senate. He used the occasion to argue that where slaves were emancipated they fell into mental illness but that slaves who were cared for in the South had improved in terms of morals and intelligence.

As the assumed nominee of the Whigs, Clay felt obligated to respond. After all, he was "the Great Compromiser," the paragon of prudential governance in the mold of Cicero. Or was he? His quarrel with Jackson had smacked of revenge. His scrap with Tyler sacrificed the National Bank for political points and nearly destroyed the Whig Party. Clay's responses to Calhoun demonstrate that his civic republicanism did not rise to the transcendence of Webster's civil religion.[16] On April 27, Clay published his "Raleigh Letter," in which he claimed that annexation of Texas would lead to war with Mexico. On the same day, Van Buren published his own condemnation of Calhoun's treaty, which fueled rumors of collusion between the presumptive nominees. This implied alliance was one of several factors that led to Van Buren's undoing at the Democratic convention. His mentor, Andrew Jackson, realized that Van Buren could not unite the party. So the ex-president worked behind the scenes to secure the nomination of dark horse James Knox Polk, the former Speaker of the House who was then governor of Tennessee.

There was bad news for Clay from New York. In competition with the Whig Party, a Liberty party had been formed that opposed any expansion of slavery. Seeing no alternative but to placate Clay, Webster encouraged its members to join with the Whigs against the expansionist Democrats. In the meantime, in a letter to Richard Pakenham, the British minister to the United States, Calhoun let it be known that slavery would be allowed to flow into Texas. This unilateral interpretation of the Missouri Compromise upset abolitionists and flew in the face of standard Senate procedure. The treaty was overwhelmingly defeated; Calhoun was now alienated from the Senate.

At their convention in Baltimore, the Whigs purposely said nothing about the Texas issue in their platform so that their nominee would have a free hand

16. See David Zarefsky, "Henry Clay and the Election of 1844: The Limits of a Rhetoric of Compromise."

to deal with it. That would turn out to be a mistake. The day after Clay's nomination, however, Webster could not know that, and he gave a speech supporting the Whig ticket. While admitting to some disagreements with the nominee, he told a cheering crowd of young Whigs that on the big issues he and Clay were one. The crowd then marched through the streets of Baltimore behind their state banners.

The Democrats' nomination of Polk stunned the newly united Whigs. They feared that he would steal votes from Clay's southern flank, something Van Buren would have had no chance of doing. Clay immediately sent his compromise position on Texas to various newspaper editors, but acting in haste led to errors. He stipulated under which conditions he might favor annexation while insisting that those conditions did not yet exist, a rather two-faced position. One of his letters, to an Alabama paper, was particularly provoking to readers. In it Clay claimed he was not courting the abolitionists. While he might "personally" oppose annexation, he said, he would do what was in the interest of the nation even though he suspected the motives of those calling for annexation. This disastrous letter offended both northerners and southerners to no purpose.

A month later, Clay sent the same newspaper a second letter in which he tried to clear up the mess. He wrote that he opposed annexation, explaining his position in light of his position during the 1820 compromise debates. In the letter's most famous passage, he wrote, "I could not but regard the annexation of Texas at this time, as compromising the honor of my country, involving it in war, in which the sympathies of all Christendom would be against us."[17] While this passage seemed to bring him back to the view expressed in his Raleigh letter, Clay did not stop there. He went on to say that he could not predict the future or what a future president would do. That only made the damage worse. Clay seemed to be not a man of principle but instead a politician who did and said almost anything to gain election. His equivocation was noxious both to those who opposed the expansion of slavery and those who supported it. An easy win against a dark-horse candidate was slipping away.

Webster saw that when it came to the presidency, Clay was snakebitten. Nonetheless, he campaigned in the North to save the congressional delegation. In Albany, for example, after a parade through the town, he spoke for

---

17. Henry Clay, "Alabama Letter," in *Candidate, Compromiser, Elder Statesman: January 1, 1844–June 29, 1852*, ed. Melba Porter Hay and Carol Reardon, 91.

three hours defending the Whigs. He tied Whig virtues to the Federalist founders and described what the American Revolution had accomplished in its conservation of rights won during the colonial period. In a bow to Ciceronian prudence, he argued that every statesman needed a sense of history. He supported the Whig agenda for a more prosperous America. He defended Clay's American System of tariffs, internal improvements, and national defense. He linked manufacturers and farmers, again arguing that Union was in their best interest and that annexation of Texas threatened that Union. He reiterated his position that prosperity benefits all, providing a higher place for those on the bottom rungs of the economic ladder.[18] Campaigning in New York was crucial because the state would have an important impact on the election. New Yorkers were unhappy that their favorite son, Martin Van Buren, had been rejected by the Democrats, but James G. Birney, the Liberty Party nominee, was expected to drain votes from Clay. Webster was trying to hold the fort for Clay and the Whigs.

Webster spoke in Faneuil Hall at the end of a grueling campaign in which he had pitched Whiggery to the voters, refused to apologize for his past, and often failed to mention Clay by name. Clay did carry Massachusetts; Polk lost his home state of Tennessee.[19] The outcome in the big states of New York, Pennsylvania, and Virginia hung in the balance for several days. When it was determined that Pennsylvania and Virginia had fallen to Polk, the election came down to New York's 36 electoral votes. Had Clay carried New York, he would have won the election by 141 electoral votes to 134. Instead he lost the state by 5,000 votes and had 105 electoral votes to Polk's 170. Birney had drained away 15,000 votes from the Whigs in New York. In the nation as a whole, Polk won by only 38,000 popular votes. Webster calculated that the Liberty Party alone had cost the Whigs 62,300 votes nationwide.

While Webster prepared to return to the Senate, Clay tried to rationalize yet another loss. The Alabama letters had driven a critical number of abolitionists into the Liberty Party, particularly in New York. The cry for American expansionism, soon to be canonized as "manifest destiny," overpowered the more sensible Whig agenda. Webster saw a new challenge emerge out of the electoral disaster: preventing the disruption of the Union. It would take up the rest of his career.

---

18. Remini, *Daniel Webster*, 596.
19. The parallels between this election and that of 2000 are eerie.

Chapter 9

War with Mexico

Amerian imperialist impulses may have first been sated when President Thomas Jefferson nearly doubled the size of the nation by purchasing the Louisiana Territory from Napoleon in 1803. Jefferson was forgiven for his constitutionally suspect move because many Americans believed that taming the wilderness was a noble goal. The orators of Webster's time built that idea into American civil religion by recounting how the early settlers had been purified by their sacrifices in New England and Virginia, how frontier heroes had emerged from across the Appalachians in the French and Indian War, how the expansion west after the English withdrawal from strategic forts continued the errand into the wilderness. Underlying the mythos of hardship and sacrifice was the mission of cultivating the land. Jefferson was not alone among the founders in taking comfort in John Locke's view that "God, when he gave the World in common to all Mankind, commanded man also to labor, and the penury of his Condition required it of him. God and his Reason commanded him to subdue the Earth, that is, improve it for the benefit of Life."[1] The American System of the Whigs had lived up to Locke's charge. The Erie Canal carried goods across the state of New York; railroads fanned out in all directions; roads carried new settlers deeper and deeper into the continent.

The expansion west was not without its hesitations. The War of 1812 blunted ambitions for Canadian territory voiced by the "War Hawks" in Congress. The Compromise of 1820 controlled the way in which the land would

---

1. Locke, *Two Treatises on Civil Government*, 309.

191

be divided between the North and South and sent a warning that expansion would be difficult. The emergence of the Texas Republic, however, rekindled the spirit of exploration, conquest, and settlement. By then several trails to the Pacific Ocean had been carved out of the deserts and mountains. John O'Sullivan's call for America to follow its "manifest destiny" resonated through the victorious Democratic Party and out to the frontier-loving public at large.[2] President Polk led the forces of expansion by involving the United States in an aggressive imperialist landgrab. The resulting war with Mexico was the first the country would fight primarily on foreign soil and the first to receive extensive media coverage.

It was a crucial moment in American history. If the march west could be stopped, questions of land use and the spread of slavery might be more easily resolved; Texas might remain a republic; California might become an independent nation; a civil war might be avoided. The banner of anti-imperialism was raised by the Whig Party and vociferously championed by one of its most venerable leaders, Senator Daniel Webster of Massachusetts, who made the core of his appeal an attack on the war policy of the president. The difficulty Webster faced was that he was out of step with the mythos of expansion that was ingrained in American civil religion by 1845: the majority of Americans favored expansion to the natural border of the Pacific Ocean.

Aside from revealing a cleft in civil religion, the imperialism of 1846 provides a definitive case study of antiwar rhetoric from the major out-party. This rhetoric exhibits a unique configuration of deliberative, epideictic, and forensic features that have resurfaced over the years in both American and British public address. Yet scholars have either ignored Webster's speeches on this war or have mistakenly attributed an imperialist policy to him, misled by southern characterizations of Webster as a northern imperialist or by later imperialist speakers, who often quoted him.[3]

---

2. O'Sullivan owned the *New York Morning News*, in which the phrase "By right of our manifest destiny" appeared on December 27, 1845. The groundwork for the romantic surge of expansionism had been laid by many others. George Bancroft's *History of the United States*, for example, was extremely popular and claimed that the development of the United States was part of the Divine Will. In August 1845 Bancroft gave the eulogy at Andrew Jackson's funeral; he claimed the president's spirit hovered not only over the United States but extended to the Rio Grande. See Lyon Rathbun, "The Debate over Annexing Texas and the Emergence of Manifest Destiny," 487.

3. See Howell and Hudson, "Daniel Webster," 665–733; Mills, "Daniel Webster's Principles of Rhetoric".

Webster's speeches delivered just before, during, and after the war with Mexico provide an opportunity to examine his use of braided genres in antiwar rhetoric and his attack on the expansionist policy of Polk. In previous chapters, we have traced the roots of Webster's anti-expansionism. His rhetorical technique continued to mature during this period, though his presidential ambitions interfered with his ability to produce transcendent eloquence. While Webster failed in his short-term goals, however, he enhanced his credibility in preparation for the debates over the 1850 Compromise, his ultimate battle.

In analyzing Webster's rhetoric, I will again rely on Aristotle's three major genres for public speeches—the deliberative, the epideictic, and the forensic— defined by the role of the audience, the subject matter, the ends, and the time emphasized (see Chapter 4). All three forms may appear in one speech or, as Aristotle notes, one form may mask another. Centuries later the *Rhetorica ad Herennium*, with which Webster was familiar, used the same tactic when it noted that "in judicial and deliberative causes extensive sections are often devoted to praise or censure."[4]

An advance in genre studies came with the construction of hybrids made from various forms.[5] The apologia, for instance, usually consists of both forensic and epideictic elements; apologists defend themselves while blaming others and sometimes praising themselves. Sermons may condemn sin, praise the virtuous life, and call for a conversion in the future. More relevant to this chapter, debates over war policy have been characterized as generic.[6]

To unravel the generic threads that Webster used to weave his hybrid form of antiwar rhetoric, I will examine four speeches from the late 1840s. These speeches are some of the least changed by Webster after delivery; only one was

4. Aristotle, *Rhetoric*, 1368b10-20; Cicero, *Rhetorica ad Herennium*, 3.8.15. Scholars now believe that Cicero was not the author of this highly influential work, which codifies Greek rhetorical theory into five canons.

5. See Karlyn K. Campbell and Kathleen H. Jamieson, *Deeds Done in Words: Presidential Rhetoric and the Genres of Governance*; Thomas M. Conley, "Ancient Rhetoric and Modern Genre Criticism"; Walter R. Fisher, "Genre: Concepts and Applications in Rhetorical Criticism"; Michael Leff, "Genre and Paradigm in the Second Book of *De Oratore*"; Stephen E. Lucas, "Genre Criticism and Historic Context: The Case of George Washington's First Inaugural Address"; Herbert W. Simons and A. A. Aghazarian, *Form, Genre, and the Study of Political Discourse*; Craig R. Smith, "A Reinterpretation of Aristotle's Notion of Rhetorical Form."

6. See Robert L. Ivie, "Presidential Motives for War"; Robert L. Ivie, "William McKinley: Advocate of Imperialism"; Vernon Jensen, "British Voices on the Eve of the American Revolution: Trapped by the Family Metaphor"; Ronald Reid, "New England Rhetoric and the French War, 1754-1760: A Case Study in the Rhetoric of War."

converted into a pamphlet for wider distribution. The first, "Admission of Texas," delivered on December 22, 1845, attacks the enabling legislation for Texas statehood. The second, "Defense of the Treaty of Washington," was delivered on April 6 and 7, 1846. The third, delivered on March 1, 1847, focuses on "The Mexican War," and the final speech, delivered on March 23, 1848, concerns the "Objects of the Mexican War."

The Admission of Texas

In the first days of March 1845, Tyler, the outgoing president, admitted Texas to the Union just before Polk gave his inaugural address. Polk indicated that the admission of Texas was only the beginning of a new wave of American expansion. He wanted the Oregon Territory. Since international matters dominated the scene, Congress did little in this area before adjourning and mourning the death of Andrew Jackson in June. When the next session of Congress began in late 1845, Webster returned to Capitol Hill and the Washington social scene. One of the most curious members of that scene was Sam Houston, one of the new senators from Texas. Houston was fond of whittling little wooden hearts while listening to speeches in the Senate. He sometimes tossed the hearts to the ladies in the galleries. He was not happy with Webster's efforts to reverse the admission of Texas to the Union.

On December 22 Webster attacked a joint resolution supporting the admission of Texas; the enabling legislation allowed Texas to split into as many as four states in the future and required the United States to pay off its bond debt and settle its border dispute with New Mexico. Webster began by establishing that he had been a friend of the Texas Republic but was consistently opposed to Texas statehood since 1837. To reinforce his credibility, he extended three arguments from his earlier speeches. They provided the columns around which Webster would braid various epideictic, deliberative, and forensic vines. This speech played a role in fomenting the resolutions of instruction passed by the Massachusetts legislature in May 1846, which referred to "a War to strengthen the 'slave power.'"[7]

Webster's first premise was that the United States was the proper size in

---

7. These resolutions, written by Charles Sumner, described slavery as "odious." Sumner also shone the light of "morality and Christianity" on the problem, once again conflating organized religion with civil religion.

terms of geography for its 20 million inhabitants. Furthermore, tampering with its boundaries threatened the Constitution: "There must be some limit to the extent of our territory, if we would make our institutions permanent."[8] Webster's conservative plea was Burkean: Imperialism threatened America's history and its social fabric. Acquisition of the vast Texas territory would undermine the Constitution, the document that organically constituted Webster's transcendent Union. This argument was balanced on praise for and preservation of the Union. Had Webster relied solely on one or the other, the argument would not have been as compelling, nor as original.

In a shift to the forensic mode, Webster claimed that the "spirit of aggrandizement" would injure America's credibility abroad. If the United States continued to acquire territory in unjust ways, it would violate its responsibility as a "republic" and suffer the condemnation of the community of nations. This forensic note echoed Pericles' praise of just causes and noble goals in pursuit of deliberative ends.

With his credibility established and his foes condemned, Webster issued a third argument, the most clearly deliberative and the lengthiest. He opposed the admission of any state that allowed the ownership of slaves: "[T]he State proposing to come in should be required to remove that inequality by abolishing slavery, or take the alternative of being excluded." What was particularly galling to Webster was that the Texas constitution specifically stated that slavery could not be abolished unless "every master" consented and was compensated. Thus, not only would slavery remain in perpetuity but the admission of this slave state would "derange the balance of the Constitution, and create inequality and unjust advantage against the North." Webster punctuated his point a few sentences later when he referred to the policy as "manifest inequality" and spoke of those "who have manifested a disposition to add Texas to the Union." Hardly a senator present could have missed the play on the phrase *manifest destiny*. Prescient about the 1850 crisis, Webster predicted that those northern senators who voted for the admission of Texas would come to regret their action. He concluded by dissenting for himself and the people of Massachusetts from the annexation and reaffirming his record "during the last eight years."

This morning gun of his campaign against acquisition of new territory put the president and the political establishment on notice that Webster intended

8. Webster, *Speeches and Formal Writings*, 2:355–60.

to be a conscience for the Congress. In that capacity, he would serve as a judge of policy by establishing an anti-imperialist context for his antiwar rhetoric. That context grew out of the noble injunctions of Pericles and Edmund Burke, two prophets in Webster's civil religion.

A Public Relations Scandal

At this juncture, Webster needed cash once again. A group of friends quickly set up a fund in March 1846. The fund would serve not only to underwrite Webster's extravagant tastes, but also to support his campaign to rebuild the Whig Party in his own image. Before that could happen, however, another scandal plagued Webster and he was obliged to deliver a major apologia. While engaging in this ostensibly forensic endeavor, he wove anti-imperialist threads into his defense.

Most observers praised Webster for his work as secretary of state in negotiating the treaty with England that ended the long and tangled Maine boundary dispute. But a few, particularly Rep. Charles Ingersoll of Philadelphia, claimed Webster had given away too much. Ingersoll initiated this charge in part because he and his fellow Democrats were annoyed by Webster's attacks on Polk with regard to his bellicose Oregon policy. They hoped to diminish Webster's effectiveness by distracting him and reducing his credibility.

Webster tried to ignore the petty charges, but when they were reissued before the House Foreign Affairs Committee and repeated by Sen. Daniel Dickinson of New York, he was forced to reply. The resulting speech, which took the better part of two days of business, featured Webster's forensic prowess, which was well known. Few, however, could predict the wealth of evidence he would bring to the occasion. Webster's defense of the Washington Treaty reflected Cicero's forensic style. Rhetorical questions kept the audience on track, and wit, ad hominem attacks, and biting sarcasm relieved the tedious and lengthy arguments. However, it was Webster's ability to shift among the genres that gave the speech its strength. These shifts not only allowed him to move from pragmatic to idealistic appeals but also to generate more arguments than he could have had he adhered to a single form. For example, in an epideictic turn, Webster played to the galleries when he attacked his chief accuser: "Sir, this person's mind is so grotesque, so *bizarre*—it is rather the caricature of a mind, than a mind. . . . [W]e sometimes apply to him a phrase borrowed from the mechanics. We say, there is a screw loose, somewhere. In this case, the screws are all loose all over. The whole machine is out of order, disjointed, rickety, crazy, creaking, as often upside down as upside up." While condemning others, Webster was not above praising himself, even in comparison with past presidents: "[T]here were difficulties and obstacles in the way of this settlement, which had not been overcome under the administration of Washington, or the elder Adams, or Mr. Jefferson, or Mr. Madison, or Mr. Monroe, or Mr. John Quincy Adams, or General Jackson, or Mr. Van Buren."[9] Webster implied that he had succeeded where these noble lights had failed.

The speech demonstrates that as secretary of state Webster was dedicated to the enforcement of international law as part of the character of a decent republic. He favored treaties that included arbitration provisions so that armed force would not be necessary when it came to enforcement. He endorsed the principle of equity as a means to achieve compromise. Of his settlement over the issue of impressing seamen, he said: "This declaration will stand . . . because it announces the true principle of public law; because it announces the great doctrine of the equality and independence of nations upon the seas; and because it announces the determination of the . . . United States to uphold those principles." To achieve peace, Webster was willing to give up territory rather than acquire it. Most important, the treaty's provisions on the slave trade were so admired internationally that they were promptly imitated by France and England under the guidance of Webster.

At the end of the speech, those in the Senate chamber knew that Webster's reputation had been enhanced. The speech was rushed into print and a public relations campaign on Webster's behalf began. But the battle was not over. Ingersoll issued a nasty rebuttal on April 9, and Rep. William L. Yancey of Alabama followed up the next day by invoking the "Black Dan" label in a disparaging way. Events took another bad turn in late April when Polk, perhaps to embarrass Webster further, refused to release secret documents surrounding the scandal. The House erupted in anger. When Rep. George Ashmun of Massachusetts rose to defend Webster, the debate got particularly mean-spirited and resolutions were passed to establish committees to investigate the charges. Webster's attackers were stunned when one committee heard testimony from former president Tyler to the effect that he had authorized Webster's use of public funds to rally support for the treaty. The committee exonerated Webster in June 1846, the same month an Oregon treaty much to Webster's liking was signed by Polk and approved by the Senate.

Webster had successfully used an apologia to mask other generic themes

9. Ibid., 2:361–434.

and to advance his anti-imperialist agenda. The apologia not only led to his vindication, it also reinforced his policy with regard to the Oregon Territory and reminded his audience of his treaty-making abilities with regard to the Maine boundary dispute. Having been vindicated—his method of treaty-making tacitly endorsed and his anti-imperialism established—Webster moved to a more specific objective: antiwar rhetoric.

Polk Goes to War

In January 1846, after Mexico had turned down money offers for the California and New Mexico territories and refused the Slidell mission, Polk had ordered Gen. Zachary Taylor's army to cross the Nueces River and proceed to the Rio Grande, which Texas claimed as its southern boundary. Whigs argued that crossing the Nueces was a violation of Mexican sovereignty. In the spring, however, legal technicalities were cast aside when Polk received word that Taylor's troops had come under attack while probing the Rio Grande Valley, that some had been captured, and that seventeen had been killed. Polk sent a message to Congress in early May justifying war with Mexico.[10] On May 13, Webster was absent from the Senate when it voted to declare war by a vote of 40 to 2. Many of Webster's Whig compatriots voted for the war, fearing that what had happened to the Federalists after the War of 1812 would happen to them. The Whig-dominated Massachusetts legislature, however, passed a resolution proclaiming the war unconstitutional and a product of "slave power."

The Conscience Whigs opposed the war with the Mexico, and Webster intended to become a leader on the issue. Before he could do that, however, he needed to maneuver another tariff bill through the Congress. The House version was unacceptable to New England, so Webster crafted a substitute. He spoke in favor of his proposal on July 25 and 27, referring to vested interests as the "King Party," which ignored the wishes of the "people." He claimed that the House version would restrict the availability of materials needed by manufacturers and thus slow the economy, throwing many laborers out of work. When he finished speaking, Webster hoped for a vote, but some Whigs thought they could gain favorable amendments in committee and the House bill was sent to the Finance Committee for rewriting. This greedy strategy backfired be-

10. Robert L. Ivie, "Progressive Form and Mexican Culpability in Polk's Justification for War."

cause it gave Polk time to lobby senators. The bill was reported back to the Senate without amendment. Webster was able to eliminate only one provision on the floor. When the vote on the bill came in tied, the vice president carried the day for Polk. The House approved the amended bill quickly and Polk approved it at the end of July.

Furious at this defeat, Webster decided to work behind the scenes in favor of the Wilmot Proviso, which had been passed by the House. This amendment to an appropriations bill would have prevented slavery in any territory gained in the war with Mexico. However, the Senate killed the proviso by filibuster and Congress adjourned on August 10.

At the Whig convention in Massachusetts, Charles Sumner gave a speech imploring the party to make opposition to slavery mandatory, and he challenged Webster to lead the abolitionist movement. When Conscience Whigs who supported abolition began to quarrel with Cotton Whigs who opposed interference with slavery where it existed, Webster was called to the hall to speak. Without endorsing abolition, Webster brought the crowd to its feet when he spoke in favor of national "liberty" and Whig "unity." Sumner later begged Webster to take a more specific stand on abolition, but Webster refused. He knew it would tear the country apart and sink his chances for national leadership. Abolition was too extreme a step for Webster. Sumner never forgave him for this breach of faith.

As the congressional elections of 1846 approached, Webster continued to attack the war policy of the administration and encourage Whig unity. He could not stop his son Edward, however, from putting together a company of volunteers and going off to Mexico. Edward soon came home ill, recovered, and returned to Mexico, much to Webster's distress.

In the December 1846 session of Congress, Rep. David Wilmot of Pennsylvania again brought his amendment before the House. Again it was passed, this time attached to a bill authorizing money for the war. Webster voted in favor of the proviso, but it was stripped from the funding bill in the Senate. Congress adjourned, having accomplished little.

Webster must have known that the chances of stopping the war and subsequent expansion were nil. The new Congress would not take over until December 1847. (In the House a lanky lawyer named Lincoln would oppose the war with Mexico.) Nonetheless, on March 1, near the close of the session, he reasserted his resistance to expansion and opposed the war with Mexico. He spoke in the context of the resurrection of the Wilmot Proviso to prohibit slavery in the territories. This bill proved divisive. Southern senators wanted new territories without restrictions on slavery; northern senators wanted restrictions. Voting for the proviso would force southern senators to oppose acquisition of new territories, while voting against the proviso would force northern senators to oppose acquisition of new territories. The situation was a precursor to the deadlock the Senate would face during the Compromise of 1850.

Surrounded by senators anxious to end the session, Webster rose to speak at midnight though he was ill and tired. His condition gave him an excuse to appeal to his colleagues' sympathy and to shorten his remarks, which were a powerful combination of forensic condemnation of and deliberative opposition to the war. He began by claiming what many in Washington knew to be true—that the distant and pointless war had been provoked by guile: "Sir, we are in the midst of a war, not waged at home in defense of our soil, but waged a thousand miles off, and in the heart of the territories of another government. Of that war no one yet sees the end, and no one counts the cost. It is not denied that this war is now prosecuted for the acquisition of territory; at least, if any deny it, others admit it, and all know it to be true." This accusation was followed by an inhospitable picture of the "pestilence"-ridden coasts and hot "alien plains" of Mexico.[11]

Next Webster turned to those senators who had been quibbling over the meaning of the "remonstrances" or state resolutions of instruction, which he claimed were clear. Reading from the Massachusetts resolution, he moved from the war to the future of slavery: " 'That the people of Massachusetts will strenuously resist the annexation of any new territory to this Union, in which the institution of slavery is to be tolerated or established.' . . . Sir, is there any possibility of misunderstanding this? . . . For the resolution, there were two hundred and thirty-two votes; against them, none." Previewing a tactic he would use in the 1850 Compromise debates, he expanded the support he had from Massachusetts to the entire North.

Quickly shifting from the deliberative to the epideictic mode, Webster moved to the offensive; he attacked Sen. John Adams Dix of New York, comparing him to Sen. Andrew P. Butler of South Carolina. These strange bedfellows were so blinded by their lust for land, he said, that they ignored their ideological responsibilities. They could have escaped the dilemma of either an un-

11. Webster, *Speeches and Formal Writings*, 2:435–46.

happy North or an unhappy South by endorsing the amendment of Sen. John M. Berrien of Georgia, which would have forbidden obtaining territory from the war with Mexico. The amendment, however, had been rejected: "Who has rejected it? . . . Sir, it has been lost by the votes of the honorable member from New York and his Northern and Eastern friends. It has been voted down by the 'Northern Democracy.' " Echoing his attacks on the administration from the fall congressional campaign, Webster explained that Berrien's amendment would have passed if just a handful of northern Democrats had supported it. Using apophasis, Webster condemned the president and his party for abandoning principles in order to acquire new land: "I arraign no man and no parties. I take no judgment into my own hands." Then, deftly moving from epideictic to deliberative appeal, he asked, "Shall we prosecute this war for the purpose of bringing on a controversy which is likely to shake the government to its centre?"

In the last part of the speech, Webster relied on his standard technique of repeating and extending his themes, as he had done with great effect in the "Eulogy to Adams and Jefferson" and the Second Reply to Hayne. Here the fugal form began with Webster's self-praise for his consistency on the admission of Texas in the context of his anti-imperialism: "I have never swerved." He again prosecuted "Northern Democracy" for allowing the addition of Texas as a slave state:

> That history and that record can neither be falsified nor erased. . . . Texas was brought into this Union, slavery and all, only by means of the aid and active cooperation of those who now call themselves the 'Northern Democracy' of the United States. . . . Where were they, I ask? Were they standing up like men against slaves and slavery? . . . [They] were counseling and assisting, aiding and abetting, the whole proceeding.

This salvo was followed by the potent use of rhetorical questions that are resolved with complex artistry, reminding the audience of Patrick Henry's "liberty or death" address: "We remonstrated, we protested, we voted; but the 'Northern Democracy' helped to outvote us, to defeat us, to overwhelm us." The asyndetonic triples balance one another while summing up the argument. The right-branching periodic phrases cap the call of conscience of one who has lost the battle but not the moral issue.

After this examination of the record, Webster again employed rhetorical questions to reveal his vision of the future: "All I can scan is contention, strife, and agitation. . . . Will the North consent to a treaty bringing in territory subject to slavery? Will the South consent to a treaty bringing in territory from which slavery is excluded? Sir, the future is full of difficulties. . . . We appear to me to be rushing upon perils headlong, and with our eyes open." Of the four speeches under examination from this period, this was perhaps the most helpful in enhancing Webster's credibility during the 1850 Compromise debates. It employed an ingenious triangulation of genre to achieve its effect. Webster accused the southern Democrats and some northern Democrats of a conspiracy to enter into a war that was unjust and unnecessary. He praised himself for his consistency and civic virtue, assuming the credibility to make predictions about the future that would serve him well three years hence.

Heading South

With the Wilmot Proviso laid to rest and the president's war funded, Congress adjourned. Webster embarked on a political tour to try to bring unity to the Whigs. He planned to travel to Virginia, North and South Carolina, Georgia, and Tennessee. After the appropriate greetings and some parading, Webster would report to a hotel, and in the evening he would give a major political address. While the trip gave him a better feel for the southern states, it also alerted him to growing divisions between the North and the South. He heard that an emerging hero of the Mexican War, Gen. Zachary Taylor, was a potential Whig nominee for 1848. Were generals to be the bane of Webster's political career? Jackson had been a demagogue who reinvented the Democratic Party, Harrison had thwarted Webster's ambitions and then died, and now Taylor and Winfield Scott, another Mexican War general, could steal the nomination of his party. Discouraged and ill, Webster cut his trip short to steam home from Savannah. By June he was recovering at Marshfield.

His other adversary within the party decided to come out of retirement. Clay's return to the Senate alerted Webster to the possibility that there was someone besides himself who could provide an alternative to the generals. In fact, it may have been Webster's illnesses and subsequent canceling of appearances that drew Clay from Kentucky in the first place.

In September 1847 the Whigs of Massachusetts met in Springfield to settle various issues. Should they bind their nominee to the Wilmot Proviso? Should they declare for Webster? How would they stay united? Suddenly Webster stepped into the fray with a speech that demonstrated he was well and as articulate as ever. He condemned the violence of the war and the Polk policy. He claimed he had supported the spirit of the Wilmot Proviso as far back as 1838. The speech was cheered. Even the great abolitionist William Lloyd Garrison praised it; in the October issue of the *Liberator* he wrote, "The Wilmot Proviso was not Mr. Wilmot's, after all, but Mr. Webster's thunder."[12] Webster was nominated by his state party, a candidate for president once again. Surely it was his turn to be the nominee, not the quadrennial runner-up Clay and certainly not any of the politically naive generals. He would be the statesman-politician, the Cicero who would seize the day. What Webster failed to see was that in embracing the proviso so strongly he had committed political suicide in the South.[13] The Cotton Whigs would never support him for the nomination.

In December Webster returned to Washington to attend Congress and to prepare for his presentation before the Supreme Court in *Luther v. Borden.* The case reached the Court in January 1848, just a month before the end of the war with Mexico. Webster represented Luther Borden, a militiaman of Rhode Island who had helped to put down Dorr's Rebellion, an 1842 attempt to establish a populist government in the state. One of the insurgents, Martin Luther, sued Borden for illegal entry and violation of his habeas corpus rights. Luther argued that the provisions of martial law declared by the state of Rhode Island had deprived him of his rights. Luther and the Dorrites were supported nationally by populist Democrats; Borden and Rhode Island were supported by states' rights Democrats and constitutional Whigs.

Webster argued that people in the states must exercise their power through elected representatives. He claimed that the states in the colonial period had been small republics, not populist bastions. The Rhode Island constitution was open to democratic amendment processes; therefore, the Dorrites had no proper grievance in this case. In fact, the Dorrites had never tried to gain remedies through the court system. They had not exhausted the legal possibilities. The state had settled this matter for itself and the federal government, particularly the Supreme Court, should not get involved. Webster relied heavily on Article IV, Section 4, of the Constitution, which guarantees that the federal government will protect states with republican forms of government in cases of insurrection. Webster portrayed the Dorrites as emotional, erratic,

12. Webster, *Writings and Speeches*, 13:345–58; *Liberator*, October 8, 1847.

13. Ironically, Lincoln would make the same mistake more than a decade later in another Springfield—Springfield, Illinois. In his "house divided" address accepting the Republican nomination for senator in 1858, he also went too far to ever have a chance of winning over the South.

and impatient, qualities he attributed to all populists. A year later, Chief Justice Taney gave the majority decision, agreeing with Webster's states' rights interpretation and limiting judicial power in such cases as these. Taney believed that this was a "political affair" best left to the state. The case set a precedent that has rarely been rejected.

The War Ends

In his annual message to Congress in December 1847, Polk asked for ten more regiments and new volunteers for the war. He believed he could force Mexico to surrender on terms generous to the United States. Sen. Jefferson Davis of Mississippi, a hero of the battle of Buena Vista, introduced the legislation in the Senate. Davis had been wounded in the foot early in the battle, but fought on to the end. Led by John Quincy Adams, the Whigs opposed the plan. On January 8, 1848, however, Ambassador Nicholas Trist ignored the president's recall orders and negotiated a settlement that reflected the original war aims of the administration. The United States would pay $15 million for "Upper California," the New Mexico Territory, and an agreement that the lower Rio Grande would serve as the southern border of Texas. In late February the draft treaty came to the Senate, where it was attacked by the Whigs. In the House the bewhiskered Adams rose to speak, only to collapse. He was carried off the floor and died while Clay held his hand.

The Senate ratified the treaty on March 10; the president signed it on March 16 and sent it back to Mexico for approval. The next day, the president's request for ten regiments was approved in the Senate over Webster's objection. On March 23, when Webster rose to speak on the goals of the war with Mexico, his frustration was evident. However, he did not let it get the best of him. As Calhoun often did, Webster aimed his speech at his supporters in the House.

The war with Mexico had the highest rate of casualties—persons injured or killed—of any war to that date by far. The casualty rate of the War of Independence was 11.6 percent and the War of 1812 had a rate of only 2.3 percent; the Mexican War had a rate of 22 percent, which has since been exceeded only by the Civil War, with a rate of 29 percent.[14] This tragic situation motivated

14. World War I had a rate of 6.8 percent, World War II 6.6 percent, and the Vietnam War 6.2 percent. Richard Holmes, ed., *The Oxford Companion to Military History*, 583.

Webster's final speech on the subject even before he heard news of a personal loss resulting from the war when his son Edward became part of the statistics.

At first the speech appeared deliberative as Webster described an anomalous situation: On the one hand, the Senate had approved a peace treaty; on the other, the president had called for more troops and more money for war. Soon, however, a forensic flavor was evident as Webster condemned the president and defended defenseless Mexico: "[W]e are summoned to fresh warlike operations; to create a new army of thirty thousand men for the further prosecution of the war; to carry the war, in the language of the president, still more dreadfully into *the vital parts of the enemy,* and to press home, by fire and sword, the claims we make and the grounds which we insist upon, against our fallen, prostrate, I had almost said, our ignoble enemy."[15]

Since the famous debate with Hayne, few people could interpret the meaning of the Constitution with more credibility than Webster. As in 1830, this powerful asset was reinforced by his ability to wither his opposition with ridicule:

> In the ordinary transaction of the foreign relations of this and of all other governments, the course has been to negotiate first, and to ratify afterwards. . . . We have chosen to reverse this order. We ratify first, and negotiate afterwards. We set up a treaty, such as we find it and choose to make it, and then send two ministers plenipotentiary to negotiate thereupon in the capital of the enemy. . . . It strikes me that the course we have adopted is strange, is even *grotesque.* So far as I know, it is unprecedented in the history of diplomatic discourse.

Perhaps that is why, claimed Webster, the House of Representatives had passed a resolution condemning the war as unconstitutionally initiated. The worst fault, however, was not the president's breach of diplomatic etiquette, but the fact that the treaty was being coerced from "fallen, fallen, fallen Mexico" in the name of acquisition. Surely this was a grave injustice.

Webster moved back to the deliberative mode when he warned that Polk was in danger of losing public support. The public, he said, "will not go for [the war's] heavy expenses; they will not find any gratification in putting the bayonet to the throats of the Mexican people." Webster then made an argument

---

15. Webster, *Speeches and Formal Writings,* 2:447–76.

common among those opposing a war, whether in Mexico, Vietnam, or the Persian Gulf. He said he resented the fact that his questioning of war aims was considered something that gave "encouragement" to the enemy. He turned the tables on Sen. Lewis Cass of Michigan, who had interrupted him with this charge, by claiming that Cass was part of the cabal trying to scare Mexico into signing the treaty. Webster's anger and sarcasm were evident:

> [Senator Cass] comes forth and tells Mexico that the principal object of the bill is to frighten her! The words have passed along the wires; they are on the Gulf, and are floating away to Vera Cruz; and when they get there, they will signify to Mexico, "After all, ye good Mexicans, my principal object is to frighten you; and to the end that you may not be frightened too much, I have given you this indication of my purpose."

Webster asked why, if American troop strength in Mexico was at 30,296, another 30,000 men were necessary? With slashing rhetorical questions, he reasserted his argument that the president's intent was coercion: "What is the object of bringing these new regiments into the field? . . . There is no army to fight. . . . Mexico is prostrate. . . . Are we going to cut the throats of her people?" Webster drove his point home by again referring to the president's unfortunate phrase: "Are we to thrust the sword deeper and deeper into the 'vital parts' of Mexico?" Continuing to blame the president, he alleged that Polk wanted to expand the war for purposes of patronage, particularly military promotions. Dripping with sarcasm, he concluded this section of the speech by saying of the applicants for promotion: "They have my good wishes that they may find the way to their homes from the Avenue and the Capitol, and from the purlieus of the president's house."

Webster returned to his main deliberative theme: "I am against all accession of territory to form new States." On this point, he was vehemently anti-imperialistic. He claimed he opposed adding the territory acquired in the war as much as he opposed adding Canada to the United States; either would allow sparsely populated areas to be overrepresented in the Senate. Expansion would damage the Constitution and throw the Senate into disarray. He claimed his opponents had confused Americans' natural desire to "emigrate" to new areas and seek new frontiers with a desire to acquire territory. He referred to the battle over the Berrien amendment, as he had in his speech of March 1, to demonstrate how close the Senate had come to rejecting territorial acquisition early in the war; that vote, he argued, better reflected public sentiment than the current discussion. Later in the speech he returned to this argument when he pointed out that in Connecticut four members of the House were thrown out by the public for supporting the president.

Next Webster refuted the opposition's argument that the president had taken a stand and could not be shaken from it. This gave Webster another chance to attack the man he hoped to unseat in the election of 1848. He recalled that the president had been adamant about the Oregon boundary but had backed down on that issue: "He is immovable. He—has—put—down—his—foot! Well, Sir, he put it down upon 'fifty-four forty,' but it didn't stay." Using his victory on the Oregon Treaty as evidence, he turned his opponents' argument against them by showing that Polk's intransigence had been compromised before and by insisting that the Senate had as much right to declare itself unshakable as the president did. He struck an epideictic note by predicting that the Democrats would not renominate Polk and that he would be a lame-duck president: "Honored in private life, valued for his private character, respectable, never eminent, in public life, he will, from the moment a new star arises, have just as little influence as you or I." He poked fun at the Democrats, saying they would claim that "manifest destiny" had "pointed out some other man" and that the accolades to this yet-to-be-determined candidate had already been written. Rather than looking ahead to the convention, he said, his Whig colleagues should be testing the president's mettle the way General Taylor had tested the enemy's at Buena Vista.

Webster's mood turned somber when he returned to the issue of converting the territories to states. His attack was lengthy and detailed. He once again established the consistency of his position on this issue. Then he raised a question that would resurface in the 1850 Compromise debates: "We admit Texas; one State for the present; but, Sir, if you refer to the resolutions providing for the annexation of Texas, you find a provision that it shall be in the power of Congress hereafter to make four new states out of Texan territory. Present and prospectively, five new States, with ten Senators, may come into the Union out of Texas." Webster was trying to persuade northern senators that the South would permanently control the Senate if new territories were converted to states, if Texas were divided into several states, or both.

Unaware that gold had been discovered in California, Webster argued that if New Mexico and California were admitted to the Union, they would have grotesquely disproportional representation in the Senate due to their sparse population: "[A]ccording to my conscientious conviction, we are now fixing on the Constitution of the United States, and its frame of government, a monstrosity, a disfiguration, an enormity!" He attempted to frighten northern Democrats by demonstrating the harm the addition of two senators from Texas already had done in the 1846 vote on the tariff. He concluded this line of attack with a prediction: "Sir, in 1850 perhaps a similar question may be agitated here."

In an effort to reduce the ardor for acquisition, Webster moved to a description of what the United States was acquiring: New Mexico and California were "not worth a dollar." He read from a report that described the territories as "poor, sterile, sandy, and barren," and reinforced this inartistic proof by pointing out that New Mexico was not exactly the land of enchantment: "It is Asiatic in scenery altogether: enormously high mountains, running up some of them ten thousand feet, with narrow valleys at their bases, through which streams sometimes trickle along." Some of his epideictic remarks mirrored his earlier prejudices: "In seclusion and remoteness, New Mexico may press hard on the character and condition of Typee.[16] And its people are infinitely less elevated, in morals and condition than the people of the Sandwich Islands." Conjuring the image of a savage, he claimed the "Indians" of New Mexico were inferior to the Native Americans with whom the nation was more familiar: "Commend me to the Cherokees, to the Choctaws; if you please, speak of the Pawnees, of the Snakes, the Flatfeet, of anything but the *Digging* Indians, and I will be satisfied not to take the people of New Mexico. . . . [I]t is farcical to talk of such people making a constitution for themselves." To reinforce his point, Webster quoted at length from a letter by John Hardin, a colonel and congressman who was killed at the battle of Buena Vista. These new territories, said Webster, would require the building of distant forts and constant battles with Native Americans. He claimed that the territories were being considered because of "fear of executive power which induces us to acquiesce in the acquisition of territory: fear, *fear*, and nothing else." It is this mix of epideictic vituperation and deliberative prophecy that characterizes this antiwar address.

Webster alleged that converting territories to states would undermine the *telos* of the Constitution, which was "designed to make [us], *one people*, one in interest, one in character, and one in political feeling." It was not just that con-

---

16. The reference is to Herman Melville's bleak novel *Typee* (1846). One is reminded of Neville Chamberlain's description of Czechoslovakia as "a far-away country" about which "we know nothing" in his speech on the appeasement of Hitler.

verting territories to states would throw the government out of balance, it was also that new cultures would interfere with Webster's call for homogeneity. He thus extended his historic position, that the Constitution established pragmatic guidelines to assure that the Union worked, to claim that the preeminent goal of the Constitution was hegemony. If America abandoned that goal, she would be no different than the most arbitrary governments that sustain rule over disparate peoples: "Russia may rule in the Ukraine and the provinces of the Caucasus and Kamtschatka by different codes, ordinances, or ukases. We can do no such thing. [The territories] must be of us, *part* of us, or else strangers." This constitutional purpose, first developed in 1833 by Webster, gave a mythological sense to his "Union," thereby raising it above provincialism. The Constitution, it seems, possessed extended purposes that served Webster through the debates over the 1850 Compromise. The Constitution was not only a pragmatic guide, a framework for Union, but also the embodiment of the people, one people, the unified American people.

In his brief, three-paragraph conclusion, Webster returned to his claim that the administration's plan would "disfigure and deform the Constitution" and cause the Union to "fall to pieces." Even though he did not have enough support to win, he said, he would continue to fight the plan because of its dire consequences. His dramatic close portrays a man on trial: "I am sustained by a deep and a conscientious sense of duty. . . . I defy auguries, and ask no omen but my country's cause!" While returning to his call of conscience, Webster ridiculed those who believed "manifest destiny" to be in America's stars.

Heeding Webster, the Whigs in the House, including Lincoln, trapped the Davis bill in committee. Lincoln had challenged the legitimacy of the war from the moment he arrived in the House. President Polk would not get his extra troops.

The Nature of Being on the Outside

Webster was inspired by the great parliamentarians who opposed imperialism, particularly Edmund Burke in his "Speech Moving His Resolutions for Conciliation with America."[17] The unstable sands of political fortune caused

---

17. Webster quoted a passage from this work to preface the pamphlet based on his July 17 address during the 1850 Compromise debates; see the editors' footnote in *Speeches and Formal Writings*, 2:553n1.

Webster to find himself in a position not unlike Burke's. In response to presidential imperialism, he had resigned as secretary of state, gone home, and eventually returned to serve in the minority party. The foregoing analysis of four speeches given at a time when Webster was out of power and often under attack demonstrates that he had mastered the strategies of partisan, anti-imperialist attack common in British parliamentary debate. He had no choice but to become a member of the loyal opposition, which inspired his partisan rhetoric, providing antiwar themes for the Whigs in the campaign of 1848. Webster integrated nonpolitical themes using forensic, epideictic, and deliberative forms to transcend partisanship. And he complicated the model by infusing his antiwar speeches with his anti-imperialist record to ground his credibility on the matter.

Webster's antiwar rhetoric also advanced his presidential ambitions. The various elements of antiwar rhetoric often take on a political flavor, such as in Webster's epideictic and forensic attacks on Polk. In the case at hand, most of the Whigs in Congress, including Lincoln, condemned the conduct of the war with Mexico while regularly voting to supply U.S. troops. By the time of these speeches, Webster had been a member of the House, a senator, and a secretary of state. The next step was obvious, since several previous secretaries of state had become president. Webster's personal attacks on Polk's public statements, intellect, and political fortunes were in part motivated by his own ambition. His rhetoric in these speeches was marked by more sarcasm, ridicule, cynicism, and refutation than was found in his previous speeches. Surely there was sarcasm and ridicule in the Reply to Hayne; as we have seen, Hayne was reduced to rubble on his lack of knowledge of Shakespeare alone. However, there was also the soaring finale that was memorized by schoolchildren and became part of America's civil religion. No such perorations mark these speeches. They are the speeches of a shadow minister vindicating his policies, calling others to account, and attacking those who have replaced him. The attacks on the president, in particular, reveal a man claiming to have a better sense of policy than does his adversary. Webster's style here is less grand and more bitter than in the periods before and after this interregnum: the previews are skimpy, the structure less logical, the conclusions not as well developed. Perhaps because of the distractions of ambition, Webster's most elevated addresses were delivered when he was farthest from the possibility of being nominated for president.

Webster's addresses on the war with Mexico do braid the classical forms effectively; his arguments gain credibility from being contextualized in an anti-imperialist frame. Antiwar rhetoric often examines issues of racism and moral superiority, just as prowar rhetoric is often ethnocentric. Over the ages imperialism has been justified on the ground that the colonized are inferior people who need to be helped to the fruits of better government, be it the common law of the British or the democratic virtues of the Americans. This forces antiwar rhetors to demonstrate that the colonized do not need the fruits of another culture, that it is not in the national interest to intervene in their affairs, or that they are so inferior or alien in culture that the result will be entrapment in a quagmire. The moral tone combined with the opposition to change, whether that change involves expansion or entering a war, gives antiwar rhetoric a conservative cast. In defending the status quo and advancing a value-laden agenda, it frequently produces epideictic appeals. Such appeals are often reinforced with geographic arguments. That American troops are serving in a place they do not belong is a typical charge of antiwar rhetors, whether condemning the taking of the Philippines or wars in such remote places as Southeast Asia or the Middle East.

Webster embraced a moral and philosophical stance that he reinforced with graphic geographic portrayals of the territory in question. He sought the moral high ground with regard to both slavery and territorial acquisition in an attempt to become the quintessential Whig civil republican, the modern embodiment of Pericles and Cicero. In waging his campaign of persuasion, he established a highly defined antiwar position couched in an overarching anti-imperialism. Together they reinforced his prior opposition to taking "alien" territories by force and his preference for negotiated settlements. The merging of epideictic, deliberative, and forensic themes allowed Webster to argue that military acquisition would not only rip the social fabric but that it would also undermine the workings of the Constitution by destroying the balance in the Senate and eviscerate the transcendent *telos* of the Constitution that made Americans into one people. These speeches predicted the disintegration of the Union if the acquired territories were made into states. In fact it was that, along with the repeal of the Missouri Compromise in 1854, which would lead to the Civil War.

Unwinding these themes reveals an agenda that endorses Anglo-Saxon values and culture, the same agenda that others would later use to defend the very imperialism Webster opposed. Webster believed in a "natural religion" that included, as he put it in 1828, "the existence and perfection of the Deity, which the contemplation of natural objects produces."[18] By 1846, like Edmund Burke, Webster strongly supported organized religion, believing it to be one of the foundations of civilized society. He demonstrated that someone who embraces Anglo-Saxon virtues and believes them to be superior to others may oppose expansion on the same grounds that imperialists use to defend it. He described the Native Americans and the geography of the region in primitive terms, and he used Polk's chauvinistic view of Mexico as an inferior country with an inferior army to buttress his own claim that acquisition of Mexican territory would pollute American values and politics. Thus, his conservative rhetoric defended the status quo and claimed moral and political superiority over a primitive enemy.

Webster knew that campaigns of persuasion need to manipulate epideictic, deliberative, and forensic elements to be effective. It should come as no surprise, then, that his antiwar campaign embodied this strategy. Whether the main genre was epideictic, deliberative, or forensic, Webster inserted elements of the other genres to support his persuasive themes. In an ostensibly deliberative speech on the floor of the Senate, for example, Webster condemned the president in forensic terms while praising the Union in epideictic terms. Clearly he found it efficacious to braid the major genres in his antiwar public addresses.

Did Webster manage to affect public events with his antiwar rhetoric? While he failed to persuade his opponents in the immediate sense, he helped to dislodge them a year later. These four speeches contained many substantial arguments that were used in the ensuing presidential campaign by other Whigs to warn about the spread of southern political power. The Whigs won the election of 1848, capturing the White House and splitting the Senate and the House. There are other measures of Webster's effectiveness during this period. After the war, William Tecumseh Sherman attributed to Webster the notion that the U.S. government is like the solar system; it works in perfect harmony when each body pulls no more nor less than its natural gravity. However, when the *demos* gives too much weight to the presidential planet, the system can implode. Sherman soon joined the Whig Party.[19]

With these speeches, Webster established a record to which he could return

18. Daniel Webster to Jacob McGraw, October 11, 1828, in *Papers of Daniel Webster: Correspondence*, 2:368–69.

19. Sherman also agreed with Webster's opinion of President Jackson. Lee Kennett, *Sherman: A Soldier's Life*, 105.

in 1850 to effect a compromise. The success of that campaign owed a good deal to the credibility Webster was able to generate from his rhetoric against the war with Mexico. Those who employ antiwar rhetoric are often disdained for their dire predictions. Later, however, they may have the last word, in effect saying, "I told you so." For Webster this worked both ways: because he had been an anti-imperialist, his antiwar rhetoric was consistent and credible; in 1850, because he had opposed war, his more general appeals for compromise were consistent and credible. As we shall see, his rhetoric worked because the crisis of 1850 blunted the cry for expansion, which had hurt him in 1846.

Webster's intertwining of the various strands of classical genres was complicated by the contextualization of antiwar themes as part of a larger, consistent, and historical anti-imperialist approach. An examination of the matrix that Webster built with these speeches is useful in revealing the motives that are typical of antiwar rhetoric. Webster failed to prevent Texas's admission to the Union and the acquisition of new territories because the mood of the nation was against him and the congressional coalition supporting President Polk had too many votes. The tides of history can lead to political exile or vindication. Had the war in Mexico gone badly or had the public and his colleagues believed Webster's warnings, trusted his description of the territories, and embraced his view of the Constitution, he might have stopped America's march west and been nominated for president. Instead he was overpowered by popular sentiment and the presidential determination to connect America from sea to shining sea. When the expanded Union began to come apart, Webster was pressed back into service to forge a compromise that would postpone the ultimate rift for another ten years.

Chapter 10

National Crisis, Capitol Gridlock

The presidential election year of 1848 saw the end of the war with Mexico, but it began tragically for Webster. He received word that his son Edward had died of typhoid fever in San Angel, Mexico, in January. Losing a son of only twenty-seven years threw Webster into a depression. The tragedy was compounded a few months later as he watched his daughter, Julia, die of consumption. On the day of her funeral, her brother's body arrived from Mexico. Only Fletcher, on whom Webster came to rely, would survive his father. (He died leading a company in the Civil War, the conflict his father fought so hard to prevent.)

The news from the political front was not welcome. Clay announced his candidacy for president in April and Taylor continued to gain popularity among Whigs who were thirsty for victory, including the young Lincoln. Their last victory in 1840 had been washed away by the death of Harrison and the desertion of Tyler, first on the bank issue and then on Texas statehood. Furthermore, the Conscience Whigs were leery of Clay because he owned slaves and had equivocated on the Texas question. Would they support Webster? Or would the party coalesce around Taylor, ignoring the slaves he kept on his Louisiana plantation? Like many other Conscience Whigs, Lincoln endorsed "Old Rough and Ready" because Clay had lost in the past and Webster failed to generate public enthusiasm.

The Whigs held their convention in Philadelphia in June. In order to block Clay and Taylor, Webster needed the support of New England and one large state. New York was the logical choice given his business connections there and the abolitionist sentiment led by William Seward, now a U.S. senator. Millard

Fillmore, a former congressman, was Webster's operative in the state. Edward Everett, ever loyal and often abused, was commissioned to line up the New England delegates and any other strays he could find. The 64-year-old Taylor sent a letter to the convention making clear that he would support the nominee of the party, whoever that might be. The letter was meant to overcome criticism that Taylor had not voted and might bolt the party if he were not nominated or if the party endorsed the Wilmot Proviso. The subtext was that Taylor's delegates wanted a similar pledge from Clay and Webster.

The first ballot did not encourage Webster's followers. He received only 22 votes to 111 for Taylor, 97 for Clay, and 43 for Winfield Scott. Worse yet, he received only one vote from New York. His managers knew they had failed him and rightly suspected a deal had been struck between Seward and Taylor. On the second ballot, Taylor and Scott picked up strength while Clay's candidacy flagged. With that, the convention adjourned for the day.

On June 9 the Connecticut delegates moved to Taylor; he was now only seven votes shy of the nomination. On the final ballot, Taylor received 171 votes to 63 for Scott and 32 for Clay. Fillmore was nominated for vice president on the second ballot, giving New York a reward for its support of Taylor and placing Webster's protégé on the ticket. That event had major consequences in the battle to achieve a compromise two summers later. One reason the compromise was so difficult to achieve was that Taylor had made certain concessions to Conscience Whigs in return for their support—not only for his candidacy but also for his plans to expand the United States.

Webster had said he could not support Taylor for president. To keep order in the party and have any influence at all in the new administration, he was forced to humble himself. He would, however, remain fairly remote from the campaign.

In August the Free Soil Party nominated Martin Van Buren for president and Charles Francis Adams for vice president. Whigs worried that this ticket might pull enough Conscience Whigs away to elect the Democratic nominee, Lewis Cass. Already, Charles Sumner and David Wilmot had joined the Free Soil campaign. In a speech on September 1 near Marshfield, Webster stated plainly that the Taylor-Fillmore ticket was the lesser of three evils: "I have read [the Whig] platform, and though I think there are some unsound places in it, I can stand upon it pretty well. But I see nothing in it both new and valuable. 'What is valuable is not new, and what is new is not valuable.'"[1] He would

---

1. Webster was quoting Lord Henry Brougham.

hold his nose and vote for the Whig ticket. Free Soilers spread the rumor that Webster had been bribed to give the speech, but the nation followed Webster's lead. Carrying Pennsylvania, New York, and a good deal of the South, Taylor was elected president and was more beholden to Seward than ever. The alliance with Seward was less unusual than many believed. Taylor had little use for sectionalism and any form of states' rights that might hinder his dream of an ocean-to-ocean nation. He allied himself with those who could help him leave this legacy.

Fillmore would be marginalized in the new administration. Webster was isolated not only from policy making but also from the appointments process, but he retained a close friendship with Fillmore.

Anatomy of a Crisis

The United States Senate has faced many crises, but few have been as difficult or protracted as the debate over slavery in 1850. Riots broke out in major cities. Southern states threatened to secede. And the president threatened to force his views upon the nation regardless of congressional preferences. To understand the significance of Webster's achievement in attaining a compromise, we need to understand the men who worked with him and against him, as well as the events that provided opportunities and obstacles through the course of the crisis.[2]

The candidates elected to the House of Representatives in 1848 included a large group of freshmen that was divided almost evenly between Whigs and Democrats, with enough Free Soilers to make consensus practically impossible. When the House tried to organize itself in 1849, it took sixty-four ballots to select a speaker.

The fractured Senate had organized more quickly, but the tension was no less severe. As the 1850 session got under way in January, 55 percent of the Senate was Democratic, 42 percent Whig, and 3 percent Free Soil. Of the Democratic total, 54 percent were from slave states; of the Whig total, 48 percent were from slave states. Further complicating the situation was the fact that since several of the southern senators were from border states such as

---

2. This reading of events is intended to provide a corrective to previous interpretations, including those of Robert F. Dalzell, *Daniel Webster and the Trial of American Nationalism, 1843–1852*, 191–216, and Elbert Smith, *The Death of Slavery*, 107–14.

Missouri and Maryland, it was not clear how they would come down on cru-cial issues. Their constituents held strong Union or slavery sympathies; fearing a split within their states, they were more open to compromise than their Deep South colleagues.[3]

The situation was further destabilized by the fact that a change of leadership was taking place. The 1850 Compromise debate would prove to be the last hurrah for Henry Clay, John C. Calhoun, and Daniel Webster. Each had been elected to the House prior to 1815, each had served as secretary of state, each had sought but never attained the presidency, and each would die shortly: Calhoun in 1850, Clay and Webster in 1852. The Compromise debate would serve to initiate such future leaders as William Seward, Stephen A. Douglas, and Jefferson Davis.[4] Seward would eventually serve as Lincoln's secretary of state. Douglas would become famous for debating Lincoln in 1858 and then losing the presidency to him in 1860. Davis, one of the heroes of the battle of Buena Vista, had become a wealthy slave owner by the time of the 1850 de-bates. His plantation, Brierfield, took in over $35,000 a year, a hefty figure at the time. Such colorful debaters as Henry Foote of Mississippi, Thomas Hart Benton of Missouri, Salmon P. Chase of Ohio, and John Hale of New Hamp-shire were also on hand.

One way to represent the fracturing is to break the Senate into groups defined by their preferred solution to the slavery question. The southern Demo-crats, headed by Calhoun and Davis, wanted to extend slavery into the territo-ries. They believed that the South had been treated unfairly, that it was inadequately represented in the House, and that it needed the extension of slavery into new states to survive. About one-quarter of the Senate belonged to this group. The United States was (or were, to use the idiom of the time) di-vided equally between fifteen free states and fifteen slaveholding states. To admit a single new state would upset the balance and put one section of the country over the other. The balance must be maintained at all costs.

A second group, led by Cass and Douglas, favored "popular sovereignty." That is, each territory should vote on its own to decide whether slaveholding would be allowed within its borders when it became a state. In the presidential campaign of 1848, Cass had called for "squatter sovereignty" to determine

3. Percentages were calculated using the figures in Holman Hamilton, *Prologue to Conflict: The Crisis and Compromise of 1850*, 34.
4. See William J. Cooper, Jr. *Jefferson Davis, American*.

whether the territory acquired from Mexico would be organized as free or slaveholding; Douglas euphemized the term to "popular sovereignty." This group generally worked behind the scenes to try to shift the slavery question from the federal government to the citizens of the states-to-be. They constituted another quarter of the Senate and were predominantly Democrats from the North. Douglas precipitated the first alarm of the crisis when he introduced a bill in December 1848 to admit all the territory gained in the war with Mexico as one state.

Another faction consisted of northern hardliners. They supported President Taylor in his effort to exclude slavery from the territories and newly admitted states, overlooking his past opposition to the Wilmot Proviso. Led by Seward, this group of Conscience Whigs conspired with the president. They would give him his new states if those states were kept free of slaves. Taylor told them he wanted California admitted as a free state and did not believe the New Mexico Territory was physically hospitable to slavery. Webster knew that such a move would inflame the South, throw the Senate out of balance, and lead to secession.

The remainder of the Senate was divided between those who, like Webster and Clay, sought equitable compromise through omnibus legislation and those who were simply undecided. The "undecideds" were mainly from the South and were crucial to hopes for a compromise.

The issues involved in the debate were as tangled as the political prejudices of the participants. They can be traced to the recently concluded war with Mexico, in which the United States defended its annexation of Texas and expanded the size of the country by approximately a quarter. Under the leadership of Sam Houston, Texas had won its independence from Mexico in 1836. Texas had immediately petitioned for annexation by the United States, but President Jackson feared that admitting Texas would have an adverse effect on the presidential election of that year. Texas therefore turned its attention to Europe in order to obtain necessary capital for development of its vast territory. England and France were eager to recognize the Republic of Texas, and the three nations established strong ties, which had repercussions in the Civil War.

By 1844 President Tyler and Secretary of State Calhoun believed annexation of Texas was possible. As we have seen, however, Calhoun's letter to British minister Richard Pakenham, with its pro-slavery, states' rights rhetoric, intensified northern opposition and led to the defeat of the treaty. Finally, by a joint resolution of both houses of Congress, Texas was admitted to the

Union in February 1845 and officially became a state in December after Congress passed enabling legislation over Webster's strenuous objections. The resolution of admission contained three provisions that would become nettlesome in the 1850 debate: 1) Texas could be subdivided into as many as four additional states; 2) it had to pay the debts it had incurred prior to joining the Union; 3) it had to turn its boundary disputes over to the U.S. Government. The joint resolution passed the House by a vote of 120 to 98 and squeaked through the Senate on a vote of 27 to 25.

When Mexico refused offers of money for California and the New Mexico Territory in 1846, President Polk ordered General Taylor's army into the disputed territory and the war began. On February 2, 1848, the treaty of Guadalupe Hidalgo was signed, whereby Mexico ceded the New Mexico Territory and California to the United States. Ironically, gold had been discovered in the Sacramento Valley in January and eighty thousand new settlers began their emigration to California. These events spurred California politicians to clamor for statehood. The gold rush brought new traffic to the Santa Fe Trail, which had seen commercial use as early as 1821. Settlers who dropped off in Albuquerque and Santa Fe began to organize the territory of New Mexico for statehood.

A period of rapid expansion led to the crisis of 1850. Besides Texas in 1845, Iowa (1846) and Wisconsin (1848) were admitted as states. Title to Oregon was affirmed in 1846, preserving the Oregon Trail. And in August 1848, after a heated debate that rehearsed the arguments of 1850, Congress passed and Polk signed the Oregon Bill, which asserted northern power by refusing to extend the Missouri Compromise line into the West.[5]

Congress had the responsibility for organizing these new territories because it implemented the Constitution in the territories. In early 1848 when Webster offered his amendment to prohibit slavery in any new states created out of the former Mexican territory, he made just this point. The amendment failed, but even Calhoun, who opposed it, embraced Webster's philosophical position— as did the compromisers, who in the long run would become Webster's allies.

In early 1849 a group of northern senators led by Sen. Joseph Root of Ohio

5. The political situation in 1850 was also complicated by the rapid increase in immigration from Europe. Most of the immigrants were Catholics, which spurred the creation of the Supreme Order of the Star-Spangled Banner, a xenophobic group that evolved into the "Know Nothing" Party, also known as the American Party. By 1854 it would win control of the Massachusetts state government.

initiated legislation through the Committee on Territories to establish territorial governments in New Mexico and California that would prohibit slavery. In direct messages to the territories President Taylor supported this initiative, against the advice of Fillmore. In so doing, he usurped the authority of the congressional majority that favored congressional control of the territories.

Nonetheless, Californians were delighted and acted precipitously. By October, only seven months after Taylor's inauguration and without waiting for the required congressional approval, they had passed an anti-slavery constitution, elected a state government, and sent members to Congress. New Mexico and the Mormon home state of Deseret (comprising what is now Utah, Nevada, and parts of Idaho and Wyoming) followed California's lead by establishing provisional governments.

As crisis loomed, Webster spoke to an audience of aristocrats and well-heeled supporters in New York to celebrate the departure of the Pilgrims from England on their way to Plymouth Rock. At sixty-seven, he appeared war-weary and tired. He rose to the occasion, however, quoting Latin phrases and providing a federalist version of American history.[6] He then retired to Marshfield to regain his strength for the opening of Congress in December 1849.

Confrontation with the President

When criticized in the Senate and the press for the secrecy surrounding his messages to potential states, Taylor became defensive. On January 23, 1850, he notified the Senate of his actions: "I did not hesitate to express to the people of those Territories my desire that each Territory should . . . form a plan of a State constitution and submit the same to Congress with a prayer for admission . . . but I did not anticipate, suggest, or authorize the establishment of any such government without the assent of Congress."[7] The ensuing controversy centered on the organization of New Mexico and Deseret and the admission of California as a state.

By the end of January, these and other issues had frozen the Senate into legislative gridlock. Members of Congress were ready to stand up to the new president, believing he had usurped their powers. They faced tough questions:

---

6. The speech was reported in the *New York Tribune* and printed on October 9 in the *National Intelligencer*.

7. Zachary Taylor, "Message to the Senate, January 23, 1850," 27.

Should the slave trade continue in the District of Columbia? Should fugitive slaves be returned to their owners? Should California be split in two? Should Texas, as was allowed under the annexation treaty, be split into five slave states? Should the federal government assume the Texas debt? This last issue would prove particularly useful to Webster because northern Whigs held most of the bonds on the debt. Should a compromise pass, they would collect at inflated rates. Should it fail, they stood to lose a good deal of money. Since the bond-holders were influential businessmen, they could exert pressure by lobbying for compromise. Webster not only took money from them, he also suggested ways by which they could succeed in changing votes. Furthermore, over glasses of port and in letters, Webster warned business leaders that no tariff legislation would be possible until a compromise was passed.

Southern interests opposed any solution short of splitting Texas into more states and extending slavery into the territories. They used every argument to defend the last vestiges of their power. For example, on the question of abolishing the slave trade in the District of Columbia, they claimed that such a move would require the permission of the state of Maryland since Maryland had donated the land for the District's formation in the first place.

The national audience was as divided as Congress. Cotton Whigs and Democrats were balanced against Conscience Whigs and Democrats. Free Soilers and abolitionists were even more strident than southern secessionists and slaveholders. Northern Free Soil and abolitionist sentiment favored legislation directly opposed to southern cotton and slaving interests. Southern hardliners supported legislation inflammatory to the northern moralists. Each group tried to put the other on the defensive. Southerners appealed for a strict reading of the Constitution; northerners appealed to a higher law.

The depth of the division over slavery was evident early and surfaced in the most sacred beliefs of Americans. By the 1840s, for example, both the Baptist and Methodist churches had split into separate northern and southern organizations over the slavery question. In 1843 Henry H. Garnet, a minister, lecturer, and ex-slave, called for slaves to resist their owners. In 1849 John Brown printed Garnet's address and distributed it in the South. It contained provocative language: "Slavery! How much misery is comprehended in that single word. . . . Unless the image of God be obliterated from the soul, all men cherish the love of liberty. . . . Brethren, the time has come when you must act for yourselves. . . . You had far better all die—die immediately, than live [as] slaves. Let your motto be resistance! Resistance! Resistance!" This incendiary document enraged southerners. One southern clergyman typified the religious defense of slavery in the summer of 1849: "The degraded state and squalid condition of poor negroes in the so called free States, show them to be greatly injured, civilly and morally. . . . Hence the wisdom and prudence of the free negro . . . as desiring to sell himself into slavery, valuing his freedom at the moderate price of $150."[8]

Passions ran high for many reasons, not the least of which was that 1.7 million of the 6 million people who lived in the South were members of slaveholding families. This total does not include the more than 3 million slaves, who were each counted as three-fifths of a person for the purpose of apportioning seats in the House of Representatives. Slaves were essential to raising cotton profitably because cotton was more labor-intensive than other crops. It required not only picking and baling, but also carding, separating, and spinning. In 1850, the South also supplied half of the nation's corn, 87 percent of its hemp, 80 percent of its beans and peas, and nearly all of its rice, but these were not the money crops. Those were tobacco, sugar, and "King Cotton." In 1860, for example, southern cotton brought $190 million on European markets alone, while rice brought only $2 million. The entire social and economic structure of the South was imperiled by the prospect of emancipation,[9] which, while not among the compromise proposals, was certainly on the minds of abolitionists and their representatives in Congress.

With the president threatening to veto anything but unconditional statehood for California, Congress became hopelessly deadlocked. Webster's warning about electing a politically naive general echoed throughout the nation. Tempers grew short in Congress and often exploded into physical confrontations. Senators Foote and Benton became so heated in one exchange that Benton charged toward Foote, who drew a pistol. Foote had insulted Benton by reminding the Senate that he had been thrown out of college for stealing. Both men had to be physically restrained by their colleagues, one of whom pushed Foote's gun hand into the air just as he pulled the trigger.

Anxiety intensified in the money markets of the nation and among concerned citizens. The newspapers fed daily on the deepening crisis. Those who sought a compromise faced an uphill battle. The House, the Senate, and the

8. Henry H. Garnet, "Rise Up and Resist," 102; southern clergyman quoted in Henry Clay, "Response to John Brown," 6.

9. Richard N. Current, T. Harry Williams, and Frank Freidel, *American History: A Survey,* 325.

nation were seriously divided by party, by region, and, perhaps most dangerous of all, by religion. This was not only a tempest in the halls of Congress, it also caused tumult in the public sphere.

Clay's Omnibus Bill

Perhaps earlier than any of the other members of the Senate, Henry Clay saw the impending danger of the 1850 legislative session. He therefore returned to his familiar desk in the Senate chamber in 1850. On a cold, wet night in January of that year, the elderly Clay toddled out of his home to be helped into his carriage and driven to the home of Daniel Webster. Over port, they discussed the crisis.

Clay was anxious to gain Webster as an ally. The two men had known one another for more than forty years. In the process they had helped to create the Whig Party, and they had battled each other three times for its nomination. On the chilly night of January 21, 1850, Clay and Webster had a good deal about which to reminisce. They had both lost sons in Mexico, Clay's bayoneted by Mexican regulars and Webster's lost to disease. They had both fought Taylor for their party's nomination, and had both been excluded from the new president's inner circle. As Clay warmed himself beside Webster's fire, he warned his old colleague that this crisis was worse than the others they had seen. The South had helped win the war with Mexico and it wanted its share of the spoils. President Taylor, though a slave owner himself, had surprised southerners by making it clear that he would refuse to extend slavery into the newly formed territories. At the end of their meeting, Webster agreed to support Clay's compromise.

The president was suspicious of Clay's motives for returning to the Senate. Taylor was a blunt man, short of stature and temper. He had been a hero in the War of 1812, in the Indian wars that followed, and in the war with Mexico, where he had captured Monterey, Buena Vista, Palo Alto, and Resaca de la Palma. Having dispatched the Mexican army, he had little patience for the U.S. Senate. When he learned of Clay's compromise plan on January 29, he was outraged. He met with Seward and encouraged him to block the omnibus proposal. Clay asked his colleagues to help him control Taylor rather than jockey among themselves for the 1852 presidential nomination.

Clay, looking thin and pale, began his lengthy oration in support of a compromise on February 5 and finished the next day. Below the Senate chamber, Webster was arguing a case before the Supreme Court. Calhoun was in his sickbed. To a crowded gallery and nearly full chamber, Clay outlined the causes of the crisis and offered his solutions: First, admit California with no predisposition as to slavery. If slavery worked in California, so be it. If it was not economically viable, then the citizens of that state would not introduce it there. (This was disingenuous of Clay since the California organizers had already declared themselves opposed to slavery.) Second, reject the Wilmot Proviso, which called for prohibiting slavery in the territories, and replace it with popular sovereignty. Third, settle the New Mexico boundary dispute with Texas, granting to New Mexico her claim east of the Rio Grande. Fourth, the United States should assume the debt that Texas had incurred during the war with Mexico. Fifth, Congress should prohibit the slave *trade* in the District of Columbia, but allow *ownership* of slaves there. Sixth, fugitive slaves should be returned to their rightful owners. Clay concluded: "I implore . . . that if the direful event of the dissolution of this Union is to happen, I shall not survive to behold the sad and heart-rending spectacle."

As early as mid-February he knew that he had failed. Abolitionists condemned the speech, southern extremists attacked his California plan, and northern Whigs supported President Taylor. Even southern Whigs, who were Clay's natural allies, began to pick the omnibus package to pieces. While Webster would support most of the proposals, he balked at "popular sovereignty."

On February 23 the president sealed the fate of Clay's plan. In a meeting with Reps. Alexander Stephens and Robert Toombs of Georgia, Taylor promised to hang all "traitors" and made clear he meant those who spoke of secession. Stephens and Toombs told their colleagues that Taylor was referring to the southern extremists. The incident disrupted all attempts at conciliation between the various factions. On March 1 Webster wrote to his son that he was ready to deliver "a Union speech."[10] He believed it was time for him to speak, but before he could put his arguments in order, word came that Calhoun would precede him. Webster visited the dying Calhoun on March 2, hoping to win him over. Men on their deathbeds, however, are unlikely to compromise.

The press had speculated that Calhoun was too weak to participate in the 1850 session. So when he came to the Senate on March 4 to oppose Clay's omnibus proposal, the gallery was packed and the chamber was electric with excitement. Calhoun's leonine mane of white hair contrasted sharply with his formal black coat. Those assembled watched as the noble "War Hawk" of the House was helped to his seat by a colleague.

10. Quoted in Baxter, *One and Inseparable*, 411.

The gaunt Calhoun rose, thanked his colleagues, and asked Senator James Mason of Virginia to read his address to the Senate. The speech was one of his most impressive. In it, he rationalized southern obstinacy on the slavery issue, stiffened resistance to compromise, and incited radicals from the North such as Seward to oppose compromise from their side. Most important, in an interesting use of metaphor and metaphysics, Calhoun seized the high ground in the debate over compromise. He would not go on the defensive, but instead aggressively argued that the South's position was morally right and was derived from the intent of the founders of the nation. Calhoun denounced Clay's proposals as well as the plan of President Taylor as hopeless. He spent little time on Clay's omnibus bill, claiming that other senators had dealt with it adequately. He went on at some length, however, with a detailed attack on the president's plan. Calhoun even called for a dual presidency: one president from the North and one from the South.

Calhoun concluded his address by offering his solution, noting (to the dismay of Webster and Clay) that the South had "no compromise to offer, but the Constitution; and no concession or surrender to make. She has already surrendered so much that she has little left to surrender." He called on the North to concede to the South "an equal right in the acquired territory"; to "do her duty" by returning fugitive slaves, ending abolitionist agitation; and "to provide for the insertion of a provision in the Constitution, by an amendment, which will restore to the South, in substance," equal power with the North.[11] Calhoun thereby shifted the burden of proof to the North. His demands were so extreme, his challenge so strong, that compromise was impossible if southern senators embraced his position.

What most concerned Webster and others seeking a compromise were Calhoun's ominous last words: "Having faithfully done my duty to the best of my ability, both to the Union and my section, throughout this agitation, I shall have the consolation, let what will come, that I am free of all responsibility." Webster knew at the moment he heard these words that Calhoun had abandoned the idea of any compromise. "Let what will come" was a clear reference to war. If the South followed Calhoun's lead, the battle was surely lost, just as Clay had feared.

To the cheers of southerners in the gallery and on the floor, Calhoun rose and, leaning on the arm of a friend, left the Senate. He could not sleep that

11. Given that each slave counted as three-fifths of a person toward southern representation in the House, Calhoun's plea for equal power rankled northerners.

night, so he wrote to a friend about his speech, which he called "among my most successful." He returned once to the Senate, to hear Webster's speech of March 7. Three weeks later, as he lay dying, he uttered his last words: "The South, the poor South." On April 1, his body lay in state in the Senate chamber while mourners, including Webster, paid their last respects. The head of the southern pride had departed from the field of battle, and now the hunt was left to the young lions.

It is not surprising that before entering the controversy of 1850, Webster enjoyed a favorable press and a large following. "Webster's name became symbolically attached to the concepts of Constitution, Union, and the wisdom and virtue of the age of Washington," according to one biographer.[12] Webster's identification with American civil religion helped him elevate his arguments on March 7 to a transcendent level, while providing him with unprecedented credibility.

The Seventh of March Address

The night before the speech, Webster worked on the draft with Fletcher and two close friends, Edward (Ned) Curtis and Peter Harvey. They faced a huge burden: Webster needed to revive Clay's compromise and dissipate the effect of Calhoun's rhetoric. He may have realized that the former was an unrealistic goal, but at least in the North and among compromisers in the South the latter was obtainable. He could, if he were patient, lay the foundation for a compromise later in the session.

He began the three-and-a-half-hour speech by evoking Marc Antony: "I speak today for the preservation of the Union. 'Hear me for my cause.' I speak today for the restoration to the country of that quiet and that harmony which make the blessings of this Union so rich and so dear to us all."[13] Webster was asking the North to preserve not some abstract form of liberty but rather the system of government that had ensured prosperity in the past. Near the end of the speech he pointed out that the alternative to Union would be a war that threatened every person, North and South.

Throughout the speech, Webster discussed the causes of the crisis and ways to avoid the specter of secession while restoring harmony and peace. Con-

12. Bartlett, *Daniel Webster*, 121.
13. Webster, *Speeches and Formal Writings*, 2:515–51.

cerning the limitation of slavery by law, he said: "There is not at this moment
... a single foot of land, the character of which, in regard to its being free soil
territory or slave territory, is not fixed by some law, and some irrepealable law,
beyond the power of action of this government." Seeing that the president
would not bow to the will of Congress and that his supporters would block the
compromise, Webster appealed to this higher "irrepealable law" in his discussion of slavery in the California and New Mexico territories: "I hold slavery to
be excluded from those territories by a law superior to that which admits and
sanctions it in Texas. I mean the law of nature, of physical geography. . . . That
law settles forever . . . that slavery cannot exist in California or New Mexico."
Like Clay, Webster was certain that these arid territories could not support the
crops that required slave labor and thus would not prove profitable for slaveholders. It would have taken a massive irrigation effort to turn California into
a major cotton-producing state. Thus the decision as to whether a state came
in free or slave was not in the hands of Congress after all; it was in the hands
of nature. With this logic Webster sought to transcend the partisan wrangle
and also appeal to the general public.

Webster next scolded "Northern Democracy" for having supported the admission of Texas in 1845 in its greed for land. He observed that according to
the agreements made, the state of Texas could be divided into several slave states;
however, he implied that it was up to Congress to decide when those states
could be formed.

Having laid the groundwork, Webster began to spin out his understanding
of states' rights by reviewing the history of slavery. In his biography of Webster,
Henry Cabot Lodge wrote that it was a waste of time to review such a familiar
subject and "merely legalistic."[14] Yet Webster not only de-escalated the moral
implications of slavery but, more important to Free Soilers and Cass supporters, he also tied the expansion of slavery to the expansion of the cotton industry. He knew that if he could convert the debate to an economics and
geography lesson, the facts would support him. He faced trouble on moral
grounds, where the South had been stung and the North was obstinate. He
therefore argued that it was social and economic conditions in the North that
led to the moral judgment against slavery and that the South defended slavery
only after it had been justified economically: "It was the cotton interest that
gave a new desire to promote slavery, to spread it, and to use its labor." With

14. Henry Cabot Lodge, *Daniel Webster*, 301.

this strategy Webster hoped to defuse the fear of "slave power" while deflating the righteous indignation of the abolitionists. He not only diminished the moral issue, but also sought to identify with his audience through pragmatic economics. He concluded this argument by stating: "Sir, wherever there is a particular good to be done, wherever there is a foot of land to be stayed back from becoming slave territory, I am ready to assert the principle of the exclusion of slavery. I am pledged to it from the year 1837; but I will not do a thing unnecessary, that wounds the feelings of others." Webster hoped the North would understand that adopting the compromise would not expand slavery but would preserve the Union.

Webster also tried to appeal to the public sphere by appealing to latent attitudes in his review of grievances produced by the North and the South, which had "alienated the minds of one portion of the country from the other." No legislative action could be taken to correct most of the offenses, he said. However, there was one southern complaint that Congress could correct: the North's unwillingness to return fugitive slaves. Webster suggested that if northerners stopped to investigate the matter, they would come to understand that they had a constitutional obligation to return fugitive slaves. This argument probably appealed to most northerners; the abolitionists were a minority. People who were interested in preserving the Union and the prosperity that went with it would want to preserve the constitutional principles that held the Union together.

Webster knew that the southern moderates would be placated further if abolitionists were criticized. So he characterized the abolitionists as people who "think what is right may be distinguished from what is wrong with the precision of an algebraic equation." If they detected a spot on the sun, Webster surmised, they would want to strike the sun from the heavens. Although he conceded that there were thousands of "perfectly well meaning men" in the abolitionist societies, they had, by their vicious attacks, helped strengthen southern support for slavery instead of weakening it. Webster's strategy was to separate the moralistic abolitionists from the rest of the North in order to minimize their influence. This tactic particularly annoyed the abolitionists and motivated their intense hostility toward the speech.[15] Webster's arguments,

---

15. In a published letter to Webster on March 20, Van Buren was particularly upset with his attacks on abolitionists, dubbing them "sophistical." Quoted in Samuel M. Smucker, *The Life, Speeches, and Memorials of Daniel Webster,* 254.

however, were consistent with prevailing northern attitudes. Like most reformers, he believed that elimination of slavery was impossible. Many northerners saw "Negro colonization"—forced emigration to Africa or Central America—as the only real answer to the slavery problem. Once Texas was no longer an option, northerners had formed the American Colonization Society, which sought to place African Americans in Liberia. Many clergymen believed that although "slavery was a moral problem, abolition was not the moral way to solve it."[16] Students at Harvard Medical School had protested when their dean, Oliver Wendell Holmes, tried to admit African Americans. Holmes's decision was reversed, revealing the bigotry of the nation's leading academic institution.

Even though Congress could not resolve northern grievances, Webster discussed them in an effort to identify with the North. He charged the South with extending and extolling the institution of slavery. He objected to several southern claims, especially the assertion that slaves were happier and in better condition than free laborers. As he had done on his speaking tours, Webster summoned the pride of many northerners: "Why, who are the laboring people of the North? They are the whole North. They are the people who cultivate their own farms with their own hands; freeholders, educated men, independent men. If they are not freeholders, they earn wages; these wages accumulate, are turned into capital, into new freeholds, and small capitalists are formed. They provide the means of independence." He complained of "free colored men" being seized from northern ships in southern ports, an unconstitutional act. Finally, he suggested that the South, like the North, had constitutional obligations to perform. Completing the symmetry of his appeal, he said: "[S]o far as any of these grievances have their foundation in matters of law, they can be redressed, . . . and so far as they have their foundation in matters of opinion, . . . all that we can do is to endeavor to allay the agitation, and cultivate a better feeling and more fraternal sentiments between the North and the South."[17]

At the end of his speech, Webster demonstrated that he was much more in touch with public sentiment than he had been in his anti–Mexican War speeches. His metaphors embraced rather than repelled; they played to

16. Lorman Ratner, *Powder Keg: Northern Opposition to the Anti-Slavery Movement*, 138.

17. This argument did not appear in the floor speech. It was added for the publication of the speech in the North.

contemporary geography rather than to tragic consequences: "Let us make our generation one of the strongest and brightest links in that golden chain which is destined . . . to grapple the people of all the States to this Constitution for ages to come. . . . This republic now extends, with a vast breadth, across the whole continent. The two great seas of the world wash the one and the other shore."

Historians and politicians such as Henry Cabot Lodge and John F. Kennedy have often relied on the reaction of abolitionists to this speech in assessing its worth.[18] Abolitionists like William Lloyd Garrison, Wendell Phillips, Theodore Parker, and Frederick Douglass viewed slavery as a moral rather than political question and were especially vicious in attacking Webster both in print and at public meetings. Garrison claimed that Webster had shocked his moral sense and "insulted the intelligence of the people." On March 25 Phillips, Parker, and Douglass spoke to a mass meeting at Faneuil Hall. Parker said that Webster's stand could be viewed only as a "bid for the Presidency."[19] In Manhattan, the parishioners of the Little Church around the Corner (the Episcopal Church of the Transfiguration on 29th Street), which operated an underground railroad, were appalled by Webster's endorsement of the Fugitive Slave Law. They had seen firsthand the damage that had been done to the hundreds of fugitive slaves who had passed through their midst.

The response of philosophical leaders in New England and New York City was also hostile. Free Soilers such as John Greenleaf Whittier, Ralph Waldo Emerson, James Russell Lowell, George Washington Julian, Horace Mann, Henry Longfellow, William Cullen Bryant, Edmund Quincy, and Henry David Thoreau all attacked Webster for his speech. Mann decried Webster's compromise, claiming his star had fallen.[20] In Congress, he read from Whittier's poem about Webster:

> Let not the land once proud of him
> Insult him now,
> Nor brand with deeper shame his dim,
> Dishonored brow.
>
> . . . .

18. John F. Kennedy, *Profiles in Courage*, 63–66.

19. Henry Mayer, *All on Fire: William Lloyd Garrison and the Abolition of Slavery*, 400; Bartlett, *Daniel Webster*, 269.

20. Lawrence Lader, *The Bold Brahmins: New England's War against Slavery, 1831–1863*, 150–53; Fuess, *Daniel Webster*, 2:221–25; Herbert D. Foster, "Webster's Seventh of March Speech and the Secessionist Movement, 1850," 245; Horace Mann, *Slavery: Letters and Speeches*, 251.

All else is gone; from those great eyes
The soul has fled:
When faith is lost, when honor dies,
The man is dead!

Then, pay the reverence of old days
To his dead fame;
Walk backward, with averted gaze,
And hide the shame![21]

When Mann returned to Boston, he gave a speech to his constituents condemning Webster and raising the issue of fugitive slaves to new prominence. Among prominent and hostile northern politicians, Charles Sumner placed Webster in "the dark list of apostates," and Seward pronounced him a "traitor to the cause of freedom," following from Parker's charge that Webster was a "Benedict Arnold." "Not one of my colleagues from New England," Webster acknowledged, "would publicly support the speech."[22]

These men had direct influence on newspapers, and a portion of the northern press was less than enthusiastic about the speech. The *Boston Atlas* said: "[Webster's] sentiments are not our sentiments. They are not, we venture to say, the sentiments of the Whigs of New England." The *New York Tribune* considered the speech "unequal to the occasion and unworthy of its author." The *New York Evening Post* described the speech as a "traitorous retreat" and Webster as "a man who deserted the cause which he lately defended." The Abolitionist *Liberator* called the speech "the scarlet infamy of Daniel Webster . . . an indescribably base and wicked speech."[23]

The effect of Webster's speech in the North, however, cannot be measured accurately by relying on the commentary of the abolitionists or those they influenced. Several other press reactions reveal that Webster's words also had a positive influence in the public sphere. The *Boston Daily Advertiser* said: "So far

21. John Greenleaf Whittier, "Ichabod," in *The Complete Poetical Works*, 186.
22. Kennedy, *Profiles*, 62; Daniel Webster to A. Huntington, December 21, 1850, in *Writings and Speeches*, 16:582. Emerson kept his powder dry—at least in public—until May 1851, when he gave a long speech in Concord in which he claimed that Webster had become morally impotent, squandering his talents and status on an unworthy position, and that his rhetoric of compromise was a corrupted reflection of the ideas of the founders. Ralph Waldo Emerson, *Complete Works*, 11:181–204, esp. 202–4.
23. *Boston Atlas*, March 11, 1850, p. 1; Kennedy, *Profiles*, 62, 65.

as we can tell, the Boston public fully support Mr. Webster, not with an enthusiastic rush of blind admiration, but with a calm belief that he has placed a
vexed question in a position in which it can and must be fairly settled." The
Boston Courier said of the speech: "As a constitutional argument to be applied
to the existing dispute between the North and the South, it is impregnable,
unassailable, irrefutable." The *Philadelphia Evening Bulletin* called the speech
"an able and patriotic effort" and praised the "practical" and "candid" nature
of Webster's argument. The *Albany Argos* was equally supportive.[24]

Several southern papers also applauded the address. The *Charleston Mercury*
called it a "great speech" that created "hope" for compromise. In front-page
stories, Whig papers such as the *Vicksburg Weekly Whig* and the *New Orleans
Picayune* claimed that Webster was protecting southern interests. A week later
the *Vicksburg Weekly Whig* went even further: "Webster's speeches seem to be
made not for a day only, but for all time: and they will be read and studied in
future generations as the orations of Grecian and Roman orators now are."[25]
These sentiments would help win over southern senators who were open to
compromise.

However, it was sentiment for compromise in the North that Webster wanted
most. In the Massachusetts General Court a motion was introduced that read:
"The Hon. Daniel Webster, in his recent speech in the Senate of the United
States, has not faithfully represented the sentiments of the people of Massachusetts."[26] It was rejected by a vote of 19 to 10. Two more resolutions were introduced directing Webster to support the Wilmot Proviso and to oppose
Senator Mason's Fugitive Slave Bill. They too were rejected. Several hundred
New York businessmen sent Webster a gold watch and a letter thanking him
for his speech. Eight hundred leading Bostonians followed suit, publishing

24. *Boston Daily Advertiser*, March 12, 1850, p. 1; *Boston Courier*, March 13, 1850, p. 1; *Philadelphia Evening Bulletin*, March 8, 1850, p. 2; *Albany Argos*, March 9, 1850, p. 2.

25. *Charleston Mercury* quoted in the *National Intelligencer*, March 19, 1850, p. 1; *Vicksburg (MS)
Weekly Whig*, March 20, 1850, p. 1; *New Orleans Picayune*, March 20, 1850, p. 1; *Vicksburg Weekly
Whig*, March 27, 1850, p. 1.

26. Herbert Darling Foster, "Webster's Seventh of March Speech and the Secessionist Movement, 1850," 29. Foster lists other measures of support in the North and South: Rev. Thomas
Worcester, an overseer of Harvard, wrote that Webster's "speech saved the Union." Rev. J. W.
Allen wrote from Alabama that the speech was in the "spirit of patriotism." South Carolina
Unionists sent letters of praise. Several ex-mayors of Boston expressed their support, as did the
sitting mayor of Salem. Foster points out that even Isaac Hill, Webster's "bitter New Hampshire
political opponent," approved of the speech. Ibid., 30–31.

their names and their letter in the *Boston Courier*. A majority of the faculty at Harvard voted to support Webster's stand. The price of bonds, a crucial indicator of the changes for compromise, were falling before the speech and rose dramatically just after it.[27] The public relations campaign that Webster launched after his speech was working; his address proved far more effective than Clay's in terms of creating an atmosphere for compromise.

The most reliable way to determine the North's reaction to Webster's appeal is to analyze all available evidence in light of the varied northern attitudes on slavery. Then we can evaluate how well Webster utilized those attitudes in his speeches to create an atmosphere of compromise in the North. These attitudes existed in a complicated political context.

Abolitionist, Whig, and Democratic groups represented the major factions on the slavery question; however, even these groups were fractured. For example, there was the American Anti-Slavery Society (AAS), whose motto was "No Union with Slave Holders." William Lloyd Garrison's condemnation of the Constitution and his refusal to use political means to end slavery caused the Society to split unevenly in 1840. By 1850 it had lost about 110,000 members, reducing its membership to 40,000.[28] The American and Foreign Anti-Slavery Society, which broke with the AAS in an attempt to gain the political power to implement its own policy, evolved into the Free Soil Party. Its candidate in 1848, former president Martin Van Buren, polled only 291,263 votes. The *Albany Argos* referred to Van Buren's party as a "decaying hybrid."[29]

The vast majority of northerners were caught between their prejudice against African Americans and the conviction that there was a "slave power" conspiracy attempting to capture political power. The abolitionists contributed to this conviction by arguing that "[s]lavery produced a ruling caste, a minority group of large slave holders, who, through the constitutional provision for counting three-fifths of the slaves in computing the basis of congressional representation, controlled the destinies of the South and the nation."[30]

Slaveholders contributed to northern fears by aggressively trying to force slavery into the territories. Acts of violence and inflammatory remarks by a few southerners heightened the belief of many northerners that the southern oligarchy was trying to destroy the Union. The abolitionist press blew these acts

27. Fuess, *Daniel Webster*, 2:241.

28. Arthur Young Lloyd, *The Slavery Controversy, 1831–1860*, 281.

29. *Albany Argos*, March 6, 1850, p. 2.

30. Ratner, *Powder Keg*, 140; Lloyd, *Slavery Controversy*, 65.

and remarks out of proportion and invented others. These reports concerned northerners who were considering migrating westward to cheap land. Conservative northerners were more influenced by the fear of "slave power" pushing into the territories than by any argument concerning the sin of slavery in the southern states.[31]

The Free Soil Party was not immune to this conservatism. The majority of Free Soilers were antislavery not because they wanted to change the system radically, but because they wanted to preserve their political, social, and economic institutions and extend them westward.[32] Votes for Van Buren were likely to be reactions against the choice of Lewis Cass, an advocate of popular sovereignty, and Zachary Taylor, a southern slave owner.

The Whig and Democratic Parties were also split. Conscience Whigs held many of the same views as Free Soilers, but avoided identification with the latter group's many radical abolitionists. Northern Cotton Whigs were mainly bankers and businessmen seeking a new tariff in 1850.

The Democratic Party in the North had a proslavery faction and a Free Soil faction. Hard-core members of the proslavery faction would become the "Copperheads" who so violently opposed Lincoln during the Civil War. Most of the Free Soil Democrats voted for Van Buren in 1848. It is important to remember in evaluating Webster's use of attitudes in the public arena that the Democrats and Whigs polled a sizeable majority in the North by running men like Cass and Taylor. In his home state of New York, where the Liberty League and Free Soil Party were founded, Van Buren polled only 120,000 votes against Cass's 114,000 and Taylor's 218,000 in the election of 1848. The Free Soil–abolitionist coalition was rejected and the conservatives carried the day, indicating a public preference for pragmatic rather than moralistic approaches to the slavery problem.

This analysis of northern attitudes indicates that Webster's Seventh of March Address was attuned to the sentiment for compromise in the North. The crucial strategy for Webster was his appeal to the pragmatic majority in the North

31. Ratner, *Powder Keg*, 68; Lloyd, *Slavery Controversy*, 66–67.

32. Major L. Wilson argues that Free Soilers in general were conservative due to nationalistic and expansionist sentiment: "The slogan 'freedom national and slavery local' precisely expressed this position. . . . They attributed to the founding fathers the geopolitical idea . . . that when slavery ceased to spread out into new and unsettled areas it would in time die out." Major L. Wilson, "The Free Soil Concept of Progress and the Irrepressible Conflict," 76; see also Rowland Berthoff, "The American Social Order: A Conservative Hypothesis."

to preserve the Union. That is why by the end of March over 120,000 copies of his address had been distributed in the North. The speech was also sent west by telegraph using Morse's new code of dots and dashes, exhausting the fingers of telegraphers by the end of the transmission.

Despite the abolitionist-inspired commentary on the speech, most other indicators reveal that the majority of northerners favored it and that in the South it deflated enthusiasm for secession.[33] On the Senate floor, senators began to ridicule the idea of secession for the first time. More than three thousand people at Faneuil Hall signed their names in support of compromise. Webster's effectiveness is all the more remarkable in that his freedom to represent northern attitudes was limited by the fact that he dared not affront moderate southern senators, who were essential to any compromise.

The speech was only the beginning of Webster's campaign to persuade the North to accept the compromise. As we have seen, the momentum for compromise was interrupted by the death of Calhoun at the end of March, an event that coalesced southern obstinacy. Then there was presidential opposition funneled to the Senate through William Seward, who spoke on March 11 attacking the compromise. Seward reactivated moral sentiment with his appeal to "higher law" and split the Whig Party. The first half of his speech concentrated on the question of statehood for California. Seward, like the president, wanted California admitted for strategic as well as economic reasons. He talked at length about how California had grown from a "Mexican province" to a major population center. Recognizing California's vote for free status, he said: "California [is] the youthful Queen of the Pacific, in her robes of freedom, gorgeously inlaid with gold. . . . There are silver and gold in the mountains and ravines of California; the granite of New England and New York is barren." He went on to answer charges that California had been organized too quickly. Defending the president's action, Seward opposed any compromise, arguing that if California were not admitted it would become an independent republic and take Oregon with it. Webster was so disturbed by this address that he interrupted it at one point to remind Seward that Texas could be divided into four more slave states.

These events led to Senator Foote's proposal to form a committee to craft a compromise. When it passed, Webster accepted assignment on the committee along with Clay.

33. Foster, "Webster's Seventh of March Speech," 252.

At the end of April, Webster toured the North to campaign for compromise. He talked to legislators and judges, wrote letters that were published in the newspapers, and gave speeches at mass meetings. He was greeted by a crowd of five thousand when he arrived in Boston. Before he could return to Washington, the Foote Committee reported a compromise omnibus bill very similar to the original Clay proposal. As he read the report, Webster had an intuition that would prove crucial to the eventual compromise: he believed that an *omnibus* bill would never pass the Senate; the legislation had to be segregated. In a few months, he would be proven right. Nonetheless, in his private letters, Webster continued to campaign for compromise. He wrote to Peter Harvey in May that southern Whigs "will not give a single vote for the tariff until this slavery business is settled."[34] Webster claimed that abolitionist agitation could shut the Lowell mills down. Northern businessmen still needed a new tariff. No wonder more than ten thousand New York businessmen pledged themselves to aid in the rendition of fugitive slaves.

Webster had written to Fletcher in 1848 that the best strategy for maintaining the Union would be to isolate extremists on each side of the slavery question.[35] In the Seventh of March Address, originally dubbed "The Constitution and the Union," Webster separated the extremists, North and South, from the pragmatic majority by attacking their legislative proposals, radical methods, and strident rhetoric. He knew they would never favor compromise and were of use to him only as examples of the division that overmoralization could cause. He then made overtures to moderates on each side, while reconceptualizing the problem from a philosophical confrontation into a pragmatic deliberation. Whigs, essentially economic conservatives, were told that prosperity came only with Union. Businessmen were promised a settlement of the bond issue and a tariff reform in the future. Those Free Soilers who Webster knew to be more fearful of the closing of the frontier than affronted by the immorality of slavery were told that the forces of nature would preclude development of cash crops in the territories, thereby stopping the expansion of slavery; thus, they need not worry about southern expansionism. Southerners were promised peace at home and return of their slaves. In short, Webster created an audience amenable to compromise, particularly among Whigs, because he was able to recognize a pervasive conservative sentiment and artic-

---

34. Current, *Daniel Webster.* 169.
35. Bartlett, *Daniel Webster,* 231.

ulate it in either a pragmatic or transcendent rhetoric acceptable to self-interested segments in the North and South.

Webster knew that his goal was not yet achieved. There would be strong opposition in the South, the president was holding fast to his course, and Seward was rallying the radicals in the Senate. Webster knew too that by rhetorically traveling from pragmatism to idealism and back again when it suited his purpose, he had moved from the realm of civil religion to political reality. That offended many in the intelligentsia who had admired him. By the end of May, however, he believed he had public sentiment on his side, particularly among northern and southern pragmatists. The question was whether time was on his side. Luckily for Webster, fate stepped in and dramatically changed the balance of power in the compromise debate.

Chapter 11

Consummating Compromise

T en days after the Seventh of March Address, Webster wrote to his son
that if the fate of the speech "should be to go to the bottom, it has no
cargo of value, and only one passenger to be drowned." Perhaps this explains
why he revised it so extensively before releasing it to the public. More than two
months after the address, Webster wrote to a friend that his influence had
ebbed, adding: "If more than six Southern senators refuse their support, the
compromise bill will fail in the Senate."[1]

Congressional debate remained acrimonious and cynical through May and
June, and proponents of the necessary elements of legislative compromise
failed to make any headway. For example, Senator Douglas tried to have
California statehood voted on separately but was defeated by a vote of 28 to
24. Webster rarely spoke during this period, but was present to keep an eye on
the maneuvering. The speeches he gave were short and conciliatory. On April 1
he gave the obligatory eulogy for Calhoun. On June 3 he spoke briefly on the
Fugitive Slave Bill, reaffirming his position that slavery was impractical in the
territories. On June 13 and 17 he addressed the compromise bill, but only to
clarify legalistic arguments.

On June 27 and 28 Webster engaged in more lengthy debate, speaking
against an amendment by Sen. Pierre Soule of Louisiana on "California Public
Lands and Boundaries." In marked contrast with the Seventh of March Address, this speech was legalistic and almost entirely refutative in nature, dem-

---

1. Daniel Webster to Fletcher Webster, March 17, 1850, and Daniel Webster to Franklin
Haven, May 18, 1850, in *Private Correspondence*, 2:359, 369.

onstrating Webster's intimate knowledge of documents, facts, and strategies surrounding the issue of compromise. Soule's amendment was defeated 36 to 19, and Webster deserved a good deal of the credit. He was much more effective with his colleagues and had much more impact on the legislative process than Clay, which may explain why Clay, after claiming he would "rather be right than be president," retreated to Kentucky when the summer began.

When not watching over the Senate, Webster kept busy writing public letters and editorials and bringing political pressure to bear on vacillating senators. Through this whole period he tried to avoid a confrontation with the president. By the end of June, he wrote that "the issue of union or disunion was still touch and go."[2] He continued to monitor the situation and advise all who would listen, including Vice President Fillmore and Senator Douglas, on how to solve the crisis.

The Seventeenth of July Address

Then came what some considered to be divine intervention. On July 4, 1850, under a hot Washington sun, President Taylor cooled himself by eating cherries soaked in bourbon and cream. He contracted a violent stomach disorder, cholera morbus, and died five days later. Millard Fillmore succeeded Taylor, becoming the last Whig president of the United States. Not only was one of the major obstacles to compromise removed with the death of Taylor, but the new president was also an avid supporter of compromise, put on the ticket to satisfy Webster's wing of the party.[3]

On July 10, along with others in the Senate, Webster eulogized the fallen president. Even on this occasion he editorialized in favor of compromise: "The circumstances under which [Taylor] conducted the government for the short time he was the head of it have been such as perhaps not to give him a very favorable opportunity of developing his principles."[4]

Fillmore's admiration for Webster was unabashed, so it is not surprising that he asked Webster to become secretary of state and head his cabinet. Webster agreed to return to the post he had held under Presidents Harrison and

2. Walker Lewis, ed., *Speak for Yourself, Daniel: A Life of Webster in His Own Words*, 413.

3. In his capacity as president of the Senate, Fillmore had told Clay he would break a tie in favor of compromise should the opportunity present itself.

4. Webster, *Writings and Speeches*, 10:142.

Tyler. Events had presented him with a remarkable opportunity to press home a compromise. A farewell address to the Senate would receive special attention, enhance his credibility, and allow him to focus his remarks on the very body essential to hopes for a compromise. On July 17 he rose to make his last formal appeal on the issue.

Dressed in his trademark blue waistcoat and buff-colored vest, Webster stared into the faces of the men with whom he had so long served and debated. He must have known that his success or failure with the national audience was not critical at this juncture: the Seventh of March Address had been for them. Now he must move his colleagues to act. This is not to say that he ignored his secondary audience, nor that the speech was incomplete. It is simply to say that Webster knew where his emphasis should lie now that the president would not veto parts of a compromise.

Because the Seventeenth of July speech is complex and subtle, it is best to examine Webster's strategies as they emerge from the progression of arguments in the text. Several tactics are worth noting. First, understanding the tangle in which the Senate was caught, Webster attempted to transcend rivalries wherever he could. Second, he argued that his solution was *better* than the others offered, not that it was the only one possible. This left him room to change positions when need be (as he would do in August when the compromise was moved as separate pieces of legislation rather than as an omnibus bill). Third, he explained specifically and vividly what legislative steps were necessary to achieve a compromise. Fourth, throughout the address he judiciously used evidence to put a Unionist interpretation on history and geography that would support his portrait of the crisis. This last tactic provided a coherent conceptualization that allowed senators to rationalize their acceptance of a compromise while transcending their differences.

In an apparent attempt to court Conscience Whigs, Webster began with a tribute to President Taylor that diverted attention from divisive issues. At the same time, he argued that the Union had survived the crisis of the president's death: Credit was unaffected, no disturbances had arisen, and the legislative body continued to function. The Union worked, he claimed, and legislators' duty to the dead president was to keep it working.

Throughout his introduction, Webster avoided any mention of Taylor's policies; instead he concentrated on his qualities as a war hero. In this way, he was able to identify the deceased president with the cause of Union. And Union benefiting the whole nation was the idea Webster wanted his colleagues to accept. Later in the speech, he would use himself to symbolize Union in an effort to reinforce the transcendent attitude he sought to foster in the Senate.

After his introductory remarks, Webster proceeded to do what had to be done. As on March 7, he chastised the abolitionists for their rigid moral stand and its consequences. Once again, he offered businessmen economic rewards for support of compromise: Texas bonds would be paid off; a tariff could be set. Once again, he presented pragmatic alternatives to disunion: Leave slavery where it was, return slaves to their rightful owners, and open the territories to new settlers. He began to identify a coalition composed of moderates from the border states, undecided senators, and those senators favoring various popular-sovereignty remedies. The trick was to build concurrent majorities around the different provisions of the compromise since hardly any of the senators supported each one of its provisions. For example, a majority of senators favored admission of California to the Union, though most southern senators opposed such a move. A majority of senators favored returning fugitive slaves to their owners, though most northern senators opposed such a law. Webster therefore focused his attention on the individual proposals and getting them through the Senate by swinging from one majority to the next. This was not a time for civil religion; it was a time for political prudence and strategic argumentation.

What seems most remarkable about the Seventeenth of July Address is Webster's judicious shifting from the philosophical to the pragmatic and back again to suit his purposes. If an issue was divisive he treated it pragmatically, as legislation necessary to the workings of the nation. He asked his colleagues to accept a few bitter pills so that compromise might pass and all might benefit. If an issue had broad support he elevated it to a transcendent level, thus giving it more importance than the divisive issues.

Webster's high-wire act was grounded in the Union. From the beginning, he supported the thesis he uttered in his last line: "No man can suffer too much, and no man can fall too soon, if he suffer or if he fall in defense of the liberties and constitution of his country."[5] The power of the Unionist appeal in this particular address lay in the fact that Webster had stood for Union in speeches dating back to his celebrated addresses on the landing at Plymouth and the groundbreaking for the Bunker Hill monument. If he could provide an example for enough senators, compromise would be achieved. His personal credibility became part of the consensus-building process.

5. Webster, *Speeches and Formal Writings*, 2:553-78.

At this juncture, Webster was not only trying to advance the cause of compromise, he was also trying to identify it and himself with the survival of the Union, thereby allowing his colleagues a way to transcend their petty differences. He said: "I wish, Sir, so far as I can, to harmonize opinions. I wish to facilitate some measure of conciliation. I wish to consummate some proposition or other, that shall bring opponents' sentiments together." This appeal led to his argumentative synthesis: All responsible members of Congress wanted the Union to survive and the current crisis to end. Webster not only gave his colleagues a rationale for voting for compromise, he also showed them the way to achieve it.

To accomplish this feat under difficult circumstances, Webster based his plea for compromise on its comparative advantage over the alternative. The legislative proposals were neither right nor wrong; one course was simply more advantageous than the other. Compromise, Webster consistently argued, was a better road to travel than the ideological sundering advocated by extremists of the North and South. For those who needed a transcendent moral position, he offered defense of the Union and the Constitution as handed down by the founders, the same founders who had allowed slavery to exist in the South.

To support his case, Webster put the issues in perspective. He interpreted history in a way that helped build his argumentative synthesis: The expansion of slavery into the territories was an economic impossibility. Therefore, opening the territories to all who wanted to go into them did not present a threat to the North. Admit California as a free state; the Union of states would expand to the Pacific and all parties would benefit. Pay off the Texas debt and solidify her boundaries. The resulting expanded Union with all of its advantages could be obtained through the legislative process; the matter was in the hands of the men he addressed.

On several occasions, Webster went into great detail to prove just how simple a compromise could be. His discussion of California is a case in point. It was connected to questions of prosperity and preservation of the Union, as it had been in the Seventh of March Address. Webster articulated the strategy that Douglas eventually used to pass a compromise: The essential bills need not be seen as an omnibus. The following exchange, which took place during the speech, reveals just how ready Webster was to engineer the legislative process in order to achieve consensus:

Mr. Webster:	The honorable member from Illinois [Douglas], who is at the head of [the Committee on Territories], sits near me,

and I take it for granted that he can say whether I am right or not in the opinion, that, if we should this day admit California alone, he would to-morrow feel it his duty to bring in a bill for the government of the Territories, or to make some disposition of them. . . .

Mr. Douglas: Mr. President, if California should be admitted by herself, I should certainly feel it my duty, as the Chairman of the Committee on Territories, to move to take up the subject of the Territories at once, and put them through, and also the Texas boundary question, and to settle them by detail if they are not settled in the aggregate. . . .

Mr. Webster: Then, Sir, it is as I supposed. We should not get rid of the subject, even for the present, by admitting California alone. Now, Sir, it is not wise to conceal our condition from ourselves. Suppose we admit California alone. My honorable friend from Illinois brings in, then, a bill for territorial government for New Mexico and Utah. We must open our eyes to the state of opinion in the two houses respectively, and endeavor to foresee what would be the probable fate of such a bill. If it be a bill containing a prohibition of slavery, we know it could not pass this house. If it be a bill without such prohibition, we know what difficulty it would encounter elsewhere. So that we very little relieve ourselves from the embarrassing circumstances in which we are placed by taking up California and acting upon it alone.[6]

These paragraphs read like an in-house memorandum and give the clearest evidence that Webster was showing his colleagues the legislative path to compromise. He employed the same strategy when he moved to a discussion of the New Mexico and Utah territories. Even his transition tended toward the pragmatic. He asked, "What is next to be done?" and then placated southern senators by admitting that he had "the strongest objection to a premature creation of states." This bit of parliamentary advice is typical of the legislative cast of the address.

6. Ibid., 2:557-58. Webster's later memos to Douglas, his influence over Fillmore, and his role with other senators demonstrate that he was the architect of compromise and Douglas was his minion.

Continuing to balance interest against interest and arguing that no other crisis had so unnecessarily tied up Congress, Webster then took up the questions surrounding Texas. Could the border dispute with New Mexico Territory be settled? Should the federal government assume Texas's debt? Again, sounding much like a legislative manager, Webster explained how Texas was central to the complex deliberations. Unless the Texas boundary was set, New Mexico could not be organized as a territory. If Texas's debt were not paid, there would be no trade-off for California's entry, nor any way to pay off Texas bonds. The money that would come to the bondholders in the North was never far from Webster's rhetorical focus, nor, as it turned out, from his own pocketbook.

Having moved from the admission of California, a northern bill, to the Texas questions, which were supported by southern interests and Whig bondholders, Webster reduced the debate to a question of proper management of legislation. At this point he once again characterized the motivations of those who opposed compromise. As in the Seventh of March Address, he described as irrational the Seward and Calhoun loyalists who "directly opposed to each other in every matter connected with the subject under consideration." He disassociated himself from those who would "fight [compromise legislation] to the last." Even more strongly than in the March address, Webster asserted that the enemies of such legislation had become allied because of a desire to see compromise destroyed for their own sectional advantage. His sarcastic attack on "the consistency of the opposition to this measure" was designed to carve away extremists from the majority he wished to coalesce. Extremists from the North and South threatened not only compromise, but the Union as well. They would destroy the system of government that had worked so well to serve so many—the Whig banker, the southern cotton merchant, the western farmer, the New England textile owner, the plantation farmer, and the industrialist. Thus, Webster established a dialectic between Union, the transcendent value that meant work and prosperity, and disunion, the course that led to destruction. On the side of Union, his utopia, he lined up the elements he needed for his compromise majority. On the side of disunion, his dystopia, he placed the extremists.

Having attacked ideological intransigence, Webster made an appeal for all senators to reexamine the procedure whereby they voted according to instructions from their state legislatures. Again, the rhetorical focus was on a pragmatic, parliamentary point. Webster knew that if compromise was to succeed, some senators would have to violate their instructions. (Senator Foote of Mississippi would do just that.) If instructions were to be followed, no flexible representation was possible and no debate was necessary. Webster said he knew that some senators would vote against their conscience because of instructions from home. He said he sympathized with these men since he had been in a similar situation.[7] He therefore could not impugn his colleagues' motives: "I cannot but regret, certainly, that gentlemen who sit around me . . . and my friends from Massachusetts in the other house, are obliged, by the sense of *duty*, to oppose a measure which I feel bound by conscience to support to the utmost of my ability. They are just as high minded, as patriotic, as pure, and every way as well intentioned as I am." However, Webster asked them to make a sacrifice nonetheless. He compared voting on instructions with "involuntary servitude," thus cleverly reducing senators who followed instructions to slaves of their states, in the knowledge that most of these men were from states opposed to slavery. There was another tactic at work here too. Some states opposed the omnibus bill as a whole; thus if the bill was broken apart, their instructions would no longer apply. In other cases specific provisions of the bill were condemned, and here Webster's different majorities would come into play.

Like Edmund Burke, Webster equated voting independently with conscience, freedom, and transcendent values. In his republican church, one was elected not to follow orders, but to represent one's congregation to the best of one's ability. As we have seen, Webster had followed his state's instructions in the past, but only when they agreed with his own position. He was able to elevate the pragmatic issue of voting on instructions to a question of conscience where it worked to his advantage. The mechanics of achieving legislative compromise were to Webster manifestations of moral principle, while protestations of regional loyalty were tools of destruction. In short, he turned Calhoun's view of compromise upside down.

Webster proceeded to discuss the value of compromise, using a powerful, progressive form of argument. He began with a single example, the state of Massachusetts, and then expanded it to include the whole of the North and eventually the entire Union, showing at each level the gain that would occur with compromise. Next he returned to an argumentative strategy, showing the

---

7. This was a difficult argument to make since Webster had used Massachusetts resolutions of instruction to his advantage during the Mexican War.

loss that would occur in each case *without* compromise. The parallel structure of this argument from consequences is compelling and at times overwhelming. It was sustained through twelve paragraphs in which Webster frankly discussed what compromise would mean to northern interests. As he rehearsed the issues of the debate, Webster showed how each provision of the compromise benefited the North: "She gains the quiet of New Mexico, and she gains the settlement of the Texas boundary. . . . More than that, Sir, she gains . . . and the whole country gains, the final adjustment of by far the greater part of all the slavery questions." That "final adjustment" would result in the "greatest of all possible benefits . . . the restoration of this government to the ordinary exercise of its functions." Once again Webster merged preservation of the Union with the pragmatic operation of Congress.

The strategy of progression-and-gain versus dissolution-and-loss is employed again in a section of the speech in which Webster sought to gain southern adherence to compromise. Before embarking on this delicate task, however, he reminded his audience in vivid and pragmatic terms of the problem confronting the nation: "Men must live; to live, they must work. And how is this to be done, if . . . all the business of society is stopped, and everything is placed in a state of stagnation." Thus, before reinforcing the comparative advantage of his position, Webster painted a picture of the crisis he wanted his colleagues to fear. He reinforced the dramatic nature of the crisis: the government, he said, was "hardly able to keep . . . alive. . . . [A]ll is paralysis. . . . [E]verything is suspended upon this one topic."

Having gained the attention of southern moderates, Webster pointed out that the North had given up the Wilmot Proviso and would enforce the Fugitive Slave Act, absorb Texas's debt, and allow free choice in the territories. These concessions, he said, were generous enough to warrant a quid pro quo from southern senators. Throughout this portion of his address, Webster maintained a delicate balance between seducing the South into compromise and retaining northern support for bills that might benefit the South. Most importantly, he again achieved a transcendent effect by arguing from the parts (legislative concessions) to the whole (southern support for compromise).

Having used Massachusetts to demonstrate the benefits of compromise to the North, he now used Maryland to demonstrate the advantages to the South. The selection of Maryland was designed to appeal to moderates because it was a border state. Webster appealed for calm, deliberate consideration of the issues upon which compromise depended and asked that the more patriotic

southern senators prevail on those who were "not as wise." He compared southerners who used the Nashville Convention on secession "as a syllabus of Southern sentiment" to northerners who were "tinctured with abolitionism." He
thus renewed his pragmatic argument, appealed to the better nature of moderates, and once again isolated the extremists, who refused to support a compromise in any case.

He ended this section of the speech with a plea to all moderates to "come
together as brethren, enjoying one renown, one destiny, and expecting one
and the same destiny hereafter." He recounted his privilege at having served in
Congress "with good union men from the South." Webster was courting southern favor much more than he had in the March address. He spoke of the valor
of southern military leaders in the war with Mexico. He praised southern sentiment and values. He separated himself from those who questioned the loyalty of his southern colleagues. As he had with northern senators, Webster
sought to identify himself with moderates from the South through an appeal
to conscience based on Unionist motives. In short, he praised where he could
afford to praise, moved away from divisive and emotional questions, and
hoped his appeals would reconcile southern consciences to the transcendent
compromise he endorsed.

Webster began his summation by calling for the preservation of the Union.
Again, he used Massachusetts as an example of a state with close ties to the
Union and the Constitution. But Union, he said, transcends statehood; it is
"the law which determines the destiny" of us all, "[l]ike that column which . . .
perpetuates the memory of the first great battle of the Revolution." At the end
of a pragmatic address that aimed at opening as many senators as possible to
compromise, Webster was suddenly attempting to seal that persuasion with an
emotional and florid conclusion. Into this highly charged moment, he once
again asserted his own credibility by discussing how he planned to function as
secretary of state: "I shall stand by the Union, and by all who stand by it. I shall
do justice to the whole country . . . in all I say . . . and mean to stand upon the
constitution. . . . The ends I aim at shall be my country's, my God's, and
Truth's. I was born an American; I will live an American; I shall die an American; and I intend to perform the duties incumbent upon me in that character
to the end of my career."

Taylor and Webster, symbolic exponents of Union, served as terminals for
the speech. The arc of the argument ran from the comparative advantage of
compromise to its "essential nature." Massachusetts and Maryland served as

synecdoches for the beneficial consequences of compromise in the North, the South, and hence in the whole Union. In between, an argumentative net was woven that used history to justify compromise and pragmatic suggestions to achieve consensus. If any part of the portrait was neglected, Webster's coalition would not perceive a coherent picture, one in which compromise was essential to national survival. Webster grounded his strategies in detailed audience analysis. He knew which interests were most salient to each of his listeners. This knowledge guided his selection of words, phrases, arguments, and values. His ability to master his subject, to understand his audience, and to fashion his speech accordingly prevented dissidents from reducing the deliberative body to quarrelsome disarray.

The nonabolitionist northern press praised the speech as it had his Seventh of March Address. The *New York Herald* said that "on the whole, Mr. Webster's speech yesterday is a credit to him, and we shall be much mistaken if it does not exercise a very great influence on the settlement of the slavery question." The *Philadelphia Evening Bulletin* was even more generous, calling the speech the "most conclusive argument [Webster] has attempted during the present session." The *Vicksburg Weekly Whig* represented southern moderate opinion when it wrote, "Daniel Webster has acted so independently that upon the slavery question he might now be classed as a supporter of our institution."[8]

Webster's colleagues, particularly some of his most ardent critics, also praised the speech. Senator Hale of New Hampshire, an antislavery extremist, referred to Webster's "graphic powers of delineation." Senator Foote of Mississippi said he was inspired to a new "spirit of concord" and would not press divisive amendments.[9] Sen. William C. Dawson of Georgia said it was time to restore harmony. For others the speech provided the perfect opportunity to save face. Following Webster's lead, they could in good conscience disobey instructions from home and form new alliances to save the Union.

Evidence is strong that Webster was successful in moving the Senate toward compromise. In the days following his speech, confusion diminished and was replaced by an atmosphere of business-as-usual.[10] On July 18, a motion by Foote to split California was defeated 34 to 20. Clay, who had left the Senate early in the summer after pronouncing the situation hopeless, returned for Webster's

8. *New York Herald*, July 18, 1850, pp. 1–2; *Philadelphia Evening Bulletin*, July 18, 1850, p. 1; *Vicksburg Weekly Whig*, July 31, 1850, p. 3.

9. Hale and Foote quoted in Hamilton, *Prologue to Conflict*, 115–16.

10. Hamilton, *Prologue to Conflict*, 115; Avery O. Craven, *The Coming of the Civil War*, 271.

address and on July 22 gave a three-hour speech for compromise. The coalition of more than thirty senators who voted for compromise held again on July 24 when a southern attempt to change the Texas border failed, and it held together again on July 25 against northern extremists who sought to prevent slavery's expansion. That issue needed to be postponed and would not be addressed squarely until Douglas got the Kansas-Nebraska Act, endorsing popular sovereignty, passed in 1854.

As soon as the new administration was organized, Webster began to work with Senator Douglas to move the crucial bills through the Senate. First, however, the omnibus strategy had to be terminated. That unpleasant task was accomplished on July 31 when Senators Benton and Seward led a coalition that destroyed Clay's legislation. When the bill was killed, Seward took a victory lap around the Senate chamber, offending many of those present.

As secretary of state, Webster wrote President Fillmore's message to Congress, spelling out how the compromise legislation should be passed. Distinguishing Fillmore from his predecessor, the message called Congress "the sole judge of the time and manner of creating" a territorial government. After creating a conciliatory mood, it expressed Fillmore's "deep and earnest conviction of the importance of an immediate decision or arrangement or settlement of the question of the boundary between Texas and the Territory of New Mexico." It argued that all other questions flowed from the settlement of the boundary:

> [N]o event would be hailed with more gratification by the people of the United States than the amicable adjustment of questions of difficulty which have now for a long time agitated the country and occupied to the exclusion of other subjects, the time and attention of Congress. . . . In the train of such an adjustment we may well hope that there will follow a return of harmony and good will, an increased attachment to the Union, and the general satisfaction of the country.

This message of August 6 reinforced Webster's Seventeenth of July Address and allowed senators to vote on each item of the compromise without endorsing the others.

It was still a close bet as to whether Webster's strategy would work. Though moderates of the North and South would provide the core of votes for a concurrent majority, their numbers were small. Perhaps no more than four Whigs supported every measure of the compromise. To produce a majority on the single bill in question, on each issue they would be joined by southerners or northerners who normally took more extreme positions.

Within a week after receiving the president's message, the Senate passed the boundary legislation and set the stage for Douglas to present the remaining parts of the compromise as separate bills. California was admitted to the Union; the slave trade was abolished in the District of Columbia; New Mexico Territory was organized after ceding over thirty-three thousand acres to Texas; the Fugitive Slave Bill was passed. The bills were sent to the House. While they awaited further action, President Fillmore made clear that he was ready to sign them.

Throughout this period, Webster dominated the president and the cabinet. Edward Curtis, as Webster's guest in Washington, observed in August 1850 that "Mr. Webster appears among [the cabinet members] like a father teaching his listening children." W. A. Graham, the secretary of the navy, claimed that Webster brought "light" to the Congress "after chaos and dissension" had dominated for so long.[11] When Webster was accused of taking a bribe, the House overwhelmingly voted down a resolution calling for an investigation. The governor of Massachusetts agreed to replace Webster in the Senate with Robert Winthrop, an advocate of compromise in the House. Then Samuel Eliot, a Whig, defeated Free Soiler Charles Sumner for that Boston House seat on August 22, and Webster claimed vindication for his support of compromise.

On September 6 the first of the compromise bills passed the House, and the rest soon followed. Fillmore gleefully signed the final bill on September 20. Washingtonians took to the streets in wild celebration. As much in relief as in joy, citizens paraded with torches and lit huge bonfires that illuminated the public buildings.

Some historians have praised Douglas for breaking Clay's omnibus bill into separate parts. However, as we have seen, many others, including Webster in his Seventeenth of July Address and in the Texas boundary message he penned for Fillmore, had thought of the same strategy. Even Clay came out for it on August 1. Douglas acknowledged this when he spoke on September 16 to thank his colleagues for their cooperation: "The particular form of the proceeding was a matter of small moment. I supported [the bills] as a joint mea-

---

11. Curtis quoted in Bartlett, *Daniel Webster*, 256; J. G. de Roulhac Hamilton, ed., *The Papers of William Alexander Graham*, 3:321.

sure, and when they failed I supported each as a separate measure. . . . The decision of that point involved no principle; it was purely a matter of policy. . . . No men and no party has acquired a triumph, except the party to the Union triumphing over abolition and disunion."[12]

Few men worked harder for that triumph than Daniel Webster. Nevertheless, he continued to suffer the vilification of former friends such as Emerson and moralists such as Horace Mann and Theodore Parker. At least he would not live to see how Douglas corrupted the 1850 Compromise. Douglas took "popular sovereignty" out of the context of the compromise—where it functioned as a stopgap measure—and converted it into a general principle with his Kansas-Nebraska Act. With that act, Congress abrogated its responsibility to the territories, causing civil unrest in the Kansas-Nebraska Territory in 1854. The slide into civil war took a short seven years.

On the night the compromise passed in September 1850, Webster, in ill health, had to be carried to his doorstep to wave at paraders and speak to crowds of admirers who refused to disperse until he appeared to receive their adulation. He had the satisfaction of knowing that his last deliberative speech in the Senate had helped shape the strategy that would preserve the Union beyond his lifetime.

12. Hamilton, *Prologue to Conflict,* 147.

Chapter 12

Twilight Time

 One of the most remarkable characteristics of Daniel Webster is that he did not become a regional extremist like Calhoun. Despite his disdain for slavery, Webster continued to work with southern senators to produce a compromise. As secretary of state under Fillmore, Webster enforced the Fugitive Slave Act, much to the chagrin of abolitionists and other moralists in the North. Webster had abandoned civil religion, or at least revised it into a pragmatic defense of Union. Two forces account for Webster's pragmatism. First, he had been co-opted by the congressional system in a way that Calhoun and Seward never were. Webster mastered the legislative process, and it mastered him. Compromise was always part of the game. Webster became convinced that successful legislation was more important than ideological posturing or moralizing. However, that position ran flat in the face of his construction of a civil religion. As a high priest of that religion, Webster appeared to have been corrupted.

That is why he might well have given up on his dream of becoming president. But he did not. From 1836 to the summer of 1852 the possibility lingered in his mind, proving that his ego was no smaller than many others in U.S. history who have sought the presidency against all odds. To achieve his goal, Webster needed a plurality of support. He had to avoid the extremes of ideology and region. He certainly believed he had achieved the right balance with the passage of the 1850 Compromise.

There is no doubt that Webster's leadership of the cabinet and the passage of the 1850 Compromise gave him renewed stature across the country. He underwent a renaissance of spirit that energized him physically. A few days after President Fillmore signed the 1850 Compromise legislation, Webster took his wife to hear a concert by Jenny Lind, the famous "Swedish Nightingale." He demonstrated his effective sense of timing by entering the opera house just as Lind was about to sing the national anthem. The audience rose to its feet and cheered the secretary of state. During the recital Webster sang along, at one point standing and bowing to Lind when she finished a song. She genuflected to him and the audience cheered again.

Back at the White House, Webster began to populate the administration with his supporters. Followers of Taylor and Seward were weeded out of the bureaucracy and replaced by compromise Whigs. Webster's other concern was seeing that the compromise legislation was carried out. The major problem was the Fugitive Slave Law, which was regularly ignored by abolitionists in the North. Ministers condemned the law from their pulpits and argued that citizens were bound by the laws of God to free the slaves. Organized religion once again spilled over into the political arena. Webster was demonized when he personally intervened in a case in November 1850 to assure that two fugitive slaves in Boston were returned to their owners in the South. However, followers of Theodore Parker managed to place the two fugitives on a ship for England.

Charles Sumner also proved difficult now that he was estranged from Webster. In a Boston address, Sumner condemned the compromise as a national crime comparable to the atrocities of Rome. He constructed his civil religion from the whole cloth of organized religion, consistently appealing to a higher law. The civil religion Webster had constructed was meant to be respectful of others' opinions and deliberative. Sumner's civil religion, however, was extremist and uncompromising, and by the time of the Kansas crisis it encouraged religious war.

The embers of division were fanned during the compromise debates and continued to glow after the legislation was signed. In February 1851 a fugitive slave named Shadrach was taken across the border to Canada; when a jury in Boston failed to convict the offenders, Webster penned a presidential proclamation demanding conformance to the rule of law. In April while Webster was visiting Boston, another fugitive was arrested. This time Webster took no chances. He ordered the police to put the slave on a ship bound for Georgia. Upon arrival in Savannah, the slave was flogged and the "Black Dan" side of Webster's reputation was reinforced in the North. The incident would undercut his presidential ambitions in the following year.

Webster found himself facing a dilemma. In the name of American civil religion, he had condemned slavery in his 1820 speech in celebration of the landing at Plymouth Rock. He had supported the Wilmot Proviso for the same reason. But in order to achieve compromise, he had agreed to the Fugitive Slave Law. Some in his constituency were not going to let him have it both ways. One can't be a politician and a priest at the same time.

Hungary, the Orient, and Central America

The Fugitive Slave Law did not draw all of Webster's attention. Before the end of 1850, Webster used his rhetorical skills to respond to a note from Austria complaining about America's potential interference in Hungary's attempt to gain independence. (Most Americans had sided with Greece in its war of independence.) Webster responded that it was America's right to recognize Hungary if it so chose. He went on to proclaim the transcendent virtues of American democracy and to decry the practices of the Austrians. The message united Americans and put Europe on notice that America's internal divisions would not crack its resolve on the international front. When the Hungarian uprising failed and its leader, Louis Kossuth, fled to Turkey, Webster implored the Turks not to allow Kossuth to be extradited to Austria. Webster escorted the visiting Turkish naval attaché around Washington and obtained a grant of $10,000 to defray his travel costs. He took the attaché to Marshfield and Boston and made it clear that the Turks' help in the Kossuth affair would improve international and American goodwill toward Turkey. Webster's public relations magic worked so well that the Turks sent Kossuth and his followers first to England and then to the United States on fund-raising tours. On December 5, 1851, the Hungarians paraded through New York City to Central Park, where throngs greeted them.

When Kossuth returned to Washington to be feted on January 7, 1852, Webster introduced him to a congressional banquet with words that infuriated the Austrians. He praised the Hungarians for their struggle and claimed that autocratic government had no future. He referred to the letter he had written to the Austrians, said he stood by it, and portrayed himself as a hero of the situation. Hungarians are not Austrians, he said, playing to nationalism. Hungary had a national destiny to fulfill: "Austria would be a better and stronger government to-morrow if she confined the limits of her power to her hereditary and German domains."[1] He concluded with a toast to Hungarian independence.

---

1. For the full text of these remarks, see Webster, *Writings and Speeches*, 13:452–62.

Some in the room believed that either Webster had had too much wine or that his presidential ambitions had gone to his head. The diplomatic corps was scandalized; the Austrians protested to Fillmore. However, the American press generally, and Horace Greeley in particular, praised Webster for his audacity. In this case, his commitment to an American civil religion and his consistent call for an indigenous nationalism served him well with the media.

Webster's policy in the Pacific was also audacious and light-years ahead of other international thinkers in America. In the Tyler administration, Webster had been responsible for opening trade agreements with China. Inspired by the advent of steam navigation and the deepwater ports of the West Coast, Webster undertook diplomatic steps to break down the remaining obstacles for entry into Japan. Through Fillmore he informed the emperor of Japan that the mission of the American squadron on its way to his country was neither military nor religious, but commercial. The message concluded by listing items that were of mutual benefit to both countries.[2] Commodore Matthew Perry delivered the message and negotiated the appropriate reciprocal agreements. Webster's most delicate negotiation in this affair was with Holland, which believed it had a monopoly on trade with Japan and special access to its coal. After an exchange of meetings and messages, the Dutch supported the American mission. Webster's initiative would culminate after his death, during the administration of Franklin Pierce. Several historians have rightly dubbed Webster the "architect" of American policy in the Pacific, not only for opening doors to Japan and China but also for protecting American interests in Hawaii.[3]

Webster also explored the possibility of a canal across Central America. The discovery of gold in California, the expansion of the American navy, and the statehood of California mandated faster transportation to the Pacific. By late summer of 1851, and despite the interference of the British, who occupied Belize, Cornelius Vanderbilt completed a series of roads, rails, and canals across Nicaragua. When the steamship *Daniel Webster* tried to enter the system, the British imposed a port fee. Webster threatened to send a naval force to protect American interests, and the British backed down.

In April 1852 Webster sat down with the British to replace the Clayton-Bulwer Treaty of 1850 because of its ambiguous language concerning Central

2. Millard Fillmore to Emperor Kōmei, May 10, 1851, in Webster, *Diplomatic Papers*, 2:289.
3. See, for example, Remini, *Daniel Webster*, 713.

American interests. While the meeting restored good relations with the British, demonstrations by nationalists led to Nicaragua's refusal to participate. When Webster tried to gain a crossing from the Gulf Coast to the Pacific across Mexico, he was flatly rejected by a nation still smarting from the war of 1846 and President Polk's land grab.[4]

Webster was more successful in dealing with Spain when a spat developed over a group of Americans who tried to foment rebellion in Cuba. He won their release by providing reparations for actions taken by Americans against private Spanish citizens in New Orleans and Key West. This incident was dicey because Spain's Cuba and, to a lesser extent, England's Belize were affronts to the Monroe Doctrine, which was yet another component of Webster's civil religion. The people of the rapidly expanding United States generally believed they should exercise their power in their country's sphere of influence. To Webster's credit, he tamed these desires, but he once again found himself at odds with popular sentiment.

The Political Cauldron

On the domestic political front, events in the North, particularly in Massachusetts, were not running in Webster's favor. The aldermen of Boston closed Faneuil Hall to Webster to protest his position on the Fugitive Slave Act. Webster was devastated because the hall had been the site of some his most important speeches. To his horror, the Democrats of Massachusetts formed an alliance with the Free Soilers and captured the state legislature and governorship. Worse yet, Charles Sumner, so recently defeated for a House seat, was selected—after much wrangling and by a single vote—to take Webster's former seat in the Senate in April 1851. Sumner would become the most outspoken abolitionist in Congress and in a few years would stir the nation with his "Crime against Kansas" oration, a reaction to the civil war in that territory. Webster was so disheartened by the extremists in the Whig Party that he considered forming a new Union party with compromise Democrats and old-line Whigs.

First, however, a public relations campaign was in order. Webster's business backers bought him a state carriage for the occasion. His speeches were pub-

---

4. It is ironic that Webster, a champion of Mexico's rights in that war, would fail in his attempts to work out problems with that country. He was also rebuffed when he asked Mexico to stop its Native American tribes from making raids into the United States.

lished. His portrait was circulated. George Healy was commissioned to paint "Webster's Reply to Senator Hayne," which was unveiled in September 1851 and widely acclaimed. It is an epideictic painting, full of praise and honor for its subject. Two months after Webster's death, it was hung in Faneuil Hall, where it remains to this day. Thus Webster permanently overcame the petty aldermen; however, as we shall see, he also overcame their ban in his lifetime.

In 1851 Webster was one of the most famous men in America. He regularly received invitations to speak, many of which he had to turn down when his gout flared up. This depressed him since one of the reasons Clay was not being considered for president was that he was too old and sickly. Webster did not want the same charge made against him. He took heart from the fact that other candidates also had deficiencies. Fillmore was an accidental president. Seward was too uncompromising, arrogant, and regionally oriented. The only man who stood in Webster's way was Gen. Winfield Scott.

Scott partisans saw Webster as an effective, bright legislator who could not translate his assets into a large number of votes. In the eyes of some, he had clearly betrayed his principles. While such people ignored Webster's popular ceremonial speeches and the effective campaign he had waged on behalf of the Whig ticket in 1840, they did understand that the Whigs had won the presidency only when they ran war heroes—William Henry "Tippecanoe" Harrison in 1840 and Zachary "Old Rough and Ready" Taylor in 1848. Privately, Webster pointed out that each of those presidencies had been a disaster: Harrison died in office, which made the apostate Tyler president; Taylor was intransigent on the Compromise of 1850 and nearly plunged the nation into war.

In May 1851, defending the compromise and Union, Webster toured New York with President Fillmore. The trip was a clear indication that Fillmore supported Webster for the presidency. They spoke in Albany and many small towns along the railroad track. In Buffalo, Webster followed Fillmore to the lectern and asserted that a "house divided" could not stand; it was not the first time he had borrowed from the New Testament, nor the first time he uttered a phrase that would later appear in a Lincoln speech. He then left the president and traveled on to Syracuse, where he condemned the abolitionists in Seward's own backyard.[5] He then returned to Buffalo to express his concern

5. For the Buffalo and Syracuse speeches, see Webster, *Writings and Speeches*, 4:242–62 and 13:408–21, respectively.

about the Union of the states, praying it would be retained by the "silken cords of mutual, fraternal, patriotic affection."[6] He reminded his audience that he had opposed taking territory from Mexico because expansion led to talk of disunion, and Union was his church. Destroy the Union, in other words, and you destroy American civil religion.

Webster arrived in Washington in early June to celebrate the publication of the speeches from his recent New York tour. Edward Everett helped with the publication of another six volumes devoted to Webster's rhetorical achievements. Webster heard that some of the president's friends were going to put him forward for the nomination, and Fillmore repeated through intermediaries that Webster was his choice. Everett put together a committee to begin Webster's last campaign for the nomination; more than seven thousand people subscribed in Boston alone.

In June Webster traveled to the South to try to broaden his base of support within the party. After all, southern Whigs had supported the Compromise of 1850 and Webster was the mastermind behind its passage. In Winchester, Virginia, Webster said, "I am as ready to fight and fall for the Constitutional rights of Virginia as I am for those of Massachusetts." The speech was printed in the Washington papers.[7]

Of course he could not turn down a chance to speak on July 4, 1851, the seventy-fifth anniversary of the Declaration of Independence, at the laying of the cornerstone for an addition to the Capitol. The Capitol was a concrete symbol of Webster's Union and a home to him in its House, Senate, and Supreme Court chambers. The occasion gave him another chance to praise George Washington as a saint. President Fillmore preceded Webster to the rostrum in an acknowledgment of who was the most important speaker of the day. Nonetheless, the Whigs of Boston refused to attend the ceremony in protest against the Fugitive Slave Law, the Achilles' heel of Webster's priesthood. When he rose to speak, the assembly realized that the secretary of state was in the twilight of a great career. He seemed aged and frail, but he soon came to life.

Like Webster's other ceremonial efforts, the "Addition to the Capitol" address contains legislative recommendations and forensic attacks, in this case on the spread of slavery into the territories. He acknowledged a warm recep-

---

6. Webster, *Speeches and Formal Writings*, 2:581–82. This passage might have inspired Lincoln's "mystic chords of memory" in his First Inaugural Address.

7. Webster, *Writings and Speeches*, 13:237–41.

tion in his opening remarks: "I see before and around me a mass of faces glow-ing with cheerfulness and patriotic pride. I see thousands of eyes, all sparkling with gratification and delight." As always, Webster adapted his rhetoric to the audience and the location. On this occasion he used a narrowing perspective that came to focus on the assemblage before him: "This is the New World! This is America! This is Washington! and this is the Capitol of the United States!"

In the body of the address, as in the First Bunker Hill Address, Webster stressed the story of the Revolution and its attendant values to reinforce his transcendent vision of a democratic Union leading the rest of the world to peace and freedom: "Fellow citizens, this inheritance which we enjoy today is not only an inheritance of liberty, but of our own peculiar American liberty." He differentiated American experiences from those of other great nations and concluded with a comparison to the ancient Greeks. That example allowed him once again to make his case for Union: "And let it ever be remembered, especially let the truth sink deep into all American minds, that it was the want of Union among her several States which finally gave the mastery of all of Greece to Philip of Macedon." He reviewed what he believed "American polit-ical principles in substance to be." The list included representative govern-ment, equality, and maintaining the will of the majority in harmony with the rule of law. Echoing Washington and presaging Theodore Roosevelt, he added, "Individual virtue is a part of public virtue."

At this juncture, Webster turned to his official duty, to commemorate the laying of the cornerstone. He noted that George Washington, his great hero, had laid the first cornerstone fifty-eight years earlier, and returned to the mo-ment at hand by comparing the state of the Union in 1793 to its state in 1851. Again he claimed that Union made all expansion and prosperity possible. He called on the South in general, and Virginia, just across the Potomac, specifi-cally, to support a working federal system. He concluded his valedictory by quoting Cicero in Latin, adding:

> And now, fellow citizens, with hearts void of hatred, envy and malice toward our own countrymen . . . or toward the subjects or citizens of other govern-ments, or toward any member of the great family of man; but exalting, never-theless, in our own peace, security, and happiness . . . let us return to our homes, and with all humility and devotion offer our thanks to the Father of all our mercies, political, social, and religious.

This closing plea is remarkable because it reverses the opening focus. Instead of addressing the immediate audience, it begins with "countrymen" and opens to "the great family of man." The progressive strategy ties the speech together and gives it an elegant unity rarely attained in American public address. Notable also is the upward movement to God as the source of all benefits. The speech was rightly placed under the new cornerstone, a fitting close to Webster's oratorical career. Events would prevent the great orator from ever again achieving such a sublime moment.

A few days later Webster attended to his duties as secretary of state, negotiating a trade agreement with Costa Rica and ending a hostile relationship with Venezuela. Then he retired to Marshfield to weather the humid summer. There his attention was drawn back toward the presidential nomination, the one achievement that had eluded him. Because he had served as secretary of state with great distinction and had been a distinguished member of the House and Senate, he felt justified in attempting to capture the Whig nomination. Could he and Fillmore overcome the Conscience Whigs and those who thought Scott presented the only hope of victory?

On November 25 a rally for Webster was held in Faneuil Hall. Rufus Choate gave an encomium to his friend and colleague that brought the throng to its feet again and again. In the meantime, Thurlow Weed and William Seward were holding rallies for Scott. Clay formally removed himself from contention by announcing his intention to leave the Senate.

The campaign accelerated in 1852. In February Webster spoke again at Niblo's Saloon, and he returned to New York City for a rally in March. It was to no avail. In April, at Seward's behest, the legislative caucus of New York endorsed Scott. Seward had worked well with the uncompromising Taylor; now he sought to play kingmaker to another general.

The Whig convention was scheduled for mid-June in Baltimore, but Webster could not devote as much of his energy to the event as he would have liked because of his duties as secretary of state. Then, on May 8, near-disaster struck when a carriage carrying Webster to a fishing trip literally fell apart. Webster was thrown from his seat and into the road. He sprained both wrists while trying unsuccessfully to break his fall, and his head hit the road, which led to internal bleeding. When a doctor was summoned, he found his patient shivering and oozing blood from the head. Webster was never the same mentally or physically.

The first public signs of Webster's decline came on May 22 when he was once again allowed to speak in Faneuil Hall. The people in attendance could see his unhealed bruises; they gasped when he had dizzy spells during the speech. He seemed impatient and petulant, and was sarcastic and unpresidential in his attacks on his enemies. Whether because of his injuries or alcohol, he gave a disjointed, rambling address and often fell into incoherence. The audience was stunned.

Soon Webster was unable to function efficiently as secretary of state, much to Fillmore's dismay. Rumors about his mental and physical health plagued his convention managers.[8] By the time the Whig convention commenced on June 16, the Democrats had nominated Franklin Pierce of New Hampshire. It took the Whigs several sessions to hammer out a platform that was acceptable to the Webster-Fillmore forces. Rufus Choate celebrated the completion of their work with a major speech praising the Webster agenda. The euphoria evaporated when Clay, from his deathbed, committed his final act of disrespect for Webster by endorsing Fillmore.

Balloting began on June 18. Seward advanced the candidacy of the sixty-six-year-old General Scott, but he was blocked in his home state of New York by Fillmore. Even though many saw Fillmore as a stalking horse for Webster, Fillmore's managers used the Clay endorsement to argue that the president was a serious candidate and that only Fillmore could defeat Pierce in New York. The first ballot showed the effect of this strategy and must have devastated Webster: Fillmore received 133 votes, Scott 131, and Webster 29. One hundred forty-seven votes were needed for nomination. Webster and Fillmore together had that majority, but Webster's managers could not guarantee delivery of enough of his votes to Fillmore. In any case, Webster was obstinate and told his delegates to stand firm.[9] Fillmore's people knew that their votes, especially in New York, would be cast for Scott should Fillmore withdraw. Forty-six ballots followed, during which southern Whigs pledged to switch their support from Fillmore to Webster if he could manage to get his total up to 41. But Webster's total never exceeded 32. All this took place over Friday and Saturday; the delegates then adjourned until Monday.

The party leaders did not believe Webster could win the election. He had been on the political stage so long that he was contradicted by his own words. Most people were willing to allow their politicians one conversion. In Webster's

8. Peterson, The Great Triumvirate, 485–86.
9. Remini, Daniel Webster, 736.

case, that conversion had occurred when he transformed himself from a New England sectionalist into a nationalist. His rhetoric of civil religion rationalized that move, but it also created a standard of idealism that no politician could sustain. Webster's attack on the war with Mexico marked him as an anti-frontier Whig; it was a clear repudiation of the "manifest destiny" that had stolen its way into the canons of American faith. Then he had backtracked on slavery in the name of Union. This was a reversal that many in the North could not stomach.

Over the weekend, a heartbroken Webster sent a message to his managers instructing them to throw his support to Fillmore. Ironically, Fillmore had already sent a message to *his* managers instructing them to throw their support to Webster. Because Fillmore's managers had no confidence that his delegates would be loyal to Webster, they held fast for Fillmore. On the forty-eighth ballot, three Missouri delegates switched to Scott and the tension on the floor of the convention hall heightened. On the forty-ninth ballot, the New Hampshire delegation deserted Webster and shifted to Scott. Scott was declared the winner on the fifty-third ballot.

As if to punctuate this rejection of the old guard, Clay died on June 29. After Clay's funeral and some reflection, Webster refused to endorse Scott, claiming his nomination would be the downfall of the party. Webster's supporters formed a "Union Whig" ticket, but it did not generate any enthusiasm outside of New England and the project was soon abandoned. When Webster returned to Boston in July, the city turned out to honor him. Looking very ill, Webster participated in a parade that took him past huge crowds, endless bunting, and shops that had closed for the celebration. His carriage slowly made its way to the Boston Common, arriving in the early evening. Weeping, Webster gave a short speech commending the Constitution and the Union. The event gave him new life. He spent some time in retreat in New Hampshire, where he tried to conduct State Department business.

On July 25 he returned to Marshfield and was welcomed by a throng of supporters. He gave a brief speech to his friends, complimenting them on their neighborliness. It was the final address of his career. He returned to Washington for the last time in August to conduct business at the State Department regarding a dispute over fishing rights with the British. Fillmore was forced to step in. Webster next tried to settle a dispute with Peru, but it proved too much for him. Again Fillmore had to intervene. Webster returned to Marshfield and sought medical attention in Boston.

On September 20 doctors told Webster he did not have long to live. He quietly retired to his home at Marshfield and began preparations for his death. On October 10 he dictated plans for his funeral and an epitaph for his tombstone.[10] He requested the same ceremony that would be accorded a simple farmer. On the eighteenth he revised his will. On the twenty-third he signed the new will while propped up in bed beside a window that overlooked a field with a pond. He asked that his favorite ox be brought to the window so he could pet her. That night he gave a talk on the life of Jesus to those assembled around the bed; he was a priest again. Daniel Webster died at 2:37 a.m. on Sunday, October 24, 1852.

Boston held a ceremony of commemoration on the twenty-seventh. Edward Everett, the newly appointed secretary of state, gave the eulogy, burnishing a distinguished career as an orator and statesman. For the funeral two days later, Webster was dressed in white gloves and his familiar dark blue coat with brass buttons. His body was viewed by a distinguished group that included Franklin Pierce, who would defeat Winfield Scott, much to the surprise of the press. The funeral, on the lawn at Marshfield, was attended by ten thousand people. The *New York Times* called Webster one of those of whom the world had "rarely had his equal since the morning of time."[11]

A Gauge of Greatness

Webster's legacy has long outlived his life of service. Historian Irving Bartlett writes: "In an age of great orators, few of Webster's contemporaries challenged his pre-eminence. . . . Later generations of American orators were brought up on Webster's speeches the way writers fed on Shakespeare." Perhaps the praise of Robert Hayne, the senator Webster vanquished in 1830, is even more telling. Hayne claimed that Webster was "the most consummate orator of either ancient or modern times." Webster's ability to use available means of persuasion to advance his policies was supported by his intimate and sophisticated use of rhetorical form. When pleading a case, he not only understood the importance of evidence and argument, but also took into account the goodwill of

10. It reads in part, "Philosophic argument, especially that drawn from the vastness of the universe, in comparison with the apparent insignificance of this Globe, has sometimes shaken my reason for the faith that is in me; but my heart has always assured and reassured me that the gospel of Jesus Christ must be Divine Reality."

11. Quoted in Ferguson, *Law and Letters*, 207.

associates on the bench, the scene of the crime, and the imagination of the jury. Robert A. Ferguson writes that "Daniel Webster dominated American courtrooms." Maurice G. Baxter claims that "[N]o lawyer had more effect upon the Supreme Court . . . than Daniel Webster."[12]

When speaking at a ceremony, Webster knew that the audience needed to feel that they were part of the occasion if they were to be persuaded to adopt the values he endorsed. When addressing the Senate, he knew that the issues had to be reconfigured so that his colleagues could transcend their division and unite behind his pragmatic proposals. In fact, Webster advanced a number of important rhetorical strategies. First, he understood what Cicero meant when he argued that *ornatus*, or fashioning with tropes and figures, should support the *decorum* of the speech, the expectations in the audience. Second, he was more sophisticated in argumentation than most because he supplemented his evidence and arguments with a fugal form of repetition and extension that often overwhelmed his listeners. Third, he became an exemplar of the little used and less noted strategies by which an orator can disguise one form of public address in another and braid all three forms of public address into one masterful speech. This strategy helped Webster with his invention, giving him more resources than his opponents because he was able to multiply his *topoi* by using more than one genre at a time. We can see this talent for invention evolve from his early speeches to his masterpieces during the debates over the 1850 Compromise.

Those who believe that Webster had a knack for public speaking may be right, but he also, as Isocrates advised, polished his natural gifts with a thorough understanding of rhetorical theory, much rehearsal, and intensive research. He was a frequent user of books borrowed from the Library of Congress to supplement his own extensive collection.[13] He read not only for information but also to improve his own style. He read hundreds of books during his tenure in Congress, ranging from Dryden's translations of Virgil to James Elmes's *Dictionary of the Fine Arts*, from the Torah to Burton's *Anatomy of Melancholy*. At his home and in his office Webster kept many volumes of classical literature as well as legal studies to help him refine his sense of style and taste.

His understanding of organizational strategies and audience adaptation

12. Bartlett, *Daniel Webster*, 3–4; Hayne quoted in Peterson, *The Great Triumvirate*, 179; Ferguson, *Law and Letters*, 207; Baxter, *Daniel Webster and the Supreme Court*, 1.
13. Remini, *Daniel Webster*, 657.

matched his mastery of the elements of style. Webster was a self-made man who constructed an enormously effective persona through his rhetoric; until he compromised on slavery, he was the high priest of an American civil religion he had helped to craft. His sense of periodic cadence and his artistic use of tropes and figures—particularly metaphor, irony, and wit—made him a preeminent man of letters in his own time. His ability to bring scenes alive before an audience reinforced the logical thrust of his narration and produced some of the most effective discourse in American history.

Webster created what Cicero called *auctoritas* and *gravitas*. The former refers to the moral authority of the speaker obtained over the course of a career; it is marked by prudence and excellence in decision-making. The latter refers to the perceived substance of the speaker's reputation. Webster's remarkable far-sightedness surely helped in this regard, as did his sweeping knowledge of the lessons of history. Almost every new speech seemed to build his reputation, a reputation on which he could rely to enhance his credibility in his next rhetorical foray. By the time he spoke in the campaign for compromise in 1850, no other speaker, not the political Clay nor the dialectical Calhoun, could master the deliberative situation with more credibility. Only Webster could ascend to high moral ground and descend to the pragmatic world of operations with such consummate skill and conviction.

Webster's *gravitas* often derived from the sheer weight of his arguments and evidence. In his apologia concerning the negotiations with England over the Maine boundary, the arguments and evidence were so detailed that they formed a veritable thicket protecting Webster from his attackers. Cicero claimed that the speaker with *gravitas* would also exhibit *patronus*, which refers to family history represented in achievements and monuments. While *patronus* was more important in ancient Rome than in the democratic America of the first half of the nineteenth century, Webster created his own by identifying himself with George Washington and giving epideictic speeches at the construction of monuments, the altars of American civil religion. Thus, as Webster added his texts to the constellation of addresses available to the public, the courts, and Congress, he worked to make them outshine the others. Their inner glow came from his sense of style, his stentorian delivery, his enormous credibility, his sophisticated use of argument and evidence, and his ability to establish in his listeners the state of mind most compatible with his purpose. Their external sheen came from the editing of their texts into pamphlets, from the letters he wrote in support of each cause, and from the network of supporters he energized, including prominent orators in their own right, such as Rufus Choate and Edward Everett.

Like the best rhetors of antiquity, Webster recognized that the stronger argument would prevail over the weaker and that the more he approximated the truth as it was perceived by the listener, the more he was likely to gain the adherence of that person. While Webster did not back away from innovative form, neither did he abandon established methods. He was equally at home using narrative development or a progressive form of argumentation that washed over the audience in waves. Few speakers in American history have been better able to appeal to the actual consciousness of listeners in terms of their needs and desires while at the same time appealing to their innate potential consciousness of spiritual values and natural laws. Perhaps that is why Webster played such a large role for such a long time; his speeches are ingrained in his country's rhetorical literature, and through them his last recorded words will be forever warranted: "I still live."

Civil Religion

One of the reasons Webster still lives is that he was able to wield the two-edged sword of civil religion with skill. He began by taking the civic republicanism of the previous generation and infusing it with a nation-building mythos. Washington became his father and the father of the new nation. Madison, with his checks and balances, became the guardian angel of the federal dream of a representative democracy that protects minority rights. Alexander Hamilton was the prophet for the federalist dream of a strong national government with commercial possibilities and judicial review.

The Old Testament of Webster's civil religion contained the books of Pericles, Aristotle, Cicero, Locke, and Burke, among others. America's Revolution began a New Testament with such prophets as Washington, Henry, Adams (father and son), Hamilton, Jefferson, and Madison. They took the theories of the Enlightenment and made them into pragmatic reality. Webster then inculcated this New Testament with his own version of civil religion. Using the mythos of the founders, he converted service to the state and federal government into patriotism. He converted citizenship at the state level into citizenship in one America, a nation that transcended the states. In a religious era, he converted loyalty to the Constitution into love of country.

Flowing from the transcendent Union was a constitutional framework that provided protection for the nation against foreign interference and foreign competition. The revenues the government collected were to be stored in a national bank and used to developed a system of roads, rails, canals, and bridges that not only enhanced commercial activity but also brought the disparate citizens of the country together. The Constitution protected the sanctity of contracts and property against the government in general and the states in particular. By 1830 Webster could sum up his civil religion in one phrase: "Liberty and Union, now and forever, one and inseparable."

In that same year, however, he saw others raise the sword of civil religion in more divisive ways. He could not stop the momentum of a national religion, one he promoted in 1820 by equating good citizenship with good Christianity. William Lloyd Garrison began agitating for the abolition of slavery on moral grounds that he claimed were higher even than those of the Constitution. While Webster had by 1830 condemned slavery and the slave trade, he would not go so far as to advocate abolition in the South because that would undo constitutional guarantees. As he soon realized, the Constitution is a compromise, and compromise is the province of politics, not religion.

For Webster, the momentum of national religion also produced "manifest destiny," the belief that America should expand to the Pacific. That he could not brook because the land to be acquired would throw the Senate out of kilter and bring aliens into the nation, thereby destroying his vision of "one people." The expansionist tendency of the country can be traced back to its errand into the wilderness, and it would lead to imperialist conquests against Spain by the end of Webster's century. Sen. Albert Beveridge of Indiana would justify the conquest of the Philippines in his famous 1898 address, "The March of the Flag," which was full of religious rationalizations for expansion.

On the right, John C. Calhoun developed the religion of states' rights, complete with the doctrine of nullification based on his reading of Jefferson and Madison's Virginia and Kentucky Resolutions. He not only tried to dam up Webster's river of civil religion; he tried to reverse it. While Calhoun failed to convince the nation of his position, he did solidify the South behind it. He gave the southern states a positive rationale for the retention and extension of slavery that would provide a warrant for secession once the North succeeded in electing a man who embodied Webster's love of Union.

That man's name was Abraham Lincoln, and he would become the messiah of Union. On June 16, 1858, in Springfield, Illinois, he combined Webster's religion with a touch of Garrison's. To a cheering mob of Republicans, Lincoln quoted Jesus to ground his version of civil religion: "'A house divided against itself cannot stand.' I believe this government cannot endure permanently half slave and half free." Though over the course of seven debates with Stephen Douglas he tried to soften this position, it became the mark of his presidential campaign in 1860. As he presided over the civil war that followed his election, Lincoln modified his civil religion. First he rationalized a suspension of civil liberties in the name of preserving the Union and its Constitution. Next he declared the slaves emancipated, and then in 1863 at Gettysburg he moved the natural rights of humans as articulated in the Declaration of Independence to the forefront. To conclude that address he echoed Webster, calling for a government not of the states, but "of the people, by the people, and for the people." He was martyred for his belief after a half million soldiers died in a civil war.

Throughout American history, presidents and others have adopted various parts of American civil religion or added their own tenets to it. Like Webster, Theodore Roosevelt believed in a hegemonic America; he would brook no "hyphenated Americans." He began the twentieth century by using his "bully pulpit" to advocate for rugged individualists engaged in competition on a level playing field. That, he believed, would lead to a virtuous life. In foreign policy, he spoke softly but carried a big stick. He successfully parlayed his civil religion into a Nobel Peace Prize and enormous popularity. Woodrow Wilson, the son of a minister, sought to make the world safe for democracy, arrogantly claiming in his First Inaugural Address that he was but the "crown of the common theme." His refusal to compromise his dream cost him the United States' membership in his beloved League of Nations and perhaps his life. Franklin Roosevelt's civil religion was evident in his war against the money changers, whom he sought to chase from the temples of capitalism. Internationally, he revived Wilson's dream with his "four freedoms" and the creation of the United Nations. However, the lasting peace he sought was never achieved. Totalitarian regimes spread their own civil religion in the form of communism. A cold war ensued.

John Kennedy espoused his own martial civil religion when he claimed that the United States would "pay any price, bear any burden, meet any hardship, support any friend, oppose any foe to assure the survival and the success of liberty." The tragic consequences of his implementation of that ideal scarred the United States for years. Lyndon Johnson attempted to return to a domestic civil religion with his "Great Society." In the name of the martyred Kennedy, he espoused a philosophy of welfare over individualism and the protection of civil rights over majoritarian tyranny. Though he made great strides in civil rights, his dream was done in by a war from which he could not extricate himself.

Recent Republican presidents have provided their own take on American civil religion with mixed results. Like John Foster Dulles, Eisenhower's secretary of state, they have tended to embrace a Manichaean rhetoric that divides the world into forces of good and evil. Dulles declared international neutrality to be immoral; like Jesus, he believed that others were either for us or against us. Ronald Reagan did battle with an "Evil Empire," successfully playing on the public's fascination with the *Star Wars* trilogy. Reagan's rhetorical prowess allowed him to parlay his holy cold war into a large defense budget and to spend his enemy into the ground.

Reagan's vice president and successor, George H. W. Bush, was an internationalist who was uncomfortable with Manichaean preaching. The diplomatic tangle, with which Bush was familiar in his roles as ambassador to the United Nations and China and director of the CIA, was not as simple as Reagan believed. When Bush went to war, it was for limited goals and with a coalition of ninety-one nations behind him. On the domestic front, however, Bush did engage in dogmatic rhetoric, promising in his acceptance speech to accept "no new taxes." When he reneged on that promise, his presidency was sunk.

His son, George W. Bush, returned to the Manichaean rhetoric of Reagan when confronted with a terrorist attack on the civilian population. He valorized his father's generation, just as Webster had *his* father's, claiming that Americans have a covenant with the "greatest generation."[14] Excoriating an "axis of evil," he went to war in a preemptive attack on his father's old enemy in Iraq, and did so seeking unconditional surrender. The coalition he formed was much smaller than that of his father and is attempting to bring civic republicanism to a nation used to religious rule.

The rhetoric of civil religion can be a high-minded way to enhance and energize the ideals of a nation. It can rally citizens to their best potential consciousness in the name of freedom, caring, individualism, civil rights, and peace. In democracies, such rhetoric is often essential for a president who seeks to motivate citizens to go to war. The same rhetoric can also play to the actual consciousness of the masses by employing the myths of popular culture. In

14. See Denise M. Bostdorff, "George W. Bush's Post–September 11 Rhetoric of Covenant Renewal: Upholding the Faith of the Greatest Generation."

Webster's day these were Great Awakenings; in our own time, they may be film trilogies. The problem with civil religion is that it puts a demagogic and dogmatic patina on politics. Once politicians begin to speak as if they were prophets, it is difficult for them to compromise on the political issues they have addressed. And yet, in a representative democracy, compromise is essential for the survival of the republic.

Webster came to realize this truth when he saved the nation from civil war in 1850. He had come a long way from his pronouncements on slavery in a small church in Plymouth in 1820. However, his work for compromise wounded him with idealists in the North who saw the immorality of slavery and with ideologues in the South who saw ownership of slaves as a right embedded in the Constitution. It was Clay who said he would rather be right than be president, but it was Webster who lived with the consequences of his conscientious action. Perhaps he was too complex for the waves of democracy that swept through the nation during his lifetime in the form of the Second Great Awakening, abolition, manifest destiny, and bandwagon political campaigning. Nonetheless, the "one people" embraced his highest rhetorical moments and incorporated them into the public consciousness. For his attempt to create a civil religion that was civil, nondemagogic, and nondogmatic, his public owed him a great deal. For the lessons he teaches us, we owe him a great deal more.

Chronology of Major Speeches

Fourth of July Address, Hanover, New Hampshire, July 4, 1800.

Fourth of July Address to the Washington Benevolent Society, Portsmouth, New Hampshire, July 4, 1812.

The Conscription Bill, House of Representatives, Washington, D.C., December 9, 1814.

The First Settlement of New England, Plymouth, Massachusetts, December 22, 1820.

The Revolution in Greece, House of Representatives, Washington, D.C., January 19, 1824.

The Tariff, House of Representatives, Washington, D.C., April 1-2, 1824.

First Bunker Hill Address, Charlestown, Massachusetts, June 17, 1825.

Eulogy to Adams and Jefferson, Boston, Massachusetts, August 2, 1826.

The Second Reply to Hayne, Senate, Washington, D.C., January 26-27, 1830.

The Knapp-White Murder Case, Salem, Massachusetts, August 6, 1830.

The Character of Washington, Washington, D.C., February 22, 1832.

The Presidential Veto of the United States Bank Bill, Senate, Washington, D.C., July 11, 1832.

Debate on the Force Bill, Senate, Washington, D.C., February 16, 1833.

Reception at Madison, Madison, Indiana, June 1, 1837.

Reply to Calhoun, Senate, Washington, D.C., March 22, 1838.

The Completion of the Bunker Hill Monument, Charlestown, Massachusetts, June 17, 1843.

Admission of Texas, Senate, Washington, D.C., December 22, 1845.

Defense of the Treaty of Washington, Senate, Washington, D.C., April 6-7, 1846.

The Mexican War, Senate, Washington, D.C., March 1, 1847.

Objects of the Mexican War, Senate, Washington, D.C., March 23, 1848.

The Seventh of March Address, Senate, Washington, D.C., March 7, 1850.

The Seventeenth of July Address, Senate, Washington, D.C., July 17, 1850.

Addition to the Capitol, Washington, D.C., July 4, 1851.

Bibliographic Essay

This essay, which is intended as a guide to the available literature on Webster, comprises five sections. The first discusses the various locations of Webster's papers. The second section discusses the question of authentication of texts. The third section examines biographies of Webster with an emphasis on their usefulness to this study and other rhetorical studies. The fourth section comments on the most important studies of Webster's public speaking. The final section comments on general sources of use to this study.

I. Research Collections and Collected Papers

The almost 2,000 documents that constitute the papers of Daniel Webster written prior to 1820 are located in Baker Library at Dartmouth College, Hanover, New Hampshire. This collection includes a draft of Webster's argument for the *Dartmouth College* case. Reference libraries often make these papers available on microfilm. A 41-reel microfilm edition was published in 1971. The most relevant reels for rhetorical scholars are numbers 30 through 37, the congressional documents. Libraries usually list these documents as *Guide and Index to the Microfilm: Microfilm Edition of the Papers of Daniel Webster,* ed. Charles M. Wiltse (Ann Arbor, MI: University Microfilms, 1971).

Another 2,500 items can be found at the New Hampshire Historical Society in Concord. Much of this is correspondence between family members and is often highly personal in nature. Of most importance to scholars of American public address are Webster's outlines for the reply to Hayne of January 1830 and the Seventh of March Address of 1850.

Webster's papers have also been collected at the Massachusetts Historical Society in Boston and the National Archives in Washington, D.C. Of more use is the collection of approximately 3,000 papers at the Library of Congress, including the *Congressional Globe* and the *Register of Debates in Congress,* ed. Joseph Gales, Jr., and William W. Seaton.

Also available at the Library of Congress is microfilm of various newspapers cited in this study. These are helpful in assessing the milieu of a speech and the reaction to it. The *New York Tribune* and *New York Evening Post* leaned toward the Democratic Party. The *New York Herald* was a Whig paper that was favorable to mercantile and industrial interests. The *Albany Argos* generally favored the American System but supported Free Soil platforms and Martin Van Buren. The *Vicksburg (MS) Weekly Whig* often praised Webster's efforts at compromise, as did the *Boston Daily Advertiser,* the *Boston Courier,* the *National Intelligencer,* the *Washington Union,* and the *Philadelphia Evening Bulletin.*

The Papers of Daniel Webster, ed. Charles M. Wiltse and others, comprise fourteen volumes (Hanover, NH: University Press of New England, 1974–1989). Wiltse has had a distinguished career as an editor and compiler of historic papers. Though his work on Jefferson and Calhoun is thorough, he will be remembered more for the stupendous job he has done on the Webster papers. In 1974, housed in Baker Library at Dartmouth, he began to compile *The Papers of Daniel Webster.* Of most interest to rhetorical scholars are the two volumes entitled *The Papers of Daniel Webster: Speeches and Formal Writings,* ed. Charles M. Wiltse and Alan R. Berolzheimer (1987). The first volume takes Webster up to the tariff battles of 1833; the second volume covers his discourse until his death in 1852.

The editors' work on the speeches is meticulous. Newspaper, pamphlet, and shorthand versions of the text were compared on a word-by-word basis. Footnotes explain the precise differences between each version of each speech. The editors print the Second Reply to Hayne twice because the differences between the delivered version, as best it can be reconstituted, and the published version are significant. Each speech is preceded by a few paragraphs that establish the historical setting for the speech and that trace its publication history, explaining which text was chosen for the volume and why.

While providing a chronology of Webster's rhetorical career, a "calendar" of speeches informs the reader, by a simple comparison with the table of contents, of which speeches are not included in the volume. Rhetorical scholars will be disappointed to learn that the only forensic speech included is that from the Knapp-White murder case. Webster's other forensic speeches are relegated to volume 3 of the *Legal Papers* in this project.

Other biases further reduced the number of speeches included in these two volumes. For example, the editors claim that they include only one speech on the tariff because Webster's speeches on the subject after 1824 are "little more than special pleading for special interests." But in fact, several speeches are included that address the tariff, notably the Second Reply to Hayne. Neither Bunker Hill address is included, yet the editors include both of the speeches Webster delivered during the 1850 Compromise debates. The Plymouth oration, with its powerful attack on slavery, is omitted, but such minor speeches as the one on the Cumberland Road Bill are included. While the first volume is subtitled *1800–1833*, Webster's first years as an orator are covered only in the calendar; the first speech reprinted in the volume is the Rockingham memorial of 1812. There seems to be a general prejudice against epideictic speeches since the "Character of Washington" address is also excluded while many deliberative speeches of lesser consequence are included.

II. Authentic Texts

One difficulty with analyzing speeches is determining the authenticity of the text. The National Edition of *The Writings and Speeches of Daniel Webster*, edited by James W. McIntyre and published in Boston in 1903 in eighteen volumes, is a standard resource for most critics and more inclusive than Wiltse's *Papers of Daniel Webster*. In fact, Wiltse uses these volumes as his "basic text." McIntyre's carefully prepared edition attempts to provide the most accurate texts; he relied on earlier collections, such as the one put together by Charles B. Haddock, a professor of rhetoric at Dartmouth and Webster's nephew through his sister Abigail.

Unfortunately, most of Webster's major speeches were edited by him after they were delivered and before they were published. Thus the published versions do not represent what he actually said on the floor of the Senate, on a patriotic holiday, or before a jury. However, eyewitness and newspaper accounts indicate that the extant texts are very close to Webster's actual speeches. His memory was phenomenal, and he was able to speak from notes and soon after reproduce the entire speech on paper. When Webster was unable or unwilling to reconstruct a speech, there were usually reporters or congressional recorders on hand. Where direct transcriptions occurred, as in the *Dartmouth College* case, it is clear that Webster's published versions were faithful and did not differ markedly from his original remarks. The same conclusion is reached by examining newspaper accounts, or by consulting the text in the *Register of Debates in Congress*, the *National Intelligencer*, or the *Congressional Globe*.

Other sources for speeches by Webster include the following:

Works of Daniel Webster (Boston: Little, Brown, 1877), is the seventeenth edition of a series that began in 1830 when Webster had another twenty-two years to live. This collection was first called *Speeches and Forensic Arguments* and was edited by Charles B. Haddock, Webster's nephew. It was revised in 1835, 1843, and again in 1851. This last authorized version was edited by Edward Everett, Webster's protégé. We can assume that Everett knew Webster's style well and had an astute appreciation of speechmaking because of his own successful career as a public speaker.

S. B. Ives and W. Ives's *The Knapp-White Trial* (Boston, 1830) contains the proceedings of both trials in Salem and Webster's summation to the jury.

Great Speeches of Daniel Webster (Boston: Little, Brown, 1879) was an attempt to create a popular book of Webster's most famous orations. Unfortunately, in almost every case it contains the most polished version of the text and therefore not the words that were actually spoken.

Robert T. Oliver and Eugene White's *Selected Speeches from American History* (Boston: Allyn & Bacon, 1966) contains only one speech by Webster. However, it is one of the few available and authenticated versions of the "Reception at Madison Address."

III. Selected Biographies

Samuel Knapp's *Life of Daniel Webster* (Boston, 1831) was published soon after the Webster-Hayne debate. Knapp was a graduate of Dartmouth and an ardent admirer of Webster. During Webster's life, six books on his speaking or speeches were published. None were distinguished, some were printed only for the royalties they would bring, and almost all of them flattered Webster to a fault.

More useful to scholars have been the books published since Webster's death. Here is a list of the most prominent:

The Private Correspondence of Daniel Webster (Boston, 1857), edited by Fletcher Webster, the only child to survive his father, contains a treasure trove of information about Webster. Volume 1 includes Webster's "Autobiography," with his heartfelt description of his early speaking, stage fright, and failure, over which he "wept bitter tears of mortification" (9–11). Later he speaks about the importance of empathy: "[M]ake me think as he thinks, and feel as he feels" (465). In volume 2 he shares the tricks of the trade with his son, including "honest quackery" (16). The *Private Correspondence* is essential reading for anyone seeking to understand Webster's early training, his assessment of other speakers, and his rhetorical roots. Webster's writings in these two volumes also indicate a healthy interest in the criticism of public address. He wanted to know what made it work; in no case was he satisfied with mystical explanations.

Charles Lanman's *The Private Life of Daniel Webster* (New York, 1852) is typical of the spate of volumes published upon Webster's death. The author attempts to get at Webster's personal life, speculating on such subjects as his love for his children and his religious conviction. Lanman is probably no more accurate than Parson Weems writing on George Washington.

Samuel M. Smucker's *The Life, Speeches, and Memorials of Daniel Webster* (Philadelphia: Duane Rulison, 1861) includes Webster's best speeches but is limited in two ways. First, the speeches were edited and were drawn from reprinted versions somewhat removed from the actual speaking event. Second, Smucker's admiration for Webster prevents him from writing objectively about his subject.

George T. Curtis, the author of *Life of Daniel Webster* (New York: Appleton, 1872), was a direct descendent of both George Ticknor and Edward Curtis, close friends and traveling companions of Webster. Grace Webster and Anna Ticknor, George's wife, were also close, though Grace was a wallflower compared to Anna, who was an outgoing hostess. This two-volume work is both a biography and a collection of Webster's letters. Since the biography was authorized and uses the letters for support, Curtis's arguments—for example, his claim that Webster emulated Jeremiah Mason's plain, direct oratorical style in court—have an air of credibility.

Peter Harvey's *Reminiscences and Anecdotes of Daniel Webster* (Boston, limited edition, 1877) was reprinted by Little, Brown & Company in 1921. Webster often confided in Harvey, wrote intimate letters to him, and considered him one of the most broad-minded and unselfish men in America. If one is looking for evidence of Webster's anguish during the 1850 Compromise debates, the place to turn is Harvey's book. Webster's admiration for English speakers such as Pitt, Burke, and Fox can also be found there. Perhaps no collection other than Fletcher Webster's provides a more personal look at Daniel Webster.

Henry Cabot Lodge's *Daniel Webster* (Boston: Houghton Mifflin, 1884) was reprinted in New York by Chelsea House in 1980 with an introduction by Charles M. Wiltse. Lodge, a senator from Massachusetts, fancied himself a historian, but in fact was much more a politician who used historical data to buttress his arguments. Using local sources and indulging his bias against slavery and the South, Lodge wrote an unflattering and often inaccurate biography that condemns Webster for being a political compromiser. The book was published as volume 21 in the American Statesmen Series commissioned by Houghton Mifflin. Given Lodge's enormous influence in Massachusetts and on its educational institutions, it should come as no surprise that his version of Webster's life prevailed for generations in New England's popular culture.

Claude H. Van Tyne's *The Letters of Daniel Webster* (New York, 1902) presents a selected view of Webster's interests. It is inferior to Fletcher Webster's two-volume set and to Curtis's work, but it does include several passages that reveal Webster's views on education. For example, Webster believed that one must have a solid philosophical foundation before writing material to be published or speaking in public. He was fond of public education and thought American lawyers should be well versed in Greek, Latin, and French along with their native English. Van Tyne focuses on Webster's penchant for a clear, clean, parsimonious style. His book may be the best in terms of representing Webster's notion that style should serve function and ostentation should be avoided. He fails to point out, however, that Webster often violated his own stylistic principles.

Claude M. Fuess's *Daniel Webster* (Boston: Little, Brown, 1930) was carefully done and was perhaps the first biography with enough distance from Webster to be called objective and genuinely reliable with regard to interpretations of events. The book was reprinted in New York by Da Capo Press in 1968 with the addition of illustrations and a bibliography.

Norman D. Brown's *Daniel Webster and the Politics of Availability* (Athens: University of Georgia Press, 1969) concentrates on the tensions within American political parties from 1815 to Webster's death in 1852. It provides an excellent look at the death of the Federalist Party and the impact that had on Webster. It also examines the rise of the Whig Party and the role Webster played in constructing the Whig platform. Brown's emphasis on presidential politics results in a clear picture of the battle for power fought between the principals of the time, particularly John Quincy Adams, Andrew Jackson, Henry Clay, William Seward, Zachary Taylor, John C. Calhoun, Lewis Cass, James Polk, Martin Van Buren, and, of course, Webster. No book does a better job of reviewing what actually occurred at the national party conventions during Webster's lifetime.

Richard N. Current's *Daniel Webster and the Rise of National Conservatism* (Boston: Little, Brown, 1955) provides an understanding of Webster's national conservatism. Current argues that Webster's development of national conservatism in the court system and in Congress was his greatest legacy. Through it, he helped John Marshall establish the authority of the Supreme Court, limit the power of the states, and strengthen the sanctity of private contracts. National conservatism also complemented Clay's American System, which gave the Whigs a platform with a truly universal appeal.

Maurice G. Baxter's *Daniel Webster and the Supreme Court* (Amherst: University of Massachusetts Press, 1966) authoritatively examines Webster's career before the bar. Its strengths include a clear explication of the law and the context of each case. It is Baxter who confirms that the Supreme Court "borrowed heavily from Webster's briefs" (v). He gives the counts of cases won and lost and the number of times Webster appeared before the Court with other lawyers.

In his book *Daniel Webster* (New York: W. W. Norton, 1978), Irving H. Bartlett admits to not fully developing Webster's legal career, though he does provide the most comprehensive personal examination of any historian to date. To read Bartlett is to get to know Webster. Passages such as this one illustrate the point: "Whenever he thought about his father he became a little boy again" (21). Bartlett stresses the importance of rhetoric and oratory in American history, and he understands how Webster's language contributed to his reputation. He writes, "The fact that Webster was read so much more widely than any other public man of his time, that he was looked upon as a literary giant as well as a great lawyer, orator, and statesman contributed heavily to his enormous visibility before the American public" (4). Bartlett even comments on the large size of Webster's brain (5).

Robert F. Dalzell's *Daniel Webster and the Trial of American Nationalism: 1843–1852* (Boston: Houghton Mifflin, 1973) is a political history that traces emerging issues from the war with Mexico through the death of Webster. This carefully written book provides an excellent background to the speeches of Webster from the time he became secretary of state in the Harrison administration to his death.

Sydney Nathans's *Daniel Webster and Jacksonian Democracy* (Baltimore: Johns Hopkins University Press, 1973) is concerned with the interaction between Webster and his archenemies in Jackson's Democratic Party as they fought over the tariff, the bank, internal improvements, and western land development. In the background, Clay, most often in support of Webster, and Calhoun, most often in opposition, play supporting roles. While other books do a better job of describing Webster's philosophical foundation and political platform, few are better at describing the Jacksonian platform and why it was at odds with Webster's.

Merrill D. Peterson's *The Great Triumvirate: Webster, Clay, and Calhoun* (New

York: Oxford University Press, 1987) is a product of the author's long and distinguished career as a professor at the University of Virginia and writer on American history. Peterson, who had previously concentrated on the founders, particularly Jefferson, here turns his attention to the second generation of American leaders. Among its other virtues, his book brings together all the previous work that had been done on these three legislative leaders and sheds light on the moments when their paths crossed, including debates in the House and Senate. Peterson devotes ten pages to the Webster-Hayne debates, Calhoun's involvement, and the issues surrounding them. He mentions the first confrontation between Clay and Webster in the House. Students of Webster will be particularly interested in what Peterson has to say about Webster's literary influences (29, 32, 35, 37, 400), his training for law practice (31–34, 97–98), his performance before the Supreme Court (98–104, 250–51, 396–97), his oratorical prowess (105–12, 175, 181, 295–96, 400–402, 462–64), and his campaigning in the election of 1840 (293–96). The material is well documented and the notes lead the reader to source material that is useful in rhetorical analysis. But readers would be wise to keep in mind that Peterson's goal is to examine the golden age of republican democracy in America, which spans the years from the war of 1812 to the Compromise of 1850. That this period of time also happens to be the golden age of American oratory is coincidental to Peterson and a minor focus of his book.

Robert V. Remini's *Daniel Webster: The Man and His Time* (New York: W. W. Norton, 1997) is the latest volume on Webster by a distinguished scholar of the time period. His work on Clay, for example, informs this work on Webster. Its 796 pages provide a copious study of the events surrounding Webster.

IV. Selected Critical Studies

Herbert D. Foster's "Webster's Seventh of March Speech and the Secession Movement, 1850" (*American Historical Review* 27 [1922]; Dartmouth Reprint Series [1923], 1–35) was an early attempt to bring the tools of historicism to bear on an event that had been treated either mythically or with prejudice by Henry Cabot Lodge and other biographers of Webster. Foster's discussion of the legislative debate is useful for the facts it provides about the sequence of events. Foster, who had a love for Dartmouth, also wrote "Webster and Choate in College: Dartmouth under the Curriculum of 1796–1819" (*Dartmouth Alumni Magazine* 19 [April-May 1927]: 509–19), in which he described the courses and textbooks Webster was exposed to in college.

Paul H. Arntson and I wrote "The Seventh of March Address: A Mediating Influence" (*Southern Speech Communication Journal* 40 [1975]: 288–301) to correct two standard interpretations of Webster's speech in the 1850 Compromise debates. The first interpretation, propagated by John F. Kennedy in *Profiles in Courage*, is that Webster was heroic to take a stand that saved the Union despite the fact that he would be vilified in Massachusetts and the North. Kennedy's error was to assume that abolitionists were in the majority and were the only opinion leaders in the North in general and Massachusetts in particular. The second interpretation, put forward by Henry Cabot Lodge in 1884, is that Webster's contemporary critics were correct and that the speech was corrupt and rightly condemned. Arntson and I examined political voting and newspapers of the time, which indicate that abolitionists were in the minority and that Webster consolidated pro-Union and conservative sentiment in the North with his first major speech in the 1850 Compromise debates.

Wilbur S. Howell and Hoyt H. Hudson's "Daniel Webster," in *A History and Criticism of American Public Address*, ed. W. Norbert Brigance, 2:665–733 (New York: Russell & Russell, 1960), provides a catalogue of Webster's best rhetorical moments. This essay is a straightforward assessment of Webster as public speaker.

John W. Black's "Webster's Peroration in the Dartmouth College Case" (*Quarterly Journal of Speech* 23 [1937]: 636–42) concentrates on style, organization, ethos, pathos, and logos. Black's detailed understanding of language—he eventually moved his academic focus to linguistics—allows him to unpack the connotations of style prevalent in Webster's speech.

Glenn E. Mills's "Daniel Webster's Principles of Rhetoric" (*Speech Monographs* 9 [1942]: 124–40) is drawn from the dissertation he completed at the University of Michigan in 1941. It differs from a standard rhetorical biography by attempting to deduce a set of rhetorical principles from the corpus of Webster's works.

Howard A. Bradley and James A. Winans's *Daniel Webster and the Salem Murder* (Columbia, MO: Artcraft Press, 1956) provides an excellent depiction of the crime, its impact upon the town of Salem, and all of the events that led up to the famous set of trials.

A. A. Eisenstadt's "Daniel Webster and the Seventh of March" (*Southern Speech Journal* 20 [1954]: 136–47) represents the traditional view of Webster's speech. The author argues that Webster gave a stylistically sound address that offended northern sensibilities.

James M. Farrell's "The Speech Within: Trope and Performance in Daniel

Webster's Eulogy to Adams and Jefferson," in *Rhetoric and Political Culture in Nineteenth-Century America*, Thomas Benson, ed., 15–38 (East Lansing, MI: Michigan State University Press, 1997), concentrates on the famous "ghost speech" section of Webster's most acclaimed eulogy. Farrell examines the dominant tropes in the speech and its function as a performance.

Stephen H. Browne's "Reading Public Memory in Daniel Webster's *Plymouth Rock Oration*" (*Western Journal of Communication* 57 [1993]: 464–77) combines new theoretical approaches to memorialization with excellent Aristotelian criticism.

V. General Sources

Holman Hamilton's *Prologue to Conflict: The Crisis and Compromise of 1850* (New York: W. W. Norton, 1964) dissects the membership of the House and Senate and is exhaustive and invaluable.

Avery O. Craven's *The Coming of the Civil War* (Chicago: University of Chicago Press, 1963) carefully traces the roots of the conflict of 1861–1865. In the course of his study, he provides useful information on the years 1833 to 1852. Craven is a revisionist in his theories of the coming war and therefore gives extra weight to rhetorical factors.

The *Dictionary of American Biography*, ed. Allen Johnson and Dumas Malone (New York: Charles Scribner's Sons, 1960), is helpful in determining the character of the persons who engaged Webster in debate and heard him speak before the Supreme Court. The eleven volumes contain extensive biographies of important Americans written by experts in history, law, political science, and the social sciences. I have used the *Dictionary's* biographies of important lawyers such as Choate and Gore and of Supreme Court justices such as Marshall, Taney, Story, and Washington to supplement other means of audience analysis. The biographies detail the background of each justice, explaining where they were raised and how they were selected for the bench, and also reveal their voting patterns and leanings on constitutional questions. The *Dictionary of American Biography* has now been expanded by *American National Biography*, 24 vols., ed. John A. Garraty and Mark C. Carnes (New York: Oxford University Press, 1999).

The *Biographical Dictionary of the Federal Judiciary*, ed. Harold Chase, Samuel Krislov, Keith O. Boyum, and Jerry N. Clark (Detroit: Gale Research, 1976), focuses on prominent jurists, particularly Supreme Court justices. It provides a careful analysis of their careers that is useful in reconstructing the audience Webster faced when he argued before the Supreme Court. The entries cover attitudes on constitutional issues, party affiliation, and voting records.

Gustavus Myers's *History of the Supreme Court of the United States* (1912; reprint, New York: Bert Franklin, 1968), concentrates solely on the Supreme Court. Myers examines major decisions and all of the justices of the Supreme Court in some detail.

Carl B. Swisher's *The Taney Period, 1836–1864*, vol. 5 of the *Oliver Wendell Holmes Devise History of the Supreme Court of the United States* (New York: Macmillan, 1974) is invaluable in reconstructing Webster's forensic world. It provides extremely useful case histories and biographical information on Supreme Court justices.

Bibliography

Adams, Charles Francis, ed. *Memoirs of John Quincy Adams.* 12 vols. Philadelphia, 1874–1877.

Akers, Charles W. *Called unto Liberty: A Life of Jonathan Mayhew, 1720–1766.* Cambridge, MA: Harvard University Press, 1964.

Appleby, Joyce. *Capitalism and a New Social Order: The Republican Vision of the 1790s.* New York: New York University Press, 1984.

Aristotle. *Rhetoric.* Trans. Rhys Roberts. New York: Random House, 1954.

Arntson, Paul H., and Craig R. Smith. "The Seventh of March Address: A Mediating Influence." *Southern Speech Communication Journal* 40 (1975): 288–301.

Aune, James Arnt. "Public Address and Rhetorical Theory." In *Texts in Context: Critical Dialogues on Significant Episodes in American Political Rhetoric,* ed. Michael C. Leff and Fred J. Kauffeld, 40–51. Davis, CA: Hermagoras Press, 1989.

Bailyn, Bernard. *The Ideological Origins of the American Revolution.* Cambridge, MA: Harvard University Press, Belknap Press, 1967.

Banning, Lance. *The Jeffersonian Persuasion: Evolution of a Party Ideology.* Ithaca, NY: Cornell University Press, 1978.

Bartlett, Irving H. *Daniel Webster.* New York: W. W. Norton, 1978.

Baxter, Maurice G. *Daniel Webster and the Supreme Court.* Amherst: University of Massachusetts Press, 1966.

——. *One and Inseparable: Daniel Webster and the Union.* Cambridge, MA: Harvard University Press, 1984.

Bellah, Robert N. *The Broken Covenant: American Civil Religion in Time of Trial.* New York: Seabury Press, 1975.

Berthoff, Rowland. "The American Social Order: A Conservative Hypothesis." *American Historical Review* 65 (1960): 498–504.

Black, John W. "Webster's Peroration in the Dartmouth College Case." *Quarterly Journal of Speech* 23 (1937): 636–42.

Bostdorff, Denise M. "George W. Bush's Post–September 11 Rhetoric of Covenant Renewal: Upholding the Faith of the Greatest Generation." *Quarterly of Journal of Speech* 89 (2003): 293–319.

Brown, Norman D. *Daniel Webster and the Politics of Availability*. Athens: University of Georgia Press, 1969.

Browne, Stephen Howard. *Angelina Grimke: Rhetoric, Identity, and the Radical Imagination*. East Lansing: Michigan State University Press, 1999.

——. "Reading Public Memory in Daniel Webster's *Plymouth Rock Oration*." *Western Journal of Communication* 57 (1993): 464–77.

——. "Webster's Eulogy and the Tropes of Public Memory." In *Rhetoric and Political Culture in Nineteenth-Century America*, ed. Thomas Benson, 39–46. East Lansing: Michigan State University Press, 1997.

Burke, Edmund. "Speech Moving His Resolutions for Conciliation with America." In *Select British Eloquence*, ed. Chauncey A. Goodrich, 265–91. New York: Bobbs-Merrill, 1963.

Burnett, Edmund C., ed. *Letters of Members of the Continental Congress*. 8 vols. Washington, DC: U.S. Government Printing Office, 1921–1936.

Campbell, Karlyn K., and Kathleen H. Jamieson. *Deeds Done in Words: Presidential Rhetoric and the Genres of Governance*. Chicago: University of Chicago Press, 1990.

Chase, Harold, Samuel Krislov, Keith O. Boyum, and Jerry N. Clark, eds. *Biographical Dictionary of the Federal Judiciary*. Detroit: Gale Research, 1976.

Cicero. *De Partitione Oratoria*. In *De Oratore, De Fato, Paradox Stoicorum, De Partitione Oratoria*, trans. H. Rackham, 310–420. Cambridge, MA: Harvard University Press, 1942.

——. *Rhetorica ad Herennium*. Trans. Harry Caplan. Cambridge, MA: Harvard University Press, 1981.

Clay, Henry. *Candidate, Compromiser, Elder Statesman: January 1, 1844–June 29, 1852*. Ed. Melba Porter Hay and Carol Reardon. Vol. 10, *Papers of Henry Clay*. Lexington: University Press of Kentucky, 1991.

——. "Response to John Brown." In *A Defense of Southern Slavery and Other Pamphlets*, ed. Iveson L. Brookes, 4–8. New York: Negro University Press, 1969.

——. "Speech on the Maysville Road Veto." In *Great Issues in American History, Vol. 1: 1765–1865*, ed. Richard Hofstadter, 267–70. New York: Vintage Books, 1958.

Cmiel, Kenneth. *Democratic Eloquence: The Fight over Popular Speech in Nineteenth-Century America*. New York: William Morrow, 1990.

Cole, Arthur C. "Daniel Webster." In *Dictionary of American Biography*, ed. Allen Johnson and Dumas Malone, 19:585–92. New York: Charles Scribner's Sons, 1960.

Conley, Thomas M. "Ancient Rhetoric and Modern Genre Criticism." *Communication Quarterly* 27 (1979): 47–53.

Cooper, William J., Jr. *Jefferson Davis, American*. New York: Knopf, 2000.

Craven, Avery O. *The Coming of the Civil War*. Chicago: University of Chicago Press, 1963.

Current, Richard N. *Daniel Webster and the Rise of National Conservatism*. Boston: Little, Brown, 1955.

Current, Richard N., T. Harry Williams, and Frank Freidel. *American History: A Survey*. New York: Knopf, 1963.

Dalzell, Robert F. *Daniel Webster and the Trial of American Nationalism, 1843–1852*. Boston: Houghton Mifflin, 1973.

Duffy, Bernard K. "The Platonic Functions of Epideictic Rhetoric." *Philosophy and Rhetoric* 16 (1983): 76–86.

Eisenstadt, A. A. "Daniel Webster and the Seventh of March." *Southern Speech Journal* 20 (1954): 136–47.

Emerson, Ralph Waldo. *The Complete Works*. 12 vols. Centenary Edition. Boston, 1903–1904.

Erickson, Paul D. *The Poetry of Events: Daniel Webster's Rhetoric of the Constitution and Union*. New York: New York University Press, 1986.

Ericson, David F. *The Shaping of American Liberalism: The Debates over Ratification, Nullification, and Slavery*. Chicago: University of Chicago Press, 1993.

Farrand, Max, ed. *The Records of the Federal Convention of 1787*. 4 vols. New Haven, CT: Yale University Press, 1911.

Farrell, James M. "The Speech Within: Trope and Performance in Daniel Webster's Eulogy to Adams and Jefferson." In *Rhetoric and Political Culture in Nineteenth-Century America*, ed. Thomas Benson, 15–38. East Lansing: Michigan State University Press, 1997.

Ferguson, Robert A. *Law and Letters in American Culture*. Cambridge, MA: Harvard University Press, 1984.

Fisher, Walter R. "Genre: Concepts and Applications in Rhetorical Criticism." *Western Journal of Communication* 44 (1980): 288–99.

Foster, Herbert D. "Webster and Choate in College: Dartmouth under the Curriculum of 1796–1819." *Dartmouth Alumni Magazine* 19 (April-May 1927): 509–19.

———. "Webster's Seventh of March Speech and the Secessionist Movement, 1850." *American Historical Review* 27 (1922). Dartmouth Reprint Series (Hanover, NH, 1923), 1–35.

Fuess, Claude M. *Daniel Webster.* 2 vols. 1930. Reprint, New York: Da Capo Press, 1968.

Garnet, Henry H. "Rise Up and Resist." In *Slavery Attacked: The Abolitionist Crusade,* ed. John L. Thomas, 100–102. Englewood Cliffs, NJ: Prentice-Hall, 1965.

Hamilton, Alexander. *Federalist,* no. 15. In *On the Constitution,* ed. Ralph H. Gabriel, 29–37. Indianapolis: Bobbs-Merrill, 1954.

Hamilton, J. G. de Roulhac, ed. *The Papers of William Alexander Graham.* 4 vols. Raleigh, NC: State Department of Archives and History, 1957–1961.

Hamilton, Holman. *Prologue to Conflict: The Crisis and Compromise of 1850.* New York: W. W. Norton, 1964.

Hartz, Louis. *The Liberal Tradition in America: An Interpretation of American Political Thought since the Revolution.* New York: Harcourt Brace Jovanovich, 1955.

Harvey, Peter. *Reminiscences and Anecdotes of Daniel Webster.* 1877. Reprint, Boston: Little, Brown, 1921.

Hofstadter, Richard, ed. *Great Issues in American History, Vol. 1: 1765–1865.* New York: Vintage Books, 1958.

Holmes, Richard, ed. *The Oxford Companion to Military History.* New York: Oxford University Press, 2001.

Howell, William S., and Hoyt H. Hudson. "Daniel Webster." In *A History and Criticism of American Public Address,* ed. W. Norbert Brigance, 2:665–733. New York: Russell & Russell, 1960.

Ivie, Robert L. "Presidential Motives for War." *Quarterly Journal of Speech* 60 (1974): 337–45.

———. "Progressive Form and Mexican Culpability in Polk's Justification for War." *Communication Studies* 30 (1979): 311–20.

———. "William McKinley: Advocate of Imperialism." *Western Journal of Communication* 36 (1972): 15–23.

Jensen, Vernon. "British Voices on the Eve of the American Revolution: Trapped by the Family Metaphor." *Quarterly Journal of Speech* 63 (1977): 43–50.

Johnson, Allen, and Dumas Malone, eds. *Dictionary of American Biography.* 11 vols. New York: Charles Scribner's Sons, 1960.

Kaminski, John P., and Gaspare J. Saladino, eds. *The Documentary History of the*

Ratification of the Constitution. 17 vols. Madison: State Historical Society of Wisconsin, 1976.

Kennedy, George A. *Classical Rhetoric and Its Christian and Secular Tradition from Ancient Times to Modern Times.* Chapel Hill: University of North Carolina Press, 1980.

Kennedy, John F. *Profiles in Courage.* New York: Pocket Books, 1957.

Kennett, Lee. *Sherman: A Soldier's Life.* New York: HarperCollins, 2001.

Lader, Lawrence. *The Bold Brahmins: New England's War against Slavery, 1831–1863.* New York: E. P. Dutton, 1961.

Lampe, Gregory. *Frederick Douglass: Freedom's Voice, 1841–1845.* East Lansing: Michigan State University Press, 1998.

Leff, Michael. "Genre and Paradigm in the Second Book of *De Oratore.*" *Southern Communication Journal* 51 (1986): 308–25.

Levinson, Sanford. "'The Constitution' in American Civil Religion." In *The Supreme Court Review, 1979,* ed. Philip B. Kurland, 123–51. Chicago: University of Chicago Press, 1980.

Lewis, Walker, ed. *Speak for Yourself, Daniel: A Life of Webster in His Own Words.* Boston: Houghton Mifflin, 1969.

Lloyd, Arthur Young. *The Slavery Controversy, 1831–1860.* Chapel Hill: University of North Carolina Press, 1939.

Locke, John. *Two Treatises on Civil Government.* Ed. Peter Laslett. Cambridge: Cambridge University Press, 1966.

Lodge, Henry Cabot. *Daniel Webster.* 1884. Reprinted with an introduction by Charles J. Wiltse. New York: Chelsea House, 1980.

Lucas, Stephen E. "Genre Criticism and Historic Context: The Case of George Washington's First Inaugural Address." *Southern Communication Journal* 51 (1986): 354–70.

Madison, James. *Letters and Other Writings of James Madison.* 4 vols. Ed. Philip R. Fendall. Philadelphia: Lippincott, 1865.

———. *The Papers of James Madison.* 8 vols. Ed. Robert A. Rutland. Charlottesville: University of Virginia Press, 1973.

Mann, Horace. *Slavery: Letters and Speeches.* Boston, 1851.

March, Charles W. *Daniel Webster and His Contemporaries.* New York, 1852.

Mayer, Henry. *All on Fire: William Lloyd Garrison and the Abolition of Slavery.* New York: St. Martin's Press, 1999.

Menand, Louis. *The Metaphysical Club: A Story of Ideas in America.* New York: Farrar, Straus & Giroux, 2001.

Mills, Glenn E. "Daniel Webster's Principles of Rhetoric." *Speech Monographs* 9 (1942): 124–40.

Nathans, Sydney. *Daniel Webster and Jacksonian Democracy.* Baltimore: Johns Hopkins University Press, 1973.

Niebuhr, H. Richard. *The Kingdom of God in America.* New York: Harper & Row, 1937.

Oliver, Robert T., and Eugene White, eds. *Selected Speeches from American History.* Boston: Allyn & Bacon, 1966.

Paltsits, Victor Hugo. *Washington's Farewell Address.* New York: New York Public Library, 1935.

Pangle, Thomas L. *The Spirit of Modern Republicanism: The Moral Vision of the American Founders and the Philosophy of Locke.* Chicago: University of Chicago Press, 1988.

Peterson, Merrill D. *The Great Triumvirate: Webster, Clay, and Calhoun.* New York: Oxford University Press, 1987.

Plumer, William, Jr. *Life of William Plumer.* Boston: Phillips, Sampson, 1856.

Pocock, J. G. A. *The Machiavellian Moment: Florentine Political Thought and the Atlantic Republican Tradition.* Princeton, NJ: Princeton University Press, 1975.

Rahe, Paul A. *Inventions of Prudence: Constituting the American Regime.* Vol. 3, *Republics Ancient and Modern.* Chapel Hill: University of North Carolina Press, 1992.

Rathbun, Lyon. "The Debate over Annexing Texas and the Emergence of Manifest Destiny." *Rhetoric and Public Affairs* 4 (2001): 459–93.

Ratner, Lorman. *Powder Keg: Northern Opposition to the Anti-Slavery Movement.* New York: Basic Books, 1968.

Reid, Ronald. "New England Rhetoric and the French War, 1754–1760: A Case Study in the Rhetoric of War." *Communication Monographs* 43 (1976): 259–86.

Remini, Robert V. *Daniel Webster: The Man and His Time.* New York: W. W. Norton, 1997.

Rodgers, Daniel T. "Republicanism: The Career of a Concept." *Journal of American History* 78 (1992): 11–38.

Rosenfield, Lawrence. "The Practical Celebration of Epideictic." In *Rhetoric in Transition: Studies in the Nature and Uses of Rhetoric,* ed. Eugene White, 131–55. University Park: Pennsylvania State University Press, 1980.

Rousseau, Jean-Jacques. *Discourse on the Origin and Foundation of the Inequality between Men.* In *The Social Contract and Discourses.* New York: Everyman's Library, 1913.

Sandel, Michael J. *Democracy's Discontent: America in Search of a Public Philosophy.* Cambridge, MA: Harvard University Press, Belknap Press, 1996.

Sargent, Nathan. *Public Men and Events.* 2 vols. Philadelphia: J. B. Lippincott, 1875.

Seelye, John. *Memory's Nation: The Place of Plymouth Rock.* Chapel Hill: University of North Carolina Press, 1998.

Selby, Gary S. "Mocking the Sacred: Frederick Douglass's 'Slaveholder's Sermon' and the Antebellum Debate over Religion and Slavery." *Quarterly Journal of Speech* 88 (2002): 326–41.

Simons, Herbert W., and A. A. Aghazarian. *Form, Genre, and the Study of Political Discourse.* Columbia: University of South Carolina Press, 1986.

Smith, Craig R. "Daniel Webster." In *American Orators before 1900: Critical Studies and Sources,* ed. Bernard K. Duffy and Halford R. Ryan, 416–26. Westport, CT: Greenwood Press, 1987.

———. *The Quest for Charisma: Christianity and Persuasion.* Westport, CT: Praeger Publishers, 2000.

———. "A Reinterpretation of Aristotle's Notion of Rhetorical Form." *Western Speech Communication Journal* 43 (1979): 14–25.

———. *To Form a More Perfect Union.* Lanham, MD: University Press of America, 1993.

Smith, Craig R., and David M. Hunsaker. *The Four Freedoms of the First Amendment: A Textbook.* Prospect Heights, IL: Waveland Press, 2003.

Smith, Elbert. *The Death of Slavery.* Chicago: University of Chicago Press, 1967.

Smith, Timothy. *Revivalism and Social Reform in Mid-Nineteenth-Century America.* New York: Abingdon Press, 1957.

Smucker, Samuel M. *The Life, Speeches, and Memorials of Daniel Webster.* Philadelphia: Duane Rulison, 1861.

Spaulding, Matthew, and Patrick J. Garrity. *A Sacred Union of Citizens: George Washington's Farewell Address and the American Character.* Lanham, MD: Rowman & Litchfield, 1996.

Swisher, Carl B. *The Taney Period, 1836–1864.* Vol. 5, *Oliver Wendell Holmes Devise History of the Supreme Court of the United States.* New York: Macmillan, 1974.

Taylor, Zachary. "Message to the Senate, January 23, 1850." In *A Compilation of the Messages and Papers of the Presidents, 1789–1902*, ed. James D. Richardson, 5:30. Washington, DC: Bureau of National Literature and Art, 1902.

Thomas, George M. *Revivalism and Cultural Change: Christianity, Nation Building, and the Market in the Nineteenth-Century United States*. Chicago: University of Chicago Press, 1997.

Walker, Daniel. *The Political Culture of the American Whigs*. Chicago: University of Chicago Press, 1979.

Ward, John William. *Andrew Jackson: Symbol for an Age*. New York: Oxford University Press, 1955.

Weaver, Richard. *The Ethics of Rhetoric*. South Bend, IN: Gateway Edmons, 1953.

Webster, Daniel. *The Papers of Daniel Webster: Correspondence*. 7 vols. Ed. Charles M. Wiltse. Hanover, NH: University Press of New England, 1974–1985.

———. *The Papers of Daniel Webster: Diplomatic Papers*. 2 vols. Ed. Kenneth E. Shewmaker, Anita McGurn, and Kenneth R. Stevens. Hanover, NH: University Press of New England, 1983–1987.

———. *The Papers of Daniel Webster: Speeches and Formal Writings*. 2 vols. Ed. Charles M. Wiltse and Alan R. Berolzheimer. Hanover, NH: University Press of New England, 1987.

———. *The Private Correspondence of Daniel Webster*. 2 vols. Ed. Fletcher Webster. Boston, 1857.

———. *Speeches and Forensic Arguments*. 3 vols. Boston: Tappan, Whittemore & Mason, 1850.

———. *The Writings and Speeches of Daniel Webster*. National Edition. 18 vols. Ed. James W. McIntyre. Boston: Little, Brown, 1903.

Weincek, Henry. *An Imperfect God: George Washington, His Slaves, and the Creation of America*. New York: Farrar, Straus & Giroux, 2003.

Wheaton, Henry. *Digest of Decisions of the Supreme Court of the United States, 1789–1820*. 12 vols. Washington, DC, 1821.

Whittier, John Greenleaf. *The Complete Poetical Works*. New York, 1894.

Wilson, Major L. "The Free Soil Concept of Progress and the Irrepressible Conflict." *American Quarterly* 22 (1970): 71–84.

Zarefsky, David. "Henry Clay and the Election of 1844: The Limits of a Rhetoric of Compromise." *Rhetoric and Public Affairs* 6 (2003): 79–96.

Index

Page numbers in bold type refer to illustrations.

Abolitionist Liberator, 231
Abolitionists, 57, 157, 158, 164, 168, 172,
    178, 180, 181–82, 185–86, 188–90,
    221–22, 224, 228, 230–31, 233–34, 241,
    252–53, 257
Adams, Charles Francis, 181
Adams, John Quincy, 4, 8, 18, 20, 23, 41–42,
    55, 63, 73–76, 82–102 passim, 156,
    158–59, 164, 179–81, 185–86, 197, 204,
    215, 266; "Address to the People of the
    Free States of the Union," 185
Adams, Samuel, 12
Albany Argos, 232–33
Alcibiades, 23
Alien and Sedition Acts, 20, 24, 34, 114
American and Foreign Anti-Slavery Society,
    233
American Anti-Slavery Society, 161, 233; *An
    Appeal to the Christian Women of the South,*
    161
American Colonization Society, 229
American expansionism, 190
American System, 68, 76, 100, 104, 108, 111,
    118–19, 133, 165–66, 172, 190–91
Amistad, 178
Annapolis Convention of 1786, 69
Anti-Federalists, 13, 16–20, 42
Anti-Masons, 128, 136, 155, 159
Antony, Marc, 8, 94, 226
Aristotle, 2–3, 16, 21, 28, 49, 56, 79, 85, 87,
    95–97, 122, 193, 266; *Poetics,* 122; *Rhetoric,*
    95, 122
Arnold, Benedict, 7, 231
Articles of Confederation, 13, 14, 69, 70,
    106, 139
Ashburton, Lord, 179–80

Ashmun, George, 197
Astor, John Jacob, 36, 105
Austin, James T., 157

Bank crisis, 143
Bank of the United States, 29, 35, 49, 53, 84,
    97, 145
Barbour, Phillip, 159
Bartlett, Irving, 263
Battle of Tippecanoe. *See* Harrison, William
    Henry
Baxter, Maurice G., 264
Benton, Thomas Hart, 99, 104–7, 110–11,
    132–35, 149, 160, 167, 217, 222, 249
Berrien, John M., 201
Berrien Amendment, 206
Beveridge, Albert, 267
Biddle, Nicholas, 3, 53, 84, 129, 132–34,
    144–47, 158. *See also* National Bank
Birney, James G., 190
Blair, Hugh, 23, 109; *Lectures on Rhetoric and
    Belles Lettres,* 23
Book of Revelation, 10
Borden, Luther, 203
Boston Atlas, 155, 183, 231
Boston Brahmins, 182
Boston Courier, 76, 232–33
Boston Daily Advertiser, 231–32
Boston Massacre, 12
Brandywine and Morristown, battles of, 43
British Bill of Rights, 9
Brown, John, 221
Browne, Stephen Howard, 63, 93, 161
Burgh, James: *Political Disquisitions,* 16
Burke, Edmund, 45, 58, 76, 140, 146,
    195–96, 209–12, 245, 266

Burke, Kenneth, 2
Bush, George H. W., 269
Bush, George W., 269
Butler, Andrew P., 200

Calhoun, John C., 3, 8, 13, 29, 34–35, 65,
   73–76, 82–83, 96–97, 101–18, 128–45,
   149, 158, 160, 167, 168–70, 178, 185, 187–
   88, 204, 217–19, 223–26, 235–38, 244–45,
   252, 265, 267; "Address to the People of
   the United States," 136; Carolina doctrine,
   108, 116; *Disquisition on Government*, 101;
   doctrine of nullification, 3, 34, 101, 104,
   106–8, 112, 115–17, 128, 130, 136,
   139–41, 156, 169, 267; Force Bill, 137,
   142–43, 146, 169; "Fort Hill Address,"
   128; South Carolina Exposition, 101
California, 184, 192, 198, 204, 207–8,
   218–22, 224, 227, 235, 238, 241–44, 248,
   250, 255
Caroline (vessel), 175, 177, 179
Cartwright, Richard, 136
Cass, Lewis, 170, 206, 215, 217, 227, 234
Ceremonial form. *See* Epideictic form
Certiorari, 162
Channing, William Ellery, 57, 164, 182;
   "Slavery," 182
Charles River Bridge Company, 162
Charleston Mercury, 232
Chase, Salmon P., 217
Cherokee, 82, 118, 160, 208. *See also* Jackson,
   Andrew
Choate, Rufus, 38, 155, 176, 186, 260–61, 266
Cicero, 2–3, 8, 10, 20–22, 88, 125, 167, 188,
   190, 196, 203, 211, 259, 264–66; attacks
   on Catiline, 22; *auctoritas*, 265; *decorum*, 2,
   109, 264; *De Oratore*, 23; *gravitas*, 265; *orna-
   tus*, 264; *patronus*, 265; *Select Orations*, 23
Cincinnati Gazette, 98
Civil religion, 2, 4–40 passim, 48; definition
   of, 8; emerging American myths, 9; *telos*, 4,
   10, 79, 95, 106, 117, 208, 211
Civic republicanism, 4, 8–9, 22, 101, 142,
   173, 188, 269; Roman history of, 8
Clay, Henry, 3, 8, 16, 29, 35, 53–54, 65–68,
   72–77, 82–84, 96–97, 100, 102, 105, 119,
   128–29, 132–37, 142–47, **150**, 156, 158,
   160, 164–73, 176–78, 182–83, 186–90,
   202–4, 214–18, 223–27, 233, 235–36, 239,

248–50, 257, 260–62, 265, 270; American
   System of internal improvements, 100,
   165; Compromise of 1820, 158, 191;
   "Great Compromiser," 188; Omnibus Bill,
   223–26, 236, 240, 245, 250; Raleigh
   Letter, 188–89
Clayton-Bulwer Treaty of 1850. *See* Treaties
Clinton, George, 18, 29
Coffee, John, 136
Cohens v. Virginia, 64
College of New Jersey. *See* Princeton
   University
Colman, Henry, 121–22, 127
Compromise of 1820. *See* Clay, Henry
Compromise of 1850, 1–2, 257–58
Compromise Tariff of 1833, 143, 180
Conscience Whigs. *See* Whig Party
Constitution: adoption of, 13, 139; Bill of
   Rights, 9, 12–20, 72, 87, 96, 163;
   commerce clause, 69–70, 73; confirmation
   of the new nation, 9; contract clause, 41,
   48, 72, 162; doctrine of original intent, 19,
   50; Fifth Amendment, 162; First
   Amendment, 187; Fourteenth
   Amendment, 19, 163; "implied powers,"
   19, 51; "necessary and proper" clause, 53,
   134; and property rights, 11, 38, 40, 44,
   97, 162–63; on protection from insurrec-
   tion, 203; ratification of, 12, 15–20, 42,
   96, 156; and separation of church and
   state, 187; on slavery, 112; on taxation, 4,
   51–53, 80; Tenth Amendment, 19, 52, 108
"Copperheads," 234
"Corrupt bargain," 75, 100–102
Cotton Whigs. *See* Whig Party
Court of St. James, 100, 128, 175
Crawford, William, 65, 73–75
Crawford Hotel, 29
Creole (slave ship), 178
Crimes Act of 1825. *See* Story, Joseph
Crittenden, John J., 171
Crowninshield, Benjamin, 120, 125
Crowninshield, George, 120, 125
Crowninshield, Richard, 120–21, 125–26
Curtis, Edward (Ned), 226, 250
Cushing, Caleb, 155, 165, 184

Dane, Nathan, 105, 111
Dartmouth, Earl of, 40

Dartmouth College case, 40–49, 56, 76, 117, 163
Dartmouth University, 22–27, 38, 41, 45, 187
Davis, Jefferson, 204, 209, 217
Davis, John, 155, 158, 183
Dawson, William C., 248
Declaration of Independence, 19, 18, 56, 72, 85–87, 90, 268; adoption of, 85; as baptism of the new nation, 9
Deliberative form, 3, 24, 32, 56, 58–63, 66, 73, 80, 86, 94–96, 192–95, 200–201, 205–12, 248, 251–53, 265
Democratic Party, 186, 192, 202, 234
Democratic-Republican Party, 27, 34, 86
Demos, 141, 212
Dexter, Franklin, 121–22
Dickinson, Daniel, 196
Dix, John Adams, 200
Donelson, Rachel, 102
Dorrites, 203
Dorr's Rebellion, 203
Douglas, Stephen, 217–18, 230, 238–39, 242, 249–51, 268
Douglass, Frederick, 181–82; "Slaveholder's Sermon," 181
Duane, William, 144
Dulles, John Foster, 269
Duvall, Gabriel, 32, 43, 48, 73, 158–59

Eaton, John, 104
Edwards, Jonathan, 55
Egyptians, 8
Eighteenth Congress, 66, 68
Election of 1824, 65, 73–77
Election of 1832, 129, 136–37
Election of 1834, 155
Election of 1840, 173
Election of 1844, 180, 187–90
Election of 1848, 207, 212, 234
Eliot, Samuel, 250
Emerson, Ralph Waldo, 2, 5, 147, 170, 181, 230–31, 251; "The American Scholar," 181; "Divinity School Address," 181
English Bill of Rights (1689), 13, 16, 20
Enlightenment, 9, 12, 16–20, 84, 134–40, 266; Scottish Enlightenment, 9
Epideictic form, 3, 7–8, 21, 25, 27, 55–58, 78, 81, 85, 94–96, 117, 257
Era of Good Feelings, 35, 54, 73
Erickson, Paul D., 2, 57, 166

Erie Canal, 39, 191
Ethos, 2, 59, 66, 106
Everett, Edward, 66, 85, 117, 155, 175, 178, 184, 215, 258, 263, 266

Falwell, Jerry, 12
Faneuil Hall, 54, 75, 80, 86, 96, 98, 136, 157, 168, 181–82, 185, 190, 230, 235, 256–57, 260, 261
Farrar, Timothy, Jr., 27, 48; Report of the Case of the Trustees of Dartmouth College, 48
Federal Club, 23
Federal Coasting Act, 69–71
Federalist (no. 32), 70
Federalist Party, 13, 16, 20, 28, 36, 39, 66, 104
Ferguson, Robert A., 2, 5, 62, 109, 263–64
Fillmore, Millard, **153,** 215–16, 220, 239, 243, 249–50, 252–53, 255, 257–58, 260–62
First Great Awakening, 55
First Reply to Hayne. *See* Webster, Daniel: Writings
Fiscal Bank Bill, 176–77
Fiscal Corporation Bill, 176
Fletcher, Grace. *See* Webster, Grace
Fletcher v. Peck, 43–44
Foot, Samuel, 104
Foote, Henry, 217, 222, 235–36, 245, 248
Forensic form, 3–6, 27, 31, 45, 56, 59, 63, 66–67, 72, 86, 95–96, 128, 177, 192–96, 200, 205, 210–12, 258
Fox, Charles James, 3
Fox, Henry, 177
Free Soil Party, 215, 233–34; Free Soilers, 164, 216, 221, 227, 230, 234, 236, 250, 256
French and Indian War, 70, 61, 191
Fries Rebellion, 116
Fryeburg Academy. *See* Webster, Daniel
Fugitive Slave Law, 1, 5, 10, 221, 224–25, 228, 230–32, 236, 238, 241, 246, 250, 252–56, 258
Fulton, Robert, 69

Gales, Joseph, 117
Gardiner, William, 121
Garnet, Henry H., 221

Garrison, William Lloyd, 157–58, 161, 181–82, 185, 203, 230, 233, 267
Gettysburg Address, 4, 66, 118, 268. *See also* Lincoln, Abraham
Gibbons, Thomas, 69
Gibbons v. Ogden, 68–73, 76
Glorious Revolution of 1688, 9
God-terms, 8. *See also* "Union, the"
Goodrich, Chauncey, 48
Goodridge, Elijah, 36
Goodridge, Sarah, 103
Gore, Christopher, 22, 25–26, 29
Gorham, Benjamin, 65
Greek independence, 66–67, 78
Greeley, Horace, 255
Grimke, Angela, 160, 161
Grimke, Sarah, 160, 161; *Epistle to the Clergy of the Southern States*, 161
Grogan, James, 177
Guadalupe Hidalgo, Treaty of. *See* Treaties

Hale, John, 217, 248
Hale, Nathan, 9
Hamilton, Alexander, 4, 14, 15, 20, 23, 24, 34, 42, 53, 70, 130, 266
Hardin, John, 208
Harrison, William Henry, 156, 159, 160, 165–67, 170–75, 183, 185, 202, 214, 239, 257
Hartford Convention, 34, 39, 108, 156
Harvard College, 65, 155, 162, 182, 229, 233
Harvey, Peter, 226, 236
Hayne, Robert, 3–4, 49, 52, 92, 99, 101, 104–18, 126–27, 130, 132, 136–38, 165–66, 170, 201, 205, 210, 257, 263–64
Healy, George, 257
Henry, Patrick, 12, 17–18, 201
Hesiod, 8
Hobbes, Thomas, 15–16, 135
Holmes, Oliver Wendell, 181–82, 229
Holy Alliance of 1815, 67
Homer, 8
Hopkinson, Joseph, 49, 52, 93
Houston, Sam, 194, 218
Hyde, Michael, 2

Ides of March, 159
Independent Treasury Bill, 169
Indian Removal Bill, 118

Ingersoll, Charles, 196–97
Isocrates, 264

Jackson, Andrew, 8, 35, 73–76, 83–84, 97–98, 101–6, 118–19, 128–37, 143–46, 155–71, 188, 192, 194, 197, 202, 212, 218; Force Bill, 137, 142–43, 146, 169; populism of, 14, 73, 75, 98, 104, 134–36, 142; Specie Circular, 169
Jay Treaty, 24
Jefferson, Thomas, 4, 9–12, 18–20, 25, 34–35, 37, 41–43, 53, 66, 74–75, 86–101, 108, 118, 140, 143–44, 187, 191, 197, 201, 204, 217, 266–67
Johnson, Lyndon, 268
Johnson, William, 32, 42
Jones, Walter, 49

Kansas-Nebraska Act, 249, 251
Kansas-Nebraska Territory, 251
Kendall, Amos, 128, 134, 144
Kennedy, John F., 230, 268
Kentucky and Virginia Resolutions (1798), 180, 267
Kinniston, Laban, 36
Kinniston, Levi, 36
Kirkland, John Thornton, 86
Kitchen cabinet, 155
Knapp, Joseph, Jr., 120–27
Knapp-White murder case, 119–28
Kossuth, Louis, 254

Lafayette, Marquis, 35, 77, 78
Laws and Liberties of Massachusetts, 17
Lectures on Revivals (periodical), 56
Lee, Richard Henry, 17
LeRoy, Caroline, 103
Liberator (newspaper), 157, 203
Liberty League, 234
Liberty Party, 188, 190
Lincoln, Abraham, 4, 8, 66, 93, 96, 106, 118, 167, 209, 214, 217, 234, 257, 267–68
Lincoln, Levi, 86, 98
Lind, Jenny, 253
Livingston, Brockholst H., 32, 42, 68
Livingston, Edward, 136
Livingston, Robert, 69
Locke, John, 9, 11, 16–17, 191, 266; *Second Treatise on Government*, 11

Lodge, Henry Cabot, 277, 230
Longfellow, Henry Wadsworth, 2, 170, 181-82, 230
Lopez de Santa Ana, Antonio, 159
Louisiana Territory, 191
Louis Philippe, King, 170
Lovejoy, Elijah, 157
Lowell, Francis Cabot, 35-37, 40, 54, 97, 137, 161, 236
Lundy, Benjamin, 156-57; "The Origin and True Causes of the Texas Revolution Commenced in the Year 1835," 156
Luther, Martin, 203
Luther v. Borden, 203
Lyman, Theodore, 73, 102, 157

Madison, Dolly, 33
Madison, James, 4, 9, 14-16, 18-19, 27-30, 33-35, 49, 74, 84, 101, 108, 115, 118, 120, 142, 167, 187, 197, 266-67; "Mr. Madison's war," 14, 29
Magna Charta, 13, 16, 19-20, 46
Maine boundary: compromise with England, 32, 177-80; dispute, 177-80
Maine caucus, 170
Manichaeanism, 10, 269
Manifest destiny, 3, 10, 60, 190, 192, 195, 207, 209, 262, 267, 270
Mann, Horace, 230-31, 251
Mansfield, Lord, 45
Marbury v. Madison, 42, 64
Marshall, John, 4, 30-32, 41-44, 47-49, 52-53, 56, 64-65, 70-73, 76, 97, 180, 159-60, 163
Martin, Luther, 17, 49, 52
Mason, George, 12, 17
Mason, James, 225, 232
Mason, Jeremiah, 27, 29, 41, 44, 183
Mason-Dixon line, 77
Massachusetts Anti-Slavery Society, 158
Massachusetts Body of Liberties (1641), 17, 20
Massachusetts Constitutional Convention, 57, 85
Mather, Cotton, 55
Mayflower Compact (1620), 17
Mayhew, Jonathan, 12; "A Discourse concerning Unlimited Submission and Non-Resistance to the Higher Powers," 12;

Observations on the Charter and Conduct of the Society for the Propagation of the Gospel in Foreign Parts, 12
Maysville Road, 119
McCormick, Cyrus, 40
McCulloch, James W., 49
McCulloch v. Maryland, 32, 49-54, 64, 76, 133-34, 176
McLane, Louis, 143
McLeod, Alexander, 175, 177
Menand, Louis, 48, 182
Mexican War, 3, 10, 33, 160, 180, 184, 188, 192-214, 218, 223-24, 229, 245, 247-62
Micah (prophet), 10
Missouri Compromise, 53-55, 86, 188, 211, 219
Monroe, James, 14, 34, 54, 66, 68, 120
Monroe Doctrine, 66, 132, 256
Monticello, 74
Mount Vernon, 42

Napoleon, 28, 33, 35, 146, 191
Napoleonic Wars, 156
National Bank, 3, 35, 49, 50-52, 73, 97, 104, 129, 132-33, 135, 143-47, 167, 169, 172, 176, 185, 188, 267
National Intelligencer, 176-77, 183
National Republican Party. *See* Whig Party
National Union Party, 76
New Deal, 71
New Hampshire bill of rights, 46
New Hampshire Constitutional Ratifying Convention, 7
New Mexico Territory, 204, 218-19, 244, 250
New Orleans Picayune, 232
New-York Evangelist, 56
New York Herald, 172, 248
Northwest Ordinance of 1787, 53, 105, 111, 158
Nullification. *See* Calhoun, John C.

Octagon House, 34
Ogden, Aaron, 69, 71
Ogden, David, 38, 72
Ogden, George, 72
Ogden v. Saunders, 72-73
Oregon Bill, 219
Oregon border dispute, 180, 183-84
Oregon Trail, 219

Oregon treaty, 197, 207
Ornatus, 264
Osborn v. Bank of the United States, 29, 53
O'Sullivan, John, 192. *See also* Manifest destiny
Otis, Harrison, 136, 183
Otis, James, 36

Paine, Thomas, 18
Pakenham, Richard, 188, 218
Palfrey, John, 155, 181
Palmer, David, 22
Palmer, John, 121
Panic of 1819, 49
Panic of 1837, 73, 169
Parker, Theodore, 5, 79, 230–31, 251, 253
Pathos, 2
Peirce, Benjamin, 182
Pericles, 8, 20, 23, 195–96, 211, 266
Perry, Matthew, 255
(Philadelphia) Aurora, 144
Philadelphia Evening Bulletin, 232, 248
Phillips, Wendell, 158, 181–82, 230; "golden trumpet" of abolition, 158
Pickering, Timothy, 29, 86, 91
Pinckney, William, 32, 44, 49, 52, 65
Pierce, Franklin, 255, 261, 263
Pilgrim Code of Law (1636), 17, 20
Pitt, William, 146
Plumer, William, 30, 41
Plymouth County Anti-Slavery Society, 181
Polk, James Knox, 188–99, 203–13, 219, 256
Pope, Alexander, 2, 21
"Popular Insurrection." *See* Whig Party: Whig campaign of 1840
Preston, Thomas, 89
Princeton University, 42, 84
Protagoras, 6
Proxemics, 60

Quincy, Edmund, 230
Quincy, Josiah, 86, 93, 155

Randolph, John, 75, 83
Reagan, Ronald, 269
Resolutions of 1798, 101, 108
Revere, Paul, 9
Revolutionary War, 41–43, 77, 79, 177
Rhetoric. See Aristotle

Rhetorica ad Herennium, 193
Rhode Island v. Massachusetts, 38
Richmond Whig, 98
Rights of Man (Paine), 18
Robards, Lewis, 102
Robertson, Pat, 12
Rockingham Convention, 28
Roosevelt, Franklin, 268
Roosevelt, Theodore, 259, 268
Root, Joseph, 219
Ross, Betsy, 9
Rousseau, Jean-Jacques, 11, 16, 97
Rush, Richard, 93

Santa Fe Trail, 219
Sargent, John O., 155
Saturday Club, 181–82
Scott, Winfield, 202, 215, 257, 260–63
Second Great Awakening, 2, 21, 55, 57, 78, 156, 270
Second National Bank, 49, 129, 133
Second Reply to Hayne. *See* Webster, Daniel: Writings
Second Treatise on Government. See Locke, John
Seminole War, 118, 160
Seward, William, **154,** 175, 214–18, 223, 225, 231, 235, 237, 244, 249, 252–53, 257, 260–61
Shadrach (slave), 253
Shakespeare, William, 2, 94, 125, 210, 263
Sherman, William Tecumseh, 160, 212
Sidney, Algernon, 16; *Discourses on Government*, 16
Smith, Francis, 178–79
Smith, Jeremiah, 28, 41, 44
Sons of Liberty, 12
Soule, Pierre, 238–39
South Carolina Canal and Railroad Company, 111
Spanish Claims Commission, 64
Stamp Act, 9
State of New Jersey v. Wilson, 43
Stephens, Alexander, 224
Story, Joseph, 31–33, 37, 42–43, 45, 48, 66, 73, 97, 122, 155, 163, 179, 187; appointment to Supreme Court, 32, 42; *Commentaries on the Constitution*, 31; Crimes Act of 1825, 43
Sturges v. Crowninshield, 72

St. Paul's Episcopal Church, 57
Sumner, Charles, **152,** 181–82, 199, 215, 231, 250, 253, 256; "Crime against Kansas," 256
Supreme Court, 1–4, 11, 14, 20, 31–32, 38, 41–43, 47, 49, 51–53, 56, 64–72, 76, 82, 84, 89, 97, 105, 107, 115, 117, 120, 122, 128, 134–35, 141, 158–59, 162, 172, 175, 187, 203, 223, 258, 264

Taney, Roger, 132, 134, 144–47, 158–59, 162–63, 204
"Tariff of Abominations." *See* Tariff of 1828
Tariff of 1816, 106–7, 115
Tariff of 1828, 101, 104, 132
Taylor, Zachary, **151,** 198, 202, 207, 214–20, 223–25, 234, 239–40, 247, 253, 257, 260
Telos. See Civil religion
Texas Republic, 160, 184, 192, 194
Texas Revolt, 156
Thompson, Smith, 68–69
Thompson, Thomas, 22, 25–27
Thucydides, 2, 23
Ticknor, George, 74, 92, 155, 183
Todd, Thomas, 32, 42
Toombs, Robert, 224
Town of Pawlet v. Clark, et al., 33
Trail of Tears, 118, 160. *See also* Cherokee; Jackson, Andrew
Treaties: Clayton-Bulwer Treaty, 255; Treaty of Guadalupe Hidalgo, 219; Treaty of Paris, 21; Treaty of Wanghia, 184
Trist, Nicholas, 204
Turner, Nat, 157
Tyler, John, 32, 99, 171, 174–88, 194, 197, 214, 218, 244, 255, 257

Uncle Tom's Cabin (Stowe), 161
"Union, the," 2–5, 8, 13, 18–21, 28, 34–39, 44, 54–55, 72, 76–78, 95–96, 140–43, 150, 164–66, 181, 184–90, 194–95, 207, 209, 211–13, 219, 224–28, 233–36, 240–51, 256–59, 262, 266–68
Union Party, 39, 256
United Fraternity, 23–25
University of Virginia, 92

Valley Forge, 9
Van Buren, Martin, 68, 97, 101, 103–4, 119, 128, 132–33, 136, 143–44, 155–56, 160, 163–68, 171, 173, 175, 185–86, 188–90, 197, 215, 228, 233–34; "Little Magician," 160
Vanderbilt, Cornelius, 255
Van Rensselaer, Catherine, 103
Vicksburg Weekly Whig, 232, 248
Victoria, Queen, 170
Virginia Debates of 1788, 42
Virginia Declaration of Rights, 20
Virginia Resolution of 1798, 108, 114–15

Ware v. Hyton, 41
War of 1812, 4, 8, 28, 49, 102, 144, 191, 198, 204, 223. *See also* Madison, James: "Mr. Madison's war"
Warren Bridge Company, 162
Washington, Bushrod, 32, 42, 48
Washington, George, 4, 7, 9, 20, 28, 42, 93, 129, 131, 137, 165, 123, 258–59, 265–66
Washington Benevolent Society, 28
Washington Treaty, 196
Webster, Abigail (mother), 21
Webster, Abigail (sister), 26
Webster, Charles (son), 64, 75
Webster, Daniel, **148;** as Anglophile, 170; birth of, 7, 21; at Dartmouth, 22–25; election to the House, 29; election to the Senate, 99; first legal position, 26; at Fryeburg Academy, 25; at Phillips Exeter Academy, 22; as secretary of state, 1, 14, 32, 173, 175, 177, 183–84, 196–97, 210, 217, 249, 252–53, 258, 260–61; studies with Christopher Gore, 25–26; "web of argumentation," 41
–Nicknames of: "Black Dan," 21, 23, 197, 253; "Defender of the Constitution," 48, 117, 146; "Defender of the Peace," 180; "Defender of the Union," 180; "the Yankee Demosthenes," 27
–Writings: "Addition to the Capitol" address, 258; "Admission of Texas," 194; apologia for the Sedition Act of 1798, 26; "An Appeal to the Old Whigs of New Hampshire," 26, 146; "The Character of Washington," 25, 130; "Creole Paper," 178; "Defense of the Treaty of Washington," 194; 1850 Compromise debates, 112, 193, 200, 202, 207, 209, 217,

264; "enlistment speech" (1814), 30–31; eulogy for Ephraim Simonds, 24; Eulogy to Adams and Jefferson, 85–96, 201; First Bunker Hill Address, 11, 24, 77–82, 94, 185, 259; First Reply to Hayne, 107, 111, 113; "The First Settlement of New England" address, 54, 57, 62, 66; Fourth of July address at Concord, 26; Fourth of July address at Hanover, 28; "ghost speech," 86, 91–92, 95–96; "A Memorial to the Congress of the United States, on the Subject of Restraining the Increase of Slavery in the New States to Be Admitted to the Union," 54; "The News Boy's Message to the Patrons of the *Dartmouth Gazette*," 25; Niblo's Saloon speech, 163, 165, 260; "Objects of the Mexican War," 194; "Reception at Madison" address, 165; Richmond speech, 172; Royal Agricultural Society speech, 170; Second Reply to Hayne, 109–18; Seventeenth of July Address (1850), 239–51; Seventh of March Address (1850), 48, 226–38, 240, 242, 244, 248
Webster, Daniel Fletcher (son), 27, 30, 99, 103, 166, 184, 214, 226, 236
Webster, Ebenezer (father), 7, 21, 26; as judge for Court of Common Pleas, 7
Webster, Edward (son), 54, 103, 199, 205, 214
Webster, Ezekiel (brother), 21
Webster, Grace (wife), 27, 30, 99
Webster, Grace (daughter), 28
Webster, Julia (daughter), 44, 103, 170, 214

Weld, Theodore, 161; *American Slavery as It Is,* 161
Wellington, Duke of, 170
Whately, Richard, 109
Wheaton, Henry, 72
Wheelock, Eleazar, 40, 45, 48
Wheelock, John, 40
Whig Party, 2–4, 14, 21, 76, 96, 172, 176, 185, 187–88, 192, 196, 212, 223, 235, 256; American Plan, 55; Conscience Whigs, 181, 198–99, 214–15, 218, 221, 234, 240, 260; Cotton Whigs, 181, 199, 203, 221, 234; Whig campaign of 1840, 171
White, Hugh Lawson, 156, 159–60
White, Joseph, 120–26
White, Stephen, 121–22
Whitefield, George, 55
Whittier, John Greenleaf, 161, 230
William and Mary College, 89
William of the Netherlands, King, 177
Wilmot, David, 199, 215
Wilmot Proviso, 199, 202–3, 215, 218, 224, 232, 246, 254
Wilson, Woodrow, 268
Winthrop, Jonathan, 10, 12, 56
Winthrop, Robert, 183, 250
Wirt, William, 37, 44, 47, 49, 69, 71–72, 128
Wood, Samuel, 22
Woodward, William H., 41, 48
Woolen protection bill, 97
Wordsworth, William, 2
Wright, Silas, 145

Yancey, William L., 197